Piercing the Fog of War

The Theory and Practice of Command in the British and German
Armies, 1918-1940

Martin Samuels

 Helion & Company Limited

Helion & Company Limited
Unit 8 Amherst Business Centre
Budbrooke Road
Warwick
CV34 5WE
England
Tel. 01926 499 619
Fax 0121 711 4075
Email: info@helion.co.uk
Website: www.helion.co.uk
Twitter: @helionbooks
Visit our blog http://blog.helion.co.uk/

Published by Helion & Company 2019
Designed and typeset by Mary Woolley (mary@battlefield-design.co.uk)
Cover designed by Paul Hewitt, Battlefield Design (www.battlefield-design.co.uk)
Printed by Lightning Source Limited, Milton Keynes, Buckinghamshire

Cover image: British armoured counter-attack near Arras, 21 May 1940 by
W. Krogman (Open source)

Every reasonable effort has been made to trace copyright holders and to obtain their
permission for the use of copyright material. The author and publisher apologize
for any errors or omissions in this work and would be grateful if notified of any
corrections that should be incorporated in future reprints or editions of this book.

ISBN 978-1-911628-90-3

British Library Cataloguing-in-Publication Data.
A catalogue record for this book is available from the British Library.

For details of other military history titles published by Helion & Company Limited
contact the above address or visit our website: http://www.helion.co.uk.

We always welcome receiving book proposals from prospective authors.

Contents

List of Maps

Acknowledgements

This book is, in several respects, a sequel to my earlier work, *Command or Control? Command, Training and Tactics in the British and German Armies, 1888-1918* (London: Cass, 1995). Not only does it follow on from that work in terms of chronology, picking up the story at the closing climax of the First World War and taking it through until the end of the initial phase of the Second, but it also develops the concepts and hypotheses around command that were first presented there. In that earlier book, I suggested that the command approaches adopted by armies were strongly influenced by whether they saw combat as inherently structured and predictable or whether they instead believed it to be fundamentally chaotic and hence non-linear. This, in turn, affected the type of tactics that each army sought to apply, and hence drove the style and level of training that its officers and men were expected to undergo.

While I stand by these hypotheses, I am acutely aware that, apart from a sense that these were in some way connected to issues of friction and shock, there was limited exploration of these questions. The theory therefore stood on a weak foundation. It is precisely the attempt to provide such a foundation that forms the central theme of this volume. Drawing on new interpretations of the nature of friction, as first described by Carl von Clausewitz almost two centuries ago, the aim here is to make clear connections between friction as a key feature of warfare, the various different command approaches that may be adopted in response to that friction, and their relative efficacy in light of the nature of warfare. The experience of the British and German Armies during the period under consideration is used primarily as a means to explain and explore these issues, though equally the intent is that a deeper understanding of those issues may provide new insights and explanations for the decisions made by commanders during the period and for the results achieved.

In undertaking this research, I have sought to draw upon my own experience, gathered over the past quarter century, of working in large, complex, organisations across several parts of the British public service, during much of which time I have held senior positions as both 'commander' and 'staff officer'. While fully recognising that my experience in public administration inevitably differs in many key respects from that which might be gained through service in a military context, I believe there are parallels, and I have sometimes been surprised by the extent to which my research into command approaches has influenced my own practice as a senior leader. One consequence of this personal experience is to cause me to be rather less critical and more understanding of the errors, confusions, and foibles of the officers I have studied as part of this research than I was when I wrote my previous book. I hope that my assessments are perhaps a little less unforgiving and more balanced as a consequence.

In presenting this work to a wider readership, I must underline my great debt of thanks to many individuals. First, I must acknowledge the enormous debt I owe to my *Doktorvater*, the late Michael Elliott-Bateman, Department of Military Studies, University of Manchester. His groundbreaking work on military cultures provided central pillars for the basic model of command approaches that is further developed here. In addition, his challenging yet intensely supportive approach, based on questioning and exploring ideas, freely highlighting the deficiencies of his own earlier work, greatly influenced my early intellectual development and set the standard for rigour of critical analysis to which I have aspired. I should also record the positive impact on, and contribution to, my thinking that was made by my fellow postgraduate students at that time: Spencer Fitz-Gibbon and Kieran Creaton.

Second, I must thank a series of students of warfare, who encouraged me to return to active academic research after an absence of almost two decades, and then patiently put up with years of responding to my requests for advice and materials, graciously giving comments on early drafts of the text presented here. Without them, this book would remain just an unrealised possibility: Aidan Walsh, Jim Storr, Bruce Gudmundsson, and Stephen Bungay. Similar thanks are due to the anonymous peer reviewers who read the draft articles taken from early versions of several of the chapters. The work has benefited greatly from the input of each of them, though, of course, it does not necessarily reflect their views, and all remaining errors are, as ever, mine.

August 2017

Permissions

Elements of several chapters were published in earlier form as standalone articles as follows:

- 'Understanding Command Approaches', *Journal of Military Operations*, 1(3) (Winter 2012), 25-29
- 'Friction, Chaos and Order(s): Clausewitz, Boyd and Command Approaches', *Journal of Military and Strategic Studies*, 15(4) (2014), 38-75
- 'Doctrine for Orders and Decentralisation in the British and German Armies, 1885-1935', *War in History*, 22(4) (November 2015), 448-477
- 'Shock and Friction as Explanations for Disaster at the Battle of Amiens, 8 August 1918', *War & Society*, 35(4) (October 2016), 275-297
- 'Erwin Rommel and German Military Doctrine, 1912-1940', *War in History*, 24(2) (July 2017), 308-335

I am grateful to the publishers of these journals for permission to reuse this material here. I should note that, since these articles were written during earlier stages of the preparation of this final text, there are points where the argument presented here differs from that set out in them.

Note on Naming Conventions

Ranks

Although there was much in common between the naming of ranks in the British and German armies, there were sufficient differences as to allow the unwary to become easily confused in seeking to identify equivalents. The table below seeks to provide a general sense of parallels.

It is important, however, to recognise from the start that there was a key difference in approach between the two armies. In the British Army, rank was generally associated with the size of unit or formation commanded – an officer appointed to command a division, for example, would normally be a major-general, and might be promoted (permanently or temporarily) for the purpose. In the German Army, by contrast, rank was generally a matter of time served and seniority amongst the officer's peers, although on occasion an officer might be promoted as a mark of favour. Officers of several different ranks might therefore hold equivalent commands. This was especially the case for staff officers.

British Army		German Army	
Rank	*Usual Command*	*Rank*	*Usual Command*
Second Lieutenant	Platoon	Leutnant	Platoon
Lieutenant	Platoon	Oberleutnant	Platoon / Company
Captain	Company Second-in-Command	Hauptmann	Company / Battalion
Major	Company	Major	Battalion
Lieutenant-Colonel	Battalion	Oberstleutnant	Battalion / Regiment
Colonel	Staff Role	Oberst	Regiment
Brigadier(-General)	Brigade	Generalmajor	Brigade / Division
Major-General	Division	Generalleutnant	Division / Corps
Lieutenant-General	Corps	General der Infanterie / Kavallerie / Artillerie / Panzertruppen	Corps / Army
General	Army	Generaloberst	Army

Units

As a general rule, the following convention has been adopted for naming formations: 5th Division, V Corps, Fifth Army.

The fact that the forces of several countries were involved in the engagements described requires the convention to be adapted in some situations. The German Army frequently referred to formations (and smaller units) by the name of their commander, such as the Gruppe Berrer (a corps-sized formation) or the Rommel Abteilung (an ad hoc group of companies). The British too briefly adopted a similar approach during the May 1940 campaign, hence Frankforce (a temporary corps-sized formation). In other cases, a national attribution for a German division might be included within its name, or not! For example, the Bavarian 5th Infantry Division, but the 26th (Württemberg) Reserve Division.

At unit level, the position becomes significantly more complex. In the German Army, the basic operational structure was the regiment, comprising several battalions, each of several companies. The battalions were designated with Roman numerals, while the companies, numbered in sequence throughout the regiment, used Arabic numerals. Thus, II/RIR57 would refer to the second battalion of Reserve-Infanterie-Regiment 57, while 9/RIR57 would be its ninth company, which would normally be part of the third battalion.

In the British Army, the basic operational units were:
- Infantry battalion, part of an administrative regiment with several battalions,
- Tank battalion, part of the administrative Tank Corps / Royal Tanks Corps / Royal Tank Regiment
- Cavalry regiment, later part of the administrative Royal Armoured Corps, and
- Artillery brigade / regiment, part of the administrative Royal Artillery Regiment.

Thus, the following abbreviations were used:
- 6/DLI for the Sixth Battalion, the Durham Light Infantry,
- 7/RTR for the Seventh Battalion, the Royal Tank Regiment,
- 23H for the Twenty-Third Hussars, and
- 92RA for the Ninety-Second Field Artillery Regiment, Royal Artillery.

Is that clear?

Abstract

Since the late 1970s, anglophone and German military literature has been fascinated by the Wehrmacht's command system, especially the practice of *Auftragstaktik*. There have been many descriptions of the doctrine, and examinations of its historical origins, as well as unflattering comparisons with the approaches of the British and American armies prior to their adoption of Mission Command in the late 1980s. Almost none of these, however, have sought to understand the different approaches to command in the context of a fundamental characteristic of warfare – friction. This would be like trying to understand flight, without any reference to aerodynamics. Inherently flawed, yet this is the norm in the military literature. This book seeks to address that gap.

First, the nature of friction, and the potential command responses to it, are considered. This allows the development of a typology of eight command approaches, each approach then being tested to identify its relative effectiveness and requirements for success. Second, the British and German armies' doctrines of command during the period are examined, in order to reveal similarities and differences in relation to their perspective on the nature of warfare and the most appropriate responses. The experience of Erwin Rommel, both as a young subaltern fighting the Italians in 1917, and then as a newly-appointed divisional commander against the French in 1940, is used to test the expression of the German doctrine in practice. Third, the interaction of these different command doctrines is explored in case studies of two key armoured battles, Amiens in August 1918 and Arras in May 1940, allowing the strengths and weaknesses of each to be highlighted and the typology to be tested. The result is intended to offer a new and deeper understanding of both the nature of command as a response to friction, and the factors that need to be in place in order to allow a given command approach to achieve success.

The book therefore in two ways represents a sequel to my earlier work, *Command or Control? Command, Training and Tactics in the British and German Armies, 1888-1918* (London: Cass, 1995), in that it both takes the conceptual model of command developed there to a deeper level, and also takes the story from the climax of 1918 up to the end of the first phase of the Second World War.

About the Author

Martin Samuels gained his PhD in Military Studies at the University of Manchester. He entered the UK public service and has subsequently filled roles at national, regional and local level in a variety of organisations in the civil service, National Health Service, and local government. He is currently a senior director in a metropolitan borough council. Having returned to the field of military studies in 2010, he has been surprised to find that his analysis of military command approaches has had an impact on his own practice as a senior leader.

1

Friction and Command: Developing a Model of Command Approaches

It is a very difficult task to construct a scientific theory for the art of war, and so many attempts have failed that most people say it is impossible, since it deals with matters that no permanent law can provide for. One would agree, and abandon the attempt, were it not for the obvious fact that a whole range of propositions can be demonstrated without difficulty [...].

Clausewitz[1]

A former writer of British military doctrine, Jim Storr, lamented that, although many books explore *what* happens in war (history) or *why* wars happen (international relations), very few focus on *how* wars should be fought (warfare).[2] He concluded this reflected warfare's status as 'a poorly developed discipline'. Consequently, 'It is incoherent, contains a range of poorly described phenomena and is pervaded by paradox.'[3] The underdeveloped discourse concerning warfare, and within it the limited consideration of different approaches to command, may be considered an important contributor to the longstanding gulf between the doctrine of Mission Command espoused by the United States and British armies and their actual operational practice,[4]

1   Carl von Clausewitz, *On War*, ed. and trans. by Michael Howard and Peter Paret (Princeton, NJ: Princeton University Press, 1976), p.71.
2   Jim Storr, *The Human Face of War* (London: Continuum, 2009), p.2.
3   Storr, *Human Face*, p.10.
4   For example, Major John D. Johnson, 'Mission Orders in the United States Army: Is the Doctrine Effective?' (unpublished master's thesis, US Army Command & General Staff College, Fort Leavenworth, KS, 1990), Major David J. Lemelin, 'Command and Control Methodology: A Sliding Scale of Centralisation' (unpublished master's thesis, US Army Command & General Staff College, Fort Leavenworth, KS, 1996), and Brigadier Nigel Aylwin-Foster, 'Changing the Army for Counterinsurgency Operations', *Military Review* (November-December 2005), 2-15.

such that the doctrine is 'realized only in some places some of the time'.[5]

Understandably, the pressing practical concerns of serving officers encourage focus on the application of doctrine, rather than its theoretical basis. But this brings significant dangers: reliance upon a descriptive paradigm ('do this *because* it works') as opposed to an analytical paradigm ('this is *why* it works') can lead to Mission Command being perceived as merely a technique, divorced from its connection to the basic nature of warfare. Consequently, discussion of command approaches may be reduced to simplistic two-dimensional models.[6]

From the mid-1980s, articles about command approaches became a feature of many military journals. Most veered towards an unproven view that what became known as 'the Manoeuvrist Approach' and, to complement it, a command approach now designated Mission Command, were 'a good thing'. Although these were codified in various doctrinal publications, their adoption was not a 'given': the landmark *Design for Military Operations: The British Military Doctrine* of 1989 did not use either term.[7]

These developments were based on a limited theoretical model, which typically differentiated between just two command approaches. These had first been described in the late nineteenth century German debates regarding the implications for command of dispersed formations:[8]

> *Auftragstaktik* (Mission Tactics): Commanders set out their intent, but leave the means of its achievement to their subordinates' initiative, based on the latter's better knowledge of the local situation.
>
> *Befehlstaktik* (Orders Tactics): Commanders rely on their better knowledge of the wider context, so issue detailed orders that their subordinates must follow rigidly, regardless of how events unfold.

When these concepts inspired anglophone doctrine, they were often reduced to mechanical lists of 'do's' and 'don'ts', largely divorced from the human circumstances to which they relate. In practice, the widespread perception that Mission Command was 'just another' managerial concept, combined with the existence of seemingly permitted exceptions, allowed significant deviation from endorsed practice.[9]

---

5   Eitan Shamir, *Transforming Command: The Pursuit of Mission Command in the U.S., British and Israeli Armies* (Stanford, CA: Stanford University Press, 2011), p. 201.
6   For example, Lieutenant-Colonel W. Lossow, 'Mission-Type Tactics versus Order-Type Tactics', *Military Review* (June 1977), 87-91, Richard E. Simpkin, *Race to the Swift: Thoughts on Twenty-First Century Warfare* (London: Brassey's, 1985), p. 228, Lemelin, 'Methodology', p.3, and Richard E. Simpkin, *Human Factors in Mechanized Warfare* (London: Brassey's, 1983), pp.153-154.
7   *Design for Military Operations: The British Military Doctrine* (Army Code 71451) (London: HMSO, 1989).
8   Stephan Leistenschneider, *Auftragstaktik im preussisch–deutschen Heer 1871 bis 1914* (Hamburg: Mittler, 2002), pp.98-122.
9   Shamir, *Transforming Command*, pp.4-5.

With hindsight, the near absence of consideration of other command approaches, or exploration of how particular command approaches develop and why they persist, was a striking feature of this debate. There was also little rigour around why Mission Command was thought to be the right choice. The evangelists for Mission Command should not be criticised too harshly, however. The almost total absence from the literature of any real theoretical analysis of command approaches (as opposed to leadership) is striking.

The German Army, from the end of the First World War and through until the middle part of the Second, has long been lauded by military theorists and academics as representing a near perfect example of the application of the *Auftragstaktik* ideal. Conversely, the British Army of that period has been criticised as an archetype of the flawed *Befehlstaktik* approach. This 'good/bad' dichotomy is surely simplistic and overly judgemental on the commanders of both armies. In seeking to understand the true nature of the command approaches employed by these two armies during the period from 1918 to 1940, it is necessary to move beyond such limited thinking.

This chapter therefore aims to take a series of steps towards establishing a conceptual foundation for discussion of command, which can then be employed as a means to examine the doctrine and practice of the British and German armies. First, it presents a typology of command approaches that treats command as a response to the essence of warfare: friction. Having thereby provided a conceptual foundation for the variations in approaches used by different armies, it then examines how each of the command approaches defined in the typology interacts with the different aspects of friction identified by Clausewitz, thereby enabling an assessment to be made of the likely effectiveness of each approach in reducing friction.

Through such theoretical analysis of the relationship between command approaches and friction, this chapter seeks to test the contention that a command system is not simply a neutral technique, but (whether consciously or not) is a response to the fundamental nature of warfare. As such, some approaches are more likely than others to deliver victory.

It is fully recognised that many factors affect the preference for, and application of, particular command approaches by different armies. These factors, which may include political expectations, cultural tunnel vision, and technology, merit further discussion beyond the scope of what is possible in this volume. Presenting the typology here may encourage such deeper examination of the subject.

It should be noted that no attempt is made to define 'command approach': if it looks, feels or smells like a command approach, then it is a command approach. In this context, 'command approach' is taken to encompass both managerial practice and leadership style, though the focus is more on the technical than the interpersonal. Indeed, the variability of possible definitions underlines how poorly the whole subject is understood.

Having developed a theoretical model of command approaches in this chapter, this is then used in Chapter Two as a tool to analyse the doctrine for command, as it developed in the British and German armies, with a particular emphasis on the period 1918 to 1940. This analysis of the theory expressed in the official doctrinal manuals of the two armies is then tested in the following three chapters, to explore the extent to which the armies actually fought in accordance with their espoused doctrine. Chapter Three considers the case of one of the German Army's most famous generals, Erwin Rommel. It is recognised that historians of the Second World War, perhaps especially those who are British, sometimes display something of an obsession with Rommel. In this case, he has been chosen as the focus of this case study due to his reputation as a maverick, whose success up to 1940 was the result of his disregard of the official doctrine. Chapters Four and Five complete the analysis of doctrine and its relationship with friction, through close examination of key elements of two important battles. Chapter Four considers the British tank attack at Amiens on 8 August 1918, the largest such offensive undertaken during the war and arguably the worst defeat suffered by the German Army at any point of the First World War. Chapter Five explores the British armoured counterattack at Arras on 21 May 1940, which was the first time British heavy tanks encountered the Germans during that war. Not only does this operation provide an insight into the command approaches adopted by the two armies in the opening phase of the Second World War, it also offers an excellent case study of the impact of friction at multiple levels. The analysis is concluded in Chapter Six, which pulls together the key threads of the argument and peers forward to the major developments in command approach that occurred during the remainder of the Second World War.

Although it is necessary to take account of trends and developments both before and after these dates, this book deliberately focuses on the period 1918 to 1940, as this represents a key phase in the military thought and practice of both armies. By the summer of 1918, both armies had reached a peak of professional expertise, with the experiences gained over the previous four years of fighting encapsulated into tactics, equipment and training that placed them far in advance of the formations deployed in 1914. The interwar period effectively represents a time during which the British and Germans each sought to distil the enduring lessons of the First World War and build these into their doctrine. The battles of 1940 were largely fought with the equipment, tactics and doctrine developed during that interwar period. It may therefore be considered that the key fulcrum of subsequent doctrinal development lies in the period after the Fall of France, as both armies then reflected upon the evidence and experience gained during those early campaigns. In addition, it is often argued that this period also marks a vital discontinuity in the development of German military doctrine, what Robert Citino termed the 'death of *Auftragstaktik*'[10] – the failure of Operation Barbarossa exposed the limits of the approach and Hitler thereafter took ever closer personal control of military operations and imposed his own philosophy, the 'Führer Prinzip', which was strongly counter to the traditional culture of low-level

---

10   Robert M. Citino, *The German Way of War: From the Thirty Years' War to the Third Reich* (Lawrence, KS: University Press of Kansas, 2005), pp. 301-303.

initiative and flexibility. The spring of 1940 may therefore be taken as marking the end of a key phase in doctrinal development, allowing this book to consider it as a whole.

Towards a Model of Command Approaches

Origins

From the late 1980s, recognising the weak conceptual foundations of the contemporary development of Mission Command (then termed 'Mission Analysis / Directive Control') in the British and US Armies, the late Michael Elliott-Bateman, with his postgraduate students, Spencer Fitz-Gibbon, Kieran Creaton, and the author, at the Department of Military Studies, University of Manchester, explored issues related to command approaches. The aim was to suggest a more robust model than the simplistic dichotomy that characterised the debate at the time.[11]

Central to our argument was the proposition that different armies perceive combat in fundamentally different ways. Some see it as inherently structured, others as essentially chaotic. This perception is expressed in the command approach that an army generally employs. We proposed that those armies that understand combat as inherently structured will seek to reduce friction by imposing control of the battle from above through 'Restrictive Control', which we felt was broadly equivalent to the German concept of *Befehlstaktik*. Conversely, armies that consider it essentially chaotic will endeavour to reduce friction by maximising subordinates' initiative to achieve the overall intent – 'Directive Command', broadly equivalent to *Auftragstaktik*.[12] We proposed the British Army generally demonstrated a preference for Restrictive Control, while the German Army leaned towards Directive Command. Exceptions existed, of course, such as Major Chris Keeble's encouragement of initiative at Goose Green in the Falklands War of 1982 and Alfred von Schlieffen's insistence on rigid obedience to orders in the 1890s. However, we argued that these examples served to prove the rule: the fact that they stood out from the norm underlined their difference from that norm.

Having identified a conceptual basis for command approaches, we identified a further variation: 'Umpiring'. Here, commanders set out their intent and leave the means of its achievement to their subordinates' initiative, yet do not intervene even when they see those subordinates acting in ways that will not deliver the intent.

---

11   The framework was most clearly set out in Martin Samuels, *Command or Control? Command, Training and Tactics in the British and German Armies, 1888-1918* (London: Cass, 1995), pp. 3-5, and Spencer Fitz-Gibbon, *Not Mentioned in Despatches… The History and Mythology of the Battle of Goose Green* (Cambridge: Lutterworth, 1995), pp. xiv-xvi.

12   This term has generally fallen from use, due to the (strictly speaking incorrect) association of 'directives' with prescriptive written orders, and been replaced by 'Mission Command' in contemporary military usage.

For example, despite his better appreciation of events during the initial landings at Gallipoli in April 1915, Sir Ian Hamilton felt unable to get involved when the assault by one of his subordinates, Aylmer Hunter-Weston, went awry.[13]

Although this model represented an important conceptualisation, it remained largely descriptive, due to the limited depth of the connection with the theory of friction. We were, however, far from alone in this. Although friction is all-pervading in human conflict, and hence a major factor to be accommodated, Martin van Creveld noted, 'Save perhaps for the occasional intercepted or misunderstood message or the broken-down radio, it is indeed possible to study military history for years and hardly notice that the problem exists.'[14]

The Prussian soldier and theorist, Carl von Clausewitz (1780-1831) was the first to understand how friction creates the gulf that so often exists between what commanders *intend* to happen and what *actually* happens.[15] As he noted in On War, 'This tremendous friction, which cannot, as in mechanics, be reduced to a few points, is everywhere in contact with chance, and brings about effects that cannot be measured, just because they are largely due to chance. [...] Friction [...] is the force that makes the apparently easy so difficult.'[16] Since friction is a basic characteristic of the (military) environment, any successful army therefore needs to address it as a matter of routine

Clausewitz recognised that friction was expressed in several different ways. Internal aspects of friction, generated within the army itself (such as insufficient knowledge of the enemy, or commanders' uncertainty about friendly forces' location and strength), is expressed through a gap between the plans of commanders and the actions undertaken by their troops. Friction generated by the environment (such as weather, terrain, and logistics) is shown through a gap between the action and its expected outcome. As Stephen Bungay, a director of the Ashridge Strategic Management Centre,[17] and a group of likeminded researchers have recently shown, the interaction between these aspects of friction produces a third gap – the actions taken by an army, even if these are according to the commander's plan, may not deliver the desired outcome.[18] This produces the following model of friction:

---

13   John Lee, *A Soldier's Life: General Sir Ian Hamilton, 1853-1947* (London: Pan, 2001), pp.164-165.
14   Martin Van Creveld, *Command in War* (Cambridge, MA: Harvard University Press, 1985), p.11.
15   Hew Strachan, *Clausewitz's On War: A Biography* (New York, NY: Atlantic Monthly, 2007) p.153.
16   Clausewitz, *On War*, pp. 120-121.
17   The author has benefitted greatly from the opportunity to discuss the ideas and concepts presented in this book with Stephen Bungay and with two other members of his group: Jim Storr and Aidan Walsh.
18   Stephen Bungay, *The Art of Action: How Leaders Close the Gaps between Plans, Actions and Results* (London: Brealey, 2011), pp. 30-35.

- Knowledge Gap: plans are imperfect because there is a gap between what commanders would *like to know* about the local situation and what they *actually know* – as Clausewitz noted, 'This difficulty of *accurate recognition* constitutes one of the most serious sources of friction in war, by making things appear entirely different from what one had expected';[19]
- Alignment Gap: actions are imperfect because there is a gap between what commanders *want* units to do and what they *actually* do – 'A battalion is made up of individuals, the least important of whom may chance to delay things or somehow make them go wrong';[20] and
- Effects Gap: outcomes are imperfect because the nature of war means an army's actions may produce *unexpected results* – 'Particular factors can often be decisive – details only known to those who were on the spot'.[21]

The model is expressed graphically in Figure 1.1.

Figure 1.1: Stephen Bungay's Three Gaps Model

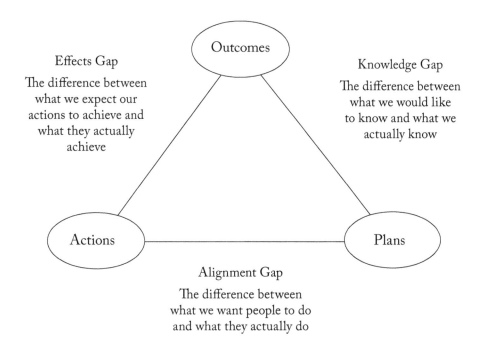

Effects Gap

The difference between what we expect our actions to achieve and what they actually achieve

Outcomes

Knowledge Gap

The difference between what we would like to know and what we actually know

Actions

Plans

Alignment Gap

The difference between what we want people to do and what they actually do

19 Clausewitz, *On War*, p. 117 (emphasis in original).
20 Clausewitz, *On War*, p. 119.
21 Clausewitz, *On War*, p. 595.

The model highlights the alternative options open to commanders:

- Knowledge Gap: commanders may know either more or less about the local situation than do their subordinates, and, if less, may seek to close this gap either by demanding more information or by adapting their command approach to cope with less;
- Alignment Gap: subordinates may implement their commanders' instructions to a greater or lesser extent, and, where these instructions may not be implemented, commanders may seek to close this gap either by limiting themselves to orders setting out their general intent, leaving implementation to their subordinates' initiative, or they may require their subordinates to follow detailed orders precisely; and
- Effects Gap: events on the battlefield may or may not turn out as the commanders had intended, and, where they do not unfold as expected, commanders may respond to this gap either by intervening or by allowing their subordinates to react to the changed situation.

The deeper model of friction developed by Bungay and his colleagues is therefore of particular importance, as it can be linked with the initial model of command approaches developed by the author and his colleagues at the University of Manchester in the late 1980s. Combining the thinking of these two groups allows a new and more sophisticated typology of command approaches to be generated, based on these representing different approaches to reducing friction, as differently perceived by different armies.

Knowledge, alignment and effects can be considered as three broadly 'either/or' axes, which produces a simple model comprising two-by-two-by-two (that is, eight) permutations. These are listed at Figure 1.2 and described in more detail at Figure 1.4

Figure 1.2: Eight Permutations

Knowledge Gap	Alignment Gap	Effects Gap	Title
Superior knows less than subordinates	Subordinates should use initiative	Superiors will intervene	1: Enthusiastic Amateur
		Superiors will not intervene	2: Directive Command
	Subordinates should do as they are told	Superiors will intervene	3: Restrictive Control
		Superiors will not intervene	4: Detached Control
Superior knows more than subordinates	Subordinates should use initiative	Superiors will intervene	5: Directive Control
		Superiors will not intervene	6: Umpiring
	Subordinates should do as they are told	Superiors will intervene	7: Logistic Control
		Superiors will not intervene	8: Neglected Control

Figure 1.3 provides an alternative way of presenting the permutations, through two four-box models, which allows the relationships between the eight command approaches to emerge more clearly.

Figure 1.3: Command Approaches

(Knowledge Gap)	*Superiors Know Less Than Subordinates*				*Superiors Know More Than Subordinates*	
	Enthusiastic Amateur	**Restrictive Control**	*Superiors Intervene*		**Directive Control**	**Logistic Control**
(Effects Gap)	**Directive Command**[22]	**Detached Control**	*Superiors Do Not Intervene*		**Umpiring**	**Neglected Control**
(Alignment Gap)	*Subordinates Should Use Initiative*	*Subordinates Should Follow Orders*			*Subordinates Should Use Initiative*	*Subordinates Should Follow Orders*

The names applied to each of the command approaches were coined for ease of reference and, where possible, to avoid negative perceptions. The aim was to identify the full typology, rather than to make judgements regarding relative effectiveness. That assessment is made in later sections of this chapter. That said, it is recognised that Command Approach 8: 'Neglected Control', *is* negative, which is insightful in relation both to this permutation specifically and the list in general. It may describe a situation in which a superior seemingly deliberately sets up their subordinate(s) to fail. Despite this seeming an unlikely occurrence, it may perhaps reflect situations where allegiances are uncertain and political considerations outweigh immediate military objectives, such as in a civil war or the Italian Army of 1940-42. The ability of the model to generate such permutations illustrates its value and (perhaps) its power.

---

22 While there are considerable similarities between Mission Command and Directive Command, the latter term is used here, partly to retain consistency with the author's earlier work and partly to draw a distinction between Directive Command as a theoretical concept and Mission Command as the espoused doctrine of various armies.

Describing the Command Approaches

Having identified the basic nature of the eight approaches, Figure 1.4 defines and describes them.

Figure 1.4: Describing Command Approaches

Title	Description	Context
1: Enthusiastic Amateur	Superiors intervene, despite the fact they know less than their subordinates do and these will use their initiative wisely.	Might be typical of the early stages of a large civil war (such as the American Civil War or English Civil War), where most commanders act enthusiastically and in accordance with the perceived common good, but where command issues relating to decentralisation have not yet been agreed.
2: Directive Command	Superiors will not intervene, because they know less than their subordinates do and are confident these will use initiative.	May be considered the default preference of the German Army for more than a century. It is widely held to be appropriate to the armed forces of many developed states, but requires significant levels of responsibility, initiative and training on the part of subordinates.
3: Restrictive Control	Superiors know less than their subordinates, but issue definitive orders (in the expectation these will be adhered to), and intervene to ensure compliance. *In practice,* they act as if they know more than their subordinates do.	May arise where a small professional army has experienced rapid expansion at the start of a major war, such as the British Army in 1914-1916 and the American Army in 1941-1942. It may also reflect arrogance on the part of superiors, where the potential ability of subordinates to use initiative is discounted, perhaps because of the selection and training of commanders.[23]

---

23 Jörg Muth, *Command Culture: Officer Education in the U.S. Army and the German Armed Forces, 1901-1940, and the Consequences for World War II* (Denton, TX: University of North Texas, 2011), p. 80.

4: Detached Control	Superiors know less than their subordinates know, but nevertheless issue definitive orders, and then leave their subordinates struggling to put these into effect without further guidance. Subordinates actually know more than superiors, but are not allowed (or expected) to use initiative to resolve the problems arising from orders based on a poor understanding of the situation.	Probably unthinking and may reflect inadequate training of superiors. They have been taught command and staff processes (perhaps by rote), but understand neither their own limitations nor the ability of subordinates to get things done. Critically, it may be what is actually practised (as opposed to intended) in modern western armies. The fault may lie in overly prescriptive doctrinal pamphlets (and training systems).
5: Directive Control	Superiors know more than their subordinates know, issue definitive orders and will intervene, but require their subordinates to use their initiative in all other situations.	An expression of the German approach of 'the commander at the *Schwerpunkt*'. It suits a situation where the senior commander takes personal control at the critical point, but has subordinates with the training, education and experience to display initiative. It is also perhaps appropriate in large-scale operations where the big picture is more important than local detail, such as the D-Day landings in Normandy.
6: Umpiring	Superiors will not intervene, even though they know more than their subordinates do, as they are confident subordinates will use initiative.	Can be seen as careless (failing to take responsibility to intervene when things go wrong) or as Directive Command gone wrong (failing to pass relevant knowledge down to subordinates, so they can use initiative effectively). It may be well intentioned, sometimes resulting from command relationships that are too familiar or insecure, such as where commanders hold the same rank as their subordinates. It may have been characteristic of formation-level commanders in the pre-1914 British Army.

7: Logistic Control	Superiors know more than their subordinates and issue definitive orders, then intervene to ensure these are acted on, recognising subordinates cannot be relied upon to use initiative safely.	A very highly centralised command system. It might be representative of the position sometimes achieved in modern high-technology warfare, where sophisticated intelligence systems may (appear) to give commanders more information than can be gained by their subordinates. The term Logistic Control was coined to suggest that, in the first instance, subordinates (and formations) are treated largely as inanimate objects to be pushed around, like parcels to be delivered. The Soviet Army may have aspired to this approach in the 1980s.
8: Neglected Control	Superiors know more than their subordinates and issue definitive orders, yet fail to intervene when events work out differently, since they are content to see subordinates fail (thereby strengthening their own position).	May describe a situation in which a superior seemingly deliberately sets up their subordinate(s) to fail. Despite seeming unlikely, it may perhaps reflect situations where allegiances are uncertain and political considerations outweigh immediate military objectives, such as in a civil war or the Italian Army of 1940-1942. An alternative explanation is that it reflects a personal or cultural avoidance of responsibility. As with Umpiring, the commander may not feel his responsibility extends to correct problems at lower levels, even though this may prejudice mission success. Whatever the case, this describes behaviour few would describe as professional.

Connecting the Command Approaches

Another way of thinking about the model is in terms of space or volume. If knowledge, alignment and effects are considered axes at right angles to each other, then a commander's (or army's) command approach can be seen to lie in a space with eight possible extremes, as expressed in Figure 1.5. A real cube, with names written on each of its faces, makes visualisation easier.

Figure 1.5: Command Approach Cube

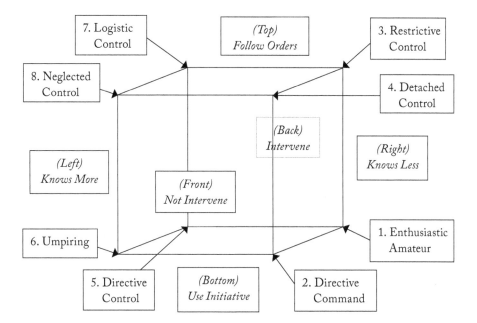

The cube reveals that (for example) approaches 2 (Directive Command) and 6 (Umpiring) are in some ways quite similar. In both cases, superiors will not intervene and subordinates display initiative. They differ only in that in Umpiring the commander ignores the fact he knows more, while in Directive Command he recognises he knows less. This implies it may be relatively simple (although not necessarily easy) to move from one approach to another, either as an individual or as an organisation.

The cube indicates four pairs of approaches are the exact opposite of each other, eight pairs are adjacent to each other (sharing two factors) and eight pairs share one factor (lying diagonally opposite each other on the same face). It is probably no accident that Directive Command and Logistic Control are opposites: they are the natural successors to *Auftragstaktik* and *Befehlstaktik*. Both can be recognised as entirely logical responses by professional commanders and armies to very different circumstances. They can now be seen as direct opposites. The cube also indicates that all the other approaches have at least one factor in common with *both* of those opposites. It also suggests an army could:

- Conceptually move from its present preferred approach to several others with just one step.
- Drift away from its preferred or official approach relatively easily, by sliding inadvertently along one of three axes.

Either case might be good or bad. In particular, it may be possible for a commander to believe he is applying one approach, only to in fact slide across to another, less effective, command approach. This highlights just how difficult the exercise of command can be in practice.

This may be of some importance in a situation where an army's culture has favoured one approach, but changes in context mean that a shift to a different command approach is required. The first step is realising the different approaches exist. The second is understanding what separates them. The third is engineering the move. For example, in the early 1990s, the British Army attempted to move towards Directive Command (which it called Mission Command) by, first, enunciating the alternatives and, next, moving from something like Umpiring to something like Directive Command (described at the time as 'Auftragstaktik with Chobham Armour').[24]

A Pause for Reflection

The model, and particularly the cube, suggests there are eight precisely defined alternative approaches. Clearly, that is simplistic. Not least, different human institutions, with different cultures and histories, do not behave in the same ways, and so different armies espousing Mission Command (equivalent to the Directive Command approach identified above) do not practice it in identical ways.[25] The model, and the cube, should be taken to indicate there are, in practice, an infinite variety of command approaches. The eight permutations are simply illustrative places on that continuum, representing zones of similarity (as, for example, between the German and Israeli practice of Mission Command).

The model suggests that commanders and armies can move between permutations. It offers some tools that may facilitate an understanding of why that might occur. The environment will typically be one of high stress (such as during a conflict or operation). Linking back to the earlier Manchester work, the model also suggests why some personality types may be predisposed to certain command approaches. Finally, the model may indicate factors facilitating or hindering armies seeking to move from one approach to another. Such factors may include officer training, the peacetime social environment, and experience of actual conflict.

The model is therefore inevitably a simplification. Perhaps its most obvious shortcoming is around the Knowledge Gap. Does that gap indicate the commander actually does know more or less, or that he *acts* as if he does? Does it refer to knowledge of the wider context or of the local situation faced by each subordinate? Or to the relative importance of context and situation? Those questions denote several possibilities, and there are probably more. When linked to the Alignment Gap, they demand consideration of whether superiors are more capable of deciding what to do

---

24   Shamir, *Transforming Command*, p.171.
25   See Shamir, *Transforming Command*, passim.

at lower levels. The British plan for the first day of the Somme in 1916 assumed they did. The result was tragic.[26] But, given pitiably low levels of training on the part of many subordinates, the assumption might be correct. Yet a commander would typically be poorly placed if he were to attempt to make every decision on behalf of his subordinates. The second- and third-order effects of delegating responsibility, not least on motivation and display of initiative, should not be discounted.

The model has implications for commanders and command systems, including the need for information to flow through the system, for trust between commanders and subordinates, and for training, not just before operations but also learning through the conduct of operations.

Command approaches are generally poorly studied, and hence poorly understood. They have emerged as a result of the military and human conditions that exist in armies and in the conflicts they undertake. It is better to understand how and why they have evolved, and their strengths and weaknesses, than to brand them as inherently 'right' or 'wrong'.

In summary, focusing on three major variables (superior knowledge, display of initiative, and intervention) suggests a model of eight broad command approaches. The variables are chosen from an analysis of the command process and its interaction with friction, specifically the gaps between reality, planning, and action. Despite this inherent simplicity, the model appears to describe much of the variation of command approach noted in history.

It is simplistic to say Directive Command is always right. It is more sensible to say, for the armies of developed nations, Directive Command generally best supports the achievement of military objectives in an environment that is inevitably human, complex, and dynamic. It is, however, entirely understandable that other armies might prefer other approaches. They might, for example, operate in conditions where their subordinates are grossly untrained, poorly motivated, or politically suspect.

The real benefit of the model is not to underpin a call for Directive Command. It is to assist the understanding of command approaches, and ensure alignment between the approaches armies employ and the contexts within which these are employed.

The model of command approaches developed above is intended to demonstrate the full range of possible options open to a commander, based on the alternative situations for each of the three gaps that together represent the causes of friction. Designed to represent the totality of the system, most of the descriptions are deliberately neutral in tone. Before moving on the consider their relative effectiveness, it should again be underlined that these represent theoretical extremes, since the 'either/or' basis for the three gaps would, in reality, be more properly represented by a spectrum. For the current purposes, however, the division into eight idealised command approaches provides a useful basis for their characteristics to be explored.

26   Samuels, *Command or Control?*, pp. 124-157.

Reducing Friction Experienced by Friendly Forces

Having developed a model of different command approaches, while fully recognising its deficiencies, the next step is to assess the effectiveness of each of the eight approaches in reducing friction, and hence its value on the battlefield. In so doing, it must be recognised that command approaches do not exist as independent variables without context.

A key element in the thinking done by the Manchester group was that two aspects of context[27] are of central importance:

- Whether warfare is inherently chaotic or else essentially structured, and commanders' different perception of this aspect of warfare's basic nature.
- The organisational culture of an army, especially the beliefs and values surrounding the relationship between commanders and subordinates.

Chaos and Structure

The essence of the Knowledge Gap is whether commanders have an understanding of the local situation relevant to the orders they give and receive.

A central characteristic of the Knowledge Gap is that it is easy for commanders and their subordinates to make incorrect assessments of their own and each other's knowledge. Consequently, commanders and subordinates may believe their own knowledge of the local situation is either greater or less than the reality, and they may be similarly incorrect regarding each other's knowledge. This unconscious factor is one of the main factors widening the Knowledge Gap, increasing friction.

The command approach adopted by an army, or an individual commander within it, is influenced by whether it is considered practical for commanders to gain a better understanding of the local situation than can their subordinates. A key consideration is whether warfare is seen as inherently chaotic or else as structured.[28] In many respects, this question may be considered closely related to that issue central to much recent management thinking: whether the problems facing leaders are 'tame' or else 'wicked'.

By the start of the twentieth century, the American management theorist Frederick Winslow Taylor was convinced 'the man in the planning room' could draw on his extensive records of a factory's processes in order to set out in advance the precise tasks required for each worker. The latter was simply required to follow those detailed instructions, which laid down 'not only what is to be done but how it is to be done and the exact time allowed for doing it'. Based on his experience as general manager of a large paper mill company, Taylor believed this separation of functions would

27   See Samuels, *Command or Control?*, pp.3-6.
28   Samuels, *Command or Control?*, pp.3-5. See also Fitz-Gibbon, *Not Mentioned in Despatches...*, pp. xiv-xvi.

lead to greater productivity and, consequently, the worker would 'grow happier and more prosperous'.[29] His approach, termed Scientific Management, soon became predominant in management thinking. As recently as the year 2000, members of the American Academy of Management voted Taylor the most influential management thinker of the twentieth century.[30]

If one uses the model of Clausewitzian friction, as developed by Bungay, as a means of analysis, it may be seen that Taylor in effect assumed that the Knowledge Gap could be closed through the collection of complete data, and the Alignment Gap eliminated by requiring the worker to act only as exactly instructed. Since the consequences of actions could be determined in advance, there could be no Effects Gap.[31] In essence, therefore, Taylor favoured a management approach equivalent to Logistic Control.

In the early 1970s, however, Horst Rittel and Melvin Webber recognised that the 'classical paradigm of science and engineering [...] is not applicable to the problems of open societal systems':[32] They realised that Scientific Management was not an effective response outside the controlled environment of the factory. Indeed, it was often not appropriate inside the factory either. Rittel and Webber identified a range of factors, bearing a remarkable similarity to those noted by Clausewitz as expressing friction in warfare, which meant that such societal problems differed from what they labelled the 'tame' nature of scientific questions. These problems' lack of a clear mission or any defined solution gave them a character that Rittel and Webber termed 'wicked'.

More recently, Keith Grint[33] has suggested that a tame problem 'may be complicated but is resolvable through unilinear acts'. These are associated with Management (the function of providing the correct process through which to implement the single right solution). By contrast, a wicked problem 'is often intractable, [has] no unilinear solution, [and] there is no "stopping" point'. Such problems are associated with Leadership (the function of asking the right questions in order to draw out the best from the many possible solutions).[34]

In a point of central importance, Grint noted it is rarely possible to determine objectively *at the time* whether a specific problem is tame or wicked. Rather, the participants' *perception* of the nature of the problem will lead them to express it in ways that focus on either its tame or wicked aspects and hence (often unconsciously) have

29 Frederick Winslow Taylor, *The Principles of Scientific Management* (New York, NY: Harper, 1911), pp. 37-39.
30 Robert F. Conti, 'Frederick Wilmslow Taylor', in *The Oxford Handbook of Management Theorists*, ed. by Morgen Witzell and Malcolm Warner (Oxford: Oxford University Press, 2013), pp.11-31 (p.11).
31 I am grateful to Aidan Walsh for drawing this argument to my attention.
32 Horst W.J. Rittel and Melvin M. Webber, 'Dilemmas in a General Theory of Planning', *Policy Sciences* 4 (1973), (155-169), p.160.
33 Professor of Public Leadership and Management, Warwick Business School.
34 Keith Grint, *Leadership, Management and Command: Rethinking D-Day* (Basingstoke: Palgrave, 2008), pp.11-12.

the effect of legitimising their chosen approach.[35] This again brings out the importance of a comparative approach: in the context of warfare, situations will involve opposing forces, each of which may perceive a specific problem in different ways, such that one side may respond as if the problem were tame, while the other may consider it wicked. Which side is 'correct' in its assessment of the situation may be less important than how the interplay of those different assessments favours one side or the other.

In passing, it should be noted that use of this model is not intended to suggest military commanders were necessarily guided by, or even aware of, Scientific Management. It merely provides a useful means for the historian to analyse their behaviour. In just the same way, the concept of the 'learning curve' has provided a powerful tool by which to explain the British Army's performance during the First World War,[36] even though its commanders themselves never used the term.

Nonetheless, there is clear evidence that Taylorism did have a definite influence on some aspects of military administration during this period. For example, the reforms of the US Army undertaken by Elihu Root when Secretary of War between 1899 and 1904 were explicitly based on the concepts of Scientific Management.[37] In Britain, some of the professional managers brought into the army during the First World War were also familiar with Taylorism and applied it in their newfound military duties. For example, Brigadier-General E.G. Wace, who from 1916 headed the army's military labour establishment, was 'an enthusiastic advocate of scientific management and a follower of [...] Taylor's system'.[38] Related approaches, based on careful statistical analysis of methods, were also widespread across the British engineering industry.[39] For example, Sir Eric Geddes, who revitalised the British Expeditionary Force's (BEF's) logistics systems,[40] received advanced training in statistics as a management tool at the North Eastern Railway.[41] More importantly for this study, the model of problems being either wicked or tame has become standard in modern management

35   Grint, *Rethinking D-Day*, pp.12-14.
36   Gary Sheffield, *Forgotten Victory: The First World War: Myths and Realities* (London: Headline, 2001), pp.xi-xii.
37   Donald Vandergriff, *The Path to Victory: America's Army and the Revolution in Human Affairs* (Novato, CA: Presidio, 2002), pp.40-51, and Jason Patrick Clark, The Many Faces of Reform: Military Progressivism in the US Army, 1866-1916 (unpublished PhD thesis, Duke University, 2009), pp.124-125.
38   Nicholas J. Griffin, 'Scientific Management in the Direction of Britain's Military Labour Establishment During World War I', *Military Affairs*, 42(4) (December 1978), (197-201), pp.197-198.
39   Lyndall Urwick, *The Development of Scientific Management in Great Britain* (London: Management Journals, 1938), pp.24-34.
40   Ian Malcolm Brown, *British Logistics on the Western Front, 1914-1919* (Westport CT: Praeger, 1998), pp.139-178.
41   Keith Grieves, *Sir Eric Geddes: Business and Government in War and Peace* (Manchester: Manchester University, 1989), pp.4-7.

thinking,[42] where friction is as much an issue as in warfare, and so there is benefit from interdisciplinary borrowing.

If warfare is basically *structured* (linear in cause and effect relationships), and hence the problems faced are generally tame, commanders can expect to have better knowledge of the local situation than is available to their subordinates. This is a consequence of senior commanders' control of greater intelligence resources, their access to regular and detailed operational reports provided by friendly forces, and their staff's ability to analyse alternative scenarios. Consequently, commanders can objectively predict emerging opportunities and obtain detailed knowledge of new situations, thereby reducing the Knowledge Gap. Linearity also implies that the outcomes of combat actions are broadly predictable, reducing the Effects Gap.

Since the main remaining aspect of friction is the Alignment Gap, armies that perceive warfare as linear may be expected to emphasise extensive planning and detailed orders, to which subordinates must adhere rigidly. This was certainly a central pillar of Scientific Management and it appears also to have been the model adopted by the Soviet Army. The Marxist belief that human interaction was subject to immutable laws (and consequently that warfare was inherently structured) led it to conclude that commanders could use their understanding of these laws to develop detailed plans in advance, which their subordinates simply needed to follow to the letter.[43]

This may lead to the 'Logistic Control' command approach being favoured as the most effective means to reduce friction. In turn, this may encourage commanders to expect that they will have greater knowledge of the situation than do their subordinates, and hence fail to recognise when this is not the case, thereby causing them to slip unwittingly into 'Restrictive Control'.

By contrast, if warfare is fundamentally *chaotic* (non-linear in cause and effect relationships), and hence the problems faced are generally wicked, commanders (given their distance, in time and location, from unfolding events) can rarely know the local situation as well as (let alone better than) do their subordinates. The Knowledge Gap is therefore wide. The absence of linear relationships between actions and results means that the outcomes of combat actions are also less predictable, widening the Effects Gap. By comparison, the Alignment Gap may be less critical to the overall level of friction.

Armies that perceive warfare as chaotic are therefore likely to emphasise the importance of subordinates showing initiative, rendering the Knowledge Gap less significant, and to focus on reducing the Effects Gap. Since these armies believe victory is gained through rapid actions to seize the fleeting and unpredictable opportunities

---

42 A search on Amazon.co.uk for 'tame wicked problems' returned 150+ books, over half from the Business category.
43 Major George W. Eisel, 'Befehlstaktik and The Red Army Experience: Are There Lessons for Us?' (unpublished master's thesis, US Army Command & General Staff College, Fort Leavenworth, KS, 1993), pp. 4-23.

generated by this chaos, subordinates must be allowed maximum scope within which to apply their initiative – guided by the commanders' overall intent. The adoption of Mission Command by the American and British armies in the 1980s was in part driven by precisely the belief that warfare was inherently chaotic, with ever changing scenarios, which therefore demanded the flexibility offered by this doctrine.[44]

This may produce a preference for the 'Directive Command' command approach as the most effective means to reduce friction. Again, this may lead commanders to overlook the possibility that sometimes they will have greater knowledge of the situation than do their subordinates, causing them to slide unwittingly into 'Umpiring'.

A perception of warfare as inherently chaotic may also encourage commanders to emphasise efforts to reduce the Knowledge Gap by securing personal observation of the local situation at the decisive point,[45] resulting in the use of 'Directive Control'.

Figure 1.6 summarises how the model of whether problems are tame or wicked, that is to say, linear or chaotic, can illuminate the three 'gaps' associated with friction, and hence the relative effectiveness of different command approaches.

Figure 1.6: The Gaps and Tame / Wicked Problems

Gap	Tame Problem (unilinear, with a single 'correct' solution)	Wicked Problem (complex, with many possible solutions)
Knowledge Gap	Commanders can extrapolate from their greater knowledge of the broader context to predict the local situation within which their subordinates will operate	Extrapolation is unlikely to be accurate and therefore widens the gap
Alignment Gap	Role of subordinates is primarily to apply the 'correct' process, as determined by the commander	Subordinates must be part of a collaborative effort that draws upon everyone's unique knowledge to secure the most effective solution
Effects Gap	Focus is on making sure the commander identifies the single 'correct' solution, even if this takes time	Role of the commander is to ensure a 'good enough' solution is implemented as quickly as possible

44   Major John F. Antal, 'Combat Orders: An Analysis of the Tactical Orders Process' (unpublished master's thesis, US Army Command & General Staff College, Fort Leavenworth, KS, 1990), pp. 14-19.

45   Muth, *Command Culture*, pp. 99-101, and *On the German Art of War: Truppenführung*, ed. by Bruce Condell and David T. Zabecki (London: Rienner, 2001), pp. 36-37.

Since an army's *perception* of the nature of warfare as being either chaotic or linear significantly influences the command approaches adopted, it is necessary to consider warfare's *actual* nature. Given that the typology of command approaches is based on Clausewitz's description of friction, it is appropriate to use him as our guide when considering the fundamental nature of warfare. The richness, depth and complexity (some might say obscurity)[46] of Clausewitz's work here is demonstrated by the extensive secondary literature that it has inspired.[47] It is possible, however, to highlight the main positions through consideration of two seminal articles.

Alan Beyerchen[48] argued that Clausewitz saw warfare as inherently non-linear, in that outputs may be disproportionate to inputs and results may be sensitive to initial conditions. Such systems are termed 'chaotic' in natural science,[49] and hence the problems emerging from them are by their nature wicked, to use Grint's terminology. Central to Beyerchen's understanding was that the outcome in warfare is, by definition, the consequence of the dynamic interplay between the opposing forces. Clausewitz used the analogy of a wrestling match[50] to highlight that the positions and moves adopted by one wrestler are often made possible only by those employed by their opponent. In passing, this alone should demonstrate that the study of one army alone can provide only a very partial understanding of a battle (just as a radio commentary of a soccer game that barely mentioned the opposing team would render the course of play virtually impossible for the listener to understand) – yet this is the norm in military history.

This interpretation was rejected by Terence Holmes,[51] who argued the passages used to support it had been misinterpreted. He suggested instead that Clausewitz believed detailed planning – a linear approach – was central to victory. Holmes took particular issue with Beyerchen's suggestion that Clausewitz considered warfare unpredictable, with the result determined by the combination of chance and the actions of the opponent. He noted that the famous saying, 'no war plan outlasts the first encounter with the enemy', comes not from Clausewitz but from Helmuth von Moltke the Elder. Instead, he argued Clausewitz placed great emphasis on effective advanced planning, focused on the desired objective, and a relentless concentration on the delivery of those elements of the plan central to the attainment of that objective. For this, Clausewitz

46   Michael Howard, 'The Influence of Clausewitz', in Clausewitz, *On War*, pp. 27-44 (p.27).
47   See the Clausewitz Homepage (http://www.clausewitz.com/) [accessed 19 March 2013].
48   Alan Beyerchen, 'Clausewitz, Nonlinearity, and the Unpredictability of War', *International Security*, 17(3) (Winter 1992/93), 59-90.
49   Several definitions of chaos are provided in a popular introduction to the topic by James Gleick, *Chaos: The Amazing Science of the Unpredictable* (London: Vantage, 1998), pp. 306-307.
50   Clausewitz, *On War*, p. 75.
51   Terence M. Holmes, 'Planning versus Chaos in Clausewitz's *On War*', *Journal of Strategic Studies*, 30(1) (February 2007), 129-151.

borrowed another term from physics, the *Schwerpunkt*, to denote an object's centre of gravity – 'the point against which all our energies should be directed'.[52]

It may be suggested Holmes was right to argue Clausewitz did not consider warfare completely unpredictable. Indeed, were this to be the case, the task of the commander would be impossible. But Beyerchen overstated the position when he suggested chaotic systems are, by definition, unpredictable. A distinction can be drawn between systems that are completely unpredictable and those that cannot be predicted with certainty. That this distinction is far from semantic may be demonstrated by analogy with the weather. As meteorologists have long recognised, the weather is certainly a non-linear system, but this does not mean it cannot be predicted. Even though it may be impossible to forecast accurately more than a few days in advance whether (in the northern hemisphere) it will snow on a particular day in January or be sunny during a specific week in August, we can be almost certain that the weather during the winter will be colder and wetter than in the summer, and we can make reasonably reliable estimates far in advance regarding the likelihood of snow or storms, and temperature. It is therefore entirely possible for Clausewitz to have regarded warfare as inherently chaotic, as Beyerchen argued, while still placing great weight on the importance of planning, as Holmes suggested.

This is perhaps best summed up by the actual quotation from Moltke: 'No plan of operations extends with certainty beyond the first encounter with the main hostile force. [...] Yet in spite of all this, the conduct of war has never degenerated into blind arbitrariness.'[53] Moltke was not saying commanders should not have a plan. Rather, they should not be surprised if events unfold differently from their intention, and should be prepared accordingly:

> Certainly the commander in chief will keep his great objective continuously in mind, undisturbed by the vicissitudes of events. But the path on which he hopes to reach it can never be firmly established in advance. Throughout the campaign he must make a series of decisions on the basis of situations that cannot be foreseen. The successive acts of the war are thus not predictable designs, but on the contrary are spontaneous acts guided by military measures.[54]

If warfare is therefore inherently chaotic, and hence the problems facing commanders are generally wicked, 'Directive Command' may be the most effective command approach for reducing the level of friction experienced by friendly forces, supplemented

---

52 Clausewitz, *On War*, pp. 595-596. It should be noted the German Army's longstanding use of the term differs from Clausewitz's definition, which is also now the current US Army usage. Major-General David T. Zabecki, *The German 1918 Offensives: A Case Study in the Operational Level of War* (London: Routledge, 2006), p. 31.

53 *Moltke on the Art of War: Selected Writings*, ed. by Daniel J. Hughes (New York, NY: Ballantine, 1993), pp.92-93.

54 *Moltke on the Art of War*, pp.45-46.

by 'Directive Control' when commanders can position themselves personally at the decisive point. Its assumption that the Alignment Gap is the least significant of the three gaps, and hence its reliance on subordinates' initiative to achieve the commander's intent, based on their greater knowledge of the local situation, highlights the second critical aspect of the context within which command is undertaken – the trust between commanders and subordinates.

Trust, Initiative and Orders

The extent to which commanders can rely upon their subordinates to carry out their instructions as intended (and hence the width of the Alignment Gap) has two main aspects: motivation and capability. These may be mutually reinforcing. For example, William DePuy emerged from the Second World War convinced American troops were 'inherently reluctant to take risks and, because of inadequate training, unable to take charge in the absence of orders from a superior.' He therefore felt he could not trust his troops to perform as required without a system of 'detailed orders and thorough supervision by commanders'.[55]

As with the Knowledge Gap, commanders' assessment of the motivation and capability of their subordinates may be incorrect, over- or under-estimating these factors. Such incorrect assessments may cause commanders to issue orders that are either too general or too detailed for the capability of their troops. If too general, the Alignment Gap widens, as subordinates are unable to identify the most appropriate actions by which to achieve the commander's intent. If too detailed, the Effects Gap increases, since subordinates follow precise orders, even if inappropriate to the local situation.

The command approach adopted by an army, or an individual commander within it, will be affected by whether it is believed realistic for commanders to have trust in their subordinates sufficient to allow them significant freedom of initiative.

Questions of capability may arise where commanders find themselves leading newly raised forces, with limited training or combat experience. Alternatively, subordinates may be operating in an unfamiliar context, whether against a different enemy or in a novel environment. This may be particularly likely early in a major war. The quest for rapid victory may place a premium on every available soldier joining the fray, as with the German volunteer corps decimated at Langemarck in October 1914, whose mere two months of training meant they were capable of little more than massed frontal charges.[56] Conversely, a small professional army may experience a traumatic expansion

---

55   Major Paul H. Herbert, *Deciding What Has to Be Done: General William E. DePuy and the 1976 Edition of FM 100-5, Operations* (Fort Leavenworth, KS: Combat Studies Institute, 1988), p. 16.
56   Alex Watson, '"For Kaiser and Reich": The Identity and Fate of the German Volunteers, 1914-1918', *War in History*, 12(1) (2005), 44-74 (pp. 62-70).

into a mass army, as when the US Army officer corps mushroomed thirtyfold in the two years to 1943.[57] In such situations, commanders may well be justified in doubting the capability of their subordinates, hence assuming they cannot be trusted to act appropriately without detailed instructions.

Questions of motivation may arise where subordinates are perceived as inherently unwilling to further the commander's intent. Such situations may occur in conscript armies when the war has limited popular support, such as during the later stages of the Vietnam War.[58] Equally, this may happen when volunteers come forward only due to the absence of alternative employment options. For example, before 1914, over ninety percent of recruits to the British Army were previously unemployed and a majority failed to reach the minimum physical standard.[59] Where subordinates have little connection with either the cause or their unit, their willingness to put themselves at risk through active initiative may be doubted.[60]

These (comparatively objective) factors affecting whether subordinates will carry out their commanders' instructions as intended may also be influenced by an army's organisational culture, specifically the relationship between commanders and commanded. Where command is considered a prerogative, initiative by subordinates may be perceived as a threat, encroaching on the commander's authority.[61] Conversely, armies with a strong sense of individual honour may feel it disrespectful to constrain subordinates through detailed orders.[62] Thus, just as with the question of whether warfare is linear or chaotic, an army's beliefs may affect its attitude regarding whether troops can be relied upon to act in accordance with the commander's intent, quite independently of their capability or motivation.

Taking this together, commanders who believe their subordinates incapable or unwilling to act with initiative to secure the overall intent are likely to seek to close the Alignment Gap by favouring command approaches featuring detailed orders, from which subordinates must not deviate. Since the essence of the philosophy is that subordinates cannot be trusted to act independently, the command approaches

---

57   Martin Van Creveld, *Fighting Power: German and U.S. Army Performance, 1939-1945* (Westport, CT: Greenwood, 1982), p. 140.
58   Richard A. Gabriel and Paul L. Savage, *Crisis in Command: Mismanagement in the Army* (New York, NY: Hill & Wang, 1978), pp. 39-46.
59   E. M. Spiers, 'The Regular Army in 1914', in *A Nation in Arms: A Social Study of the British Army in the First World War*, ed. by Ian F. W. Beckett and Keith Simpson (Manchester: Manchester University Press, 1985), 37-62 (p. 44).
60   E. A. Shils and Morris Janowitz, 'Cohesion and Disintegration in the Wehrmacht in World War II', *Public Opinion Quarterly* (Summer 1948), 280-315 (pp. 314-315).
61   Colonel S. L. A. Marshall, *Men Against Fire: The Problem of Battle Command* (Norman, OK: University of Oklahoma Press, 2000), pp. 61-62.
62   For example, Frederick Charles, Prince of Prussia, 'The Origins and Development of the Spirit of the Prussian Officer, its Manifestations and its Effect' (1860), reprinted in K. Demeter, *The German Officer Corps in State and Society: 1650-1945* (London: Weidenfeld & Nicolson, 1965), pp. 257-266 (pp. 260-261).

of 'Detached Control' and 'Neglected Control' would appear to be inherently dysfunctional, as in these the commander does not follow up their orders by intervening to close the Effects Gap, leaving their subordinates adrift.

As has been noted, armies that consider warfare to be inherently structured are likely to have few reservations about seeking to close the Alignment Gap through reliance on detailed orders. They expect commanders to have sufficient knowledge of the local situation (leading to a narrow Knowledge Gap) and to be able to predict the outcome of their 'timetable tactics' (narrowing the Effects Gap). Hence, they may seek to operate through 'Logistic Control'.

However, if warfare is in fact fundamentally chaotic, commanders' knowledge will normally be less than is that of their subordinates, such that the Knowledge Gap is wide. Reliance upon detailed orders in these circumstances would mean the approach adopted was instead 'Restrictive Control'. This carries the significant risk that closing the Alignment Gap may come at the expense of increasing the Effects Gap. The commander's intervention, based on inferior knowledge, may merely worsen the situation. Nonetheless, in some situations, the choice of 'Restrictive Control' may be forced upon commanders, encouraging reliance upon highly-stylised tactical schemes, typified by a reliance upon overwhelming force and a low rate of tempo (an issue considered in detail below). For example, senior British commanders in the First World War recognised that Kitchener's New Army formations, hastily raised from volunteers at the outbreak of war and almost devoid of Regular officers,[63] were at first incapable of any but the simplest manoeuvres based on detailed orders.[64]

It should also be noted that commanders' insistence that subordinates adhere rigidly to detailed orders may hinder development of the very capability and motivation to act with initiative whose absence generates the need for detailed orders in the first place, thereby creating a vicious circle. Equally, commanders may become so accustomed to issuing detailed orders that they fail to recognise when their subordinates become reliable. Not only may 'Logistic Control' decline into 'Restrictive Control', therefore, it may also be retained when circumstances no longer require it.

Conversely, where commanders believe their subordinates have the capability and motivation to achieve the overall intent, they will focus on approaches emphasising maximum scope for lower level initiative. This suggests that the 'Enthusiastic Amateur' command approach is inherently dysfunctional, as in this situation commanders intervene even though they recognise that they have less knowledge of the local situation than do their subordinates, and that these can be

---

63   For example, all of 21st Division's battalion commanders had been called out of retirement, as had fourteen other regimental officers. All the other officers were newly commissioned. Peter Simkins, *Kitchener's Army: The Raising of the New Armies 1914-16* (Manchester: Manchester University Press, 1988), p.218.

64   Brigadier-General James E. Edmonds, *The Official History of the Great War: Military Operations: France & Belgium, 1915, vol. 2: Battles of Aubers Ridge, Festubert, and Loos* (London: Macmillan, 1928), p.vii.

trusted to act appropriately. Enthusiastic Amateurs simply hinder their competent and better-informed subordinates, creating disorder through widening the Effects Gap. Conversely, commanders' confidence in their subordinates can lead them to overlook situations where they do in fact have greater local knowledge than do those subordinates, leading to the dysfunctional 'Umpiring' command approach.

Relative Effectiveness of Command Approaches

This discussion of whether warfare is inherently structured or fundamentally chaotic, and whether commanders can trust their subordinates to act appropriately on their own initiative, suggests that four command approaches ('Enthusiastic Amateur', 'Detached Control', Umpiring', and 'Neglected Control') are inevitably dysfunctional. They are clearly misaligned with the nature of warfare, regardless of whether it is perceived as structured or chaotic, and hence its problems tame or wicked, and so lead to a widening of the Effects Gap. The history of war, however, shows many commanders have nonetheless adopted these approaches, normally inadvertently. But their relevance to the current discussion is limited and they will not be considered further in this chapter.

Under 'Logistic Control', commanders believe they have greater (or more relevant) knowledge of the local situation than do their subordinates (so the Knowledge Gap is narrow), their troops are unable or unwilling to exercise effective initiative (widening the Alignment Gap), and there is a linear relationship between commanders' instructions and the results achieved (narrowing the Effects Gap). Since the main source of friction is therefore the Alignment Gap, the appropriate response is for the commander to issue detailed orders, to which subordinates must comply unwaveringly – what the Germans called *Kadavergehorsamkeit* (corpse-like obedience).[65]

Even competent and motivated subordinates may be unable to exercise initiative effectively in some circumstances, such as when they have less knowledge of the local situation than does their commander. For example, during a complex manoeuvre in August 1870, during the Franco-Prussian War, the Elder Moltke issued detailed orders directly to several corps, bypassing two army commanders. He recognised that his superior knowledge of the road network and of the location of the various formations meant relying on the initiative of his subordinate commanders, no matter how competent, would simply have led to gridlock.[66] Commanders may also create such imbalances of knowledge deliberately, as when secrecy is required prior to an attack, in order to minimise the risk of information leaks and thereby maintain surprise.

---

65   Dennis E. Showalter, *Tannenberg: Clash of Empires, 1914* (Washington, DC: Brassey's, 2004), pp. 114-115.
66   Bungay, *Art of Action*, pp. 220-222.

Although 'Logistic Control' can therefore be an effective command approach under the right conditions, the chaotic nature of warfare means that these conditions are likely to be relatively unusual, especially when forces are in contact with the enemy. Commanders will normally have less knowledge of the local situation than do their subordinates (widening the Knowledge Gap), such that attempts to employ 'Logistic Control' will actually result in 'Restrictive Control'. In these circumstances, closing the Alignment Gap through detailed orders may simply widen the Effects Gap. The commander's lesser knowledge of the local situation means the orders are unlikely to reflect that situation properly, a state of affairs compounded by the limited correlation between plans and results. Together, these factors mean the original orders are unlikely to lead to the desired results, rendering the commander's orders irrelevant and leaving subordinates unable or unwilling to continue to act in accordance with them. In the absence of an expectation, supported by previous training, that troops should exercise initiative, they are likely to remain passive until fresh orders are received, passing the initiative to the enemy. In order to minimise these risks, commanders intending to adopt 'Logistic Control' should seek assurance that their knowledge of the local situation, and their ability to predict the results produced through subordinates following their orders precisely, are both soundly based. In essence, commanders should adopt the presumption that situations in which 'Logistic Control' would be the most appropriate command approach are rare and should be treated with some suspicion.

The weaknesses of 'Restrictive Control', as an attempt to apply 'Logistic Control' in an inappropriate context, should not obscure the fact that this command approach may yet sometimes be the most suitable available command approach in certain circumstances. Commanders may find themselves with subordinates unable or unwilling to exercise initiative effectively, yet be unable themselves to secure sufficient knowledge of the local situation. As has been noted, such situations may often arise in the case of formations hastily established from raw recruits at the start of a war. Equally, they may be prevalent towards the end of a war, where troops are convinced their cause is lost and so become apathetic: in the autumn of 1918, 'exhausted German soldiers simply waited for the advancing Allies to roll over them'.[67]

Given the unwelcome nature of the circumstances that force commanders into 'Restrictive Control', they may be expected to make significant efforts to change this state of affairs. Armies that consider warfare to be inherently structured may be more likely to focus on closing the Knowledge Gap, in order to shift into 'Logistic Control'. This is an attractive option, as increasing commanders' knowledge may appear easier and quicker than increasing the capability and motivation of subordinates, which may accordingly be relegated to a lower priority. However, the chaotic nature of warfare suggests that attempts to gain greater knowledge are unlikely to be effective, while

---

67   Alexander Watson, *Enduring the Great War: Combat, Morale and Collapse in the German and British Armies, 1914-1918* (Cambridge: Cambridge University, 2008), pp. 230-231.

downplaying efforts to increase subordinates' initiative may trap commanders into continued reliance on 'Restrictive Control'.

By contrast, commanders confident their subordinates will exercise initiative effectively are in a much stronger position. This renders the Knowledge Gap much less important and makes 'Directive Command' the most appropriate means by which to reduce friction. But reliance on subordinates' initiative to close the Alignment Gap must be grounded on their competence and motivation. The mere granting of freedom to subordinates to use their initiative does not in itself mean they will do so in practice, or will choose the most effective course of action. Instead, the trust commanders have in their troops must be derived from a solid foundation of training, which has developed subordinates' capacity and capability to the level required to enable them to act effectively and reliably on their own initiative. One important aspect of this is that commanders must accept subordinates will sometimes make mistakes.[68] It is noteworthy that the question of whether commanders were safe to make these assumptions, and so trust their subordinates, was a focal point in the debate between the supporters of *Auftragstaktik* and those of *Normaltaktik* in Germany during the late nineteenth century.[69] In the absence of reliable subordinates, attempts to employ 'Directive Command' are likely to lead to significant friction, through widening the Alignment Gap.

This question of trust, and especially the inevitable requirement that commanders who place trust in their subordinates' judgement must accept mistakes will sometimes happen, is an important one, which deserves fuller consideration than is possible here. However, a brief excursion is justified. While the basic model of the eight command approaches has been developed through idealised extremes, in order to highlight contrasts, it has been noted reality is rarely so clear-cut. Commanders may well find themselves having to make a judgement regarding the competence of their subordinates. A key factor in such situations may be the perceived consequences of what may be termed the 'well-intentioned mistake'. As Storr has noted, if a mistake (whether well-intentioned or not) may result in significantly negative consequences for the commander, human nature is such that the commander will default into retaining close personal control of the situation and leave minimal scope for initiative to subordinates. Storr argued counteracting the insidious impact of this tendency requires armies to be consciously aware of the issue and then to take active and explicit steps to make clear their firm support for any soldiers, whether commanders or subordinates, in the event of well-intentioned mistakes leading to undesired results. If this is not done, 'the good will leave and only the obedient, subservient and unimaginative will stay'.[70] While there can be little doubt this is indeed the only

---

68   See Major Jim Storr, 'A Command Philosophy for the Information Age: The Continuing Relevance of Mission Command', *Defence Studies*, 3(3) (Autumn 2003), 119-129 (pp. 124-125).
69   Samuels, *Command or Control?*, pp. 68-77.
70   Storr, 'Command Philosophy', pp. 124-125.

practical solution, questions must remain whether this is always realistic, given the prevalent culture in many countries that leads to political and media expectations that mistakes by definition imply fault, which should be addressed through blame, and resignation or dismissal.

As well as being sensitive to the reliability of their subordinates (and the consequences of well-intentioned mistakes), commanders seeking to employ 'Directive Command' need to recognise there are some situations where they may indeed have greater knowledge of the local situation than do their subordinates. As has been noted, failure to recognise or act on such greater knowledge may cause commanders to slide into dysfunctional 'Umpiring'.

That said, the use of initiative by subordinates must be recognised as no more than a means to achieve the end of delivering their commanders' intent. Commanders should not use their confidence in their subordinates as a reason not to grasp every opportunity to increase their knowledge of the local situation, thereby allowing them to shift into 'Directive Control'. As Richard Simpkin put it, 'By being on the spot [the commander] gets the true feel of the situation, the thing that makes folks go to ballgames rather than watch them on television. [… But,] however he intervenes, he is going to tread on somebody's toes'.[71] For example, on 14 May 1940, when the German breakthrough in the Ardennes was at its most vulnerable stage, General der Panzertruppen Heinz Guderian, commander of the key XIX Panzer Corps, visited the forward regiments of his divisions and was then himself visited by Generaloberst Gerd von Rundstedt, commander of Army Group A.[72] In both cases, these commanders were operating 'two-down', in order to ensure their personal understanding of the situation and to drive the troops onwards, while recognising their subordinates could in general be relied upon to use their initiative effectively. The intervention of commanders at the critical point reduces both the Knowledge Gap and the Alignment Gap, and consequently enables the Effects Gap to be narrowed. These issues are examined in detail in Chapter Three, which considers the command style of Erwin Rommel as a case study.

This summation of these four command approaches brings out a central factor in the framework: the correct assessment by commanders of their level of knowledge, compared to that of their troops, is the driving force behind the subsequent steps taken to reduce friction.

If commanders have less knowledge of the local situation than do their subordinates (likely to be the norm, given the chaotic nature of warfare and the 'wicked' character of the resulting problems), the most effective response is to adopt a system of command by intent, which relies on troops using their initiative and skill to exploit the emerging

---

71   Richard E. Simpkin, *Human Factors in Mechanized Warfare* (London: Brassey's, 1983), p. 149.
72   General Heinz Guderian, *Panzer Leader*, trans. by Constantine Fitzgibbon (London: Futura, 1974), pp. 104-105.

opportunities only they can perceive: 'Directive Command'. Where it is not possible to rely on such initiative, detailed orders, based on commanders' greater professional knowledge, must be employed: 'Restrictive Control'.

By contrast, if commanders have better knowledge of the situation than their subordinates and the problems to be addressed are generally 'tame', so the outcome of actions can be predicted, then a system of close control through detailed orders that must be followed precisely offers the best route by which to reduce friction: 'Logistic Control'. Where it is not possible to predict outcomes with certainty, close personal control coupled with the exercise of initiative by subordinates may be more appropriate: 'Directive Control'.

The conclusion of this assessment of the effectiveness of the different command approaches must therefore be that none is inherently superior to the others, as they are all dependent upon context. All should therefore be acceptable in practice. This conclusion stands in stark contrast to that reached by most military theorists, who have generally sought to demonstrate one approach or another is the 'correct' one for an army to follow.

Nonetheless, if it is accepted that the nature of warfare is inherently chaotic, with the problems facing commanders therefore largely wicked in nature, this suggests armies that focus on developing the initiative of their troops, and hence their capability and motivation, and which emphasise 'Directive Command' as the default approach to command, are more likely to be able to reduce the level of friction experienced.

Increasing Friction for the Enemy

Reducing friction for friendly forces, however, is only one side of the picture. It is equally necessary to consider the friction experienced *by the enemy*. Indeed, the most important consideration regarding friction in warfare may not be the *absolute* level affecting a given army. Rather, it may be the *relative* level of friction experienced by the respective opponents. Clausewitz's analogy with wrestling, noted earlier, underlines that warfare is not like those sports where athletes individually seek to achieve the best absolute time or distance, with minimum interaction between the competitors, such as in sprinting, golf, or gymnastics. Rather, warfare is like soccer, fencing, or tennis, where victory is secured through one participant directly defeating the other, with success based on comparative performance.

Clausewitz argued victory was achieved through the 'destruction of the enemy's forces', putting them 'in such condition that they can no longer carry on the fight'.[73] This can be defined as 'rendering the enemy force operationally irrelevant'[74] or 'a reduction in strength relatively larger than our own'. While recognising that inflicting

---

73   Clausewitz, *On War*, p.90.
74   Richard E. Simpkin, *Race to the Swift Thoughts on Twenty-First Century Warfare* (London: Brassey's, 1985), p.139.

physical casualties is an important element of destruction,[75] Clausewitz noted 'the loss of morale has proved the major decisive factor.'[76]

As Marshal Ferdinand Foch, quoting Joseph de Maistre, put it, 'A battle lost is a battle one thinks one has lost; for a battle cannot be lost physically'.[77] While not literally true, of course, Foch was correct to highlight that the loss of confidence in victory on the part of the commander is a key tipping point. The history of war proves repeatedly that this is the case: indeed, the very fact so many orders and regulations exhort troops to carry out their tasks 'regardless of cost' suggest this rarely happens in practice. For example, when Crete fell to German airborne assault in May 1941, British battle casualties numbered 3,479 men, but over twelve thousand were ordered to surrender after their commanders concluded the position had become hopeless.[78] That Foch and de Maistre were not completely correct, of course, may be demonstrated by the defence of Okinawa in the spring of 1945: 'there was only one kind of Japanese casualty – the dead'.[79] This being the exception that proves the rule, maximising the *psychological* impact of operations on the enemy must therefore be of central importance. As Simpkin argued, 'a commander's ultimate aim should be to implant a picture of defeat in his opponent's mind'.[80]

Yet, in considering friction, Clausewitz was primarily concerned with *decreasing* its impact on friendly forces. It was Colonel John Boyd of the US Air Force, drawing especially on his reading of Sun Tzu,[81] who suggested this was one-sided. Instead, he argued commanders should equally aim to *increase* the friction experienced by the enemy, in order to achieve destruction of their strength.[82]

The OODA Loop

Despite the widespread impact of Boyd's theories, it was long difficult to be precise about his thought since his prose work comprised only a single, unpublished essay:

---

75   Storr, *Human Face*, pp.70-73.
76   Clausewitz, *On War*, pp.230-231.
77   Marshal Ferdinand Foch, *The Principles of War*, trans. by Hilaire Belloc (New York, NY: Holt, 1920), p. 286. See also the discussion in Simpkin, *Race to the Swift*, pp.214-215.
78   David Fraser, *And We Shall Shock Them: The British Army in the Second World War* (London: Hodder & Stoughton, 1983), pp.145-147. This is not to argue the commanders were wrong in their assessment of the situation.
79   Quoted by John Terraine, *White Heat: The New Warfare 1914-18* (London: Sidgwick & Jackson, 1982), p.17.
80   Simpkin, *Race to the Swift*, p.227.
81   One of several editions used by Boyd was Sun Tzu, *The Art of War*, ed. by James Clavell (London: Hodder & Stoughton, 1981).
82   John R. Boyd, Patterns of Conflict, p. 41. This and other related briefings by Boyd are available at http://dnipogo.org/strategy-and-force-employment/boyd-and-military-strategy/ [accessed 5 April 2012].

Destruction and Creation.[83] In part, this was due to the anti-intellectual culture of Boyd's background as a fighter pilot, combined with a deep sense of the imperfection of his own thought. But perhaps the key factor was that he normally communicated through the military model of the oral briefing.[84] Boyd therefore primarily encapsulated his thinking in the slides prepared for four standard briefings: Patterns of Conflict, Organic Design for Command and Control, The Strategic Game of ? And ?, and The Essence of Winning and Losing. These slides essentially provided prompts from which Boyd elaborated his argument. They were repeatedly revised as his thinking developed as he delivered these briefings hundreds of times over many years. As a result, their precise meaning is not always immediately clear when considered in isolation. It is therefore to be greatly welcomed that Frans Osinga, an officer of the Royal Netherlands Air Force, has produced a detailed, at times slide-by-slide, exposition of Boyd's thinking in these seminal briefings.[85] This allows their full meaning to become available to those who were not fortunate enough to hear Boyd speak.

Boyd argued the commander's intent should be 'to shatter cohesion, produce paralysis, and bring about collapse of the adversary by generating confusion, panic, and chaos'.[86] In achieving this, his starting position was a model of combat that proposed each participant, whether an individual pilot or an entire army, repeatedly goes through a four-stage cycle:[87]

- *Observation*, where information about the current situation is gathered;
- *Orientation*, where that information is processed in order to produce an understanding of the situation;
- *Decision*, where that understanding is used to develop plans; and
- *Action*, where those plans are implemented.

Termed the 'Boyd (or OODA) Loop',[88] the concept has been widely adopted, not least by the British and American armed forces, especially the US Marine Corps.[89]

Before proceeding further, however, it should be recognised there are weaknesses in the conceptual basis of the Loop. While Boyd drew his original inspiration from studies of aerial combat in Korea, more recent analysis of the methods used by the most

83   Grant T. Hammond, *The Mind of War: John Boyd and American Security* (Washington, DC: Smithsonian, 2001), pp. 118-120. The piece is reproduced in Robert Coram, *Boyd: The Fighter Pilot Who Changed the Art of War* (Boston: Little Brown, 2002), pp. 451-462.
84   Hammond, *Mind of War*, p. 17.
85   Frans Osinga, *Science, Strategy and War: The Strategic Theory of John Boyd* (Delft: Eburon, 2005).
86   Coram, *Boyd*, pp. 332-334.
87   William Lind, *Maneuver War Handbook* (Boulder, CO: Westview, 1985), pp. 4-5.
88   Boyd personally preferred the usage 'O-O-D-A Loop', but found himself forced to accept the more common form. Coram, *Boyd*, p. 334.
89   Hammond, *Mind of War*, pp. 194-195.

successful fighter pilots shows they rarely participated in classic dogfights. Rather, fighter aces usually destroyed their targets during a single pass, not the iterative model proposed by Boyd. There must therefore be some caution whether the Loop reflects the reality of aerial combat, and hence can safely be extrapolated to other contexts.[90]

Yet this by no means requires that we discard the Boyd Loop. Despite its perhaps questionable empirical basis, the Loop provides 'a descriptive framework on which to hang discussions of command and control'[91] – an example of George Box's famous maxim that 'all models are wrong, but some are useful'.[92] This is all the more apparent when it is recognised that Boyd presented the Loop in graphic format only once, and this in the last of his briefings, The Essence of Winning and Losing,[93] prepared in 1995, just two years before his death.[94] Whereas descriptions by other authors had reduced the Loop to a superficial four-step cycle, Boyd in this final briefing demonstrated its true richness. As demonstrated in Figure 1.7, he showed the Loop not only as a double-loop learning process, but with a double-loop process within the Orientation phase.[95]

Figure 1.7: Boyd Loop

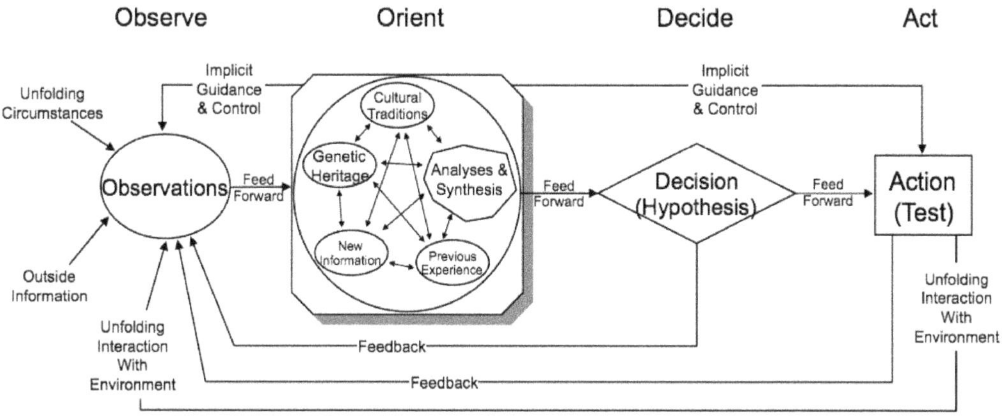

90   Storr, *Human Face*, pp. 12-14.
91   Storr, *Human Face*, p. 33.
92   George E.P. Box and Norman R. Draper, *Empirical Model Building and Response Surfaces* (London: Wiley-Blackwell, 1986), p. 424.
93   John R. Boyd, The Essence of Winning and Losing, p. 3.
94   Osinga, *Science, Strategy and War*, p. 268.
95   Osinga, *Science, Strategy and War*, p. 271.

In considering the relevance of the Boyd Loop for the framework for command approaches, two aspects are of particular importance: the central importance of the Orientation phase,[96] and the impact of getting 'inside the adversary's time cycle or loop'.[97] It is here argued that these aspects relate closely to two of the gaps central to friction: the Knowledge Gap and the Alignment Gap.

Orientation and Decision-Making

In our earlier discussion of the Knowledge Gap, it was identified that the correct assessment by commanders of their level of knowledge, compared to that of their troops, is critical to the subsequent steps taken to reduce friction. That discussion focused on the quantity and quality of information: plans are imperfect because there is a gap between what commanders would *like* to know and what they *actually* know. Armies have often sought to pierce the fog of war, and so close the Knowledge Gap, by increasing the volume of information available to commanders, a trend reinforced by developments in modern information technology.[98]

Statistical analysis of decision-making reveals that, if both sides make decisions at the same speed, the most likely outcome is a stalemate. This is to be expected. What is unexpected, however, is that this is true even if one side's decision-making is of much higher quality than the other's. By contrast, if one side makes decisions twice as fast as the other, it is almost certain to secure victory, even if its decisions are of lower quality than those of its opponent (subject to a minimum standard).[99] What is apparent from this analysis is that a decision that is 'about right' (not simply a quick guess!), but made and implemented at speed, is much more likely to lead to an increase in the level of friction experienced by the enemy than is a decision that is completely right, but slow. As General George Patton recognised, 'A good solution applied with vigour *now* is better than a perfect solution ten minutes later'.[100]

Boyd understood this and therefore argued that the commander should aim to 'operate at a faster tempo or rhythm than [his] adversaries.'[101] This has often been misunderstood, with the Loop reduced to 'a simplistic, one-dimensional cycle [... where] speed is the most important element of the cycle, [such] that whoever can go through the cycle fastest will prevail'.[102] For example, Simpkin erroneously defined tempo as the 'operational rate of advance [...,] the distance from the initial line of contact to the back of the final operational objective'[103] – that is, speed of movement

---

96   John R. Boyd, Organic Design for Command and Control, p. 16.
97   Boyd, Patterns of Conflict, p. 5.
98   Shamir, *Transforming Command*, pp. 166-168.
99   Storr, *Human Face*, pp. 132-137.
100 Charles M. Province, *The Unknown Patton* (New York, NY: Hippocrene, 1983), p. 165.
101 Hammond, *Mind of War*, p. 123.
102 Coram, *Boyd*, p. 334.
103 Simpkin, *Race to the Swift*, pp. 106-107.

(not even speed of reaction). That mere speed, by itself, does not necessarily lead to an increase in the enemy's level of friction may be demonstrated by Rommel's famous 'dash to the wire' during Operation Crusader in November 1941. In this action, the Afrika Korps moved around the exposed southern flank of the British Eighth Army with the intention of threatening its supply lines and consequently prompting its precipitous withdrawal. This underlined again the superior speed of Rommel's operations, but the manoeuvre failed to disconcert Auchinleck and so ultimately led to Britain's first victory of the war over German ground forces.[104] In fact, as Osinga shows, 'Boyd advances the idea that success in war [...] hinges upon the quality and tempo of the cognitive processes of leaders and their organizations'[105] – a much more complex model.

The pace with which commanders can go through the Loop is therefore of great importance. Here, the key factor is the emphasis placed by Boyd on the Orientation phase – 'without orientation there is no command and control worthy of the name'[106] – and its impact on the Knowledge Gap. In this context, the Knowledge Gap should be understood not simply in terms of the quantity and quality of information (Observation). Rather, its essence is the commander's ability to make use of the information available, in order to make and implement a 'good enough' decision *quickly*, even in the absence of significant elements of the whole picture (Orientation).

Boyd defined the Orientation stage as 'an interactive process of many-sided implicit cross-referencing projections, empathies, correlations, and rejections that is shaped by and shapes the interplay of genetic heritage, cultural tradition, previous experiences, and unfolding circumstances. [...] Orientation is the *Schwerpunkt*. It shapes the way we interact with the environment – hence orientation shapes the way we observe, the way we decide, the way we act'.[107] In a truly postmodernist appreciation, Boyd recognised Orientation is not simply a process of objective analysis of the information collected during the Observation phase. Rather, it involves the interaction of information and individual to create a subjective interpretation of reality.[108]

Boyd argued superior Orientation was central to the rapid decision-making required to confuse the enemy. As Rommel noted, 'it is often not a question of which of the opposing commanders is the higher qualified mentally, or which of them has the greater experience, but which of them has the better grasp of the battlefield'.[109] Boyd recognised that this 'grasp of the battlefield' was not achieved simply by laboriously going through each of the four stages of the Loop in turn at a faster pace. Instead, the ideal was to short-circuit the process.

104 *The Rommel Papers*, ed. by B. H. Liddell Hart (London: Collins, 1953), pp. 163-167.
105 Osinga, *Science, Strategy and War*, p. 3.
106 Boyd, Organic Design, p. 25.
107 Boyd, Organic Design, pp. 15-16. Boyd here uses *Schwerpunkt* in the Clausewitzian sense of 'centre of gravity', rather than the classic German military sense of 'point of main effort'.
108 Osinga, *Science, Strategy and War*, p. 237.
109 *Rommel Papers*, p. 122.

There is significant evidence to suggest battlefield commanders in practice base decisions on only a small proportion of the information available.[110] Indeed, receiving too much information can overwhelm commanders and their staffs, leading to paralysis.[111] Clausewitz understood this, noting 'war has a way of masking the stage with scenery crudely daubed with fearsome apparitions'. He concluded, therefore, that the challenge facing commanders was not so much to secure full information, but rather to achieve 'accurate recognition'.[112] This is not simply a question of the quantity and quality of the information *received*, but of its *use*.

Boyd adopted the term *Fingerspitzengefühl* (finger-tip feeling),[113] which may be defined as 'an instinctive sixth sense for terrain and tactics',[114] to describe the ability of the commander 'to bypass the explicit "Orientation" and "Decision" part of the Loop, to "Observe" and "Act" almost simultaneously. The speed must come from a deep intuitive understanding of one's relationship to the rapidly changing environment'.[115]

Boyd argued superior Orientation – the ability to 'create mental images, or impressions, hence patterns that match with [the] activity of [the] world' – enables commanders to inflict friction by 'deny[ing the] adversary the possibility of uncovering or discerning patterns that match our activity, or other aspects of reality in the world'.[116] The result is that commanders' actions 'appear ambiguous (unpredictable) [and] thereby generate confusion' among the enemy.[117] Thus, the ability to make a good decision quickly, based on a minimum of information, thereby narrowing one's own Knowledge Gap, has the effect of widening the gap affecting the enemy and consequently increasing the level of friction experienced by them.

Having explored the connection between Orientation and the Knowledge Gap, it is necessary to consider the effectiveness of the four key command approaches in facilitating rapid and effective decision-making.

Under 'Logistic Control', commanders' greater knowledge should allow them to achieve better orientation and, as such, the quality of their decisions should be higher. When considering the ability of commanders to use this narrowing of the Knowledge Gap to maximise the friction experienced by the enemy, the question is whether 'Logistic Control' is compatible with *Fingerspitzengefühl* and tempo.

It seems likely that the commander employing 'Logistic Control' will be at a headquarters some distance behind the frontline, at the nodal point of a network of information-gathering systems, supported by a large staff. Gathering significant

110 Storr, *Human Face*, p. 131.
111 Storr, *Human Face*, p. 140.
112 Clausewitz, *On War*, pp. 117-118.
113 John R. Boyd, The Strategic Game of ? And ?, p. 45.
114 *Generals Balck and Von Mellenthin on Tactics: Implications for NATO Military Doctrine*, edited by General William DePuy (McLean, VA: BDM, 1980), p. 21.
115 Coram, *Boyd*, pp. 335-336.
116 Boyd, Organic Design, p. 16.
117 Boyd, Patterns of Conflict, p. 5.

amounts of information during the Observation stage, and collating, analysing, and synthesising it during the Orientation stage, will take a considerable amount of time. This reliance upon superior information runs counter to the essence of *Fingerspitzengefühl*, which commanders using 'Logistic Control' may consider rash and unsystematic – intuition rather than deliberation. In addition, because, under this command approach, subordinates are expected to follow orders to the letter, the orders themselves are likely to be more detailed and hence take longer to prepare, thereby adding further to the time required between Observation and Action. For example, Simpkin noted the Soviet Army of the 1980s sought to use the power of information technology to enable senior commanders to operate a system he dubbed 'forward command from the rear' and which was essentially 'Logistic Control', but that this failed to offer sufficient 'speed and aptness of response to the actual situation'.[118]

While commanders' orientation under 'Logistic Control' may therefore be superior to that of their opponents, it is probably rather slower, making it less likely they will achieve tempo and thereby inflict significant friction on the enemy.

Under 'Directive Control', by contrast, commanders' greater knowledge of the local situation is likely to come from personal observation on the ground, such as that sought by Otto von Moser, a corps commander during the surprise German counterattack at Cambrai on 30 November 1917.[119] In part due to his closure of the Knowledge Gap, the assault regained much of the ground that had been lost to the massed British tank attack ten days earlier and took over two and a half thousand prisoners.[120] This command approach is likely to be highly compatible with *Fingerspitzengefühl*. At the same time, the ability of commanders to rely upon their troops to act appropriately in order to achieve the intent, even in the absence of detailed orders, indicates the amount of time required between Decision and Action will be short. This combination of strong Orientation and rapid Action may give the best chance of achieving tempo. For example, on 25 September 1915, following a major French assault in Champagne that had brought the German defence to breaking point, the newly appointed chief of staff of Third Army, Colonel Fritz von Loßberg, made a personal observation of the new front line. This detailed understanding of the situation led him to undertake an immediate redesign of the defensive system, such that only days later French attempts to take advantage of their initial successes came to nothing.[121]

The combination of rapid, accurate Orientation, coupled with quick implementation due to the ability to issue brief orders that capable subordinates can apply with

---

118 Simpkin, *Race to the Swift*, pp. 43 & 52.

119 General Otto von Moser, *Feldzugsaufzeichnungen als Brigade-, Divisionskommandeur und als kommandierender General, 1914-1918* (Stuttgart: Belsersche, 1920), p. 323.

120 Bryn Hammond, *Cambrai 1917: The Myth of the First Great Tank Battle* (London: Weidenfeld & Nicolson, 2008), pp. 325-383 and Jack Sheldon, *The German Army at Cambrai* (Barnsley: Pen & Sword, 2009), pp. 227-272.

121 Captain Greame C. Wynne, *If Germany Attacks: The Battle in Depth in the West* (1940, reprinted Westport, CT: Greenwood, 1976), pp. 90-98.

initiative, offers a high probability that commanders employing 'Directive Control' will achieve tempo.

Under 'Directive Command', the key difference is that commanders have less knowledge of the situation than their subordinates do. While it is by no means impossible for them to achieve *Fingerspitzengefühl*, this is likely to be more difficult and slower than under 'Directive Control', as they have less information on which to base their Orientation and this is likely to take longer to reach them than if they were able to observe directly. However, since their subordinates can be relied upon to use their initiative to achieve the intent, orders can be short and issued quickly.

Perhaps the most famous example of this approach came in August 1914, when Erich Ludendorff was appointed chief of staff of the Eighth Army, which was in full retreat in the face of a two-pronged Russian invasion of East Prussia. In Coblenz, eight hundred miles away, Ludendorff received only a basic briefing on the situation, yet he was able to develop the plan that led to the annihilation of the Russian Second Army at Tannenberg. Even then, however, he recognised the Knowledge Gap meant, 'an actual decision as to the plan to be adopted could be given only on the spot'.[122]

Taken together, skilled commanders, able to use with insight what information they have, coupled with reliable troops, may achieve a fairly high tempo through 'Directive Command'.

Finally, under 'Restrictive Control', commanders find themselves in the unenviable position of having less knowledge of the local situation than do their troops, yet unable to rely on them acting appropriately on their own initiative. This may cause commanders to devote time to efforts to gain additional information about the situation, in order to narrow the Knowledge Gap, while also spending significant time on the preparation of detailed orders. Thus, during the attack on Thiepval, part of the opening day of the Battle of the Somme on 1 July 1916, the significant initial gains made by 109th Brigade of 36th (Ulster) Division were lost to German counterattacks after the corps commander rejected requests by all three of his divisional commanders to commit his reserve at that point of the line. He felt he needed further information before issuing detailed orders to troops he believed were of questionable capability.[123] In the event, the shattered ruins of Thiepval were not to fall into British hands until 27 September.[124]

The combination of difficult orientation with the lengthy time required to prepare detailed orders means commanders relying on 'Restrictive Control' are almost certain to experience a slow cycle time, making it unlikely they will achieve the tempo required to inflict friction on the enemy.

122 General Erich Ludendorff, *Ludendorff's Own Story, August 1914-November 1918; the Great War from the siege of Liège to the signing of the armistice as viewed from the grand headquarters of the German Army*, 2 vols. (New York, NY: Harper, 1919), vol. 1, pp. 49-55.
123 Samuels, *Command or Control?*, pp. 150-151.
124 William Philpott, *Bloody Victory: The Sacrifice on the Somme* (London: Abacus, 2009), p. 375.

Taking this together, through their reliance upon the commander's intent as a guide for subordinates, the speed of decision-making under both 'Directive Command' and 'Directive Control' is likely to be faster than under 'Logistic Control' or 'Restrictive Control', since the time required to develop and issue high level directives will normally be much less than for detailed orders. However, the quality of decision-making is likely to be lower in the case of 'Directive Command' and 'Restrictive Control', as the commanders in those situations have a wider Knowledge Gap and hence their Orientation is likely to be less effective than under 'Logistic Control' or 'Directive Control'.

In summary, an army employing 'Directive Control' can expect to make good decisions (based on personal observation) rapidly, thereby getting inside their adversary's Loop. By contrast, an army applying 'Restrictive Control' is likely to make poor decisions (due to an incorrect assessment of the relative knowledge of commander and subordinates, or an inability to rely on subordinates' initiative) at a slow pace. The chances of getting inside the enemy's Loop in order to inflict friction are therefore low.

In terms of likelihood of achieving tempo, therefore, 'Directive Control' would appear best placed and 'Restrictive Control' worst. Given the relationship between speed and quality of decision-making, the quality of decision-making under 'Logistic Control' would need to be very much higher than under 'Directive Command', in order to counteract the differential in speed. This is expressed in Figure 1.8.

Figure 1.8: Tempo and Command Approaches

	Logistic Control	Directive Control	Directive Command	Restrictive Control
Speed of Decision Making	Slow	Quickest	Quick	Slowest
Quality of Decision Making	High	Highest	Low	Lowest
Likelihood of Achieving Tempo	Medium to Low	Highest	Medium to High	Lowest

Tempo and Shock

The ability to short-circuit the Loop (narrow the Knowledge Gap) through *Fingerspitzengefühl* and hence superior Orientation, enables commanders to achieve 'tempo', getting 'inside' the enemy's Boyd Loop. But this is only half the picture.

Central to the concept of tempo is its impact on the enemy. This leads to its definition as 'the actuality of total domination of the "Being" of the enemy'.[125]

Boyd argued that 'operat[ing] at a faster tempo or rhythm than our adversaries [...] will make us appear ambiguous (unpredictable), thereby generating confusion and disorder among our adversaries. This will cause our adversaries to be unable to generate mental images that agree with the menacing and faster transient rhythm or patterns they are competing against'.[126] Similarly, he suggested getting inside their Loop has the effect of 'folding our adversaries back inside themselves, morally-mentally-physically — so that they can neither appreciate nor cope with what's happening — without [us] suffering the same fate ourselves.'[127] Consequently, the enemy becomes 'unable to adapt to rapidly changing circumstances thereby convincing him to give up'.[128]

What Boyd was describing, and hence the means by which tempo achieves an increase in the level of friction experienced by the enemy, appears to be the combination, often mutually reinforcing, of surprise and shock.

In seeking to connect surprise and shock with tempo, it is helpful to start with J.F.C. Fuller's definition: 'Surprise may be considered under two main headings: surprise effected by doing something that the enemy does not expect, and surprise effected by doing something that the enemy cannot counter. The first may be denoted as moral surprise, the second as material.'[129]

These definitions fit closely with, and are given further depth by, those for surprise and shock developed by David Rowland and his colleagues at the former Defence Operational Analysis Establishment and set out in his remarkable book, *The Stress of Battle*.[130] Rowland defined surprise as: 'The achievement of the unexpected in timing, place or direction of an initiative [...]. It can also include the effect of [...] weapon type, their combined use, strength, numbers or speed.'[131] This connects with Fuller's concept of 'moral surprise'.

'Moral surprise' may be achieved through timing, direction, means, or methods. Rowland noted that the effect of such surprise is that 'soldiers cannot perform', due to lack of time and space. Based on extensive historical analysis, he was able to demonstrate that the achievement of surprise on average reduced the effectiveness of the defence by around sixty per cent and hence reduced the attacker's casualties by

125 Michael Elliott-Bateman (in conjunction with Spencer Fitz-Gibbon and Martin Samuels), 'Vocabulary: the Second Problem of Military Reform – I. Concepts', *Defense Analysis*, 6(3) (1990), 263-275 (p. 267).
126 Hammond, *Mind of War*, p. 123.
127 Boyd, Strategic Game of ? And ?, p. 45.
128 Boyd, quoted by Hammond, *Mind of War*, p. 143.
129 Colonel John F.C. Fuller, *The Reformation of War* (London: Hutchinson, 1923), p. 50.
130 David Rowland, *The Stress of Battle: Quantifying Human Performance in Combat* (London: TSO, 2006).
131 Rowland, *Stress*, p.169.

two thirds.[132] Further, statistical analysis of battles has revealed that frontal assaults on average result in the attacker suffering twice as many casualties as the defender, whereas unexpected attacks against the enemy's flanks reverse that ratio, and attacks against the enemy rear double it again – making an unexpected rear assault on average eight times as effective as a frontal attack.

Storr suggested these results derive in part from the immediate effects of surprise: physiological arousal, uncertainty, 'attentional blink', and the cessation of ongoing activity. In combination, these make surprised troops briefly unable to take an active part in combat, thereby giving the attacker the advantage. Over a longer period, surprise also leads to stress, which in turn may prompt irrational attempts to reduce uncertainty, expressed through 'big-picture blindness' or micro-management.[133] For example, at the climax of the Battle of Mars-La-Tour on 16 August 1870, the overall French commander, Marshal Bazaine, focused his attention on the placing of a single artillery battery, clearly unable to cope psychologically with the unexpected disaster unfolding around him.[134]

With regard to shock, this reduces the effectiveness of the defence by about forty percent. Storr identified the main causes of shock as being 'surprise, rapid bombardment, sudden approach, the use of armour, and the use of certain types of weapons'. As with surprise, shocked troops withdraw from active or useful participation in combat, but this appears to be due to a state of psychological numbness, deeper than the 'blink' of surprise.[135] Rowland defined shock as 'morale conditions causing stunning, paralysis or debilitating effect'.[136] Whereas surprised troops 'cannot' react (due to lack of time or capability), shocked troops could, but do not.[137] This led to a further connection, between shock and panic, where panic is the instant reaction to a fear-inducing event, while shock follows when no effective reaction (such as flight) is possible.[138] Together, this suggests a connection with the second element of Fuller's definition: 'material surprise'.

Shock appears to be more likely when troops are presented with a sudden intervention they believe themselves unable to counter, be this a saturating bombardment, an attack by seemingly invulnerable tanks, or in conditions of poor visibility.[139] This suggests a connection with knowledge, in that although the troops may *believe* they have no counter to the enemy's actions, subsequent analysis often reveals they did, but did not think of it. This may also be related to what Boyd termed 'menace', defined as

---

132 Rowland, *Stress*, pp.169-174.
133 Storr, *Human Face*, pp. 84-86.
134 Michael Howard, *The Franco-Prussian War* (London: Routledge, 1988), pp. 155-156.
135 Storr, *Human Face*, pp. 87-88.
136 Rowland, *Stress*, p.178.
137 Rowland, *Stress*, p.169.
138 Rowland, *Stress*, pp.189-191.
139 See also Clausewitz's comments about the psychological impact of threats of encirclement. Clausewitz, *On War*, p. 233.

'impressions of danger to one's well being and survival',[140] which can cause moral strength to 'evaporate'.[141]

It is clear inflicting surprise and shock upon the enemy greatly increases the friction they experience.[142] This is principally through widening the Alignment Gap, as troops become unable or unwilling to carry out the tasks desired of them. Similarly, if commanders are themselves shocked or surprised, there may arise a gap between the orders they *ought* to give to achieve the intent and those they *actually* give (or fail to give).

Boyd's emphasis on 'getting inside the enemy's decision loop' can therefore be seen as being based on the conviction that the ability to make 'good enough' decisions quickly, and then implement them faster than the enemy, makes it easier for commanders to achieve surprise and inflict shock on their opponents. This causes the enemy to experience both a wider Knowledge Gap (as events outpace their commanders' knowledge of the local situation) and a wider Alignment Gap (as surprised and shocked subordinates become unable to undertake their tasks effectively).

The consequence is a great increase in the differential combat potential of the two forces, and hence the probability of achieving victory is significantly improved. As Clausewitz noted,

> All in all, loss of moral equilibrium must not be underestimated merely because it has no absolute value and does not always show up in the final balance. It can attain such massive proportions that it overpowers everything by its irresistible force. For this reason *it may in itself become a main objective of the action*.[143]

Finally, if the purpose of achieving tempo is to make it easier to inflict surprise and shock on the enemy, given the dramatic reduction in combat capability this can cause, it is necessary to complete the circle and return to consideration of one's own forces, in order to evaluate the effectiveness of the different command approaches in protecting friendly forces against surprise and shock.

'Logistic Control' and 'Restrictive Control' seek to narrow the Alignment Gap by requiring subordinates to follow detailed orders, and to await further orders if their original orders become inappropriate. However, troops waiting for revised orders are likely to be passive or following orders that are no longer aligned to the changed situation. As a result, actions by the enemy that are better suited to the situation as it has now become are likely to come as a surprise. In addition, troops accustomed to relying on orders before acting may be more likely to feel unable to counter an unexpected action by the enemy, and hence more likely to experience shock.

---

140 Boyd, Patterns of Conflict, p. 122.
141 Osinga, *Science, Strategy and War*, p. 214.
142 Boyd, Patterns of Conflict, p. 98.
143 Clausewitz, *On War*, p. 232 (emphasis added).

Consequently, reliance on 'Logistic Control' or 'Restrictive Control' may make troops more susceptible to surprise and shock, thereby widening the Alignment Gap.

Conversely, under 'Directive Control' and 'Directive Command', the expectation is that subordinates will continuously assess their local situation in order to identify the best means by which to achieve their commanders' intent. As a result, those subordinates are likely to use their initiative to reduce the chances of their being surprised by the enemy. They are also likely to have a greater sense of being able to respond to 'material surprise', thereby reducing shock. Consequently, it will be harder for the enemy to inflict friction on them through widening their Knowledge and Alignment Gaps.

Concluding Thoughts

This chapter has sought to take three steps towards establishing a conceptual foundation for discussion of command approaches.

First, through considering the possible responses of commanders and their forces to the different ways in which friction arises, it has developed a typology of command approaches. This enables a move beyond a descriptive consideration of command towards an analytical exploration. Despite the longstanding recognition of the importance of friction in warfare, such a connection between friction and command approaches appears not to have been made previously in the literature on warfare.

Second, it has examined how each of the eight idealised command approaches interacts with the different aspects of friction identified by Clausewitz, as expressed through the 'gaps' model presented by Stephen Bungay. This makes possible an assessment of the likely effectiveness of each approach in reducing friction. In so doing, the chapter has considered the fundamental nature of warfare, exploring whether it is inherently structured and linear, such that the problems facing commanders are essentially 'tame', or instead fundamentally chaotic and non-linear, such that its problems are 'wicked'. This exploration concluded the latter is a more accurate assessment of the reality of warfare, and this allowed an examination of the consequences of this for command approaches.

Finally, the chapter then turned the issue of friction on its head and, drawing on the work of John Boyd, explored how each command approach responds to the challenge of actively *increasing* the friction experienced *by the enemy*, in order to achieve destruction of their strength. In so doing, connections were made with two other vital elements of warfare: surprise and shock.

The basic contention has been that a command system is not simply a neutral technique, but (whether consciously or not) is a response to the fundamental nature of warfare. As such, some approaches are more likely than others to deliver victory.

This analysis has suggested four of the command approaches are intrinsically dysfunctional, as they are deeply misaligned with the nature of warfare, regardless of whether it is perceived as structured or chaotic, and so inevitably widen the Effects Gap. In 'Detached Control' and 'Neglected Control', commanders believe subordinates cannot be trusted to act independently, yet do not intervene to close the Effects Gap, leaving them adrift. In 'Umpiring', commanders also fail to intervene to close the Effects Gap, but this time because their confidence in their subordinates means they overlook their own greater local knowledge. By contrast, 'Enthusiastic Amateurs' intervene even though they recognise they have less knowledge of the local situation than do their subordinates, and these can be trusted to act appropriately. Enthusiastic Amateurs simply impede their competent and better-informed subordinates, creating disorder through widening the Effects Gap.

Of the remaining four approaches, the analysis demonstrates the most effective is likely to be 'Directive Control' and the least effective 'Restrictive Control', with 'Directive Command' and 'Logistic Control' between them.

Both 'Directive Control' and 'Directive Command' are likely to reduce the friction experienced by friendly forces, while at the same time increasing the friction affecting the enemy. In both cases, commanders draw upon the information available to them to achieve rapid Orientation and quickly issue brief orders, centred on their intent. Both rely on troops having the capacity and willingness to exercise initiative to further the commander's intent, and the skills to do so effectively. This places great emphasis on the training of even relatively junior troops. It also underlines the importance of commanders being able to recognise the delicate balance, when giving their subordinates scope for initiative, between the benefits to be gained from the greater responsiveness this brings and the risk of those subordinates making mistakes that might undermine the commander's intent. Especially during periods of rapid expansion, such as at the start of a major war or when heavy casualties cause a high turnover of manpower, achievement of the required level of training may be difficult, if not impossible. In these circumstances, if commanders persist in expecting subordinates to exercise significant initiative, the result may be a descent into 'Umpiring', where commanders incorrectly assess their troops' knowledge, or 'Detached Control', where subordinates are left to exercise initiative beyond their capability.

'Directive Command' in particular also relies on commanders feeling comfortable with uncertainty, yet this may be difficult to achieve during periods of peacetime, when the structured nature of military life may make it especially attractive to authoritarians, for whom the principles behind this command approach are an anathema. This tendency may be reinforced if the consequences of subordinates making even well intentioned mistakes may be severely negative, whether directly to the success of the engagement, or to the future career prospects of the commander. The solution – an explicit corporate recognition that mistakes happen and that those making well-intentioned errors should be protected – may be easier to promote in theory than to apply in practice.

By contrast, 'Logistic Control' relies on commanders having greater knowledge of the local situation than do their subordinates. Given the chaotic nature of warfare, such circumstances will rarely occur for more than brief periods, despite rapid advances in information technology. In the absence of such greater knowledge, commanders seeking to control their subordinates absolutely may instead slide into 'Restrictive

Control'. Yet this is not necessarily a dysfunctional command approach. Commanders may find themselves responsible for subordinates with only the most basic training, such that they possess minimal capacity and capability for action beyond that prescribed in advance. But lower standards of training are easier to achieve, especially during financial stringency, rapid expansion of forces, or following heavy casualties. In addition, the attractiveness of peacetime military life to personalities that feel comfortable with order, hierarchy, and certainty may mean both 'Logistic Control' and 'Restrictive Control' fit with the cultural grain.

There seem to be clear advantages in effectiveness from commanders seeking to achieve tempo through rapid Orientation, ideally based on personal observation of the battlefield through the principle of 'the commander at the *Schwerpunkt*'. This should be followed by speedy issuing of brief directives, leaving space for capable and trustworthy subordinates to exercise initiative to exploit emerging opportunities, in order to get inside the enemy's Boyd Loop and inflict friction through surprise and shock.

Yet it must be recognised that all of these approaches are dependent upon context. Where subordinates cannot be relied upon, commanders may be better advised to fall back upon detailed orders and rigid control. This may be less likely to achieve tempo, but it is also more likely to avoid the high levels of friction associated with 'Umpiring' or 'Detached Control'.

Taking account of the model of the problems facing commanders in warfare as being 'wicked' or 'tame', and connecting it with the three 'gaps' and the range of command approaches resulting from these, three factors seem to be of greatest importance:

- Whether an army expects the problems encountered in warfare to be 'wicked', such that it is unlikely senior commanders will be able to predict the local situation within which their subordinates operate (making approaches that emphasise subordinates' initiative liable to be more effective), or whether they are expected to be 'tame', such that senior commanders can determine local situations in advance (making approaches that use detailed orders more effective);
- Whether commanders can rely on their subordinates to interpret general directives within their local situation, in order to achieve the overall intent (enabling approaches that maximise low-level initiative), or whether deficiencies in capability or motivation mean commanders cannot trust their subordinates to act independently (requiring reliance on rigid adherence to orders); and
- Whether commanders seek to achieve certainty through extensive collection and collation of intelligence about the situation and detailed analysis of all the available options, in order to identify the 'correct' solution to a 'tame' problem, or whether they emphasise speed of decision-making, even in the absence of a large part of the picture, in order to implement quickly 'good enough' decisions to 'wicked' problems, thereby achieving tempo and inflicting surprise and shock on the enemy.

These factors provide a 'lens' though which to examine the different approaches adopted by the German and British armies during the period 1918 to 1940. This undertaking forms the core of the remaining chapters of this book.

Indeed, it may be suggested the absence of such a conceptual model or 'lens', which highlights the potential for ontological and epistemological differences between (and within) armies, is a significant weakness of much academic literature on doctrine. Since doctrine is ultimately a question of how an army interprets the fundamental nature of warfare, and hence determines the most appropriate means by which to respond successfully, doctrine cannot be properly understood without reference to that interpretation.

Command Approaches and Auftragstaktik

At this point, it is appropriate to consider directly the relationship of the command approaches developed above and the system of *Auftragstaktik* used by the German Army and its predecessors. The first thing to note is that, although this book is (in part) concerned with the development and application of command doctrine in the German Army, it is not intended to be an analysis of *Auftragstaktik* per se, although there are of course clear connections. Within this, it should also be noted that there existed an inevitable distinction between *Auftragstaktik* as a theoretical command style and the actual practice of commanders and units within the German Army.

For readers wishing to explore the origins and nature of *Auftragstaktik* directly, the most accessible starting point in English is by Lieutenant Colonel Dr Jochen Wittmann, a reserve officer in the German Army.[144] In this brief volume, Wittmann provided a brief summary of the theoretical background to the technique, its linkages to operational art, and its basic nature. He then used this as the basis for a series of analyses using a range of well-known tools from the field of organisational theory, drawing for example on chaos theory, with the intention of moving beyond the descriptive nature of the majority of previous studies of *Auftragstaktik*.[145] Wittmann's work complements the more general consideration presented in Robert Citino's magisterial *The German Way of Warfare*,[146] which emphasised the principles of the aggressive conduct of operations and the absolute independence of commanders as comprising the essence of the technique.[147]

Readers seeking a more in-depth understanding should consult three seminal works, all written in German. The first appeared in 1993, when Dirk Oetting, a long-time lecturer at the leadership schools of the Bundeswehr and immediately

---

144 Jochen Wittmann, *Auftragstaktik – Just a Command Technique or the Core Pillar of Mastering the Military Operational Art?* (Berlin: Miles, 2012).
145 Wittmann, *Auftragstaktik*, p.57.
146 Robert M. Citino, *The German Way of War: From the Thirty Years' War to the Third Reich* (Lawrence, KS: University Press of Kansas, 2005).
147 Citino, *German Way*, pp.308-309.

thereafter commander of Panzer Grenadier Brigade 1, published a full-length study of *Auftragstaktik*.[148] The work was primarily descriptive, seeking to trace the origins of the concept from its earliest emergence in the dark days of 1806 through until the present day. Nonetheless, chapters explored key facets of the concept, such as independence, the need to consider the situation as a whole, and the importance of not restricting freedom of initiative. The second came in 2002, through the work of Major Stephan Leistenschneider,[149] a General Staff officer in the Bundeswehr. In contrast to Oetting's more general work, Leistenschneider focused on the heated debates concerning the nature and approach to command that took place within the German Army during the period between the end of the Franco-Prussian War and the outbreak of the First World War.

The most important study, however, is that presented in 2014 in Swiss-German academic Marco Sigg's definitive volume, *Der Unterführer als Feldherr in Taschenformat*[150] (The Junior Leader as Master of the Battlefield in Pocket Format). Here Sigg first undertook a comprehensive examination of the understanding of warfare held by Clausewitz and Moltke the Elder and its expression in successive editions of the German Army's key doctrinal manuals. Building on this, he then drew upon key principles underlying *Auftragstaktik* identified by Leistenschneider and by Ralf Raths in his examination of the development of German tactics in the decade between 1906 and 1918, *Vom Massensturm zur Stoßtrupptaktik*[151] (From Massed Attack to Assault Squad Tactics), in order to present a complete conceptual model of the key elements underlying the command approach. This is set out in Figure 1.9.[152]

148 Dirk W. Oetting, *Auftragstaktik. Geschichte und Gegenwart einer Führungskonzeption* (Frankfurt: Report-Verlag, 1993).

149 Stephan Leistenschneider, *Auftragstaktik im preußisch-deutschen Heer, 1871 bis 1914* (Berlin: Mittler, 2002).

150 Marco Sigg, *Der Unterführer als Feldherr in Taschenformat: Theorie und Praxis der Auftragstaktik im deutschen Heer, 1869 bis 1945* (Paderborn: Schöningh, 2014).

151 Ralf Raths, *Vom Massensturm zur Stoßtrupptaktik: Die deutsche Landkriegtaktik im Spiegel von Dienstvorschriften und Publizistik, 1906 bis 1918* (Freiburg: Rombach, 2009).

152 Adapted from Sigg, *Unterführer*, pp.173.

Figure 1.9: Marco Sigg's Idealised Model of Auftragstaktik

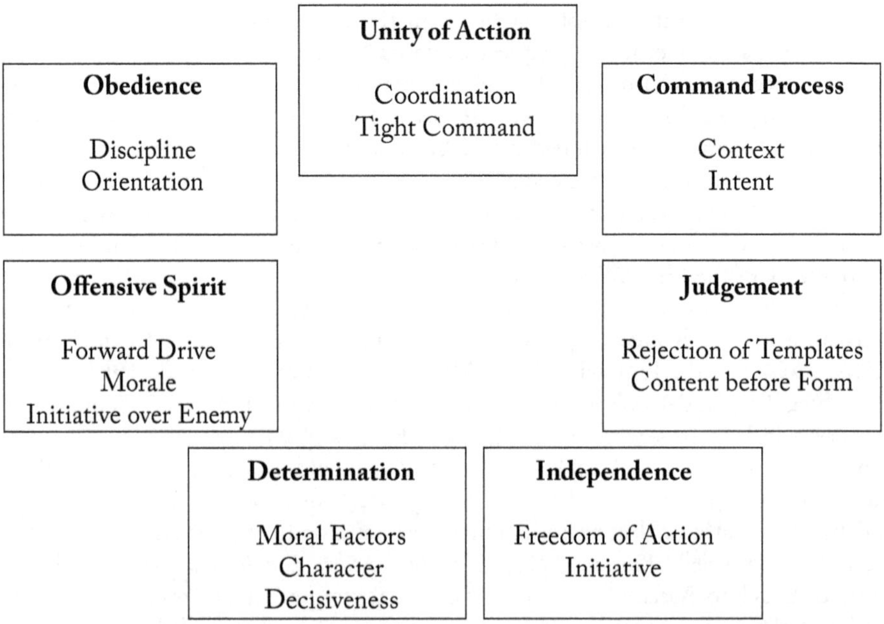

	Unity of Action	
Obedience	Coordination	**Command Process**
	Tight Command	
Discipline		Context
Orientation		Intent

Offensive Spirit	**Judgement**
Forward Drive	Rejection of Templates
Morale	Content before Form
Initiative over Enemy	

Determination	**Independence**
Moral Factors	Freedom of Action
Character	Initiative
Decisiveness	

Sigg then explored the extent to which this idealised concept of *Auftragstaktik* was ever actually applied in the German Army, using a series of case studies from the German-Danish War of 1864 through to Guderian's crossing of the Meuse in 1940, highlighting an ongoing tension between independence and arbitrariness in decision-making.[153] The book then provided three detailed examinations of division-level operations on the Eastern Front during 1942/43, the period during which *Auftragstaktik* is often held to have been abandoned by the German Army and replaced by Hitler's personal control and preference for rigid tactics and obedience.[154]

The works noted above provided vital stimulation and evidence for the consideration in this book of command approaches, and their expression in the doctrine and application in practice by the British and German armies during the period 1918 to 1940. However, their specific focus on *Auftragstaktik* as a methodology means their approach and scope is rather different from that adopted here. Nonetheless, it should be noted there are important consistencies in analysis and conclusions between these earlier studies and those presented here.

For example, while the 'fit' is not exact, given the different purposes of the approaches, it may be suggested a significant consistency may be observed between

---

153 Sigg, *Unterführer*, pp.177-252.
154 Sigg, *Unterführer*, pp.253-456.

Sigg's idealised model of *Auftragstaktik* and the 'three gaps' model developed by Bungay considered earlier in this chapter:

- Knowledge Gap – addressed through Command Process and Judgement
- Alignment Gap – addressed through Obedience and Independence
- Effects Gap – addressed through Offensive Spirit and Determination

As a consequence, it is clear *Auftragstaktik* has strong parallels with the command approaches of 'Directive Command' and 'Directive Control', as expressed in the typology developed earlier in this chapter.

And Yet...

Before closing this consideration of theoretical models of command and moving onto to their application to the historical example of the British and German armies during the period 1918 to 1940, it is important to emphasise two key points. First, command approaches are not absolutes. As has already been noted, they are contextual, in terms of their relative effectiveness. Warfare is not a race against the clock, rather it is a game of 'rock, paper, scissors'.

Second, although this chapter has sought to explore the relative effectiveness of the various command approaches identified through a model of responses to friction, it should end by noting one of Clausewitz's most important warnings:

> Given the nature of the subject, we must remind ourselves that it is simply not possible to construct a model for the art of war that can serve as a scaffolding on which the commander can rely for support at any time... *talent and genius operate outside the rules, and theory conflicts with practice.*[155]

---

155 Clausewitz, *On War*, p. 140 (emphasis in original).

2

Doctrine for Orders and Decentralisation

An order should contain all that a subordinate needs to know to be able to execute his mission – and nothing more.

Truppenführung (1933)[1]

In 1989, the Ministry of Defence issued *Design for Military Operations – The British Military Doctrine*.[2] This slim volume has been hailed as the first British attempt to 'articulate doctrine at a level above the tactical'.[3] Indeed, its foreword recognised the longstanding hostility[4] to formal doctrine in the army, noting, 'there may be some who say that laying down doctrine like this is not the British way'. Almost apologetically, it reassured readers, 'This does not mean that initiative needs to be restricted by the imposition of a set of rules'.[5]

Design for Military Operations was a product of the reawakening in Britain and the United States of an interest in what was later officially dubbed the Manoeuvrist Approach to warfare[6] as a means to counter the growing Soviet military threat in

---

1 *Heeresdienstvorschrift (HDv) 300/1: Truppenführung* (1933), para. 73.
2 *Design for Military Operations – The British Military Doctrine*, Army Code 71451 (1989). Although published under the signature of General Sir John Chapple, Chief of the General Staff, it was written during the tenure of his predecessor, Field Marshal Sir Nigel Bagnall (see p. vii).
3 *Design for Military Operations – The British Military Doctrine*, Army Code 71451 (1996), Foreword (unnumbered pages).
4 For the longstanding hostility to doctrine, see for example, 'The British Army and Modern Conceptions of War', *Edinburgh Review*, 213 (1911), 321-346 (p. 322), and Brigadier Shelford Bidwell and Dominic Graham, *Firepower: British Army Weapons and Theories of War, 1904-1945* (London: Allen & Unwin, 1982), p. 19.
5 *Design for Military Operations* (1989), p. vii.
6 *Army Doctrine Publication: Operations*, Army Code 71632 (2010), p. iii.

Central Europe.[7] Ironically, the doctrine appeared just months before the collapse of Soviet control of Eastern Europe led to the disappearance of that threat, although it was to be employed with significant success in the Gulf War of 1991.[8]

A major feature of the debate that produced the new British doctrine, as well as its American equivalent,[9] was the emphasis given to the perceived operational excellence of the German Wehrmacht during the Second World War, deemed to provide numerous examples of the application of manoeuvrist thinking to defeat numerically-superior Soviet forces.[10] Within this, special attention was given to the understanding of warfare presented in the writings of Clausewitz – *Design for Military Operations* referred to him more than to any other military thinker, specifically referencing his teachings on friction, warfare as a clash of wills, and the importance of surprise at the decisive point.[11]

In turn, this led to a focus on the manual, *Heeresdienstvorschrift (HDv) 300/1: Truppenführung* (Army Service Regulation 300/1: Unit Command of Troops). Published in 1933, this statement of doctrine was to guide the German conduct of military operations throughout the Second World War, providing the Wehrmacht with 'both the cognitive basis and the technological derivation for its wartime tactical excellence'.[12] The manual has been lauded by Williamson Murray as 'one of the most thoughtful examinations of the conduct of operations and leadership ever written',[13] by Mungo Melvin as 'arguably one of the finest pieces of doctrinal writing in military history',[14] and by Shimon Naveh as 'the best evidence confirming the existence of operational cognition prior to the year 1938 [… . It set out] the most advanced operational theory of command ever created'.[15]

Truppenführung has accordingly been subject to considerable academic examination, including by Martin van Creveld,[16] Robert Citino,[17] Bruce Condell and David

7   General Donn A. Starry, 'Foreword', in Richard E. Simpkin, *Race to the Swift: Thoughts on Twenty-First Century Warfare* (London: Brassey's, 1985), pp. vii-ix.
8   Eitan Shamir, *Transforming Command: The Pursuit of Mission Command in the U.S., British and Israeli Armies* (Stanford, CA: Stanford University Press, 2011), pp. 142-144.
9   Headquarters, Department of the Army, *FM 100-5: Operations* (5 May 1986).
10   Martin van Creveld, 'On Learning from the Wehrmacht and Other Things', *Military Review* (January 1988), 62-71.
11   *Design for Military Operations* (1989), pp. 31, 32 and 56-57.
12   Martin Van Creveld, *Fighting Power: German and U.S. Army Performance, 1939-1945* (Westport, CT: Greenwood, 1982), p. 30.
13   Williamson Murray, 'Leading the Troops: A German Manual of 1933', *Marines Corps Gazette* (September 1999), 95-98 (p. 95).
14   Mungo Melvin, 'The German Perspective', in *The Normandy Campaign 1944: Sixty Years On*, ed. by John Buckley, (London: Routledge, 2006), (22-34), p. 22.
15   Shimon Naveh, *In Pursuit of Military Excellence: The Evolution of Operational Theory* (London: Cass, 1997), p. 116.
16   Creveld, *Fighting Power*, pp.28-41.
17   Robert Citino, *The Path to Blitzkrieg: Doctrine and Training in the German Army, 1920-39* (Mechanicsburg, PA: Stackpole, 2008), pp.223-229.

Zabecki,[18] and Matthias Strohn.[19] Although all emphasised the importance of *Truppenführung*'s statements on command, there has been limited consideration of these in relation to one of Clausewitz's central concepts: friction. In addition, there has been only limited analysis of the manual in the context of German doctrinal statements over the previous half century, from Helmuth von Moltke the Elder onwards. It therefore remains unclear the extent to which the philosophy of command set out in *Truppenführung* represented a break with past thinking or else expressed continuity. This chapter seeks to address both of these gaps in the literature, building on the exploration of Clausewitzian friction and its implications for different command approaches undertaken in Chapter One.

In addition, no previous study has systematically compared the German Army's doctrinal statements with those in the manuals of their foes. Indeed, van Creveld's[20] brief contrast of *Truppenführung*'s philosophy with the very different approach set out in the 1941[21] and 1944[22] editions of the United States Army's FM 100-5, even though these included entire sentences lifted from the German manual,[23] provides the partial lone exception. Yet, as was noted in Chapter One, Clausewitz's emphasis on warfare as a clash between two independent wills,[24] especially as subsequently developed by Colonel John Boyd, suggests the effectiveness of different command philosophies is relative rather than absolute.

This chapter therefore seeks to shed light on the German concepts by contrasting them with those in British military manuals over the same period, particularly examining a change in approach in the latter in 1909. This comparison is especially appropriate, given claims the British manuals began as mere paraphrases of their German equivalents.[25] Perhaps surprisingly, the literature is even more limited in its consideration of British doctrine regarding command and orders, brief studies

18 Bruce Condell and David T. Zabecki, 'Editors' Introduction', in *On the German Art of War: Truppenführung*, ed. and trans. by Bruce Condell and David T. Zabecki (London: Rienner, 2001), pp.1-14.
19 Matthias Strohn, *The German Army and the Defence of the Reich: Military Doctrine and the Conduct of the Defensive Battle, 1918-1939* (Cambridge: Cambridge University, 2011), p.185-202.
20 Creveld, *Fighting Power*, pp.28-41.
21 War Department, *Field Service Regulations: FM 100-5: Operations* (22 May 1941).
22 War Department, *Field Service Regulations: FM 100-5: Operations* (Washington DC: US Government Printing Office, 15 June 1944).
23 Condell and Zabecki, 'Editors' Introduction', pp. 10-11.
24 Carl von Clausewitz, *On War*, ed. and trans. by Michael Howard and Peter Paret (Princeton, NJ: Princeton University, 1976), p.75
25 *Report of a Conference of General Staff Officers at the Royal Military College, 13th to 16th January, 1913, Held Under the Orders and Direction of the Chief of the Imperial General Staff* (Camberley, 1913), p.15

by David French[26] and Christopher Pugsley[27] representing notable exceptions. This comparative approach is employed to bring out a deeper understanding of the strengths and limitations of the statements in those manuals, thereby highlighting factors affecting the relative performance of the British and German armies when pitted against each other in combat during the period 1918 to 1940 that is the focus of this book.

In undertaking this analysis, it should be explicitly recognised that statements in doctrinal manuals are, of course, no more than that: statements. The risk of a gap between officially espoused doctrine and actual troop practice was implicitly acknowledged by the frequency with which manuals insisted their principles should not be subject to local limitations during peacetime training.[28] Nonetheless, if doctrine is defined as 'what is taught' and is intended to have the function of establishing 'the framework of understanding of the approach to warfare in order to provide the foundation for its practical application',[29] then it is worthy of close consideration. While the processes by which the manuals were written are considered briefly, both here and in the next chapter, a more extensive examination than possible here might expose more fully whether their doctrine was broadly accepted or subject to debate. In addition, this might reveal whether evidence regarding the validity of certain doctrinal statements was actively sought or deliberately ignored.[30] Certainly, the period between the Franco-Prussian War and the start of the First World War saw vigorous debate regarding doctrine and the lessons to be drawn from practical experience, both within the German Army and between the military establishment and civilian academics, notably Hans Delbrück.[31]

As has been noted, the behaviour of operational units and their commanders in practice may differ from that expressed in doctrinal manuals. For example, in the early

26   David French, *Raising Churchill's Army: The British Army and the War against Germany, 1919-1945* (Oxford: Oxford University, 2000), pp.12-23.

27   Christopher Pugsley, 'We Have Been Here Before: the Evolution of the Doctrine of Decentralised Command in the British Army, 1905-1989', *Sandhurst Occasional Papers* (9) (2011), pp. 7 -27.

28   For example, *The Order of Field Service of the German Army*, trans. by Major J. M. Gawne and Spenser Wilkinson (London: Stanford, 1893), p. 5, *Infantry Training (Provisional)* (London: War Office, 1902), p. 4, and *HDv 130: Ausbildungsvorschrift für die Infanterie* (Berlin: Reichsdruckerei, 1922), p. 5.

29   *Design for Military Operations* (1989), p. 3.

30   For such an examination, regarding the development of tactical doctrine for the defence during the First World War, see Martin Samuels, *Command or Control? Command, Training and Tactics in the British and German Armies, 1888-1918* (London: Cass, 1995), pp.158-229.

31   See, for example, Robert T. Foley, *German Strategy and the Path to Verdun: Erich von Falkenhayn and the Development of Attrition, 1870-1916* (Cambridge: Cambridge University, 2005), pp. 38-55, Dirk W. Oetting, *Auftragstaktik: Geschichte und Gegenwart einer Führungs konzeption* (Frankfurt am Main: Report, 1993), pp.121-140, and Stephan Leistenschneider, *Auftragstaktik im preussisch-deutschen Heer 1871 bis 1914* (Hamburg: Mittler, 2002), pp.98-122.

years of the twentieth century, supporters of the new British General Staff argued its primary role was to develop a fresh doctrine.[32] Almost by definition, therefore, the doctrine expressed in its manuals would differ from common usage, at least initially.[33] Equally, David Zabecki has highlighted the gulf between Ludendorff's doctrine of decentralisation and his actual command practice during the 1918 offensives.[34] A detailed examination of the application (or not) of the doctrines expressed in the manuals can offer valuable further insight into the experience of the two armies.[35] Chapters Three (on Rommel), Four (on Amiens, August 1918) and Five (on Arras, May 1940) provide a series of case studies of operational practice over the period 1918 to 1940 as the basis for precisely such an exploration.

It is also necessary to articulate the definition of 'doctrine' used here. The British *Army Doctrine Primer* of 2011 quoted Richard Holmes on doctrine being 'an approved set of principles and methods, intended to provide large military organisations with a common outlook and a uniform basis for action'.[36] A distinction may be drawn between doctrine and culture, which the army defined as 'the socially transmitted pattern of human behaviour within the organisation',[37] and which may be responsible for gaps between doctrine and behaviour.

While recognising the scope for further examination of connected issues, this chapter deliberately focuses on the doctrine expressed in the manuals of the two armies, and its continuity and change over time, based on close textual analysis. The manuals expressed what the most senior British and German generals believed should be the guiding philosophies of their respective forces. These slim volumes represented the most powerful means by which each army's leadership sought to convert its theoretical ideals into reality,[38] since most officers based their understanding of that doctrine on what they read in those manuals. Detailed examination of these publications therefore offers an insight into the thinking of those senior leaders, whether or not they achieved their goals in practice, through the ongoing interaction with the changing cultures of their respective armies.

---

32   Hew Strachan, 'The British Army, its General Staff and the Continental Commitment, 1904-14', in *The British General Staff: Reform and Innovation, c.1890-1939*, ed. by David French and Brian Holden Reid (London: Cass, 2002), p.86.

33   For an example of such dissemination, see Major Paul H. Herbert, *Deciding What Has to Be Done: General William E. DePuy and the 1976 Edition of FM 100-5, Operations* (Fort Leavenworth, KS: Combat Studies Institute, 1988).

34   Major-General David T. Zabecki, *The German 1918 Offensives: A Case Study in the Operational Level of War* (London: Routledge, 2006).

35   For such an examination, regarding gaps between doctrine and practice in the British Army after 1918, see French, *Raising Churchill's Army*, pp.12-47.

36   *Army Doctrine Publication: Army Doctrine Primer (AC 71954)* (May 2011), p.1-1.

37   *Army Doctrine Publication: Operations* (2010), p.2-18.

38   Ralf Raths, *Vom Massensturm zur Stoßtrupptaktik: Die deutsche Landkriegtaktik im Spiegel von Dienstvorschriften und Publizistik 1906 bis 1918* (Freiburg: Rombach, 2009), pp.15-16.

Truppenführung

When considering the philosophy of command and friction presented in *Truppenführung*, the key statements are contained in its Introduction (paragraphs 1-15) and in its Chapter Two (paragraphs 27-119), which covers Command.

The fifteen 'highly philosophical paragraphs'[39] of the Introduction, comprising just four and a half pages of the original pocket-sized volume,[40] set the manual's tone. Since issues of tone and phraseology are central to the argument, the text is quoted at some length. Further, given that, as Lord Chesterfield famously noted, 'every thing suffers by a translation, except a bishop',[41] readers are strongly recommended to compare the English version[42] to the original German text:

1. War is an art, a free and creative activity founded on scientific principles. It makes the very highest demands on the human personality.
2. The conduct of war is subject to continual development. [...]
3. Combat situations are of an unlimited variety. They change frequently and suddenly and can seldom be assessed in advance. Incalculable elements often have a decisive influence. One's own will is pitted against the independent will of the enemy. Friction[43] and errors are daily occurrences.
4. Lessons in the conduct of war cannot be exhaustively compiled in the form of regulations. The principles enunciated must be applied in accordance with the situation. [...]
6. The command of an army [...] requires leaders capable of judgement, with clear vision and foresight, and the ability to make independent and decisive decisions and carry them out unwaveringly and positively. Such leaders must be impervious to the changes in the fortunes of war and possess full awareness of the high degree of responsibility placed on their shoulders. [...]
9. Every leader in every situation must exert himself totally and not avoid responsibility. Willingness to accept responsibility is the most important quality of a leader. It should not, however, be based upon individualism without consideration of the whole, nor used as a justification for failing to carry out orders where seeming to know better may affect obedience. Independence of spirit must not become arbitrariness. By contrast, independence of action within acceptable boundaries is the key to great success.

39 Condell and Zabecki, 'Editors' Introduction', p. 3.
40 *HDv 300/1: Truppenführung*, pp. 1-5.
41 Henry Kett, *The Flowers of Wit* (Hartford: Cooke, 1825), p. 57.
42 From *On the German Art of War*, pp. 17-19.
43 The manual here uses the German term *Reibungen* rather than Clausewitz's *Friktion*, which he had borrowed from English.

10. [...] The emptiness of the battlefield requires soldiers who can think and act independently, who can make calculated, decisive, and daring use of every situation, and who understand that victory depends on each individual. [...]

12. Leaders must live with their troops and share in their dangers [...]. Only thus can they acquire a first-hand knowledge of the combat capabilities and needs of their soldiers. [...]

14. [...] Orders that are impossible to execute will reduce confidence in the leadership and damage morale.

15. Every man, from the youngest soldier upward, must be required at all times and in all situations to commit his whole mental, spiritual, and physical strength. Only in this way will the full force of a unit be brought to bear in decisive action. [...] *The first criterion in war remains decisive action. Everyone, from the highest commander down to the youngest soldier, must constantly be aware that inaction and neglect incriminate him more severely than any error in the choice of means.*[44]

Consideration of these paragraphs, along with the relevant text from the manual's Chapter Two, allows an assessment of the German perspective on the three key factors identified at the end of our previous chapter as determining the relative effectiveness of the different command approaches:

- Whether an army expects the problems encountered in warfare to be wicked, such that it is unlikely that senior commanders will be able to predict the local situation within which their subordinates operate (making approaches that emphasise subordinates' initiative liable to be more effective), or whether they are expected to be tame, such that senior commanders can determine local situations in advance (making approaches that use detailed orders more effective);
- Whether commanders can rely on their subordinates to interpret general directives within their local situation, in order to achieve the overall intent (enabling approaches that maximise low-level initiative), or whether deficiencies in capability or motivation mean commanders cannot trust their subordinates to act independently (requiring reliance on rigid adherence to orders); and
- Whether commanders seek to achieve certainty through extensive collection and collation of intelligence about the situation and detailed analysis of all the available options, in order to identify the 'correct' solution to a tame problem, or whether they emphasise speed of decision-making, even in the absence of a large part of the picture, in order to implement quickly 'good enough' decisions to wicked problems, thereby achieving tempo and inflicting surprise and shock on the enemy.

---

44   Emphasis in original.

It is clear the authors of *Truppenführung* considered the problems of warfare to be inherently 'wicked' (nonlinear, and hence chaotic). The Introduction's emphasis on war as an art (para. 1) and the unlimited variety of combat situations produced by the interaction with the independent will of the enemy (para. 3) was reinforced in the second chapter by para. 36 ('uncertainty always will be present. It rarely is possible to obtain exact information on the enemy situation'), para. 37 ('if the assigned mission no longer suffices for action, or if it is overtaken by events, the course of action must take these circumstances into account'), and para. 48 ('one must reckon with incomplete and inaccurate information').

The drive towards reliance on subordinates' initiative, resulting from this perception of the problems faced in warfare as being wicked, was set out clearly. Leaders at all levels were required to accept responsibility (para. 9), soldiers were expected to think and act independently (para. 10), and there was a firm emphasis on failure to act being a more serious fault than error in the choice of means (para. 15). This was underlined in the second chapter by para. 37 ('the commander must allow his subordinates freedom of action'), para. 73 ('an order should contain all that a subordinate needs to know to be able to execute his mission – and nothing more'), and para. 76 ('the general intent must be stated for the execution of impending operations, but the method of execution is left to the subordinate commanders').

Finally, the importance placed upon speed of decision-making was underlined by the recognition that combat situations change frequently and suddenly (para. 3), and the requirement for decisive and daring use of every situation (para. 10). This was reinforced by para. 27 ('great success requires boldness and daring'), para. 29 ('favourable situations must be quickly recognised and decisively exploited'), para. 32 ('actions based on surprise are only successful if the enemy is given no time to take effective counter measures'), and para. 63 ('the commander most likely to succeed is the one who makes the quickest and most skilful use of [...] the situation').

Taken together, these statements strongly suggest the doctrine set out in *Truppenführung* was equivalent to the command approach we have earlier termed 'Directive Command'. As set out in Chapter One, this is based on the belief that the inherently chaotic (wicked) nature of warfare means commanders rarely have better knowledge of the local situation than their subordinates (resulting in a wide Knowledge Gap). As such, they must rely on the initiative of those subordinates (thereby narrowing the Alignment Gap) to achieve the commander's overall intent by exploiting unpredictable opportunities (in this way reducing the Effects Gap) through rapid decision-making (in so doing, achieving tempo). This makes it easier to inflict surprise and shock on the enemy, in this way increasing the level of friction that they experience.

Further than this, however, the manual also placed great emphasis on the need for senior commanders to place themselves very close to their troops, especially during the attack (paras. 109-115), in order, to ensure they were personally at the decisive point (*entscheidende Stelle*) at the earliest possible time (para. 113). In this way, the commander would increase his direct knowledge of the local situation, his decision-making would be fastest, and his attention and resources most focused at the decisive point of the battle, narrowing all the gaps expressing friction within his own forces. At the same time, he maximised the potential for achieving tempo over the enemy, thereby increasing their friction. This approach, which may be considered closely aligned with that we have termed 'Directive Control', may also be seen as a response to a third type of problem, identified by Keith Grint as an extension of Horst Rittel and Melvin Webber's original typology: the 'critical' problem, characterised by its self-evident nature and need for rapid, authoritarian decision-making, associated with Command.[45]

Although Directive Control offers the potential to narrow all of the gaps that might express friction within the commander's own forces, while also maximising the potential for achieving tempo over the enemy and thereby increasing the friction experienced by them, it equally carries a significant negative aspect. Such direct personal control at the critical point brings with it the risk the commander might lose a broader awareness of the overall situation, and might impair the initiative of his subordinates – Moltke, for one, was clear on the dangers that excessive personal intervention on the battlefield could bring.[46]

Continuity and Change

To what extent were the authors[47] of *Truppenführung* breaking new ground? Matthias Strohn suggested an 'obvious' influence[48] from Hans von Seeckt's 1921 manual, *HDv 487: Führung und Gefecht der verbundenen Waffen* (Command and Combat of the Combined Arms),[49] colloquially known as *Das FuG*. Similarly, Robert Citino stated *Truppenführung* 'bear[s] the stamp' of the previous regulations,[50] while James Corum argued much of the new manual was no more than 'a paraphrase' of *Das FuG*.[51] Conversely, Condell and Zabecki noted those fifteen paragraphs in the introduction to the new manual were a vital novelty.[52] But this comparison is only partial, in that

---

45   Keith Grint, *Leadership, Management and Command: Rethinking D-Day* (Basingstoke: Palgrave, 2008), p.12. In light of the debate above, the author would prefer the term 'Control' to Grint's use of 'Command'.

46   *Moltke on the Art of War: Selected Writings*, ed. by Daniel J. Hughes, trans. by Daniel J. Hughes and Harry Bell (New York, NY: Ballantine, 1993), p. 132.

47   Ludwig Beck (commander of 1st Cavalry Division and then head of the *Truppenamt*), Werner von Fritsch (commander of 3rd Infantry Division and then *Wehrkreis* III), and Carl Heinrich von Stülpnagel (head of the Foreign Armies section of the *Truppenamt*). See Matthias Strohn, *The German Army and the Defence of the Reich: Military Doctrine and the Conduct of the Defensive Battle, 1918-1939* (Cambridge: Cambridge University Press, 2011), p. 186.

48   Strohn, *Defence of the Reich*, p.188.

49   *HDv 487/1: Führung und Gefecht der verbundenen Waffen* (Berlin, 1921).

50   Robert Citino, *The Path to Blitzkrieg: Doctrine and Training in the German Army, 1920-39* Mechanicsburg, PA: Stackpole, 2008), p. 223.

51   James S. Corum, *The Roots of Blitzkrieg: Hans von Seeckt and German Military Reform* (Lawrence, KS: University Press of Kansas, 1992), p.199.

52   Condell and Zabecki, 'Editors' Introduction', pp.2-3.

it treats the German command philosophy as if originating only with the publication of *Das FuG*, effectively discarding as irrelevant the doctrinal statements made prior to 1914.

Felddienst-Ordnung

Taking account of this longer history, it becomes clear the absence in *Das FuG* of an introduction like that in *Truppenführung* was itself a break with tradition – the successive editions of the Kaiserheer's *Felddienst-Ordnung* (*FO*) (Field Service Regulations) of 1887,[53] 1894,[54] 1900,[55] and 1908[56] all included a ten-page introduction.[57] Although the precise wording varied slightly between each of the editions,[58] several statements were carried forward throughout the period. Of key relevance to the issues considered here were the following (using the wording of the 1908 edition):

> Foreword: The latitude allowed for the performance of duties in the field is intended to give scope for original thought and initiative on the part of commanders. Superior officers are forbidden to issue orders restricting this latitude. [...]
> 1. The training of troops in peacetime is regulated by what will be required of them in war. [...]
> 4. Every officer should exert the whole force of his character in every situation, even the most unusual without fear of responsibility. It is the duty of superior officers to stimulate and to foster this spirit in their subordinates. [...]
> 13. Lectures delivered to officers [...] serve both to instruct and to stimulate new ideas [...]. It is desirable that each lecture should be followed by a discussion, in order to give as many officers as possible an opportunity of expressing their opinions. [...]

53 *Felddienst-Ordnung* (Berlin: Mittler, 1887) and *The Order of Field Service of the German Army*, trans. by Major J.M.Gawne and Spenser Wilkinson (London: Stanford, 1893).

54 *DVE 438: Felddienst-Ordnung* (Berlin: Mittler, 1894).

55 *Felddienst-Ordnung* (Berlin: Mittler, 1900) and *The Field Service Regulations (Feld Dienst Ordnung, 1900) of the German Army*, trans. by Colonel H.S. Brownrigg (London: HMSO, 1900).

56 *DVE 267: Felddienst-Ordnung* (Berlin: Mittler, 1908) and *Field Service Regulations (Felddienst Ordnung, 1908) of the German Army*, trans. by General Staff, War Office (London: HMSO, 1908).

57 The introduction to the 1887 edition of *FO* differed substantially from the *Verordnungen über die Ausbildung der Truppen für den Felddienst und über die größeren Truppenübungen* (Berlin: Königlichen Geheimen Ober-Hofbuchdruckerei, 17 June 1870) (Regulations for the Instruction of the Troops in Field Service and the Exercise of the Larger Units), which may be considered a 'prototype' Field Service Regulations.

58 See *Neues aus der Felddienstordnung* (Oldenburg: Stalling, 1900), pp.3-6, and *Was bringen Felddienst-Ordnung und Manöver-Ordnung vom 22. März 1908 Neues?* (Berlin: Mittler, 1908), pp.8-14.

25. It is no less important to educate the soldier to think and to act for himself. His self-reliance and sense of honour will then induce him to do his duty even when he is no longer under the eye of his commanding officer. [...]

37. All peace exercises lack what in war is the principal factor, namely, the enemy, the will and offensive power of whom have to be reckoned with until both are broken down. It must never be forgotten that the situations encountered in war will differ in many respects from those met with in peace exercises, and will impose a far more unequal and a severer test on moral endurance. [...]

38. Resolute action is consequently of first importance in war. Every individual from the highest commander to the youngest soldier, must always remember that supine inaction and neglect of opportunities will entail severer censure than an error in conception of the choice of means.

While less succinct and philosophical in tone than *Truppenführung*, important continuities are apparent. For example, para. 4 of *FO* 1908 (on the officer's role as the leader and teacher of his troops and the need for him to accept responsibility without fear) was carried forward almost unchanged into paras. 7 and 9 of *Truppenführung*. Similarly, paras. 37 and 38 of *FO* 1908 (on the importance of resolute action, and on inaction being far worse than errors in the choice of means) were repeated almost verbatim in para. 15 of *Truppenführung*.

As with *Truppenführung*, these paragraphs from the introduction to the various editions of *FO*, along with the relevant statements in their chapter on orders, permit an assessment of the pre-First World War German perspective on the three key factors identified earlier as determining the relative effectiveness of the different command approaches.

The perception in *Truppenführung* of warfare as inherently 'wicked' or chaotic represents continuity with *FO*, as shown by the latter's reference to the importance of the enemy's will and the difference between situations encountered in war compared to those in peace (para. 37). This was picked up in para. 50 ('circumstances may have changed before the order can be carried out').

Although the sense of warfare as unpredictable was much less strong in the various editions of *FO* than was the case in *Truppenführung*, the emphasis on the need for commanders to make maximum use of the initiative of their subordinates was just as firm. The prohibition on commanders restricting their subordinates' scope for original thought and initiative (Foreword) was reinforced through a series of further statements in the body of the manual. These underlined the need for leaders at all levels to accept responsibility (para. 4), for soldiers to think and act independently (para. 25), and the stress on failure to act being a more serious fault than error in the choice of means (para. 38). This was underlined by the text regarding the issue of orders: para. 49 ('an order should contain, and only contain, everything which the recipient requires to know to enable him to carry out independently the task assigned to him'), and para. 50 ('the general views of the commander for the conduct of the intended operations should be given, but the method of execution must be left open'). The German text of these statements makes it absolutely clear that the requirement for orders not to go beyond what the recipient needed to know was not intended as a means of restricting their knowledge of the commander's intent in order to maintain secrecy. Rather, it was a matter of not limiting their scope for initiative and their ability to adapt to the local situation. Here, the various editions of *FO* again clearly provided the template for *Truppenführung*.

By contrast, the issue of surprise, achieved through rapid decision-making facilitated by the presence of commanders placed far forward with their troops, was completely absent from the various editions of *FO*. There was accordingly no sense in *FO* of the importance of speed and surprise – indeed, every one of the frequent references to surprise (paras. 110, 125, 134, 152, 172, and 300) was in connection with the importance of forces avoiding being themselves surprised. There was no allusion at all to friendly forces seeking to surprise the enemy.

Instructions for Large Unit Commanders

Before concluding this assessment of the German pre-1914 doctrine of command and its relationship with that set out in the 1933 manual, it should be recognised that *FO* was complemented by a second manual, covering command at the strategic and higher operational level. As with *FO*, this went through a series of editions, starting with the *Verordnungen für die höheren Truppenführer* (Instructions for Large Unit Commanders) of 24 June 1869,[59] which was written under Helmuth von Moltke's direct supervision and included a number of his personal amendments.[60] The *Instructions* were revised in 1885,[61] and again in 1910, when they were renamed *Grundzüge der höheren Truppenführung* (Principles of Large Unit Command).[62] Both revisions again preserved much of Moltke's original wording from 1869.[63] Following the First World War, drafts of a revised manual, again drawing heavily on Moltke's text, were prepared in 1924, 1930, and 1938. None were published, however, in part because the text was considered too focused on the mass armies forbidden to

---

59   Much of the manual was published in *Moltkes Militärische Werke: II, Die Thätigkeit als Chef des Generalstabes der Armee im Frieden, 2. Moltkes Taktisch-Strategische Aufsätze aus den Jahren 1857 bis 1871*, ed. by Großen Generalstab, Abteilung für Kriegsgeschichte I (Berlin: Mittler, 1900), pp. 171-215. A translation may be found in *Moltke on the Art of War*, pp. 172-224.

60   *Moltkes Militärische Werke, II (2)*, pp. 167-169.

61   No original copy of this edition appears to have survived, but it formed the basis for much of the text in *Moltkes Militärische Werke: IV, Kriegslehren, 2. Die taktischen Vorbereitungen zur Schlacht*, ed. by Großen Generalstab, Abteilung für Kriegsgeschichte I (Berlin: Mittler, 1911), pp. 1-167. A translation of the relevant sections may be found in *Moltke on the Art of War*, pp. 225-265.

62   *DVE 53: Grundzüge der höheren Truppenführung vom 1. Januar 1910* (Berlin: Reichsdruckerei, 1910).

63   Harry Horstmann, *Die Entwicklung deutscher Führungsgrundsätze im 20. Jahrhundert: Eine vergleichende Betrachtung zwischen Beständigkeit und Wandel* (Norderstedt: Grin, 2009), p. 4.

Germany by the Versailles Treaty,[64] but it is clear that the 1924 draft at least remained 'completely faithful' to the pre-war philosophy.[65]

The *Instructions*, especially the 1885 and 1910 editions, were clearly based on the belief that warfare was inherently unpredictable. The 1885 edition noted, 'From out of such darkness the correct thing has to be felt out and frequently guessed at, to enable the issuing of orders whose execution may encounter unforeseen eventualities and obstacles.'[66] This led the manual to highlight one of the key risks of ignoring this reality of warfare. As the 1910 edition stated, 'any disposition made far in advance and going into too much detail can only seldom be carried out completely. It shakes the trust of subordinates and gives the units a feeling of uncertainty if things happen entirely differently from what orders from higher headquarters had presumed.'[67]

The 1885 edition then moved on to give, for the first time, that sentence so central to every subsequent manual up to and including *Truppenführung* (with the surprising exception, as has been noted, of *Das FuG*): 'It should be the rule that orders contain everything – but only that – which the subordinate commander cannot independently determine for the attainment of a certain goal.'[68] Linked to this, 'One must never forget that if one orders too much, the most important part, that which unconditionally should be done, easily is pushed into the background by minor things and may be carried out only in part or even not at all.'[69] The focus was clearly on the need for the commander to rely on the initiative of his subordinates, setting out his intent but leaving maximum scope for them to apply their initiative, based on their better knowledge of the local situation.

Finally, the *Instructions* underlined the importance of decisions being made quickly. They noted that comparison between orders issued during manoeuvres and those in war revealed the detail of the former and the brevity of the latter. This, they argued, was due to the lack of time in war.[70] The 1869 edition emphasised the confusion and stress of battle,[71] the 'momentarily changing situation',[72] and that situations 'change very rapidly in war'.[73] Taken together, these suggest that Moltke believed commanders should seek to make decisions at speed, though there was no suggestion this was

64   Strohn, *Defence*, pp.154-155 & 190.
65   Gerhard P. Gross, *The Myth and Reality of German Warfare: Operational Thinking from Moltke the Elder to Heusinger*, ed. by Major-General David T. Zabecki (Lexington, KY: University Press of Kentucky, 2016), pp.144-146.
66   *Moltke on the Art of War*, p. 229.
67   *Moltke on the Art of War*, p.230. See also *Grundzüge*, para.55.
68   *Moltke on the Art of War*, p. 231. The equivalent section in the 1869 edition states: 'In general, one does well to order no more than is absolutely necessary', *Moltke on the Art of War*, p.184.
69   *Moltke on the Art of War*, p 230. See also *Grundzüge*, para.55.
70   *Moltke on the Art of War*, p. 231.
71   *Moltke on the Art of War*, p. 173.
72   *Moltke on the Art of War*, p. 175.
73   *Moltke on the Art of War*, p. 184.

designed to achieve tempo, and thereby surprise, and so inflict shock on the enemy, hence increasing their level of friction.

Furthermore, there was no intimation that senior commanders should place themselves far forward, at the decisive point, in order to maximise their personal impact. In fact, quite the reverse, as the 1869 edition insisted, 'Bypassing an intermediate authority destroys its effectiveness and causes it to appear superfluous. [...] The advantage, moreover, which the commander believes to achieve through continuous personal intervention, is mostly only an apparent one. He thereby takes over functions for whose fulfilment other persons are designated. He more or less denigrates their ability and increases his own duties to such a degree that he can no longer fulfil them completely.'[74] A similar prohibition was included in the 1885 edition, though with the recognition circumstances might on occasion be such that the need for speedy execution of orders might sometimes make bypassing intermediate headquarters necessary.[75] It is possible, however, that Moltke's concern here was primarily with protecting subordinates' freedom of action against excessively detailed instruction from above, rather than with whether senior commanders were near the front line. Elsewhere, however, Moltke was clear senior commanders should place themselves with their most forward units, in order to gain personal knowledge of the enemy's strength, position and movement, though he recognised the risk that, in so doing, they might lose control of their own forces. He therefore urged them to return to the rear once battle opened.[76]

This examination of the manuals that set out the German Army's doctrine in the thirty years from 1885 to 1914 suggests strongly that the army, strongly influenced by Moltke's views, saw warfare as inherently chaotic. This placed a premium on the need for commanders to leave significant scope for freedom of manoeuvre for their subordinates, albeit within a clear context of the commander's overall intent, with decisions taken at speed. Taken together, these again indicate the army sought to adopt a command approach equivalent to that here termed Directive Command. By contrast with the position in *Truppenführung*, however, the lack of emphasis in the earlier doctrine on the need to surprise the enemy, and the advice that commanders should not place themselves too far forward once battle had begun, indicates there was little official support for the approach here called Directive Control.

Die Abwehr and Der Angriff im Stellungskriege

Although neither *FO* nor the *Instructions* were revised during the First World War, matters of command were considered in two of Ludendorff's key doctrinal manuals:

---

74 *Moltke on the Art of War*, pp.183-184. See also *Grundzüge*, para.53.
75 *Moltke on the Art of War*, pp. 228-229.
76 *Moltkes Militärische Werke: IV. Kriegslehren, 3. Die Schlacht*, ed. by Großen Generalstab, Abteilung für Kriegsgeschichte I (Berlin: Mittler, 1912), pp. 43-44.

Grundsätze für die Abwehr im Stellungskriege (Principles for the Defence in Position Warfare) and *Der Angriff im Stellungskriege* (The Attack in Position Warfare).

Die Abwehr went through four editions between December 1916 and September 1918.[77] Although this period was marked by robust debate within the General Staff, and there was often a significant gap between the doctrine and operational practice,[78] the wording regarding the system of command to be employed showed considerable continuity over time: later editions strengthened and expanded key sections, rather than change the approach. Reflecting the short period during which the Germans were on the offensive, only one edition of *Der Angriff* was published, in January 1918, though minor amendments were issued in September of that year.[79]

The philosophy expressed in the two manuals was mutually consistent. Given their narrow focus on specific aspects of combat associated with position warfare, however, they concentrated on practicalities rather than the statements of principle that characterised the pre-war manuals.

The nature of position warfare meant both manuals made repeated reference to the need for careful planning in advance.[80] However, *Der Angriff* noted commanders would often find they had to make decisions based on incomplete reports and, especially as the depth of the advance increased, senior commanders would be too far removed to influence events personally.[81] This indicates some sense that, even in this limited context, the problems of command might be 'wicked'.

This was reinforced by an emphasis in both manuals on the central importance of initiative at all levels. *Die Abwehr* noted commanders, even of middling rank, must be granted 'a degree of freedom' and underlined the need for troops at all levels to use every opportunity arising during the battle.[82] This was still more explicit in *Der Angriff*, which stated, 'every attack offers opportunity for freedom of activity and an eager readiness for decisive action (*entschlußfreudigem Handeln*) even for the individual soldier'. Similarly, decisive results were gained through the initiative of individual

---

77   The editions were published on 1 December 1916, 1 March 1917, 23 October, 1917, and 20 September 1918. See Captain Greame C. Wynne, 'The Development of the German Defensive Battle in 1917, and its Influence on British Defensive Tactics, Part III: Field Service Regulation (1935)', *Army Quarterly*, 35 (1) (October 1937), 14-27 (pp.15-17), and Captain Greame C. Wynne, 'The Hindenburg Line', *Army Quarterly*, 37(2) (January 1939), 205-228 (p.227). A translation of the second edition was published as *SS 561: Manual of Position Warfare for All Arms: Part 8: The Principles of Command in the Defensive Battle in Position Warfare* (1 March 1917, trans. May 1917). The final (September 1918) edition was reprinted in General Erich Ludendorff, *Urkunden der Obersten Heeresleitung über ihre Tätigkeit, 1916-18* (Berlin: Mittler, 1920), pp.604-640.

78   See Samuels, *Command or Control?*, pp.178-197.

79   Reprinted in Ludendorff, *Urkunden*, pp.641-686.

80   For example *Grundsätze für die Abwehr im Stellungskriege*, para.9 (March 1917), and para.13 (September 1918) and *Der Angriff im Stellungskriege* (1918), para.3.

81   *Angriff*, paras.24 and 65.

82   *Abwehr* (September 1918), paras.6d and 40.

assault squads and platoons in seizing opportunities, underlining the importance of 'independent and readily responsible action (*verantwortungsfreudiges Handeln*) by junior commanders'.[83]

In contrast to the pre-war doctrine in *FO*, speed and surprise, based on personal knowledge of the situation, were central to both manuals. *Die Abwehr* stated it was 'the duty of every commander to gain, by means of personal reconnaissance, a thorough knowledge of the ground [...]. Only thus will he be in a position to conduct the fight properly and maintain the necessary personal touch with the troops'.[84] Opportunities were to be taken quickly by the troops on the spot, without waiting for further orders.[85] This was emphasised even more strongly in *Der Angriff*; 'Everything depends on fast and independent action by all ranks, in the context of the whole'. The importance of surprise was also recognised and senior officers were therefore encouraged to place themselves far forward.[86]

While there was clearly continuity in these wartime manuals from those before 1914, two developments stand out. First, the need for initiative at every level, even down to the individual soldier, was more strongly stated than before, reflecting the further decentralisation forced by the overwhelming firepower of the Western Front. Second, whereas surprise had been almost entirely absent from *FO*, by 1918 it was a major feature of the army's doctrine, giving added impetus to the emerging principle that commanders should place themselves forward.

Das FuG

The German Army's first post-war field manual was *Das FuG* of 1921, written under the personal supervision of the Reichswehr's commander-in-chief, Hans von Seeckt.[87] In one vital respect, *Das FuG* stood in a different position from both its many predecessors and also from the manual that replaced it. Whereas the various editions of both *FO* and the *Instructions*, as well as *Truppenführung* itself, were the product of peacetime development, *Das FuG* alone was prepared following a period of active warfare. As Corum has pointed out, *Das FuG* emerged from an extensive analysis of the German Army's experiences during the First World War, undertaken through eighty-six committees, between them involving more than five hundred officers.[88] Given that the army as a whole was only permitted a maximum of four thousand officers (including officer cadets) by the terms of the Versailles Treaty,[89]

83   *Angriff*, paras.3, 60, and 65.
84   *Abwehr*: para.10 (March 1917) and para.19 (September 1918).
85   *Abwehr*: para.15 (March 1917) and para.40 (September 1918).
86   *Angriff*, paras.6, 7, 24, 53, 65, and 26.
87   Strohn, *Defence of the Reich*, p. 112.
88   Corum, *Roots of Blitzkrieg*, pp.37-39.
89   *Treaty of Peace with Germany*, International Conciliation, 142 (New York, NY: American Association for International Conciliation, September 1919), arts.160(1) and 176..

these committees brought more than one in eight of the entire officer corps into the process of analysis. This was a truly inclusive exercise.

Das FuG reveals much continuity with the manuals that preceded and followed it, but also some important differences. Unlike both *Truppenführung* and *FO*, the new manual did not include an introduction. Its Chapter Two dealt with matters of command. Here, the manual stated (para.5) it was insufficient for a commander 'to rely on regulations, which have to apply to every circumstance, to guide his tactical handling. This would lead to a formulaic approach, which would be counter to the many-faceted nature of war.' Similarly, it was noted (para. 8), 'The situation will rarely be so clear as to give an exact insight into the situation of the enemy. Uncertainty in war is the norm. [...] In the changing situations of combat [...], inflexibly clinging to a course of action can lead to failure. The art of leadership consists of the timely recognition of the moment when a new decision is required.' Taken together, these statements suggest Seeckt was fully in agreement with the traditional German view of warfare as inherently unpredictable and hence 'wicked'.

With regard to reliance on subordinates' initiative, *Das FuG* did *not* include the iconic statement about orders including everything required by subordinates, but nothing more. This is surprising, given that the identical wording had featured in every edition of *FO* since 1887 and the *Instructions* since 1885, and was reintroduced in *Truppenführung*. This is all the more noteworthy, given that a 1919 text for what appears to have been a prototype for a post-war set of field service regulations did present equivalent wording: 'Any order must contain that, but only that, which the subordinate must know in order to act independently. It must be short, concise and clear, and must conform to the recipients' knowledge and under certain conditions to his peculiarities.'[90] Instead, *Das FuG* included the statement (para. 35), 'A decision is translated into action through an *order*. This must express simply, and without room for doubt, the will of the commander and the missions for the lower commanders. The independent execution of the lower commanders must not be restrained.' It did, however, retain the statement (para. 5), 'Willingness to accept responsibility remains the most important quality of a leader. All leaders must constantly bear in mind, and emphasise to their subordinates, that neglect and carelessness will weigh more heavily against them than error in the choice of means.' This provides a further example to suggest that *Truppenführung* in some respects displayed greater continuity with *FO* than it did with *Das FuG*.

Finally, *Das FuG* followed the tradition of the pre-war *FO* in making no mention of surprise as a key goal in warfare. Again, this is unexpected, given the emphasis on surprise in the wartime manuals. It did, however, pick up from them the doctrine, retained in *Truppenführung*, that the place of the commander was at the front. Thus it was stated (para. 62), 'The Divisional Commander must constantly be amongst

90   Major Rohrbeck, *Tactics: A Handbook Based on Lessons of the World War*, trans. by US General Service School (Fort Leavenworth, KS: General Service School, 1921), para. 42.

his troops. During an advance, his place is far forward' – wording very similar to that used in *Truppenführung* (para. 111). A similar requirement was placed upon his subordinate commanders (para. 63). *Das FuG*, unlike the wartime manuals, however, appears to have been more focused on the personal influence of the commander on his troops for reasons of morale (paras. 61 and 63), than with rapid decision-making.

Taking all of these considerations together, it appears *Truppenführung* was indeed building on well-established foundations in many areas of doctrine regarding command, and so represented significant continuity in its philosophy. In several key areas, where it differed from *Das FuG*, *Truppenführung* was closer than its predecessor to the precepts established during the First World War, a surprising situation, given that war experience tends to fade with time, such that armies often find their later manuals are less influenced by the hard-won lessons of combat.

In summary, German manuals from the 1880s onwards stressed that the nature of warfare as a clash between two independent wills meant it was characterised by rapidly changing situations. As a consequence, commanders could not see far into the future and often had to operate on the basis of partial and uncertain information, features characteristic of 'wicked' problems and reflecting the tendency for the Knowledge Gap to be wide. It was therefore essential to close the Effects Gap by relying upon the initiative of subordinates. In order to ensure the Alignment Gap did not become a major source of friction, the doctrine emphasised subordinates must ensure their actions were based on their commitment to, and understanding of, the higher commander's overall intent and their ability to interpret the best way in which to achieve this, drawing on their better knowledge of the local situation. This was most clearly expressed in two key rules: commanders were required to include in their orders 'all that a subordinate needs to know to be able to execute his mission – and nothing more'; and subordinates were sternly reminded 'inaction and neglect incriminate [them] more severely than any error in the choice of means'. These phrases were repeated in successive editions of the manuals over a period of fifty years.

While the simplicity and directness of the language of *Truppenführung* perhaps expressed some of these beliefs and doctrines more succinctly and memorably than had been the case with the previous manuals, it is clear the command approach presented throughout the half century prior to 1933 was equivalent to that here termed Directive Command.

Where *Truppenführung*, building on wartime experience, broke new ground was in its focus on surprise as a key goal. This also led to an emphasis on the need to secure tempo over the enemy through rapid decision-making, based on senior commanders positioning themselves personally at the decisive point of the battle at its climax (the *entscheidende Stelle*). While *Das FuG* started to point in that direction, its focus was still on the moral impact on the troops of seeing their commanders sharing in their joys and sorrows (para. 5). By contrast, the emphasis in *Truppenführung* was on the ability of the commander to make better decisions faster (para. 113). This doctrine, which had first emerged in the manuals of 1917 and 1918 but was overlooked in *Das FuG*, marked a vital new departure in German doctrine. It pushed commanders towards the command approach here termed Directive Control, though only in the limited circumstances of the decisive point.

Field Service Regulations (1935)

Having considered the perspectives and command approaches presented in the German manuals, it is necessary to look across the Channel to explore the position in the British Army.

By coincidence, the final pre-Second World War edition of *Field Service Regulations: Volume II – Operations* (FSR II) appeared only a year or so after *Truppenführung*. Prepared under the auspices of Major-General Cecil Heywood, Director of Staff Duties at the War Office, FSR II (1935)[91] was drafted by Archibald Wavell while on half pay prior to his assignment to command 2nd Division.[92]

Like *Das FuG*, but unlike the German manual's predecessors and successor, FSR II (1935) did not open with an introduction. Instead, it began with a description of the different fighting arms (ss. 1-10), before moving onto statements concerning command. The first four sections (ss. 11-14) of that chapter are of particular relevance to the question of which command approach was favoured by the manual.

Taking again the three factors identified as central to the determination of command approaches, and starting with whether the problems experienced in warfare were expected to be generally as 'tame' or 'wicked', FSR II (1935) set out a very structured series of steps through which commanders should develop their plans (s. 11(2)). However, while noting these steps were very similar to those relevant to everyday civilian life, the manual argued that the nature of warfare made them far harder to execute in the context of battle. It pointed to 'the continual succession of unforeseen incidents and obstacles' which arise (s. 11(3)), listing a series of causes for these that almost paraphrased those given by Clausewitz in his description of friction.[93] Echoing Clausewitz's analogy of warfare as being like a wrestling match,[94] the manual referred repeatedly to the need for the commander to be like a boxer (a sport likely to have been more familiar to British officers), engaging with and responding to the enemy's moves. Taken together, these statements suggest Wavell considered the problems faced by commanders during warfare were likely to be unpredictable and hence 'wicked'.

Moving onto the question of whether subordinates should be expected to use their initiative or instead follow detailed orders, the manual stated:

---

91   *Field Service Regulations, Vol. II: Operations – General* (London: HMSO, 1935).
92   John Connell (pseudonym of John Henry Robertson), *Wavell: Scholar and Soldier – To June 1941* (London: Collins, 1964), pp. 170-171.
93   Clausewitz, *On War*, pp. 119-120.
94   Clausewitz, *On War*, p. 75.

14(1). An order must contain only what the recipient requires to know, in order to carry out his task. Any attempt to prescribe to a subordinate at a distance anything that he, with a fuller knowledge of local conditions, should be able to decide on the spot will be avoided.

14(2). In framing orders for operations, the general principle is that the object to be attained, with such information as affects its attainment, will be briefly but clearly stated; the actual method of attaining the object will be given in sufficient detail to ensure co-ordination of effort, but so as not to interfere with the initiative of subordinate commanders, who should be left freedom of action in all matters which they can or should arrange for themselves.

These words are very similar to those in the various German manuals, and suggest a doctrine based on the importance of subordinate initiative. As has been seen, the German manuals complemented their statements with a warning that inaction and neglect by subordinates would be treated more severely than errors in the choice of means. The equivalent section in FSR II (1935) merits quoting in full:

14(5). Notwithstanding the greatest skill and care in framing orders, unexpected circumstances may render the precise execution of an order unsuitable or impracticable. In such circumstances the following principles will guide the recipient of an order in deciding his course of action:

i. A formal order will never be departed from either in letter or spirit so long as the officer who issued it is present, or there is time to report to him and await a reply without losing an opportunity or endangering the force commanded.

ii. If the above conditions cannot be fulfilled, a departure from either the spirit or the letter of an order is justified if the subordinate who assumes the responsibility bases his decision on some fact which could not be known to the officer who issued the order, and if he is satisfied that he is acting as his superior would order him to act were he present.

iii. If a subordinate neglects to depart from the letter of his orders when such departure, in the circumstances of sub-para. ii, above, is clearly demanded, he will be held responsible for any failure which may ensue.

iv. Should a subordinate find it necessary to depart from an order, he will immediately inform the issuer of it, and the commanders of any neighbouring units likely to be affected.

While s.14(5)iii paralleled the German doctrine, and appeared to give significant scope for subordinates to use their initiative, the text around it represented a vital difference in philosophy, expressed in both the tone and precise wording of the text.

First, s.14(5)i required subordinates in the first instance to report back to the commander and await new orders. Independent action was permitted *only* if doing so would risk losing the opportunity or endangering the force. Yet, the dynamic nature of warfare would often make it almost impossible for a subordinate to judge whether the opportunity before him would remain open for the time required to receive revised instructions. This created the risk that a commander whose views had not been sought might (with all the benefits of hindsight) reach a different conclusion, and the word 'never' suggested commanders might well do so.

Second, even if the subordinate was convinced that it was impractical to seek guidance from his commander, the hurdle to independent action set by s.14(5)ii was very high indeed. The subordinate might expect to be able to fulfil the first condition set by the sub-paragraph, since he ought to be able act 'as his superior would order him to act were he present', if that superior had properly explained his overall intent, as required by s.14(2). The second condition, however, was virtually impossible to surmount: almost by definition, the subordinate could never be certain that he was basing his decision 'on some fact which could not be known to the officer who issued the order', especially as s.14(2) also enjoined commanders not to constrain their subordinates by giving them too much detail.

In the face of two near-impossibilities – seeing into the future in order to know how long an opportunity would remain open, and having certainty that the commander could not have known a given fact when issuing his orders – the statement in s.14(5) iii, that the subordinate would be held responsible for any failure resulting from not acting, merely served to leave him wriggling on the hook. If events turned out badly, the commander could blame the subordinate *whether he had acted* (on the grounds that there would have been time to await new orders or that the situation was not unknown to the commander when issuing his original orders) *or not* (on the grounds that he should have used his initiative).

In short, despite some similarities in wording with *Truppenführung*, the effect of s.14 was to constrain severely the scope for subordinates to exercise initiative in the face of changing situations. Thereby, as David French has noted, it created 'a recipe for delay and lethargy'.[95]

This assessment is reinforced by examination of the relevant section in *FSR III – Higher Formations* (1935),[96] which was also drafted by Wavell.[97] FSR III (1935) is noteworthy as being the first time the British Army had published a doctrinal manual for commanders at this level, some sixty-six years after Moltke had first issued his *Instructions*.

FSR III (1935) (s.4(2)) noted that the commander's 'outlook must be a broad one. It is certain that any future war will bring many surprises, many novelties, many fresh methods. New weapons, or the improvement of old ones, and other developments in equipment may necessitate far-reaching changes of organization. A commander who has not prepared his mind to deal with the unexpected and thinks only in terms of past experience will be at a loss.' As with FSR II (1935), this suggests a perception of

---

95 French, *Raising Churchill's Army*, p. 23.
96 *Field Service Regulations, Vol. III: Operations – Higher Formations* (London: HMSO, 1935).
97 Connell, *Wavell*, p.177.

warfare as dynamic, with one consequence being that commanders would be unlikely to have better knowledge of the local situation than would their subordinates. The problems to be addressed were therefore likely to be 'wicked' in nature, rather than 'tame'. As a consequence, the Knowledge Gap was likely to be wide.

FSR III (1935) (s.4(3)) therefore advised a formation commander to issue orders 'clearly explaining his intentions, and [...] then allow [his subordinates] liberty of action in arranging the methods by which they will carry out these tasks. Undue centralization and interference with subordinates is harmful, since they are apt either to chafe at excessive control or to become afraid of taking responsibility.' This would counteract the Knowledge Gap by reducing the Effects Gap.

This stress on local initiative, however, was somewhat undermined by the suggestion (s.4(1)) that the commander should have regard for 'the ordinary unmilitary citizen, who may compose the bulk of the forces under his command and will have had only a short military training', with the implication that the commander should not expect too much of his subordinates. This was reinforced by the requirement (s.4(3)) for the commander to assign his subordinates 'definite tasks' and issue 'clear and definite orders', which might be expected to reduce the scope within which those subordinates could exercise the liberty of action recommended earlier. While emphasising the wicked nature of the problems arising in warfare, therefore, FSR III (1935) had clear concerns regarding the extent to which it was safe to expect subordinates to make the right decisions if given significant scope for local initiative. In effect, the manual hesitated over whether subordinates could be trusted to act in ways that closed the Alignment Gap.

In terms of whether commanders should aim for certainty, or for making a good decision quickly, FSR II (1935) (s.11(3)) leaned towards the need for speed. It noted, 'speed in action must be cultivated; the power to think quickly in an emergency is one of the greatest assets both of the boxer and of the commander; and the power to move quickly often gives to a body of troops, as to a boxer, the advantage of surprise.' It went on (s.11(5)) to emphasise the importance of surprise and mobility as two of the four fundamental principles of war, noting, 'Time is the most precious element in war, and the saving of it by all possible means is the surest test of a good commander.' This was echoed in s.31(1): 'A commander must realize that he will usually have to act on imperfect knowledge of a situation; it is his business to seek continually by every means in his power to supplement, confirm or correct his information; but to postpone action, when information is required, on the plea of waiting for fuller information, will lead to the loss of valuable time and the risk of failure.'

Although it underlined the importance of speed, and the effective use of time as a precious resource, as means to inflict surprise on the enemy, FSR II (1935) did not clearly address the implications of this for the location of the commander during the battle. For example, s.15(3) suggested commanders assemble their subordinates prior to the battle, in order to impress their will and inspire confidence through their personality. The language suggests, however, this would be achieved by bringing them back to the commander's position, rather than through the commander going forward towards the front line. During the battle itself, commanders were expected (s.12(1)vi) to place themselves where they could 'best control the course of the action, remembering that at the crisis personal example and leadership are the best means to ensure success', values shared by FSR III (1935) (s.4(3)). In this, therefore, both FSR II (1935) and FSR III (1935) were broadly consistent with the longstanding position of the German manuals prior to 1933. This highlights the novelty of *Truppenführung*'s emphasis, though partly echoing the German wartime manuals, on the need for the commander to place himself far forward, in order to enhance his ability to make better decisions faster (para. 113).

Taking all these factors together, it may be suggested that Wavell in FSR II (1935) and FSR III (1935) saw the problems generated in warfare as inherently unpredictable and hence subject to friction through creating a wide Knowledge Gap. Consequently, speed of reaction was an essential means by which to inflict surprise on the enemy, thereby widening his Knowledge Gap in turn. Conversely, it appears Wavell lacked confidence in the ability of subordinates to close the Alignment Gap by responding beyond narrow limits to the changing opportunities of warfare through the exercise of initiative. Since he assumed these subordinates would be inexperienced civilians drafted into the army at the start of any major war, this may have been a well-founded concern. Commanders were therefore expected to assign detailed tasks to their subordinates, who were required to follow those orders, even though the situation might have rendered them 'unsuitable or impracticable', other than in exceptional circumstances. This may be broadly aligned to the command approach here termed Restrictive Control.

However, before drawing conclusions about which command approach was favoured by Wavell personally, it should be noted he wrote in the context of significant pressures and constraints, which affected the basic thinking of the army between the wars. David French has highlight that the General Staff was concerned whether the urban citizens who would fill the ranks of a mass army would display in combat the steadfastness of their rural ancestors. The army also believed it possible to reduce warfare to a set of fixed principles, expressed a desire for order on the battlefield, and retained a focus on consolidation rather than exploitation.[98] All these factors encouraged an approach emphasising the 'tame', predictable nature of warfare.

Wavell's text was also very much in the tradition of earlier editions of FSR. As can be seen from Figure 2:1 below, his wording on the need for orders to contain only what the recipient needed to know, in order not to interfere with his initiative (s.14(1-2)) was very similar indeed to that used in the editions of 1929 (s.134(3-4)), 1924 (s.189(4)), and 1920 (s.67(4-5)). And his text on situations when subordinates could depart from their orders (s.14(5)) was almost identical to that used in the 1929 (s.129(6)) and 1923 (s.88(1)) editions.

98   French, *Churchill's Army*, pp.12-47.

Indeed, the wording of both sub-sections goes back earlier still. Jim Beach has recently explored the process of doctrinal writing at Haig's GHQ, noting how this became more coherent under Cuthbert Headlam from March 1918.[99] From July of that year, Headlam concentrated on a new version of the BEF's core statement of offensive doctrine,[100] the British equivalent of Ludendorff's *Die Abwehr* and *Der Angriff*, which like them had gone through several previous editions.[101] A key feature of the manual, finally published in November as *SS 135: The Division in Attack*,[102] was its 'genuflection' to the pre-war edition of FSR I.[103] This was underlined in its introduction: 'There has been a tendency during the present war to [...] a disregard of many of the fundamental principles, laid down in the training manuals issued before this war [...]. We have now, however, returned our allegiance to the principles of training employed before this war, and must be careful not to depart from them again.'[104]

Headlam's manual made repeated references to FSR I (1909),[105] for example to the issuing of orders, where it was emphasised 'operation orders should be based on the principles laid down' in FSR I (1909).[106] As Figure 2:1 shows, the wording there (s.12) was virtually identical to that used by Wavell in 1935. Headlam strengthened his appeal to FSR I (1909) by quoting a single sentence from that manual: 'An operation order should contain just what the recipient requires to know and nothing more'.[107] Perhaps tellingly, there was no reference to FSR's explanation of the reason for orders being brief: 'It should tell him nothing which he can and should arrange for himself'. Headlam's emphasis on secrecy[108] may suggest the purpose of brevity had now become control of information, rather than avoiding constraints on initiative, though this was, to some extent, restored in the post-war editions of FSR.

Wavell in 1935 was therefore presenting a philosophy that had been passed on from one edition of FSR to the next in an unbroken sequence of continuity since at least 1909.

---

99   Jim Beach, 'Issued by the General Staff: Doctrine Writing at British GHQ, 1917-1918', *War in History*, 19(4) (2012), 464-491 (p.482).
100   Beach, 'Doctrine Writing', p.488.
101   These included *SS 109: Training of Divisions for Offensive Action* (May 1916), *SS 135: Instructions for the Training of Divisions for Offensive Action* (December 1916), and *SS 135: The Training and Employment of Divisions* (January 1918).
102   *SS 135: The Division in Attack* (November 1918)
103   The order of the volumes of FSR changed after the First World War. Originally, FSR Part I addressed issues around operations, while FSR Part II dealt with administrative matters. After the war, FSR Volume I covered administration and FSR Volume II considered operations. FSR I (1923) and FSR II (1924) represent a transitional period, with some topics (including elements of the policy for orders) appearing in the 'wrong' volume.
104   *SS 135* (November 1918), pp.3-4.
105   Beach, 'General Staff', pp.488-490.
106   *SS 135* (November 1918), p.18 and FSR I (1909), s.12.
107   FSR I (1909), s.12(2).
108   For example, *SS 135* (November 1918), p.18.

Figure 2:1 – Wording on Orders in FSR (1909 to 1935)

1909	1920	1923/24	1929	1935
12 (2). An operation order should contain just what the recipient requires to know and nothing more. It should tell him nothing which he can and should arrange for himself. The general principle is that the object to be attained, with such information as affects its attainment, should be briefly but clearly stated; while the method of attaining the object should be left to the utmost extent possible to the recipient. with due repaid to his personal characteristics. Operation orders, especially in the case of large forces should not enter into details except when details are absolutely necessary. It is usually dangerous to prescribe to a subordinate at a distance anything that	67 (4) An operation order must contain just what the recipient requires to know and nothing more. It should tell him nothing which he can and should arrange for himself, and, especially in the case of large forces, will only enter into details when details are absolutely necessary. Any attempt to prescribe to a subordinate at a distance anything which he, with a fuller knowledge of local conditions, should be better able to decide on the spot, is likely to cramp his initiative in dealing with unforeseen developments, and will be avoided. [...] In framing an operation order, therefore, the general principle is that the object to be attained, with such	1924 – 189 (4) **An operation order must contain just what the recipient requires to know and nothing more.** It should tell him nothing which he can and should arrange for himself, and, especially in the case of larger forces, will enter into details only when details are absolutely necessary. Any attempt to prescribe to a subordinate at a distance anything which he, with the fuller knowledge of local conditions, should be better able to decide on the spot, is likely to cramp his initiative in dealing with unforeseen developments, and will be avoided. [...] In framing an operation order, therefore, the general principle is that the object to be attained, with such	134 (3) An operation order must contain just what the recipient requires to know and nothing more. It should tell him nothing which he can and should arrange for himself, and, especially in the case of large forces will enter into details only when details are absolutely necessary. Any attempt to prescribe to a subordinate at a distance anything which he, with a fuller knowledge of local conditions, should be better able to decide on the spot, is likely to destroy his initiative in dealing with unforeseen developments, and will be avoided. [...] (4) In framing an operation order, therefore, the general principle is that the object to be attained, with such	14 (1) An order must contain only what the recipient requires to know, in order to carry out his task. Any attempt to prescribe to a subordinate at a distance anything that he, with a fuller knowledge of local conditions, should be able to decide on the spot will be avoided. (2) In framing orders for operations, the general principle is that the object to be attained, with such

he should be better able to decide on the spot, with a fuller knowledge of local conditions, for any attempt to do so may cramp his initiative in dealing with unforeseen developments. [...] It is necessary to train subordinates not only to work intelligently and resolutely in accordance with brief and very general instructions, but also to take upon themselves, whenever it may be necessary, the responsibility of departing from, or of varying, the orders they may have received (see Sec. 12, 13).	information as affects its attainment, will be briefly but clearly stated; while the method of attaining the object will be left to the utmost extent possible to the recipient, with due regard to his personal characteristics. (5) It is essential that subordinates should not only be able to work intelligently and resolutely in accordance with brief orders or instructions, but should also be able to take upon themselves, whenever necessary, the responsibility of departing from, or of varying, the orders they may have received.	information as affects its attainment, will be briefly but clearly stated; while the method of attaining the object will be left to the utmost extent possible. (5) It is essential that subordinates should not only be able to work intelligently and resolutely in accordance with brief orders or instructions, but should also be able to take upon themselves, whenever necessary, the responsibility of departing from, or of varying, the orders they may have received.	information as affects its attainment, will be briefly but clearly stated; the actual method of attaining the object will be given in sufficient detail to ensure co-ordination of effort, but co-operation, but without interfering with the initiative of subordinate commanders.	information as affects its attainment, will be briefly but clearly stated; the actual method of attaining the object will be given in sufficient detail to ensure co-ordination of effort, but so as not to interfere with the initiative of subordinate commanders, who should be left freedom of action in all matters which they can or should arrange for themselves..
12 (13) Notwithstanding the greatest care and skill in framing orders, unexpected local circumstances may render the precise execution of the orders given to a subordinate unsuitable or impracticable.		1923 – 88 (1) Notwithstanding the greatest care and skill in framing orders, unexpected local circumstances may render the precise execution of the orders given to a subordinate unsuitable or impracticable.	129 (6) Notwithstanding the greatest care and skill in framing orders, unexpected local circumstances may render the precise execution of the orders given to a subordinate unsuitable or impracticable.	14 (5) Notwithstanding the greatest skill and care in framing orders, unexpected circumstances may render the precise execution of an order unsuitable or impracticable.

14 (5) (cont)	129 (6) (cont)	1923 – 88 (1) (cont)	12 (13) (cont)
In such circumstances the following principles will guide the recipient of an order in deciding his course of action :	In such circumstances the following principles will guide the recipient of an order in deciding his course of action :	In such circumstances the following principles should guide an officer in deciding on his course of action :	Under such circumstances the following principles should guide an officer in deciding on his course of action :
i A formal order will never be departed from either in letter or spirit so long as the officer who issued it is present, or there is time to report to him and await a reply without losing an opportunity or endangering the force commanded.	i A formal order will never be departed from either in letter or spirit:- (a) so long as the officer who issued it is present (b) if the officer who issued it is not present, so long as there is time to report to him and await a reply without losing an opportunity or endangering the command.	i A formal order should never be departed from, either in letter or spirit (a) so long as the officer who issued it is present; (b) if the officer who issued the order is not present, provided that there is time to report to him and await a reply without losing an opportunity or endangering the command.	i. A formal order should never be departed from, either in letter or spirit (a) so long as the officer who issued it is present; (b) if the officer who issued the order is not present, provided that there is time to report to him and await a reply without losing an opportunity or endangering the command.
ii If the above conditions cannot be fulfilled, a departure from either the spirit or the letter of an order is justified if the subordinate who assumes the responsibility bases his decision on some fact which could not be known to the officer who issued the order, and if he is satisfied that he is acting as his superior would order him to act were he present.	ii If the above conditions cannot be fulfilled a departure from either the spirit or the letter of an order is justified if the subordinate, who assumes the responsibility, bases his decision on some fact which could not be known to the officer who issued the order, and if he is satisfied that he is acting as his superior would order him to act were he present	ii A departure from either the spirit or the letter of an order is justified if the subordinate who assumes the responsibility bases his decision on some fact which could not be known to the officer who issued the order, and if he is conscientiously satisfied that he is acting as his superior, if present, would order him to act.	ii A departure from either the spirit or the letter of an order is justified if the subordinate who assumes the responsibility bases his decision on some fact which could not be known to the officer who issued the order, and if he is conscientiously satisfied that he is acting as his superior, if present, would order him to act.

iii. If a subordinate, in the absence of a superior, neglects to depart from the letter of his orders, when such departure is clearly demanded by circumstances, and failure ensues, he will be held responsible for such failure. iv. Should a subordinate find it necessary to depart from an order, he should at once inform the issuer of it, and the commanders of any neighbouring units likely to be affected.	iii If a subordinate, in the absence of a superior, neglects to depart from the letter of his orders, when such departure is clearly demanded by circumstances, and failure ensues, he will be held responsible for such failure. iv Should a subordinate find it necessary to depart from an order, he should at once inform the issuer of it, and the commanders of any neighbouring units likely to be affected.	iii If a subordinate neglects to depart from the letter of his orders when such departure, in the circumstances of (ii) above, is clearly demanded, he will be held responsible for any failure which may ensue. iv Should a subordinate find it necessary to depart from an order he will immediately inform the issuer of it, and the commanders of any neighbouring units likely to be affected.
		iii If a subordinate neglects to depart from the letter of his orders when such departure, in the circumstances of sub-para. ii, above, is clearly demanded, he will be held responsible for any failure which may ensue. iv Should a subordinate find it necessary to depart from an order, he will immediately inform the issuer of it, and the commanders of any neighbouring units likely to be affected.

Implementing Doctrine

Before exploring the development of British command doctrine prior to 1909, it is necessary to consider briefly the means by which doctrine was implemented in the British and German armies, converting it from exhortation to reality.

As has been noted, the German *FO* was a development of a manual focused on training troops and senior commanders through manoeuvres - the *Verordnungen über die Ausbildung der Truppen für den Felddienst und über die größeren Truppenübungen* ('Regulations for the Instruction of the Troops in Field Service and the Exercise of the Larger Units') of June 1870. This tradition of connecting the doctrinal statements in *FO* with practical training was carried forward through successive editions of the manual, each of which included some sixty pages on the handling of large-scale manoeuvres. The two topics were separated only in 1908, with the publication of the *Bestimungen für die größeren Truppenübungen (Manöver-Ordnungen)* ('Provisions for Larger Military Exercises (Manoeuvre Regulations)'),[109] a manual that complemented *FO 1908*.

In addition to this direct linkage to training, the German Army, both officially and indirectly, supported a major body of literature that explained and expounded on the statements in the manuals. Soon after each successive edition of *FO* appeared, volumes were published that set out the exact wording changes and explained the implications.[110] Issues were also discussed in the *Militär-Wochenblatt* (Military Weekly News), which was sponsored by the General Staff,[111] and in the extensive wider military press.[112]

This tradition was continued after the First World War.[113] Following the publication of *Das FuG* in 1921, Oberstleutnant Friedrich von Cochenhausen, a member of the Army Training Branch of the *Truppenamt*,[114] authored a book (confusing titled *Die Truppenführung*), which sought to explain the new doctrine in a manner clear to intermediate and lower levels of command.[115] In addition, the army itself published an annual booklet setting out Seeckt's comments on training, designed to explain *Das*

---

109 *Regulations for Manoeuvres (Manöver-Ordnung, 1908) German Army*, trans. by General Staff, War Office (London: HMSO, 1908).

110 For example, *Neues aus der Felddienstordnung* (Oldenburg: Stalling, 1900), and *Was bringen Felddienst-Ordnung und Manöver-Ordnung vom 22. März 1908 Neues?* (Berlin: Mittler, 1908).

111 'Über militärisches Schrifttum im preußisch-deutschen Heere von Scharnhorst bis zum Weltkriege', *Militärwissenschaftliche Rundschau* 3(4) (1938), 463-482 (p. 468).

112 Raths, *Vom Massensturm*, pp. 16-19.

113 Strohn, *Defence of the Reich*, pp.115-116.

114 Citino, *Path to Blitzkrieg*, p. 64.

115 Oberstleutnant [Friedrich] von Cochenhausen, *Die Truppenführung: Ein Handbuch für den Truppenführer und seine Gehilfen* , 3rd ed. (Berlin: Mittler, 1926).

FuG,[116] as well as a volume providing an introduction and index to the manual.[117] A similar approach was followed after the publication of the replacement to *Das FuG*, *Truppenführung*, in 1933.

Further, commanders' understanding of the doctrine was developed through a significant reliance on staff rides and exercises as a central element of officer training. A vital and consistent characteristic of these exercises was the absence of a 'school solution' that presented the sole 'correct' solution. Instead, all of those involved in the exercise, both participants and directing staff, were invited to present their solutions and the reasons for them, and all of these responses were then debated by the group as a whole, with no particular status being given to the solution presented by the directing staff. Indeed, often one of the students' solutions, rather than that of the directing staff, would be used as the basis for the next stage of the exercise.[118] It would hardly be possible to find a better example of what Grint termed a 'Leadership' response to a wicked problem.

In short, throughout the period under consideration, the German Army made great efforts to ensure that the doctrine set out in the manuals was both understood and imbibed by commanders at all levels as an essential element of their training. This was not simply as a series of principles to be memorised, but as a guide to the practical resolution of the problems thrown up by the dynamic nature of warfare. In this way, commanders could gain the assurance necessary for them to accept the best way to respond to the inevitable Knowledge Gap was to rely on the initiative and commitment of their subordinates to close the Alignment Gap and hence avoid a wide Effects Gap.

The British approach could hardly have been more different. As Hew Strachan has noted, the British General Staff 'tended to impute to the German General Staff a more cerebral and more principled approach to the study of war than it did in fact implement'.[119] This was reflected in the approach taken by the British in promulgating their doctrine.

First, the successive editions of FSR were heavily focused on the principles of war. FSR I (1909) opened with the statement (s.1(1)), 'The principles given in this manual have been evolved by experience as generally applicable to the leading of troops.' It went on to argue (s.1(2)), 'The fundamental principles of war are neither very numerous

---

116 These were subsequently collected and published as *Bemerkungen des Chefs der Heeresleitung, Generaloberst von Seeckt, bei Besichtigungen und Manövern aus den Jahren 1920 bis 1926* (Remarks of the Commander-in-Chief of the Army, Generaloberst von Seeckt, at Inspections and Exercises in the Years 1920 to 1926) (Berlin: 1927).

117 *Einführung und Stichwortverzeichnis zu Abschnitt I-XVII von Führung und Gefecht der verbunden Waffen (F.u.G.) (Berlin: 1924).*

118 Jörg Muth, *Command Culture: Officer Education in the U.S. Army and the German Armed Forces, 1901-1940, and the Consequences for World War II* (Denton, TX: University of North Texas, 2011), p. 165.

119 Hew Strachan, 'The British Army, its General Staff and the Continental Commitment, 1904-14', in *The British General Staff: Reform and Innovation, c.1890-1939*, ed. by David French and Brian Holden Reid (London: Cass, 2002), pp. 75-94 (86).

nor in themselves very abstruse, but the application of them is difficult and cannot be made subject to rules.' David French's barbed comment that this emphasis on the importance of principles was somewhat undermined by the failure of the manual to state what those principles actually were[120] is perhaps a little unfair, given that most of the subsequent chapters opened with a section entitled 'General Principles'. But, clearly, the point was not lost on those officers responsible for drafting subsequent editions, as each of these did indeed include a list of the principles of war, though the impact was reduced by the limited consistency between the successive lists.[121]

Second, the doctrine in FSR was separate from the guidance on training and military manoeuvres, which (reflecting the German post-1908 practice) was treated in a separate manual.[122] The close connection between doctrine and training that existed in the German system was therefore absent.

Third, the British General Staff stood resolute against the idea of publishing an authoritative exposition of the doctrine set out in FSR, even when explicitly requested to do so (with reference to the German model!), on the grounds that this might stifle local flexibility.[123] The inevitable consequence was an outpouring of private and semi-official paraphrases and explanations, such as Captain Gall's series of *Questions and Answers* volumes,[124] and Trench's *Manoeuvre Orders* (in its twelfth edition by 1916).[125] That this need for supplementary material continued after the First World War is demonstrated by the publication of J.F.C. Fuller's *Lectures on FSR II* in 1931. There, he noted, 'when in command of an infantry brigade[,] I found that the Field Service Regulations were read for purposes of examination, but consistently neglected in the field, especially if action were in any way hurried. The reason for this was no doubt due to lack of professional interest, but also in part to the extreme dullness of the book'.[126]

Fuller's last point highlights an important weakness in the General Staff's logic regarding exposition of FSR. Even though it was suggested as early as 1913 that the manuals themselves 'required so much skilled interpretation that they were about as useful [...] as the cuneiform inscriptions on a Babylonian brick', this was rejected by most staff officers, who were more concerned with the risk that amplification of the principles would lead to stereotyped solutions.[127] This view also remained constant throughout the interwar period. As a consequence, there was no attempt either to

---

120 David French, 'Doctrine and Organization in the British Army, 1919-1932', *Historical Journal*, 44(2) (2001), 497-515 (p. 504).
121 FSR II (1920), s.2, FSR II (1924), s.2, FSR II (1929), ss.7-8, and FSR II (1935), s.11(5).
122 *Training and Manoeuvre Regulations* (London: HMSO, 1913).
123 *Report of a Conference of General Staff Officers at the Staff College, 9th to 12th January, 1911, Held Under the Direction of the Chief of the Imperial General Staff*, pp. 5-9, & 28.
124 For example, Captain Herbert Reay Gall, *Questions and Answers on Field Service Regulations: Part I (Operations) 1909* (London: Rees, 1910).
125 Lieutenant-Colonel B.M. Bateman, *Trench's Manoeuvre Orders 1914*, 12th rev. ed. (London: Clowes, 1916).
126 Major-General J.F.C. Fuller, *Lectures on F.S.R. II* (London: Praed, 1931), p. vii.
127 *GSO Conference, 1913*, pp. 11-17.

make the language more accessible (as, for example, was achieved by Beck and his colleagues in *Truppenführung*) or to provide an authoritative explanation of the text. Whatever the quality of the unofficial works that filled the gap, there can be little doubt one consequence was a wide variation in the interpretation of the wording of FSR, and hence a weakening of its ability to provide a single uniformly accepted doctrine for the army.

Discontinuity in British Doctrine

FSR (1909) is often treated as the first expression of a formal British military doctrine. However, although the staff manual (Part II) was indeed the first such publication, the volume dealing with operations (Part I) was in fact the *second* edition of such a manual. The very first edition of FSR I had actually appeared in 1905: *Field Service Regulations: Part I – Combined Training*.[128] This, in turn, was a revised version of a still earlier manual: *Combined Training (Provisional)* (1902).[129] Examination of these two manuals, drawing on the three key factors highlighted at the start of this chapter, reveals a number of significant differences from the doctrine expounded in the subsequent editions.

The first factor is the likelihood of orders being rendered unsuitable, which links to the question of whether warfare is seen as being inherently chaotic or linear, and hence whether the Knowledge Gap is likely to be wide. The relevant wording from the 1905 and 1909 editions of FSR is set out in Figure 2:2.

Figure 2:2 – FSR 1905 and 1909 on Orders Being Rendered Unsuitable

FSR I (1905)	FSR I (1909)
3(2): It will often happen that local circumstances, impossible to foresee, may render the precise execution of the orders given to the subordinate leaders not only unsuitable but impracticable. Moreover, when it is impossible, as must often be the case, to issue more than very general instructions, the attainment of the object aimed at must be left to the initiative and intelligence of these leaders.	12(13): Notwithstanding the greatest care and skill in framing orders, unexpected local circumstances may render the precise execution of the orders given to a subordinate unsuitable or impracticable.

---

128 *Field Service Regulations: Part I – Combined Training* (London: HMSO, 1905).
129 *Combined Training (Provisional)* (London: HMSO, 1902).

While subtle, the differences in wording are significant. As has been demonstrated in Figure 2:1 above, in successive editions of FSR from 1909 onwards, the likelihood of orders being rendered unsuitable was caveated by an emphasis on the 'greatest skill and care in framing orders'. By contrast, FSR I (1905), drawn verbatim from Combined Training (1902) (s.43(2)), indicated this was a situation that would 'often' arise. The wording in FSR I (1909) shifted the emphasis significantly. From orders being rendered unsuitable 'often', the emphasis on the 'greatest skill and care in framing orders' suggested such a situation would happen only rarely. In addition, FSR (1905)'s second sentence, underlining it would normally be impossible to issue more than general instructions, was omitted in the 1909 edition.

The second issue concerns decentralisation, as a means to narrow the Effects Gap. The relevant wording from the 1905 and 1909 editions of FSR is set out in Figure 2:3.

Figure 2:3 – FSR 1905 and 1909 on Decentralisation

FSR I (1905)	FSR I (1909)
3(2): Decentralisation of command, and a full recognition of the responsibilities of subordinates in action, are thus absolutely necessary; and leaders must train their subordinates not only to work intelligently and resolutely in accordance with brief and very general instructions, but also to take upon themselves, whenever it may be necessary, the responsibility of departing from, or of varying, the orders they may have received.	12(2): It is necessary to train subordinates not only to work intelligently and resolutely in accordance with brief and very general instructions, but also to take upon themselves, whenever it may be necessary, the responsibility of departing from, or of varying, the orders they may have received.

Although the second part of the text was largely retained in the 1909 edition, the wording on the importance of decentralisation of command, which FSR (1905) used in order to explain the need for subordinates to be trained to exercise their initiative, was removed. The entire paragraph was omitted in subsequent editions.

A similar shift may be found in the relevant editions of the manual on infantry training. Infantry Training (1905) (s.124(4)) stated:

> Since the conditions of modern warfare render decentralisation of command in action an absolute necessity, no good results are to be expected unless the subordinate leaders have been trained to use their intelligence, and unless they have been given ample opportunities of acting on their own judgement in attack and defence, and have constantly, in peace practices, been called upon to consider the necessity of departing from their original orders.

This repeated the wording introduced in Infantry Training (Provisional) (1902) (s.211(4)). The sentence was omitted from the equivalent text in Infantry Training (1911) (s.120).

The third issue covers the scope of orders, addressing the question of the Alignment Gap. The relevant wording from Combined Training (1902) and FSR (1909) is set out in Figures 2:4 and 2:5.

Figure 2:4 – Combined Training (1902) and FSR (1909) on the Content of Orders

Combined Training (1902)	*FSR I (1909)*
45(10)iv: The order will not touch on anything that subordinate commanders can, and should, arrange for themselves. […]	12(2): An operation order should contain just what the recipient requires to know and nothing more. It should tell him nothing which he can and should arrange for himself. […]
vii. The subordinate commanders will, in turn, frame their own orders on receipt of the superior's order, of which only just so much will be embodied as is necessary. Their orders should, however, be sufficiently full to enable those under them to properly appreciate the situation, and to understand how they may co-operate with others.[130]	Operation orders, especially in the case of large forces should not enter into details except when details are absolutely necessary. It is usually dangerous to prescribe to a subordinate at a distance anything that he should be better able to decide on the spot, with a fuller knowledge of local conditions, for any attempt to do so may cramp his initiative in dealing with unforeseen developments.[131]

Again, while the 1909 wording at first sight appears consistent with the idea of leaving subordinates maximum scope to apply their initiative to the implementation of their orders, omission of Combined Training's requirement that the commander should ensure his orders were sufficiently full to enable subordinates to properly appreciate the situation represented a vital shift in emphasis. In the absence of a full understanding of the commander's context and intent, it would be impossible for subordinates to use their greater knowledge of the local situation in order to recognise when to abandon their orders and instead use their initiative as a means to achieve the higher intent.

Finally, the criteria for departing from an order were again subtly different in Combined Training (1902) when compared to editions from 1909 onwards:

---

130 See also FSR I (1905), ss.3(6) and 3(15).
131 See also FSR II (1929), s.14(1), and (1935), s.14(1).

Figure 2:5 – Combined Training (1902) and FSR (1909) on Departing from Orders

Combined Training (1902)	FSR I (1909)
43(3): The following rules are to be observed:	12(13): Under such circumstances the following principles should guide an officer in deciding on his course of action:
i. A formal order is never to be departed from, either in letter or spirit, so long as the officer who issued it is present, and can see what is going on; or, if he cannot see what is going on, provided that there is time to report to him without losing an opportunity or endangering the command.	i. A formal order should never be departed from, either in letter or spirit (a) so long as the officer who issued it is present; (b) if the officer who issued the order is not present, provided that there is time to report to him and await a reply without losing an opportunity or endangering the command.
ii. A departure from either the spirit or the letter of an order is justified if the subordinate who assumes the responsibility is conscientiously satisfied that he is acting as his superior would order him to act if he were present.	ii A departure from either the spirit or the letter of an order is justified if the subordinate who assumes the responsibility bases his decision on some fact which could not be known to the officer who issued the order, and if he is conscientiously satisfied that he is acting as his superior, if present, would order him to act.
iii. If a subordinate, in the absence of a superior, neglects to depart from the letter of his orders, when such a departure is clearly justified by circumstances, and failure ensures, he will be held responsible for such failure.	iii. If a subordinate, in the absence of a superior, neglects to depart from the letter of his orders, when such departure is clearly demanded by circumstances, and failure ensues, he will be held responsible for such failure.
	iv. Should a subordinate find it necessary to depart from an order, he should at once inform the issuer of it, and the commanders of any neighbouring units likely to be affected.

Although the wording of Combined Training (1902) and FSR I (1905)[132] was very similar to that carried forward into later editions of FSR, there is one very significant

132 FSR I (1905), p. 6.

difference: the later addition of the requirement for the subordinate to base his decision 'on some fact which could not be known to the officer who issued the order'. As has been noted, this requirement represented an almost impossible hurdle for subordinates to cross, especially given the shift towards commanders restricting the amount of information given to subordinates.

Taking all these differences together, it may be suggested Pugsley was wrong to suggest that 'the guiding command philosophy remain[ed] unchanged' between the 1905 and 1909 editions of FSR I.[133] There were in fact several fundamentally important (though subtle) shifts. These were then carried forward throughout each subsequent edition, up to and including FSR II (1935).

First, the sense of warfare as an unpredictable (and hence 'wicked') phenomenon was less pronounced from 1909 onwards. The likelihood of unexpected situations arising was downgraded from this being the case 'often' to where it *might* occur 'notwithstanding the greatest care and skill' (in other words, 'rarely'). Indeed, the emphasis on this in FSR II (1935) suggests an important shift was made in Wavell's text compared to its predecessors.

Second, although the emphasis on the importance of commanders not seeking to prescribe to their subordinates from a distance was stronger from 1909 onwards, this was counteracted by a requirement for commanders to keep to a minimum the information concerning the wider context that they gave to their subordinates, yet permitting those subordinates to depart from their orders only if they were certain that in doing so they were basing their decisions on information that could not have been known to their commander.

In short, the command approach set out in the various editions of FSR from 1909 until 1929 may be considered equivalent to that earlier termed Logistic Control, where warfare is seen as being 'tame', allowing commanders to issue detailed orders on the basis of their better knowledge of the situation, which subordinates were required to follow precisely, other than in very limited circumstances. By contrast, that expressed in Combined Training (1902) and FSR I (1905) leant more closely to Directive Command. This assessment is reinforced by the preface to Combined Training (1902):

> Success in war cannot be expected unless all ranks have been trained in peace to use their wits. Generals and commanding officers are, therefore, not only to encourage their subordinates in so doing by affording them constant opportunities of acting on their own responsibility, but they will also check all practices which interfere with the free exercise of the judgement, and will break down, by every means in their power, the paralysing habit of an unreasoning and mechanical adherence to the letter of orders and to routine, when acting under service conditions.[134]

133 Pugsley, 'We Have Been Here Before', p.10.
134 *Combined Training (Provisional)* (1902), p. 4.

These words almost paraphrase the prefaces of successive editions of the German *FO*.[135] They were not repeated in any subsequent edition of FSR.

Having noted many of the changes introduced in FSR (1909) were carried forward into Wavell's text for FSR (1935), there are also some grounds to suggest that Wavell did introduce some important shifts in thinking, which amounted to a substantive change in the command approach set out in the doctrine. As has been demonstrated above, the authors of the 1909 edition had significantly toned down or eliminated the emphasis in FSR (1905) on the chaotic nature of battle. This suggests they believed that the problems facing commanders would generally be tame, rather than wicked. As such, the Knowledge Gap would be relatively narrow, and hence the Effects Gap was also unlikely to be a major source of friction, as the course of engagements could be predicted. As a result, the main potential source of friction would come from a wide Alignment Gap, if subordinates failed to implement their commanders' orders correctly. It is therefore not surprising that, in comparison with that of FSR (1905), the revised text of FSR (1909) also significantly reduced the importance placed on subordinates showing initiative and constrained its scope. In short, whereas FSR (1905) had favoured a command approach equivalent to Directive Command, FSR (1909) moved to one of Logistic Control. By contrast, as has been noted earlier, Wavell introduced new text in FSR (1935) that placed much greater weight on the chaotic and unpredictable nature of warfare. He hesitated, however, from demanding significant reliance on subordinates' initiative, due to his belief that these were likely to be largely comprised of hastily trained civilians, unable to respond effectively to such demands. The approach set out in FSR II and III (1935) was therefore more along the lines of Restrictive Control.

Haig, Henderson, and Initiative

Having identified a significant discontinuity in command philosophy between the 1905 and 1909 editions of FSR, representing a shift from one command approach to another, it is necessary to explore the reasons for this.

Prior to the publication of *Combined Training (Provisional)* in 1902, the British Army had no manual for higher command or for the combined action of different arms. *Infantry Drill* (1889),[136] issued under the signature of Lord Wolseley as Adjutant-General, had to some small extent filled that gap, giving brief guidance for higher formations up to and including corps level (Part VIII: ss.24-26). It may be noted in passing that the corps level of command had been reintroduced only as recently as 1876,[137] having been abandoned by the army after the Napoleonic Wars,

---

135 FO (1887), p. 5, FO (1894), p. 3, FO (1900), p. iv, and FO (1908), p. iv.
136 *Infantry Drill* (London: HMSO, 1889).
137 'The Mobilization of the Army, and National Defence', *Blackwood's Edinburgh Magazine*, 120 (July to December 1876), 509-520 (p. 511).

while in 1886 Henry Brackenbury had discovered that mobilising more than one such formation was beyond Britain's current capability.[138] The need for doctrinal guidance for the commanders of such formations did not appear pressing.

The manual included little on the broader nature of warfare, on the question of subordinates' initiative, or on matters of surprise, being far more concerned with details of the formations to be adopted by units. The limited approach of *Infantry Drill* (1889) was encapsulated in the statement, 'The general rules laid down for the company and the battalion apply equally to a brigade or larger force.' Although the 1896 edition, issued by Wolseley as Commander-in-Chief,[139] had begun to move in the direction of recognising there was a role for subordinates displaying initiative, it is questionable whether this generated any significant change in operational practice.

The Second Boer War (1899-1902) cruelly highlighted the many deficiencies of *Infantry Drill* (1896) in the context of modern warfare. This was especially clear to Lord Roberts, who commanded the operations that destroyed the main Boer field forces. As commander-in-chief from 1900, in succession to Wolseley, he was in a position to address this issue. The man he selected for the task of bringing the Drill Book up to date was Colonel G.F.R. (Frank) Henderson. This officer had been Professor of Military Art and History at the Staff College (1892-1899) until Roberts had chosen him to be his Director of Intelligence in South Africa, though ill health soon forced a return to England.[140]

Soon after starting the task of writing the new manual, however, Henderson travelled back to South Africa, in connection with his work on the official history of the war. Before departing, he asked a colleague, Colonel Gerald Ellison, to complete the work on the new Drill Book. As Ellison subsequently recorded,[141] much of what Henderson had already written applied as much to the other arms as to the infantry. Roberts (who had been closely involved in the project to date) therefore 'decided that a manual laying down authoritatively a doctrine regarding the tactical employment of all arms should be drawn up and published'.

To do this, Roberts established a small committee at Aldershot, chaired by the Director of Military Training at the War Office, Lieutenant-General Sir Henry Hildyard,[142] supported by Colonel Henry Rawlinson and Major Henry Wilson,

---

138 Christopher Brice, *The Thinking Man's Soldier: The Life and Career of General Sir Henry Brackenbury, 1837-1914* (Solihull: Helion, 2012), pp.169-170.

139 *Infantry Drill* (London: HMSO, 1896).

140 Field-Marshal Earl Roberts, 'Memoir', in Colonel G.F.R. Henderson, *The Science of War*, ed. by Captain Neill Malcolm, 5th imprint (London, 1912), xiii-xxxviii (pp.xxvii-xxviii and xxxv).

141 Gerald F. Ellison, 'Lord Roberts and the General Staff', *The Nineteenth Century* (December 1932), 722-732 (pp. 728-729).

142 The president of the committee is incorrectly given as General Stopford (at that time Deputy Adjutant-General at Aldershot) by Colonel John K. Dunlop, *The Development of the British Army: 1899-1914* (London: Methuen, 1938), p. 227.

both from that directorate, with Ellison as secretary.[143] These four offered perhaps an ideal team for the preparation of the required doctrinal manual: Hildyard had been Commandant of the Staff College for much of Henderson's time there;[144] Rawlinson was to take up that post soon after the committee completed its work and was succeeded in that role by Wilson in 1907; while Ellison moved on to become secretary to the Esher Committee, whose recommendations led to the establishment of the General Staff. Seldom can four officers have been so central to the doctrinal education of the army.

The committee members took the material Henderson had produced before his departure for to South Africa and used this as the basis for *Combined Training (Provisional)*, which was published under Roberts's signature on 1 May 1902. That Hildyard's committee was able to produce the manual in less than three months suggests the text they were working from was already well advanced. Indeed, it appears to have been so advanced that Roberts was also able to publish in April 1902 the replacement for *Infantry Drill* (1896), the significantly re-titled *Infantry Training (Provisional)*.[145] Equally, Henderson had produced his own text at high speed, as he had been able to devote at most six months to the project, having returned to duty only in August 1901, following the collapse of his health in South Africa.[146] The time he had available for the two manuals was in practice even less, since during the same period Henderson had drafted several chapters of the official history.

One explanation for the speed (and broad scope) of Henderson's work was offered at the General Staff Conference in January 1913 by Colonel James Edmonds, later the Official Historian of the First World War: 'Our first Field Service Manual was taken from the German. As fast as the German Felddienstordnung could be translated, the sheets were handed over to Colonel Frank Henderson, and he invested the translation with artistic merit for British use.'[147] A new edition of the German *FO* had been issued on 1 January 1900 and this was indeed rapidly translated by the War Office.[148] However, Edmonds was exaggerating somewhat in his statement, as the translation was published at least eight months before Henderson began his work on the new British manual.

Nonetheless, there are definite parallels between the text of *Combined Training* (1902) and *FO* (1900):

143 Keith Jeffery, *Field Marshal Sir Henry Wilson: A Political Soldier* (Oxford: Oxford University Press, 2008), p.55, and Jay Stone, 'The Anglo-Boer War and Military Reforms in the United Kingdom', in *The Boer War and Military Reforms*, by Jay Stone and Erwin A. Schmidl (London: University Press of America, 1988), pp. 1-160 (118).
144 Roberts, 'Memoir', p. xxviii.
145 *Infantry Training (Provisional)* (London: HMSO, 1902).
146 Roberts, 'Memoir', p. xxxvii.
147 *General Staff Conference, 1913*, p.15.
148 *The Field Service Regulations (Feld Dienst Ordnung, 1900) of the German Army*, trans. by Colonel H. S. Brownrigg (London: HMSO, 1900).

Felddienstordnung (1900)	*Combined Training* (1902)
Introduction. 38. Everyone, from the youngest soldier upwards, must be required to throw himself with all his mental and physical force into the performance of his duty. On this condition only, will a body of troops, acting in unison, yield the utmost effort of which it is capable. The orders given by the superiors specify the tasks which each man in his place must exert himself to accomplish. Determined action to gain the object in view must be demanded above everything else. *Everyone, from the highest leader to the youngest soldier, must always bear in mind that neglect and carelessness will weigh more heavily against him than error in the choice of means.*	43(2) Decentralisation of command, and a full recognition of the responsibilities of subordinates in action, are thus absolutely necessary; and leaders must train their subordinates not only to work intelligently and resolutely in accordance with brief and very general instructions, but also to take upon themselves, whenever it may be necessary, the responsibility of departing from, or of varying, the orders they may have received.
Part I. B. 50. Orders, during the transmission of which the situation may change, or the carrying out of which must depend upon circumstances which cannot be foreseen, must especially avoid detail. In such cases a letter of guidance should take the place of orders. It must lay stress on the object to be attained and leave open the means to be employed.	43(2) It will often happen that local circumstances, impossible to foresee, may render the precise execution of the orders given to the subordinate leaders not only unsuitable but impracticable. Moreover, when it is impossible, as must often be the case, to issue more than very general instructions, the attainment of the object aimed at must be left to the initiative and intelligence of these leaders.
Part I. B. 49. It is a general rule that an *order* must contain everything that the subordinate should know, so that he can arrange for the attainment of the object, and nothing more. Accordingly, the order must be short, clear, and definite, and suitable to the receiver's range of vision. [...] 62. The more accurately informed the subordinate as regards the immediate intentions of his superior, the easier it will be for him in dealing with information, to sift the essential from the non-essential.	45(10)iv. The order will not touch on anything that subordinate commanders can, and should, arrange for themselves. [...] vii. The subordinate commanders will, in turn, frame their own orders on receipt of the superior's order, of which only just so much will be embodied as is necessary. Their orders should, however, be sufficiently full to enable those under them to properly appreciate the situation, and to understand how they may co-operate with others.

While the wording of the two manuals is clearly not the same – indicating Edmonds was doing Henderson a disservice when he claimed all Frank had done was add 'artistic merit' – it may be suggested the command philosophies expressed in them were broadly comparable, both favouring what has here been termed Directive Command.

It is impossible to determine whether Henderson based his work on the German manual or independently reached similar conclusions through his own analysis. He was certainly very familiar with German military thought, having studied the battles of 1870 in considerable detail. Nonetheless, the very favourable description of the German command system in his contribution to the 1902 supplement to the *Encyclopaedia Britannica*[149] suggests he was in full agreement with its emphasis on initiative and delegation. It would therefore have been surprising if his text for the new British manual had *not* taken a similar approach, although it is clear he was not working alone, given Roberts's close personal engagement in the work.[150] It is uncertain whether Henderson was aware of the fierce debate within the German Army regarding the decentralised *Auftragstaktik* and the tighter *Normaltaktik*, though his comment that 'it was long before the system was cordially accepted, even in Germany itself; and it has been fiercely criticised'[151] suggests he was.

Given that the wording and approach adopted in Henderson's draft was largely carried forward intact when Combined Training (1902) was revised to become FSR I (1905), it is to the period after that date where we have to look for the change in command philosophy.

The 1909 edition of FSR I was prepared under the supervision of Douglas Haig, in his roles as Director of Military Training from 24 August 1906[152] and then Director of Staff Duties from 9 November 1907. His remit encompassed responsibility for providing 'a central doctrine for the training for war, and the organization in war, of the whole British Army.'[153]

It is difficult to be precise regarding the extent of Haig's direct contribution to the preparation of the new edition of FSR, in part due to the poor state of the remaining War Office files from that period.[154] His personal diaries contain only passing references to this aspect of his work,[155] though it is clear from other sources

---

149 Colonel G. F. R. Henderson, 'War', reprinted in Henderson, *Science of War*, pp. 1-38 (pp. 4-9).
150 Ellison, 'Lord Roberts and the General Staff', p.729.
151 Henderson, 'War', p.5.
152 John Gooch, *The Plans of War: The General Staff and British Military Strategy c.1900-1916* (London: Routledge & Kegan Paul, 1974), p. 108.
153 Dunlop, *Development of the British Army*, p. 291, where the date of Haig's move to become DSD is incorrectly given as 1906.
154 See Matthew S. Seligmann, '*Hors de Combat*? The Management, Mismanagement and Mutilation of the War Office Archive', *Journal of the Society for Army Historical Research*, 84 (2006), 52-58.
155 For example, *Douglas Haig: The Preparatory Prologue, 1861-1914. Diaries and Letters*, ed. by Douglas Scott (Barnsley: Pen & Sword, 2006), pp. 274-275.

he took a close personal interest in the preparation of FSR II,[156] which dealt with staff duties. However, while a number of other officers were deeply involved in the work, notably Lancelot Kiggell, Frederick Maurice, and Walter Adye,[157] it is clear Haig was a strong champion for the manual, such that Gary Sheffield and John Bourne have argued Haig 'had done much to compile' it.[158] Indeed, in his *Final Despatch* of April 1919, Haig stated, 'The principles of command, Staff work, and organisation elaborated before the war have stood the test imposed upon them and are sound.'[159] Whether or not he personally wrote the final text of FSR (1909), therefore, it is clear the words and philosophy behind it, especially those in Part II, had his full support. The switch from the command approach of Directive Command, espoused in the 1902 and 1905 manuals, to that of Logistic Control, set out in the 1909 edition, representing a shift from warfare being considered inherently unpredictable to being instead seen as predictable, must therefore have been made, at minimum, with Haig's active agreement.[160]

There is some irony in Henderson's revolutionary emphasis on decentralisation of command as the essential means by which the chaos of battle should be addressed being reversed by Haig, since he had been one of Henderson's students at the Staff College. However, as Tim Travers has shown, Haig may have believed he was in fact being true to the principles Frank had taught him:[161] Henderson was, for most of his time at Camberley, a passionate *critic* of decentralised command.[162]

His early writings included many statements pointing out the dangers of giving subordinates scope to exercise their own initiative, drawing on the German experience in 1870. In the 1891 article that won him his post at the Staff College, he had castigated 'the reckless impetuosity of the German officers of every rank' and their 'unreasonable initiative'.[163] His proposed solution was to *prevent* the chaos of war, not to *adapt* to it. He noted with favour that, 'instead of encouraging excessive exercise of initiative, the paramount importance of order, of the cohesion of the attacking body, and of

156 Gooch, *Plans of War*, pp. 113-115.

157 Dunlop, *Development of the British Army*, p. 291.

158 Gary Sheffield and John Bourne, 'Introduction', in *Douglas Haig: War Diaries and Letters, 1914-1918*, ed. by Gary Sheffield and John Bourne (London: Phoenix, 2006), pp.1-43 (p.23).

159 *Sir Douglas Haig's Despatches (December 1915 – April 1919)*, ed. by Lieutenant-Colonel J. H. Boraston (London: Dent, 1919), p. 343.

160 NB: Sheffield and Bourne argue the approach set out in FSR (1909) 'favoured what later became known as "mission tactics"', Sheffield and Bourne, 'Introduction', p.23. It will be clear from the analysis above the author disagrees with this interpretation.

161 T.H.E. Travers, *The Killing Ground: The British Army, The Western Front and The Emergence of Modern Warfare, 1900-1918* (London, 1987), pp.85-100.

162 Samuels, *Command or Control?*, pp.94-99.

163 Colonel G. F. R. Henderson, 'Military Criticism and Modern Tactics', *United Services Magazine* (1891), reprinted in Henderson, *Science of War*, pp. 108-164 (pp. 119 and 146).

maintaining the true direction is inculcated on every page' of *Infantry Drill* (1889).[164] As a consequence, 'English soldiers are brought up with the idea that obedience is of more importance than initiative.'[165] The line of sight between these statements and those in FSR I (1909) is clear.

Yet, around the time Haig graduated from the Staff College in 1897, Henderson underwent a dramatic realignment in his views. In his 1899 article, 'The Training of Infantry for the Attack', he argued, 'All systems [...] which depend on explicit regulations make but small demands on the intelligence of the individual officer, and for that reason, if for no other, they are quite inadequate to the exigencies of modern warfare.'[166] Henderson went on to welcome the moves towards decentralisation and initiative made in *Infantry Drill* (1896) (s.114(6)).[167]

The cause of this reversal in Henderson's approach is unclear. It may have been a gradual process – Jay Luvaas noted Frank 'probably learned more about war during his tenure at the Staff College than did any of his students'.[168] Equally, the possibility must be acknowledged it was the result of a more direct engagement with the German Army than he had gained through his earlier study of the battles of 1870. In 1895, Henderson had the opportunity to observe the annual German manoeuvres. His official report noted the troops 'act like intelligent beings, who thoroughly understand their duty, and the fact speaks volumes for the way in which even the privates are taught to use their initiative'.[169] Alternatively, it may have been his deeper analysis of the American Civil War, culminating in his famous study of Stonewall Jackson,[170] his first major publication following those German manoeuvres, which sparked his change of heart. Certainly, these two events mark a turning point in Henderson's philosophy, with his subsequent work consistently emphasising the importance of decentralised command and flexibility, in contrast to his earlier publications.

Perhaps it was precisely because of this newfound support for decentralised command that Roberts selected Henderson for his staff in South Africa. Certainly, the many hours they spent in discussion together during the long sea voyage out to Cape Town[171] would have given many opportunities for the issue of decentralisation of command to have arisen. Roberts's decision to ask Henderson to update *Infantry Drill* (1896), along with his instruction that Frank's incomplete text be used as the basis for

---

164 Henderson, 'Military Criticism', pp. 152-153.
165 Henderson, 'Military Criticism', pp. 161.
166 Henderson, 'The Training of Infantry for the Attack', *United Services Magazine* (1899), reprinted in Henderson, *Science of War*, pp. 338-64 (p. 344).
167 Henderson, 'Training of Infantry', pp. 348-349.
168 Jay Luvaas, *The Education of an Army* (London: Cassell, 1965), p.229.
169 Quoted in Luvaas, *Education*, p. 236.
170 Lieutenant-Colonel G.F.R. Henderson, *Stonewall Jackson and the American Civil War* (London: Longmans Green, 1898).
171 Luvaas, *Education*, p. 237.

both *Infantry Training (Provisional)* (1902) and *Combined Training* (1902), suggest that the Commander-in-Chief was in full agreement with his subordinate's views.

Even though Henderson's former students frequently sought him out in South Africa, in order to seek their mentor's views on the practical problems they faced when fighting the Boers,[172] the sudden collapse of his health and the brevity of his return to work before his premature death in 1903 meant he had very little time in which to promulgate his new ideas. As a consequence, although he had sought to encapsulate his latest thinking, reinforced by his experience of combat in South Africa, in *Infantry Training* and *Combined Training*, it was therefore his previous understanding of the nature of warfare, as linear and tame, rather than chaotic and wicked, that held sway in the minds of Haig and his colleagues when they came to revise the manual in 1909. The result was a return to the philosophy Henderson himself had once taught, but then rejected: a philosophy that was to remain the official doctrine of the British Army, as expressed in successive editions of the FSR, throughout the interwar period and into the Second World War, though with the subtle shifts in emphasis made by Wavell in 1935.

One can only speculate how the history of the army might have been different had Henderson not died at the age of only forty-eight. He evidently enjoyed the trust and confidence of Roberts, and his closeness to Ellison might have enabled him to survive the purges that followed his patron's dismissal in 1904 following the Esher Report. Indeed, given Ellison's position from 1906 as private secretary to the Secretary of State for War (the reform-minded Lord Haldane), it is possible Frank might have been selected for a senior role in the newly-established General Staff.

Henderson's close connection to Roberts suggests Ellison's view[173] may be correct that the latter's role in the development of the new doctrine has been underplayed, even by recent historians, such as Spencer Jones,[174] and Timothy Bowman and Mark Connelly.[175] Roberts' abrupt dismissal as part of the process to establish the General Staff may have been more of a backward step than has perhaps been recognised.

Conclusions

While recognising the very real limitations of a study of official military doctrine, as expressed in Field Service Regulations and its German equivalents, this analysis has revealed some key lines of continuity within the development of command philosophy in the British and German Armies in the half century prior to 1935.

---

172 Roberts, 'Memoir', pp. xxxvi-xxxviii.
173 Ellison, 'Lord Roberts', pp.722-723.
174 Spencer Jones, *From Boer War to World War: Tactical Reform of the British Army, 1902-1914* (Oklahoma, OK: University of Oklahoma, 2012), especially Chapter 1.
175 Timothy Bowman and Mark Connelly, *The Edwardian Army: Recruiting, Training, and Deploying the British Army 1902-1914* (Oxford: Oxford University, 2012), especially Chapter 3.

From at least 1885, the successive editions of the *FO* and the *Instructions* suggest the German doctrine saw warfare as inherently unpredictable, such that commanders could not extrapolate from their greater knowledge of the broader context in order to understand the local situation (widening the Knowledge Gap). As a consequence, the doctrine demanded commanders give their subordinates a clear sense of direction, but leave the achievement of that intent to their initiative (narrowing the Alignment Gap). When compared to the different options open to commanders when faced with the three dimensions of friction, this philosophy equates best with that command approach here termed Directive Command.

By contrast, the British Army maintained a strong emphasis on the need to minimise the chaos of warfare, by dint of commanders retaining tight control over their subordinates, a philosophy that equates to the command approach of Logistic Control. It was this model of command that was upheld by Frank Henderson throughout the 1890s, as he taught successive cohorts of Staff College students. Those officers went on to reach the most senior levels in the army following Haldane's reforms, where they shaped and then commanded the formations that fought in the First World War.

From the mid-1890s, however, Henderson's detailed study of the battles of 1870, coupled with his analysis of the German doctrine of command that had developed over the following decades, ultimately led him to reject the previous orthodoxy. This was then expressed in his draft text for a replacement of *Infantry Drill* (1896), which became FSR I (1905) via *Combined Training* (1902). While by no means a simple paraphrase of the German *FO*, the new manual drew very similar conclusions about the nature of warfare and accordingly promulgated similar solutions.

Following the experience of the First World War, the German Army concluded Directive Command remained an appropriate response to the reality of modern warfare and this was expressed in its first post-war statement of command doctrine – *Das FuG*. However, following further analysis and the development of thinking around armoured forces, the fundamentally chaotic nature of warfare became even more central to the army's thinking, leading to the conclusion the existing tradition of forward command needed to be strengthened still further. This would enable rapid decision-making at the decisive point of the battle, which would allow commanders to achieve tempo and inflict surprise on the enemy. As a result, *Truppenführung* set out a command approach equating to Directive Control.

By contrast, in the British Army, Henderson's own former students led the revision of his manual that saw his emphasis on decentralisation severely weakened, with FSR I (1909) effectively reverting to the former tradition of Logistic Control. Although there is much evidence to demonstrate a correlation during the First World War between the BEF's progressive adoption of decentralised command and its increasing combat effectiveness, the official doctrine remained at heart one of Logistic Control based on a belief in the need to minimise the chaos of warfare by commanders retaining tight control over their subordinates. This change was sustained through successive editions of FSR, until Wavell returned to an understanding of warfare as inherently chaotic. The impact of this on the approach to command was limited, however, by his concerns about the reliability of the hastily trained civilians he expected to form the bulk of the army during any major European conflict. This led to his promoting an approach equivalent to Restrictive Control in FSR (1935).

If it is accepted many of the problems that arise during modern warfare are indeed fundamentally unpredictable and hence 'wicked', the result of the collision in May 1940 between German forces employing Directive Control and British forces reliant upon Restrictive Control was perhaps inevitable. That the German doctrinal manual of that time, *Truppenführung*, continues to be hailed as a landmark in military thought, while the British turned their back on the FSR, and indeed any formal written doctrine, for almost half a century, is perhaps also unsurprising.

This all serves to reinforce Paul Johnston's conclusion: 'It is not enough to write a new doctrine, if the purpose is to change the way an army will fight. Ultimately, an army's behavior in battle will almost certainly be more a reflection of its character or culture than of the contents of its doctrine manuals.'[176] The German Army perceived warfare as chaotic, or 'wicked', and their doctrine reflected this over an extended period of major change. Most British commanders saw it as structured, or 'tame'. Since Henderson's new doctrine did not fit with the cultural norm of the army, it was rejected.

---

176 Paul Johnston, 'Doctrine is Not Enough: The Effect of Doctrine on the Behavior of Armies', *Parameters* (Autumn 2000), 30-39 (pp.35-36).

3

Erwin Rommel and the Application of German Doctrine

I had the impression that I must not stand still, or we were lost.

Rommel[1]

There exists a real danger that our friend Rommel is becoming a kind of magician or bogey-man to our troops.

Auchinleck[2]

As the men of Kradschützen-Bataillon 7 (7th Motorcycle Battalion) crossed the border into Belgium on the morning of 10 May 1940, their commander, Major Friedrich-Carl von Steinkeller, would have been forgiven for harbouring doubts about his divisional commander. Appointed just twelve weeks earlier, the general was a highly decorated veteran of the First World War. But this was his first divisional command, and he had spent most of the last ten years in a series of staff roles, away from the troops. Furthermore, all his previous experience had been with the infantry, yet now he was commanding a panzer division. It was abundantly clear the appointment owed much to the general's strong personal connections with Hitler. Would his abilities as an operational commander meet the test of the forthcoming battle?

Steinkeller[3] need not have worried. By the time France capitulated just six weeks later, the division had taken almost one hundred thousand prisoners, along with more than three hundred guns and over four hundred and fifty armoured vehicles, as well as countless soft-skinned vehicles. Its own losses were fewer than one thousand men

---

1 General Field Marshal Erwin Rommel, *Infantry Attacks* (Barton-under-Needwood: Wren's Park, 2002), p.221
2 Quoted in Desmond Young, *Rommel* (London: Collins, 1950), p.23.
3 For details of Steinkeller's career, see Samuel W. Mitcham, *Rommel's Lieutenants: The Men Who Served the Desert Fox, France, 1940* (Mechanicsburg, PA: Stackpole, 2009), pp.107-108.

killed or missing, and just forty-two tanks destroyed.[4] Its units so frequently appeared unexpectedly behind enemy lines, it was nicknamed the 'ghost division'.[5] The formation was, of course, 7th Panzer Division and its commander Erwin Rommel, who thereby shot to international attention.

Having considered the development of the German Army's doctrine over the decades leading up to 1940 in Chapter Two, and especially the nature of the preferred command approach, it is appropriate to take the hero of the Battle of France as a case study to examine whether that doctrine was reflected in actual practice. As he led 7th Panzer Division's daring thrusts into the depths of the French positions, did Rommel's command approach display the characteristics of Directive Control or was his success the result of a different approach?

An Outsider to the Military Establishment?

Rommel certainly enjoyed an exceptional reputation amongst his opponents during the Second World War. Speaking in Parliament, Churchill referred to him as 'a very daring and skilful opponent', while Eisenhower called him 'a great general'. There was, however, no suggestion that his approach was inherently different from the norm of German commanders. For example, the British 1943 propaganda film, *Desert Victory*, portrayed him as skilled, but autocratic, centralised in his decision making, and indifferent to the fate of his men, and as such from the same mould as Hitler himself.[6]

Interest in Rommel faded after his wounding in July 1944 and subsequent death, as attention focused on the victorious campaign to end the war.[7] It reignited in January 1950 following the publication of his first biography. Its author, former brigadier Desmond Young, had returned after the war to his interest in writing, becoming a professional journalist and biographer. Business was not good and yet he found himself turning down the opportunity to write a biography of former prime minister, Andrew Bonar Law, on the basis that he did not feel able to do a good job of it. Over 'an economy lunch at the Ritz grill' in late 1948, a chance mention of Rommel by his wife caught his imagination. He felt the topic was somewhat limited in its appeal, but thought the book might sell ten thousand copies. It was Ronald Politzer, head of publicity at his publishers, Collins, who identified the potential commercial opportunity of a biography of Britain's famous opponent.[8] The book was indeed an

---

4   Field Marshal Erwin Rommel, *The Rommel Papers*, ed. by Basil H. Liddell Hart, trans. by Paul Findlay (London: Collins, 1953), p.84.

5   Horst Scheibert, *Die Gespenster-Division: Die Geschichte der 7. Panzer-Division* (Eggolsheim: Dörfler, 2006), pp.42-44.

6   Mark Connelly, 'Rommel as Icon', in *Rommel: A Reappraisal*, ed. by Ian F.W. Beckett (Barnsley: Pen and Sword, 2013), 157-178 (pp.160-161).

7   Connelly, 'Rommel as Icon', p.162.

8   Desmond Young, *Try Anything Twice* (London: Hamilton, 1963), pp.343-347.

instant success, selling more than two hundred thousand copies in Britain alone,[9] and spawning a Hollywood film, *The Desert Fox*. In contrast to the wartime depiction, Young presented Rommel in a very favourable light, almost hagiographic. He judged him 'the perfect fighting animal, cold, cunning, ruthless, untiring, quick of decision, incredibly brave'. Rommel was simply 'on the wrong side',[10] as Young found many 'British' characteristics in this German officer. This perspective was reflected in *The Desert Fox*, where James Mason portrayed him as 'stern, but chivalrous and respectful'.[11]

One of the many figures from the British military establishment who had assisted Young in preparing his book was Basil Liddell Hart.[12] Liddell Hart's reputation as Britain's leading military thinker had been severely damaged by the Fall of France in 1940.[13] In 1945, however, he had been the beneficiary of an enormous stroke of luck: many of the captured German generals in British hands had been sent to No.1 PoW Camp at Grizedale Hall in Cumbria, which just happened to be only five miles from his home. Making use of family connections, Liddell Hart secured a pass to the camp and, between August 1945 and January 1946, he made at least fifteen visits, during which he interviewed twelve of the generals. The result appeared in 1948 as *The Other Side of the Hill*,[14] in which he presented his interviewees in a broadly positive light, as 'technicians' who had been 'hoodwinked' by Hitler.[15]

The Other Side of the Hill played a major role in reviving Liddell Hart's reputation as a historian. It had also positioned Liddell Hart in Germany as a well-known British writer with a supportive attitude to the Wehrmacht's commanders,[16] making him a natural choice when Young was seeking help in preparing his own, highly positive, biography of a German general. It is therefore perhaps unsurprising that, a few weeks before his biography was published, Young contacted Liddell Hart on behalf of Rommel's family, asking whether he would be willing to edit the general's personal papers. Liddell Hart agreed, apologising to them that he had not been sufficiently kind about Rommel in his own writings.[17] It is of note that the second (1951) edition of *The Other Side of the Hill* included an additional paragraph at the end of the chapter on Rommel: 'The more deeply his record is examined the clearer it becomes that both his gifts and his performance [...] qualified him for a place in the role of the

9   Connelly, 'Rommel as Icon', pp.162-163.
10 Young, *Rommel*, p.32.
11 Stephen Bungay, *Alamein* (London: Aurum, 2002), pp.233-234.
12 Young, *Rommel*, p.5.
13 John J. Mearsheimer, *Liddell Hart and the Weight of History* (London: Brassey's, 1988), p.178.
14 Captain Basil H. Liddell Hart, *The Other Side of the Hill: Germany's Generals, Their Rise and Fall, with Their Own Account of Military Events 1939-1945* (London: Cassell, 1948).
15 Liddell Hart, *Other Side* (1948), pp.ix-x.
16 Alaric Searle, 'A Very Special Relationship: Basil Liddell Hart, Wehrmacht Generals and the Debate on West German Rearmament, 1945-1953', *War in History*, 5(3) (1998), 327-357 (pp.330-336).
17 Mearsheimer, *Liddell Hart*, pp.192 & 199.

"Great Captains" of history'.[18] Liddell Hart's labours on behalf of the general's family appeared in 1953 as *The Rommel Papers*.[19]

These three books together set a trend for presenting Rommel as a maverick. Young argued Rommel's tactical brilliance (especially his famous *Fingerspitzengefühl*[20] – literally 'finger-tip feeling', equivalent to 'finger on the pulse') and unorthodox approach secured victory despite the hesitancy of his superiors.[21] Reinforcing this perceived separation from the mainstream, Field Marshal Sir Claude Auchinleck wrote in Young's foreword, 'Rommel was certainly exceptional. Germany produces many ruthlessly efficient generals: Rommel stood out amongst them because he had overcome the innate rigidity of the German military mind and was a master of improvisation.'[22] In *The Rommel Papers*, Liddell Hart repeatedly referred to Rommel's originality, and its index included the heading 'Originality (and Unorthodoxy)'.[23] In *The Other Side of the Hill*, he described Rommel as 'an outsider', who had been passed over by the military establishment as not fit for 'the select circle of the future General Staff'. Rommel had only achieved promotion through his contacts with Hitler, who had found him 'a refreshingly unorthodox soldier'.[24] Reinforcing this depiction, Young claimed Chief of the General Staff Franz Halder's dislike of Rommel was 'obvious'.[25] These themes were echoed in another book appearing around that time, in which Rommel's chief of staff in North Africa, Siegfried Westphal, argued the German military establishment had been hostile to Rommel, due to his 'strongly-developed spirit of contrariness'.[26]

This sense of Rommel as an outsider to the German military establishment characterised the 'string of effusive and often uncritical biographies'[27] appearing during subsequent decades. Ronald Lewin's biography (1968) commented on the way Rommel's mind appeared 'fresh, uninhibited, experimental, untrammelled by precedent'.[28] Similarly, Charles Douglas-Home (1973) argued he was 'a man apart' from the German military tradition, 'an outsider as far as the general staff was concerned', separate from its thinking and writing.[29] Kenneth Macksey (1979) again underlined his position as an outsider, recording Westphal had commented on

18 Compare Liddell Hart, *Other Side* (1948), p.61, with Liddell Hart, *Other Side*, 2nd edn (1951, reprinted London: Pan, 1978), p.85.
19 Field Marshal Erwin Rommel, *The Rommel Papers*, ed. by Basil H. Liddell Hart, trans. by Paul Findlay (London: Collins, 1953).
20 Young, *Rommel*, p.138.
21 Young, *Rommel*, pp.140-141.
22 Field Marshal Sir Claude Auchinleck, 'Foreword', in Young, *Rommel*, pp.9-11 (p.9).
23 *Rommel Papers*, pp.xviii & 538.
24 Liddell Hart, *Other Side* (1948), pp.52-53.
25 Young, *Rommel*, p.83.
26 General Siegfried Westphal, *The German Army in the West* (London: Cassell, 1951), pp.126-128.
27 Alaric Searle, 'Rommel and the Rise of the Nazis', in Beckett, *Rommel*, 7-29 (p.7).
28 Ronald Lewin, *Rommel as a Military Commander* (New York, NK: Barnes & Noble, 1968), p.5.
29 Charles Douglas-Home, *Rommel* (London: Book Club Associates, 1973), pp.18-20.

how surprising it was that, in 1919, Rommel, unlike the handful of other subaltern recipients of the *Pour le Mérite*,[30] was not selected for staff training at the famous War Academy. Westphal suggested this was because his approach did not 'fit' with the General Staff and noted Rommel had taken the decision as a serious rebuff, leaving him bitter towards the military establishment.[31]

An important element in Rommel's perceived status as a maverick, operating outside the mainstream of German military thinking, was the oft-repeated assertion that his success in 1940 owed nothing to Guderian's doctrine for the use of armoured forces. Not only had he had no prior involvement with the panzers prior to his appointment to command 7th Panzer Division in February 1940, Liddell Hart even argued Rommel had been an active opponent of the new gospel.[32] Instead, it was suggested, he simply reverted to the techniques employed in 1917, his last experience of combat, when he was a subaltern in the Wurttemberg Mountain Battalion.[33] Indeed, Kurt Hesse, a colleague at the Dresden Infantry School, wrote, 'Basically, he [Rommel] always remained the same lieutenant, appreciating the situation in the blink of an eye and then seizing its opportunities through lightning-quick action.'[34]

This orthodoxy of Rommel as a brilliant outsider, drawing on his own experience in preference to following established doctrine, was first challenged in 1977. In a revisionist biography, David Irving argued Rommel was far from being the maverick of previous accounts. Rather, this picture was in large measure the deliberate creation of Hans Speidel, his chief of staff in Normandy.[35] Although analysis by Richard Evans has revealed fundamental flaws in Irving's technique and approach, such that his publications must be treated with extreme caution,[36] subsequent historians have broadly supported Irving on this specific point.

30 Imperial Germany's highest military honour, broadly equivalent to the British Victoria Cross, though generally awarded for command achievements rather than bravery. Rommel was the sixth of only eleven company commanders to receive the award. Of the 534 awards made to officers in the land army, only 84 went to individuals at or below battalion level. Jürgen Brinkmann, *Die Ritter des Ordens "Pour le Merité" 1914-1918* (Bückeburg: self-published, 1982).

31 Kenneth Macksey, *Rommel: Battles and Campaigns* (London: Book Club Associates, 1979), p.22.

32 Liddell Hart, *Other Side* (1951), p.77.

33 Young, *Rommel*, p.35, Lewin, *Rommel*, p.11, Douglas-Home, *Rommel*, pp.29 & 55, and Macksey, *Rommel*, p.28.

34 Kurt Hesse, Wandlung eines Mannes und eines Typus (1945), in Irving Collection, <www.britishonlinearchives.co.uk> [accessed 24 August 2015] Documents Discussing Rommel Mostly by Those Close to Him, img.320.

35 David Irving, *The Trail of the Fox: The Life of Field-Marshal Erwin Rommel* (London: Weidenfeld and Nicolson, 1977), pp.407-408.

36 Richard J. Evans, *David Irving, Hitler and Holocaust Denial*, electronic edition <http://hdot.org/en/trial/defense/evans/6.html> [accessed 28 July 2015], para.6.21.

Through Rommel's family, Speidel too had assisted Young with his biography,[37] thereby meeting Liddell Hart and gaining the opportunity to influence the books that established Rommel's post-war reputation. In doing so, Speidel had motives beyond simple historical accuracy or the improvement of conditions for Rommel's family. Soon after the war had ended, tensions with the Soviet Union had given Britain and America new concerns, raising the question whether Germany should be rearmed.[38] For this to happen, the German Army needed to be rehabilitated. That depended in part on identifying Wehrmacht commanders who had resisted the Nazis and so retained their honour. As early as 1946, Speidel had told his fellow former generals in captivity that he intended to make Rommel, whose association with the 20 July bomb plot had led to his forced suicide, 'the hero of the German people'.[39] Through his involvement with Liddell Hart and Young, Speidel was able to make this goal a reality, ensuring Rommel became the archetypal 'good German', who had opposed Hitler and thereby lent legitimacy to Germany's war experience[40] and hence new Bundeswehr.[41] For him to be perceived as a brilliant field commander, yet an outsider to the General Staff (declared a criminal organisation at the Nuremberg trials), made Rommel even more perfect for this role.

As military adviser to the German Chancellor, Konrad Adenauer, Speidel went on to play an important role in the development of a 'shadow' army, formed in direct contravention of Allied regulations, as a precursor to the establishment of the Bundeswehr, in which he became a central figure. He was facilitated in this by the fact that Rommel's positive reputation led the Allies to assume that his former associates were also trustworthy, especially those who had served directly under him, such as Speidel.[42] He thereby gained a double connection to Rommel and hence enjoyed further ability to promote his dream of a reborn German Army. In short, there were strong reasons during the late 1940s and early 1950s for Rommel to have been presented as an outsider to the German military elite, a maverick who rejected their (and Hitler's) doctrines. Not only did this offer the prospect of securing better treatment for his family and former colleagues,[43] it also facilitated the process of German rearmament.

Most subsequent biographers and historians have agreed with Irving that Rommel was rather more within the mainstream of German military practice than had at first been suggested. Russel Stolfi suggested the characteristics displayed by Rommel and 7th Panzer Division were typical of the German Army as a whole, while nonetheless

37   Young, *Rommel*, p.6.
38   Searle, 'Special Relationship', pp.340-341.
39   Quoted in Searle, 'Rise of the Nazis', p.9.
40   Lieb, 'Rommel', p.342.
41   Bungay, *Alamein*, pp.233-235.
42   Agilof Kesselring, *Die Organisation Gehlen und Die Verteidigung Westdeutschlands: Alte Elitedivisionen und neue Militärstrukturen, 1949-1953* (Marburg: Bundesnachrichtendienst, 2014), pp.47-48.
43   Searle, 'Special Relationship', p.356.

highlighting his reliance on experience from the First World War.[44] Dirk Oetting noted Rommel sometimes acted like a First World War stormtroop lieutenant, but similarly suggested his command from the front and his readiness to seize fleeting opportunities remained within the compass of the army's doctrine.[45] Dennis Showalter equally argued Rommel's technique in 1940 drew on his experiences in 1917, but suggested this 'owed a good deal to the German army's doctrine', which had likewise drawn lessons from the more mobile campaigns of that war. He also dismissed claims Rommel was an outsider to the military establishment.[46] Claus Telp again emphasised Rommel in 1940 operated within the mainstream of German military thought. Indeed, contrary to suggestions Rommel was ignorant of, and indeed hostile to, armoured tactics prior to his appointment to command 7th Panzer Division, Telp highlighted his study of armoured theory, suggesting this aligned with his experience as a light infantryman in 1917.[47] Similarly, Daniel Butler underlined the impression made on Rommel by his observation of motorised forces during the conquest of Poland in 1939, while suggesting he saw their characteristic speed and surprise as offering an opportunity to apply his favoured command style from the previous war.[48]

But this view of Rommel as an orthodox adherent to the German Army's doctrine and an insider to its establishment is by no means accepted by all recent historians. Telp himself suggested Rommel's leadership style during the campaign in France was 'only broadly in line with established doctrine'.[49] Similarly, Peter Caddick-Adams, while noting Rommel's familiarity with the tactics enshrined in the army's doctrine, argued his behaviour in practice deserved the label of 'maverick'.[50] David Fraser too suggested Rommel 'could only command in his own way, in the way he had learned from his own experience against [...] the Italians [in 1917]'.[51] Maurice Remy claimed Rommel simply refused to listen to his superiors and rushed forward like a man possessed, despite their best efforts to stop him.[52] Marco Sigg perhaps went the furthest of recent historians, arguing Rommel was guilty of '*Eigenmächtigkeit*' (wilfulness), breaking free of all control from his superiors, and hence acting beyond the scope of the accepted

44   Russel H.S. Stolfi, *A Bias for Action: The German 7th Panzer Division in France & Russia, 1940-1941* (Quantico, VA: Command & Staff College Foundation, 1991), pp.15 & 38-41.
45   Dirk W. Oetting, *Auftragstaktik: Geschichte und Gegenwart einer Führungskonzeption* (Frankfurt am Main: Report, 1993), pp.201 & 203.
46   Dennis Showalter, *Patton and Rommel: Men of War in the Twentieth Century* (New York, NY: Berkley Caliber, 2005), pp.62 & 147.
47   Claus Telp, 'Rommel and 1940' in Beckett, *Rommel*, pp.30-59 (pp.31 & 49).
48   Daniel Allen Butler, *Field Marshal: The Life and Death of Erwin Rommel* (Havertown, PA: Casemate, 2015), pp146-147.
49   Telp, 'Rommel', p.49.
50   Peter Caddick-Adams, *Monty and Rommel: Parallel Lives* (London: Arrow, 2012), pp.221 & 239.
51   David Fraser, *Knight's Cross: A Life of Field Marshal Erwin Rommel* (London: HarperCollins, 1994), p.209.
52   Maurice Philip Remy, *Mythos Rommel* (Munich: List, 2002), pp.48-49.

doctrine.[53] Perhaps most importantly, the head of the Bundeswehr's department for the history of the two world wars, Colonel Karl-Heinz Frieser, argued, 'Rommel won breathtaking victories, ironically because he knew so little about Panzer operational principles. The old rules, spelled out in regulations, no longer applied [...]. Instead [... he] led his Panzers like an infantry assault detachment and employed the same infiltration tactics he had [...] during World War I. This unorthodox way of employing the Panzer force became the nightmare of his methodical French counterparts.'[54]

Although recent historians have therefore largely rejected the simplistic picture, presented in the immediate post-war literature, of Rommel as a maverick, his true relationship with the army's doctrine and its inner establishment remains the subject of debate. There is general agreement that the tactics and command approach Rommel applied as a panzer division commander in France in May 1940 showed great continuity with those he had used as an infantry subaltern in Italy in 1917. There is, however, rather less consensus over whether those tactics and his command approach were typical of, or contrary to, those set out in the German Army's doctrine. This reflects a broader trend in recent German historiography on Rommel, which increasingly reveals the complexities and subtleties of his approach and thinking, and thereby defies the simplistic categorisation of much of the earlier anglophone literature. The thoughtful thematic biography by Ralf Georg Reuth[55] and Peter Lieb's analysis of Rommel's changing relationship with Nazi ideology[56] especially reflect this latest approach.

This chapter therefore seeks to address these areas of disagreement. It provides an analysis of Rommel's command approach in 1940, as displayed through his actions during the critical phase of the campaign: the crossing of the Meuse at Dinant and the subsequent penetration of the French defensive zone, 12-15 May. The central elements of this command approach are then compared to his exploits in 1917 against the Italians in a key phase of the Caporetto campaign: the capture of Mount Matajur, 24-26 October. This allows the issue of continuity to be considered in detail. Rommel's command approach, as demonstrated in these two actions, is then compared with the statements in the successive editions of the German Army's most important infantry training and field service regulations, from the date when he was first commissioned, in 1912, through until he came to international notice, in 1940. This provides the basis for an assessment of whether he acted within or outside the doctrine as it developed over the period. In addition, this comparison of Rommel's practice with official theory allows insights into the doctrine itself.

53 Marco Sigg, *Der Unterführer als Feldherr im Taschenformat: Theorie und Praxis der Auftragstaktik im deutschen Heer 1869 bis 1945* (Paderborn: Schöningh, 2014), pp.243-246 & 251.
54 Karl-Heinz Frieser with John T. Greenwood, *The Blitzkrieg Legend: The 1940 Campaign in the West* (Annapolis, Maryland: Naval Institute, 2005), p.224.
55 Ralf Georg Reuth, *Rommel: The End of a Legend* (London: Haus, 2008).
56 Lieb, 'Rommel', passim.

Tutor to the Army

Before embarking on this analysis, however, it is appropriate to explore in more detail the precise nature of Rommel's postings between the two world wars, in order to understand his position with regard to the German military establishment.

With the formation of the Reichswehr, Rommel's pre-war unit, Infanterie-Regiment 124 of the Wurttemberg Army, was dissolved and its tradition carried on by Infanterie-Regiment 13 (IR13). Retained as one of the four thousand officers required for the new army, Rommel was assigned to the regiment as a company commander on 1 January 1921.[57] He remained in Stuttgart in this relatively obscure posting for almost a decade, his career proceeding in an unremarkable manner,[58] until October 1929, when he became a tactics instructor at the *Infanterieschule* (Infantry School). This was the turning point in his progression and marked his entry into the army's central elite. He was to spend most of the next decade in a series of such roles:[59]

- 1 October 1929 to 30 September 1933: tactics instructor at the Infantry School at Dresden;
- 15 October 1935 to 9 November 1938: course instructor at the *Kriegsschule* (War School) at Potsdam; and
- 10 November 1938 to 14 February 1940: commandant of the new War School at Wiener Neustadt, based in the Maria Theresa Military Academy of the former Austrian Army.[60]

During this period, Rommel's only substantive posting to a non-instructional role[61] was two years (1933-1935) as commander of III Bataillon, Infanterie-Regiment 17 (III/IR17), a specialist mountain battalion, known as the Goslar Jäger ('the Huntsmen from Goslar'). This phase in his career ended on 15 February 1940, when on promotion to *Generalmajor* (brigadier) he took over command of 7th Panzer Division.[62] Just twelve weeks later, he led it across the Meuse and into the history books.

Drawing largely on unattributed reminiscences first presented by Irving,[63] scholarly accounts of this phase in Rommel's career have focused primarily on his obvious

---

57 Young, *Rommel*, p.46.
58 Lieb, 'Rommel', p.307.
59 Young, *Rommel*, pp.50, 53 & 57.
60 Remy, *Rommel*, p.41.
61 Rommel also undertook four short temporary attachments towards the end of this period: as trainer to the *Hitlerjugend* (Hitler Youth) in 1937 and as commander of the *Führerbegleitbataillon* (Hitler's escort battalion) during operations in the Sudetenland in October 1938, Prague in March 1939, and Poland in September 1939. Young, *Rommel*, pp.56-62.
62 Young, *Rommel*, p.66.
63 Irving, *Fox*, pp.21-24. Extracts by Irving from annual evaluations of Rommel by his superiors have recently been made available: Beurteilungen, 1929-1938, in David Irving's

ability as a teacher and his outstanding reputation with his students.[64] Little has been written concerning the training institutions themselves or their place within the German Army. How important was Rommel's role?

During the Reichswehr period (1919-1935), officer candidates were first appointed to the ranks. There, they undertook nine months of basic training along with other new recruits, followed by a further six months training in NCO skills. Those who passed the Officer Candidate Examination then attended the Infantry School, regardless of their intended arm of service, for a ten-and-a-half-month course. Following a brief period back with their regiments, candidates destined for the infantry then underwent a further nine-month course at the school, after which they were commissioned. The essence of both courses was to develop the candidates' leadership skills, principally through classroom discussion and practical exploration of all-arms tactical problems.

A central feature of the training in Dresden was the absence of any 'school' solution, the aim being to develop the cadets' initiative and speed of decision-making.[65] Shortly before Rommel joined the teaching staff at the establishment, one of the students was Captain William Hones, US Army, who attended as part of the regular exchange arrangements between the two armies.[66] In a report submitted to the US Army Command and General Staff School after his return, Hones noted that the Dresden course was focused on 'the training of the student [... through] problems in leadership and tactics, designed to inculcate in him the ability to command. [... A] maximum amount of time [... is] devoted to exercises in which the student is given opportunities to make decisions, issue orders and command'.[67] Field exercises were an 'almost daily occurrence' and particularly emphasised the influence of terrain and the handling of tanks.[68]

This last point must cast doubt on the oft-repeated suggestion, made for example by General Wilhelm von Thoma, commander of the Afrika Korps at El Alamein, that Rommel never understood the 'technique' of tanks, but merely applied his instinctive feel for infantry tactics.[69] Indeed, although it has been argued Rommel

Private Research Collection, Selected Documents on the Life and Campaigns of Field-Marshal Erwin Rommel (hereafter Irving Collection), Rommel's Career as Recorded in His Personnel File and His Words <http://www.britishonlinearchives.co.uk/group. php?cat=&sid=&cid=9781851172511&date_option=equal&page=&pid=72511f> [accessed 24 August 2015], imgs.112-135.

64   Fraser, *Knight's Cross*, pp.98 & 117, Caddick-Adams, *Rommel*, pp.177-180 & 188-190, and Butler, *Field Marshal*, pp.105-107 & 130-137.

65   David N. Spires, *Image and Reality: The Making of the German Officer, 1921-1933* (Westport, CT: Greenwood, 1984), pp.17-20.

66   Thomas G. Mahnken, *Uncovering Ways of War: U.S. Intelligence and Foreign Military Innovation, 1918-1941* (Ithaca, NY: Cornell University Press, 2009), pp.88-90.

67   Captain William Hones, The German Infantry School (unpublished student paper, US Army Command & General Staff School, 1931), <http://cgsc.contentdm.oclc.org/cdm/ singleitem/collection /p4013coll14/id/1132/rec/21>. [accessed 2 November 2014], p.6

68   Hones, German Infantry School, pp.10-12.

69   Young, *Rommel*, p.66.

was an opponent of Guderian's proposals for the establishment of the new panzer divisions,[70] little evidence has been presented to support this claim. As an instructor at the Infantry School, Rommel would have been expected to have as good an understanding of armoured tactics as was possible for anyone in the Reichswehr at that time: in late 1928, Major Heinz Guderian was appointed as the first instructor in tank tactics at the school established by the Transport Department of the *Truppenamt* (the disguised Great General Staff), despite never having even seen inside one![71] Rommel's awareness of tanks may be indicated by the fact that he included armoured vehicles in four of the nineteen exercises set out in his 1934 handbook for junior officers.[72]

Rommel's superiors recorded with approval how his teaching, presented in a highly stimulating manner and drawn from his own combat experience, was focused on developing 'initiative, fresh audacity, and a willingness to take responsibility' on the part of the cadets.[73] Although Showalter noted Rommel 'was impatient of any reference to doctrine or authority at the expense of a student's own mental processes',[74] the point was that doctrine should not be used as a replacement for thought ('I don't want to hear what Clausewitz thinks, tell me what *you* think!'),[75] rather than that doctrine was of itself of no value.

The Reichswehr placed great emphasis on raising the standard of officer candidate education. Care was therefore taken to ensure only the best line officers, alongside selected General Staff officers, served as one of the forty[76] military instructors at the Infantry School. As the institution through which all officer candidates passed, this establishment was considered the most important of all the four branch schools (the others served the cavalry, artillery and pioneers respectively). Showalter noted assignment to the Infantry School was therefore 'in the same category' as service with the *Truppenamt*.[77] Selection for Dresden, therefore, was a prestigious posting for Rommel, placing him near the heart of the army's establishment and marking him out for future promotion,[78] a career route already recommended in his final annual evaluation report from IR13 in 1929.[79]

70   Mearsheimer, *Liddell Hart*, p.191.
71   General Heinz Guderian, *Panzer Leader*, trans. by Constantine Fitzgibbon (London: Futura, 1974), pp.22-23 and Kenneth Macksey, *Guderian: Panzer General* (London: Macdonald & Jane's, 1974), p.47.
72   Generalfeldmarschall Erwin Rommel, *Aufgaben für Zug und Kompanie (Gefechtsaufgaben, Gefechtsschiessen, Geländebesprechung), Ihre Anlange und Leitung*, 5th edn (Berlin: Mittler, 1944), exercises 7, 8, 10 & 17.
73   Beurteilung, 1 August 1932, in Irving Collection, Rommel's Career, img. 117.
74   Showalter, *Patton and Rommel*, p.159.
75   Quoted by Butler, *Field Marshal*, p.131, emphasis in original.
76   Hones, German Infantry School, p.3.
77   Showalter, *Patton and Rommel*, p.145.
78   James S. Corum, *The Roots of Blitzkrieg: Hans von Seeckt and the German Military Reform* (Lawrence, KS: University Press of Kansas, 1992), pp.78-80.
79   Beurteilungen, 1 September 1929 and 30 September 1929, in Irving Collection, Rommel's

Indeed, the decision not to select Rommel for General Staff training may have reflected a sound assessment of his character by the army's personnel office. Rommel had found his time as a staff officer in 1918 a severe trial, the steady nature of planning being fundamentally at odds with his impatient character.[80] Assigning him instead to a role where he could make the most of his gift for leadership and practical training should not necessarily be seen as evidence of a rejection by the establishment,[81] even though of course that is certainly how Rommel himself took it. As Reuth noted, Rommel 'was disturbed by the dominant role of the nobility in the officer corps. He believed officers of this class often gained general staff positions as their birthright rather than any accomplishments on the battlefield.'[82] Given such a perspective, Rommel's affront at his exclusion from the General Staff was to be expected. There is, however, significant evidence to suggest selection for that august body was in fact largely driven by considerations of merit. Perhaps the key to understanding Rommel's discontent was his belief that performance on the battlefield should be the prime measure of an officer's ability. By contrast, the General Staff placed equal emphasis on achievements in headquarters roles when selecting its future leaders.[83]

A key element of the positive impact on Rommel's future career prospects of this posting to the Infantry School were the connections that he made in Dresden.[84] These included:

- Alexander von Falkenhausen, commandant of the Infantry School when Rommel arrived, who was later Military Governor of Belgium from 1940 to 1944;
- Wilhelm List, successor to Falkenhausen as commandant, who commanded Twelfth Army in France in May 1940 and Army Group A in Russia from July 1942;
- Karl-Heinrich von Stülpnagel, head of the training division, who served as deputy to Franz Halder, Chief of the General Staff, from November 1938 to May 1940, commanded Seventeenth Army in Russia, and became Military Governor of France in 1942.

Selection for the directing staff at the Infantry School therefore gave Rommel an excellent network of influential contacts across the four-thousand-strong officer corps of the small Reichswehr. This network would have become still more important during the rapid expansion of the army from 1935, as many of his contacts secured influential senior positions, with considerable ability to affect Rommel's career opportunities.

Career, imgs.114-115.
80 Caddick-Adams, *Rommel*, pp.141-142.
81 Showalter, *Patton and Rommel*, p.148.
82 Reuth, *Rommel*, p.22.
83 Martin Samuels, *Command or Control? Command, Training and Tactics in the British and German Armies, 1888-1918* (London: Cass, 1995), pp.18-20 & 28-29.
84 Caddick-Adams, *Monty & Rommel*, p.178.

Moreover, Rommel's posting to the Infantry School may itself have benefitted from existing connections with senior officers. He had long been a protégé of Generalleutnant Eberhard von Hofacker, commander of the 26th (Wurttemberg) Division at Caporetto in October 1917 and (as will be seen in Chapter Four) of LI Corps at Amiens in August 1918, under whom he had worked when the latter was responsible for the Wurttemberg War Ministry in 1919.[85] In addition, he was a favourite of Wilhelm List[86] from well before the latter's appointment as commandant of the Infantry School. Indeed, List may have had a direct hand in Rommel's original appointment to Dresden, since he was head of the Truppenamt's T4 *Heeresausbildungsabteilung* (Army Training Branch) in 1929. List's previous posting had been as commander of III/IR19, a specialist mountain battalion. It seems entirely possible this role had led List to become aware of Rommel, a fellow Wurttemberger and a renowned member of its elite mountain battalion during the recent war, whose IR13 was part of the Reichswehr's 5th Infantry Division and was based in the neighbouring area to the 7th Infantry Division, which included IR19.

Rommel's networking continued after he left Dresden: his battalion command, III/IR17, was the successor unit to Jäger-Bataillon 10 of the Kaiserheer. Guderian had been commissioned into this unit in 1907, had commanded one of its companies between 1920 and 1922, and thereafter maintained close links with it.[87] By 1935, therefore, Rommel had been brought into the army's establishment and had forged a number of key relationships. He was clearly no outsider, though it is true his exclusion from the General Staff and his comments about its members showed he was not a member of its most inner elite.

Following the reintroduction of conscription in March 1935, the Infantry School, designed for the two hundred new officers required annually for the hundred-thousand-man Reichswehr,[88] could not cope with the flood of subalterns needed for the new Wehrmacht. The four (later five) War Schools were the solution, each training a thousand officer candidates at a time.[89] As before, and despite the massive demand for new officers, the training remained rigorous, with the course remaining two years in duration. The tone of the content was also maintained, with a strong focus on tactics. Here, as before, the officer candidates learned to develop their powers of command through field exercises and simulated problems, during which they took on roles up to and including that of a battalion commander.[90]

85   Caddick-Adams, *Rommel*, pp.127 & 162.
86   Richard Brett-Smith, *Hitler's Generals* (London: Osprey, 1976), p.252 and Caddick-Adams, *Monty and Rommel*, p.178.
87   Guderian, *Panzer Leader*, pp.16-18 and Fraser, *Knight's Cross*, p.103.
88   Spires, *Image and Reality*, p.7.
89   Caddick-Adams, *Monty & Rommel*, p.188.
90   *German Military Training: A Study of German Military Training*. Produced at GMDS by a combined British, Canadian and US Staff (*May 1946*), *pp.55-56*.

As an instructor, and then commandant, in these various establishments for eight years, Rommel played a key role in the initial command training of perhaps a thousand Reichswehr officer candidates and up to five thousand in the Wehrmacht. By the time he left Wiener Neustadt in February 1940, therefore, Rommel had personally instructed perhaps a quarter of all the Active officers in the German Army, and a higher proportion still of those below field rank.[91] This impact on the thinking of a whole generation of junior officers, unequalled by any of his peers, has been largely overlooked in the historical literature.

Yet Rommel's influence went even wider than this. In 1934, shortly after he left Dresden, he published a short instructional handbook, *Gefechts-Aufgaben für Zug und Kompagnie* (Combat Problems for Platoon and Company).[92] This was followed in 1937, while he was at Potsdam, by a second volume, *Infanterie Greift An!* (Infantry Attacks).[93] This text brought together a number of pamphlets based on his lecture notes, which drew on his personal experiences during the First World War.

There is some uncertainty regarding the impact of these books. Caddick-Adams noted *Infantry Attacks* had sold half a million copies by 1944,[94] while Irving reported Rommel's embarrassment at the scale of the resulting royalties.[95] Conversely, the foreword to the (unauthorised) translation published in America in 1944 by the *Infantry Journal* stated neither volume made much impression when first published, receiving only perfunctory reviews in the German military periodicals.[96] This implies sales exploded only *after* Rommel had achieved international fame through his exploits in May 1940. In other words, the book became a bestseller through the celebrity of its author, rather than vice versa. Nonetheless, while he may not have reached a wider audience initially, *Infantry Attacks* became a textbook at the War Schools,[97] such that almost every newly-commissioned officer in the Wehrmacht would have been familiar with it, and hence its author. One non-military reader was Hitler himself, with favourable consequences for Rommel's career.[98] Here too, Rommel's influence on the officer corps through his roles as an instructor helped: one of his students from Dresden, Nicolas von Below, had become Hitler's Luftwaffe adjutant and presented

91 In October 1938, the German Active Officer Corps totalled 16,358, of whom 90 percent were of the rank of Major or below, see Martin van Creveld, *Fighting Power: German and U.S. Army Performance, 1939-1945* (London: Arms & Armour, 1983), table 11.7, p.153.
92 Major Rommel, *Gefechts-Aufgaben für Zug und Kompagnie: Ein Handbuch für Offizierunterricht* (Berlin: Mittler, 1934).
93 General Field Marshal Erwin Rommel, *Infantry Attacks* (Barton-under-Needwood: Wren's Park, 2002).
94 Caddick-Adams, *Monty & Rommel*, p.190.
95 Irving, *Fox*, p.27.
96 'Publishers' Note', in Rommel, *Infantry Attacks*, xi-xiii (p.xi).
97 Caddick-Adams, *Monty & Rommel*, p.190.
98 Lieb, 'Rommel', p.307.

his former teacher to the Führer as an exemplar of the new generation of officers he was seeking.[99]

Both Caddick-Adams[100] and Jörg Muth[101] have suggested that, in writing *Infantry Attacks*, Rommel was 'almost certainly inspired' by *Infantry in Battle*, a handbook published in 1934 by the *Infantry Journal* on behalf of the US Army Infantry School, under the direction of Colonel George C. Marshall.[102] Although they note Marshall's volume was reviewed favourably in Germany, and so may well have come to Rommel's attention, whether it formed the inspiration for his own book must be questioned. First, whereas *Infantry in Battle* was organised by topic, with examples drawn from a multitude of different situations, Rommel adopted a completely different approach in *Infantry Attacks*, which provided a chronological narrative, based on his own personal experience alone. Second, in presenting his experiences in a format designed to develop the knowledge and expertise of young officers, Rommel was merely following a longstanding German military tradition. As James Corum has highlighted,[103] numerous serving officers had published guides and tactical handbooks throughout the 1920s:[104] *Infantry Attacks* was unusual only in the quality of its writing and its placing of the author at the centre of every engagement.[105] The active involvement of the General Staff in the production of this major body of literature designed to explain and expound on the official manuals (maintaining a tradition that stretched back long before even 1914),[106] ensured such expositions remained true to the philosophy behind the doctrine, thereby clarifying rather than confusing.[107] There was therefore no need for Rommel to seek inspiration from an American handbook. In fact, the reverse may have been true, with the Americans perhaps being motivated to produce their own book after learning about the German practice: Marshall had worked closely with Hauptmann Adolf von Schell, a Reichswehr officer who attended the US Army Infantry School at Fort Benning as an exchange student in 1930.[108]

99   Reuth, *Rommel*, p.33.
100 Caddick-Adams, *Monty & Rommel*, p.516n23.
101 Jörg Muth, *Command Culture: Officer Education in the U.S. Army and the German Armed Forces, 1901-1940, and the Consequences for World War II* (Denton, TX: University of North Texas, 2011), p.142.
102 *Infantry in Battle*, 2nd ed. (Washington, DC: Infantry Journal, 1939), Introduction.
103 Corum, *Roots*, pp.86-88.
104 For example, Oberstleutnant Hüttmann, *Die Kampfweise der Infanterie auf Grund der neuen Ausbildungsvorschrift für die Infanterie vom 26.10.1922* (Berlin: Mittler, 1924) and Oberstleutnant von Cochenhausen, *Die Truppenführung: Ein Handbuch für den Truppenführer und seine Gehilfen* (Berlin: Mittler, 1926).
105 Searle, 'Rise of the Nazis', p.19.
106 Ralf Raths, *Vom Massensturm zur Stoßtrupptaktik: Die deutsche Landkriegtaktik im Spiegel von Dienstvorschriften und Publizistik 1906 bis 1918* (Freiburg: Rombach, 2009), pp.16-19.
107 Matthias Strohn, *The German Army and the Defence of the Reich: Military Doctrine and the Conduct of the Defensive Battle, 1918-1939* (Cambridge: Cambridge University Press, 2011), p.116.
108 Muth, *Command Culture*, p.142.

In addition to these semi-official influences on the thinking of young officers, there is a small possibility Rommel may have played a more direct role in the development of the army's doctrine. As the Reichswehr and then the Wehrmacht came to review and revise their manuals after 1918, the Infantry School, and its equivalents for the other arms, played a central role in the production of the new publications.[109] A new edition of the *Ausbildungsvorschrift für die Infanterie* (Training Regulations for the Infantry), which included a volume dealing with command of an infantry battalion,[110] appeared during Rommel's time as an instructor. As commandant of one of the five War Schools, which would rely on the new manual as a centrepiece of their curriculum, he may have played a part in its preparation.

In summary, therefore, although Rommel was not selected for the General Staff and long smarted from the perceived rejection, he secured a series of prestigious postings that played to his strengths. In these, he took a leading role in the early training of successive cohorts of the army's new officers. His lectures, based on his personal experiences and approach to combat, were hugely popular. Far from being considered controversial, he was regarded with favour by his superiors, and received promotion and further key appointments in the officer training system. Published in book form, his lectures became virtually required reading for all officer candidates. It would be difficult to find a career path closer to the military establishment for an officer who was not a member of the General Staff, or one with greater potential to shape the thinking and command approach of junior officers throughout the army. While not a member of the innermost elite, the suggestion Rommel was an outsider should therefore be rejected.

France, May 1940: Crossing the Meuse at Dinant

Given that Rommel's command approach, as presented in his lectures and books, was received with such favour by the military establishment, it is necessary to identify its key elements, as demonstrated in the action that brought him to international attention in May 1940 – the crossing of the Meuse at Dinant.

Significant source material is available concerning this action. Apart from Rommel's own account of events[111] and the (generally rather brief) narratives presented by his many biographers,[112] the crossing is covered in some detail by several histories of both

109 Edgar Graf von Matuschka, 'Organisationsgeschichte des Heeres', in *Handbuch zur deutschen Militärgeschichte, 1648-1939, vol. VI: Reichswehr und Republik (1918-1933)*, ed. by Militärgeschichtliches Forschungsamt (Munich: Bernard & Graefe, 1970), p. 339.

110 *HDv130/9: Ausbildungsvorschrift für die Infanterie, Heft 9: Führung und Kampf der Infanterie. Das Infanterie-Bataillon* (Berlin: Offene Worte, 1940).

111 *Rommel Papers*, pp.3-14.

112 Young, *Rommel*, pp.66-67, Irving, *Fox*, pp.38-46, Lewin, *Rommel*, pp.13-15, Fraser, *Knight's Cross*, pp.166-173, Caddick-Adams, *Rommel*, pp.223-224, Butler, *Field Marshal*, pp.154-162, Remy, *Rommel*, pp.48-51, and Showalter, *Patton and Rommel*, pp.177-183.

the wider campaign[113] and of 7th Panzer Division.[114]

The broad course of events during the critical period, from 12 to 15 May, is simply outlined (Map 3:1):

- 12 May: Having advanced 115km through the Ardennes in two and a half days, lead elements of 7th Panzer Division reached the Meuse in the early evening. Attempts to 'bounce' the defence failed, however, as the French succeeded in demolishing the bridges at Dinant and Yvoir, the latter literally as the first enemy scout car was crossing. Nonetheless, men of 8th Reconnaissance Battalion[115] became the first Germans to cross the river at any point when they slipped across an unguarded weir[116] at Houx just before midnight.

- 13 May: Despite this success, Rommel decided to focus his efforts on two other crossing sites, one immediately south of Houx and the other just to the north of Dinant. Although the French occupied a string of concrete bunkers along the heights overlooking the river and enjoyed excellent artillery observation, by evening 7th Panzer Division, with only minimal air support, had successfully forced bridgeheads at both points.

- 14 May: Rommel pushed elements of 7th Rifle Regiment forward to Onhaye, 5km west of Dinant, only to have to rush to their rescue with the few tanks that had so far been ferried across the river, when reports suggested they were surrounded. Fortunately, the news was simply a mishearing of a radio message. Rommel, however, pressed on further, reaching Morville, 12km beyond the Meuse, by nightfall.

- 15 May: In the morning, Rommel's 25th Panzer Regiment encountered the French 1st Armoured Division at Flavion. Once German reinforcements had arrived, Rommel pushed 7th Panzer Division around the enemy flank and drove headlong westwards, reaching Cerfontaine, 50km beyond the Meuse.[117]

---

113 John Williams, *The Ides of May. The Defeat of France, May-June 1940* (London: Constable, 1968), pp.138-203, Alistair Horne, *To Lose a Battle: France 1940* (Harmondsworth: Penguin, 1979), pp.295-300 & 308-321, Frieser, *Blitzkrieg Legend*, pp.223-239, and Faris R. Kirkland, 'The French Officer Corps and the Fall of France, 1920-1940' (unpublished doctoral dissertation, Pennsylvania University, 1982), pp.356-381.

114 Alfred Tschimpke, *Die Gespenster-Division: Mit der Panzerwaffe durch Belgien und Frankreich*, 2nd ed. (Munich: NSDAP, 1940), pp.44-64, Stolfi, *Bias for Action*, pp.1-18, and Scheibert, *Gespenster-Division*, pp.26-29.

115 Part of 5th Panzer Division, temporarily under Rommel's command, rather than 7th Panzer Division proper, Frieser, *Blitzkrieg Legend*, p.228-229.

116 The weir lay at the boundary between the French II and XI Corps, so neither was focused on this vulnerable point.

117 Guy Chapman, *Why France Collapsed* (London: Cassell, 1968), pp.130-137.

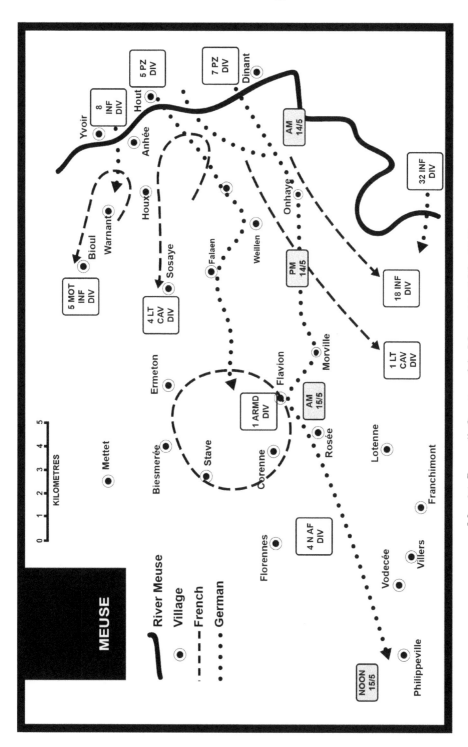

Map 3:1: Rommel's Crossing of the Meuse, 12–15 May 1940

Penetration of such depth, coupled with a similar advance by Guderian's forces advancing from Sedan in the south, caused the French Ninth Army to collapse, tearing a gap in the defensive front over 100km wide and sowing the seeds of defeat in the minds of France's leaders.

What of Rommel's personal command approach? A number of factors have been highlighted in the literature. Fraser noted his tendency to lead from the front, placing himself at the critical point of the battle, and his 'rapidity and energy'.[118] Telp also emphasised Rommel's leadership from the front, his concern for maintaining momentum, and his personal courage.[119] Stolfi remarked on his presence, leadership, speed and relentlessness.[120] Showalter commented on Rommel's aggressive spirit and personal leadership from the front, coupled with a reliance on subordinates to act independently when he was elsewhere.[121] Oetting underlined Rommel's feel for tactics, his confident leadership from the front, and his overriding drive to advance.[122] Sigg highlighted his rapid and aggressive pressure to advance, his leadership from the front, and his willingness to ignore orders if the local situation suggested a better course of action.[123] Butler emphasised his focus on attacking the 'enemy's will to fight: [through] rapid movement, flanking attacks, concentrated firepower, surprise'.[124]

Taken together, and reflecting on the events of these four days, it is here suggested three aspects stand out:

- His personal presence at the key points of the battle, even in the face of great physical danger;
- His insistence on speed, both of action and movement, and hence maintaining tempo; and
- His coolness and decisiveness in the face of unexpected and changing situations.

These characteristics are most typical of the command approach here termed Directive Control, where the commander recognises he can best reduce the Knowledge Gap through his personal presence at the key point, but reduces the Alignment Gap by expecting his subordinates elsewhere to act on their own initiative. As noted in Chapter One, the combination of this forward command and reliance on initiative permits a very rapid tempo of operations, allowing the commander to get inside the enemy's decision loop and hence achieve surprise, thereby increasing the level of friction experienced by the enemy and so reducing their combat effectiveness.[125]

118 Fraser, *Knight's Cross*, pp.206-209.
119 Telp, 'Rommel and 1940', pp.49-53.
120 Stolfi, *Bias for Action*, pp.8-9.
121 Showalter, *Patton and Rommel*, pp.175-177.
122 Oetting, *Auftragstaktik*, p.201.
123 Sigg, *Unterführer*, 243-244.
124 Butler, *Field Marshal*, p.159.
125 See Showalter, *Patton and Rommel*, pp.170-171.

Rommel's ubiquitous presence throughout the battle is striking – as the history of 7th Panzer Division prepared under his direction put it, 'He keeps appearing there, where it is fiercest'.[126] Wherever events were in doubt, Rommel would soon turn up, make the crucial decision, and lead its implementation from the front. Shuttling between the two crossing points on 13 May, Rommel saw both assaults were coming under heavy fire. At one, he ordered houses set alight to provide a smokescreen. At the other, he brought forward tanks to suppress the defenders. Recognising the unexpected opportunity for rapid exploitation once the bridgeheads had been achieved, he ordered the engineer battalion to stop building light 8-tonne pontoons and instead focus on the heavier 16-tonne ones that could ferry tanks across. He himself waded into the water to help get the work started. The following day, he personally led the tanks to rescue the advanced infantry believed surrounded at Onhaye. On 15 May, Rommel rode with the tanks of 25th Panzer Regiment as they engaged, and then bypassed, the French 1st Armoured Division at Flavion. Soon after, he personally led a company of tanks back from the deepest point of the penetration, in order to establish contact with the infantry following behind. What stands out is both Rommel's ability to be at the key point at the critical moment – a demonstration of his *Fingerspitzengefühl* – and his clear belief in the principle of 'the leader at the *Schwerpunkt*'. Rommel also clearly wanted this practice to be noted by his superiors: in the division's after action report for these critical days of battle, his personal presence at the front is noted in every single paragraph.[127] As Showalter noted, 'Rommel's style of command depended on the control exercised by a general who appeared from nowhere and took charge of critical situations.'[128]

The physical danger into which Rommel placed himself was significant, as he repeatedly came under enemy fire. He was in one of the first boats to cross the Meuse, in the face of heavy defensive fire. The next day, his tank was hit twice and came to rest, almost on its side, in full view of French anti-tank guns. In both cases, men around him were killed and he himself was slightly wounded.[129] Oberleutnant Hans von Luck, a company commander in 37th Reconnaissance Battalion, recorded these actions had a striking effect on the men of the division: '"Is Rommel immune?" we asked ourselves.'[130]

Not only did this extreme visibility of the new divisional commander steady the troops when they wavered in the face of heavy French fire,[131] it also allowed Rommel to maintain a very rapid tempo of operations. Even though the first German

126 Tschimpke, *Gespenster-Division*, p.53.
127 Kurzer Gefechtsbericht der 7.Pz.Div. für die Zeit v.10.-29.5.40, in Irving Collection, Rommel's Career, imgs.142-143.
128 Showalter, *Patton and Rommel*, p.192.
129 *Rommel Papers*, pp.8-15.
130 Hans von Luck, *Panzer Commander: The Memoirs of Colonel Hans von Luck* (London: Cassell, 2002), p.38.
131 Tschimpke, *Gespenster-Division*, pp.53-55.

reconnaissance troops only reached the Meuse at 1745 hours on 12 May,[132] and made the initial tentative crossing over the weir at Houx just before midnight, Rommel ensured both of his infantry regiments launched their assaults at 0530 hours the next morning. This was despite the fact they had only a few hours, during the middle of the night, in which to prepare their orders and move into position. Once the bridgeheads had been gained, he insisted his exhausted infantry push forward through the night, advancing 5km to reach Onhaye before dawn on 14 May. When it seemed these troops had been surrounded, Rommel's insistence that tanks be quickly ferried across the river, rather than wait for a bridge to be built, paid dividends, as he was able to respond immediately with an armoured force of just fifteen panzers. Again, rather than consolidate at Onhaye after French counterattacks had been repulsed, Rommel advanced at 1930 hours, penetrating a further 7 km to reach Morville at 2230 hours. On 15 May, once 31st Panzer Regiment of 5th Panzer Division had pinned the French 1st Armoured Division at Flavion, Rommel immediately disengaged 7th Panzer Division, in order to press on still further westwards, only halting for the night around 1900 hours.[133] By then, his troops had advanced 160km in just six days, despite continual enemy resistance.

These advances meant Rommel was now operating deep within the French zone of forces, repeatedly crossing new lines of resistance declared by the enemy higher command even before these could be manned by the confused defenders. 7th Panzer Division had completely lost touch with the German troops on its flanks and with 5th Panzer Division some 25km to its rear. Despite this exposed position, as in many other unexpected situations during the previous days, Rommel remained entirely calm.

When the initial crossings on 13 May had begun to falter, the assault pioneers declaring they could make no further progress, 'The General [Rommel][134] does not allow himself to be disconcerted. The word "impossible" does not exist for him. Not even for a second does he hesitate. Control of the action lies with the attacker, he does not allow it to be wrested from him.'[135] When French tanks attacked the weak bridgehead, Rommel instantly ordered his men to fire tracer rounds from their machineguns – the enemy thought they faced anti-tank guns and retreated. When his infantry were believed surrounded at Onhaye, Rommel at once set off to relieve them with the few tanks immediately to hand. When he stumbled upon an entire French armoured division, he pushed past as soon as the enemy force could be fixed by a following panzer regiment, even though this had only thirty Panzer IIIs and IVs against almost one hundred and seventy French battle tanks.[136] As the divisional

132 German time. French time was an hour behind.
133 Stolfi, *Bias for Action*, pp.7-19.
134 Interestingly, Tschimpke's account never mentions Rommel by name, even though it was written under his personal direction.
135 Tschimpke, *Gespenster-Division*, p.52.
136 By the following morning, only 16 of the French tanks remained operational. Frieser, *Blitzkrieg Legend*, pp.236-239.

history recorded, success came from 'the lightning fast decisiveness of a single man, with the cool head of a leader and the combative heart of a frontline soldier.'[137]

Rommel was clearly comfortable with the tendency of combat to throw up sudden surprises, never allowing these to shake his calm understanding of the battle and surefooted control of his forces in order to seize every opportunity. This was a decisive factor in the ability of 7th Panzer Division to make progress, when it would have been so easy for the advance to have come to a standstill.[138] As Fraser encapsulated it, Rommel recognised that 'the pace of *offensive* battle is set by the decision of the commander, and that there is one critical point only where the decision can be taken – the point of contact. No man has ever been more alive to the importance of opportunism in battle. No man has ever been more conscious of time, of the fleeting nature of opportunity, of the rapidity with which the commander must act or react.'[139]

It should be noted Rommel's constant appearance at the critical point, and personal assumption of control at the climactic moment, did not reflect any lack of confidence in his subordinates.[140] He himself recognised his style of command was possible only because the 'officers of a panzer division must learn to think and act independently within the framework of the general plan and not wait until they receive orders'.[141] That his approach saved the lives of his subordinates can be in no doubt: during the four days under consideration, 7th Panzer Division suffered only one hundred and thirty fatalities (plus six missing) and four hundred and fifty-one wounded. More than three-quarters of these were lost during the crossing of the Meuse.[142] This represents a surprisingly low casualty bill for an opposed river crossing, let alone one followed by a pitched battle with an entire enemy armoured division.

Effect on the French

What was the impact of Rommel's approach on the French? It was designed to secure tempo and hence inflict surprise and shock his enemy, thereby reducing their effectiveness through overwhelming friction. Was this achieved?

In contrast with the richness of material regarding the German exploits, the French sources are quite sparse. This is unsurprising, since Ninth Army was officially disgraced, its commanders dismissed, its units broken up, and its personnel scattered. None of the senior officers within the formation published memoirs. A detailed account, however, was written immediately after the war by General Joseph

---

137 Tschimpke, *Gespenster-Division*, p.55.
138 Lieutenant-Colonel Ove Pappila, 'Rommel and the German 7th Panzer Division in France 1940: The Initial Days of the Campaign', *Kungl Krigsvetenskapsakademiens Handlingar Och Tidskrift* (2009), 73-101 (pp.97-99).
139 Fraser, *Knight's Cross*, p.172. Emphasis in original.
140 Showalter, *Patton and Rommel*, p.176.
141 Rommel, *Rommel Papers*, p.17.
142 Stolfi, *Bias for Action*, p.22.

Doumenc.[143] During the campaign, Doumenc had been chief of staff to the overall French commander-in-chief, General Maurice Gamelin, and had acted as his main link to General Alphonse-Joseph Georges, commander-in-chief of the Northeast Front.[144] He therefore had direct knowledge of events and access to the relevant official reports, yet was not personally implicated in the disaster.[145]

Despite widespread concerns regarding the morale of the French forces,[146] it is clear the troops on the ground, actually facing the German assault across the Meuse, generally fought with considerable determination and bravery. For example, First Lieutenant de Wispelaere of the Belgian engineers dashed forward under heavy fire to ignite the charges that successfully demolished the bridge at Yvoir while the Germans were in the act of crossing it, falling mortally wounded.[147] Similarly, Rommel's own account makes clear the fire brought down by the French 18th Division at Houx and Dinant was so heavy the men of 7th Panzer Division faltered: 'The crossing had now come to a complete standstill, with the officers badly shaken by the casualties which their men had suffered.'[148] The robust performance of the French infantry is all the more noteworthy, given they had not expected the Germans to reach the river for another three days, and had believed the enemy would require several further days to prepare an assault crossing. When Rommel attacked on 13 May, therefore, 18th Division was still in the midst of deploying, along an over-extended front.[149]

The performance of their commanders was less creditable. As a formation, 18th Division was already in a state of near chaos even before Rommel attacked, despite having made its approach march to the Meuse through friendly territory and by means of a pre-planned manoeuvre. Although the formation had been mobilised in September 1939, eight months earlier, only now was it discovered the divisional headquarters' radios did not work and there were no motorcycles to act as despatch riders. Out of touch with its sub-units, the division was essentially passive in the face of the German crossings – in contrast to Rommel, its commander, General de Brigade Camille Duffet, made no attempt to resolve his communication problems by personally viewing the front line.

Similarly, it was only around noon, more than six hours after 7th Panzer Division had begun its twin assaults, that the commanders of the two French corps (II and XI) facing the attacks reacted, ordering their reserves to launch major combined arms counterattacks to drive the Germans back across the river at Houx and Dinant

---

143 General Joseph Edouard Aimé Doumenc, *Histoire de la Neuvième Armee* (Paris: Arthaud, 1945).

144 Williams, *Ides*, p.109.

145 Kirkland, 'French Officer Corps', pp.357-358. Kirkland's account is largely drawn from Doumenc.

146 Horne, *Lose*, pp.138-141.

147 Frieser, *Blitzkrieg Legend*, p.226.

148 Rommel, *Rommel Papers*, p.9.

149 Kirkland, 'French Officer Corps', p.362.

respectively. Despite the growing urgency, these actions were repeatedly delayed, as units struggled to get into position. In the end, all that was achieved was a tentative probe by a single unsupported company of tanks – which Rommel drove off with tracer rounds. The artillery then insisted the entire operation be postponed until the next day, due to the falling darkness. The commander of Ninth Army, General André-George Corap, labelled the whole effort a 'comedy'.[150]

It is clear the French commanders were bewildered by the pace of the German advance, which had brought them to the Meuse several days earlier than expected, and were unable to react with any speed or coordination. Rommel's repeated decisions to advance ever further west, rather than consolidate (thereby maintaining his fast tempo), left the French constantly wrong-footed. Opportunities to counterattack the Germans where they were vulnerable were therefore missed and units were instead themselves surprised and overrun by the panzers. The disaster that engulfed 1st Armoured Division exemplifies both aspects.

On 13 May, the division, with around one hundred and seventy powerful modern tanks, was at Charleroi, only 40km from the crossings at Houx and Dinant. It was therefore in a good location from which to launch a counterattack that would have had every prospect of driving Rommel's infantry back into the river before any supporting tanks could be ferried across. Waiting for orders, however, it did nothing. Finally, alerted at midnight that it should prepare precisely such an attack, it still remained motionless for a further sixteen hours. Even when it did finally stir, the division took another five hours to move the 35km to Flavion. While Rommel was pushing his troops to their limits, insisting his infantry advance through the darkness, supported by only a few dozen tanks, 1st Armoured Division settled down for the night. On the morning of 15 May, the French were in the midst of refuelling when 25th Panzer Regiment suddenly burst in amongst them. Once again, the French soldiers fought with extraordinary bravery, but they had been placed in an impossible position by their commanders: more than one hundred and thirty tanks were destroyed in the resulting melee.[151]

While it is clear that the French Army had reached a nadir in its military culture, fixated by the dogma of the methodical linear defence,[152] nonetheless these weaknesses might not have proven fatal had Rommel not employed such a rapid and dynamic approach. Despite the courage of the French troops and the superior quality of much of their equipment, Ninth Army was left flat-footed by the tempo of 7th Panzer Division's advance. The psychological confusion this generated in Corap and his

150 Kirkland, 'French Officer Corps', pp.364-366, Chapman, *Collapsed*, p.111, and Frieser, *Blitzkrieg Legend*, pp.233-235.
151 Frieser, *Blitzkrieg Legend*, pp.235-239.
152 Robert Allan Doughty, *The Breaking Point: Sedan and the Fall of France, 1940* (Hamden, CT: Archon, 1990), pp. 324-326.

subordinates meant their formations acted with extreme timidity, leaving themselves open to be repeatedly surprised by Rommel's bold moves and hence defeated in detail.

Reaction of Rommel's Superiors

How did Rommel's superiors react to these bold moves by their newest panzer division commander?

On 13 May, Rommel returned to his divisional headquarters after one of his frequent visits to the attempted river crossings to find waiting for him both his immediate superior, General der Infanterie Hermann Hoth (XV Motorised Corps), and the army commander, Generaloberst Hans-Günther von Kluge (Fourth Army). The meeting appears to have been intended purely to ensure Hoth and Kluge understood the situation, rather than reflect any lack of confidence in their impetuous subordinate, as Rommel immediately drove back to the front and continued his efforts to inspire the troops crossing the Meuse.[153] This interpretation of the meeting is supported by the fact that, in similar circumstances on the following day, Guderian, commanding XIX Panzer Corps, visited the commanders of two of his divisions. He was then himself visited by Generaloberst Gerd von Rundstedt, commander of Army Group A.[154]

It was only after the Meuse had been crossed that Rommel's behaviour as a commander became especially bold, as shown by his daring thrusts ever deeper into the French interior and his driving of his troops well past nightfall. Yet, notwithstanding Sigg's negative comments about 'wilfulness',[155] there is no sense he took these actions without the full support of his commanders. At 0900 on 14 May, Hoth gave Rommel command of the elements of 5th Panzer Division that had managed to cross the Meuse, ignoring the complaints of that division's commander.[156] On 16 May, Kluge again visited Rommel's headquarters, who noted he 'gave complete approval to our plan'.[157] A few days later, on Hitler's personal instruction, Rommel was awarded the Knight's Cross, one of Germany's highest military honours,[158] the first divisional commander to be so recognised in the campaign.[159]

After the campaign had been won, Hoth, in an 'after action' report regarding XV Motorised Corps, centred his account on the exploits of 7th Panzer Division. He emphasised both his own efforts to ensure it pressed forward quickly and deeply into the enemy forces, and the contribution this made to the campaign as a whole.[160] Similarly, Kluge, commenting on the draft official history of the division's experiences, ended

---

153 *Rommel Papers*, p.9.
154 Guderian, *Panzer Leader*, p.11.
155 Sigg, *Unterführer*, pp.243-246.
156 Frieser, *Blitzkrieg Myth*, pp.232-233 & Stolfi, *Bias for Action*, p.10.
157 *Rommel Papers*, p.17.
158 *Rommel Papers*, pp.39 & 42.
159 Showalter, *Patton and Rommel*, p.193.
160 Stolfi, *Bias for Action*, pp.38-41.

his letter with the words, 'Be reassured, my dear Rommel, that I will always remember with especial thanks my experience with the 7th Panzer Division, and especially with you, and nothing would be dearer to me than were I to find this especially valued formation under my command again.'[161]

Had Rommel been perceived as acting unacceptably outside the German doctrine, there was ample opportunity for his superiors to rein him in. Neither Hoth nor Kluge did so. Indeed, they reinforced his successes at the expense of other formations, suggesting they regarded his behaviour as entirely acceptable. His actions may have left his own superiors as uncertain of 7th Panzer Division's location as were his opponents, but the outstanding results that came from this behaviour gave him the right to continue in that same vein.[162] Rommel's application of Directive Control was therefore certainly not considered unacceptable.

Caporetto, October 1917 – Capturing Mount Matajur

As noted earlier, the literature reflects a general consensus that Rommel, lacking direct experience with armoured forces until taking up command of 7th Panzer Division in February 1940, instead drew heavily upon his experience as a mountain infantryman during the First World War. The analysis above has demonstrated that the key features of his approach during the Meuse battle were his personal presence and intervention at the key points of the engagement, his emphasis on speed and hence tempo, and his calmness in the face of the chaos and opportunity of battle. It is therefore necessary to explore whether these did indeed similarly characterise his technique two decades earlier, when serving with the *Königliches Württembergisches Gebirgs-Bataillon* (Royal Wurttemberg Mountain Battalion) (hereafter WMB).

Rommel's greatest military success during the First World War was without doubt his capture of Mount Matajur, during the opening stages of the Caporetto campaign in October 1917.[163] In contrast to the events in France in 1940, the sources for Rommel's experiences during this battle are much more limited, with most of his biographers[164] principally relying on the highly personalised account given in *Infantry Attacks*.[165] This is understandable, given that Rommel was at that time an unknown Oberleutnant (Lieutenant), whose exploits would normally be unlikely to merit reference in wider accounts.

161 Kluge to Rommel, 30 November 1940, in Irving Collection, Items Chronicling Rommel's Military Career, 1917-1941, img.112.
162 Oetting, *Auftragstaktik*, p.203.
163 Remy, *Rommel*, p.19.
164 Young, *Rommel*, pp.36-37, Irving, *Fox*, pp.13-15, Fraser, *Knight's Cross*, pp.62-73, Caddick-Adams, *Rommel*, pp.95-127, Remy, *Rommel*, pp.19-23, Showalter, *Patton and Rommel*, pp.62-73, and Butler, *Field Marshal*, pp.67-77.
165 Rommel, *Infantry Attacks*, pp.168-227.

Yet, in fact, there is rather more evidence available. The WMB's immediate after action report, written by its commander, Major Theodor Sprösser, survives.[166] Sprösser also edited a history of the unit,[167] which allows a crosscheck of Rommel's own narrative at key points and provides a slightly larger context to his very narrow focus. Further, a monograph on the battalion's exploits in the Caporetto campaign was subsequently written by one of Sprösser's co-authors, Helmut Schittenhelm. He appears to have been a member of Rommel's force during the battle and Rommel plays the central role in his account.[168]

Looking more broadly, since Mount Matajur was the centre of gravity (*Schwerpunkt*) of the entire Italian defensive position, its capture was described in the German official history, *Der Weltkrieg*.[169] The strategic perspective of that publication, however, meant its account did not go below divisional level. It merely attributed the success to the Bavarian Alpenkorps (Alpine Corps, actually a division-sized mountain formation), to which the WMB was attached. The account in *Der Weltkrieg*, however, was complemented by a volume in the Reichsarchiv's series of detailed campaign studies, *Schlachten des Weltkrieges* (Battles of the World War). Written by Konrad Krafft von Dellmensingen, who had raised the Alpenkorps in late 1914 and served as chief of staff of the Fourteenth Army at Caporetto, this presented a detailed account of the events surrounding the capture of Mount Matajur and of the part played by the WMB within this, mentioning Rommel several times by name.[170]

It is should be noted Sprösser publicly denounced Krafft's account, which he argued overplayed the actions of the Bavarian Life Guards within the Alpenkorps and overlooked the central role of the WMB, and in particular of Rommel (who, at the time of publication in 1926, was still only a captain, commanding a machine-gun company). Not only did Krafft use the second volume of his study to rebuff Sprösser's claims, but a footnote (which appears to have been written by staff from the Reichsarchiv) strongly criticised Sprösser's behaviour in making such public smears on the reputation of other units.[171] An element of care is therefore required when

---

166 Gefechts-Bericht über die Zeit vom 04.-31.10.1917 (1 November 1917), Irving Collection, Rommel's Career, imgs.257-267.

167 Generalmajor Theodor Sprösser, *Die Geschichte der Württembergischen Gebirgsschützen* (Die württembergischen Regimenter im Weltkrieg 1914-1918, Band 49) (Stuttgart: Belser, 1933).

168 Helmut Schittenhelm, *Wir zogen nach Friaul: Erlebnisse einer Kriegskameradschaft zwischen Isonzo und Piave* (Stuttgart: Thienemanns, 1939).

169 Kriegsgeschichtlichen Forschungsanstalt des Heeres, *Der Weltkrieg, 1914 bis 1918, Band 13: Die Kriegführung im Sommer und Herbst 1917, Die Ereignisse außerhalb der Westfront bis November 1918* (Berlin: Mittler, 1942), pp.230-250.

170 General der Artillerie Konrad Krafft von Dellmensingen, *Der Durchbruch am Isonzo, Teil 1: Die Schlact von Tolmein und Flitsch (24. bis 27. Oktober 1917)* (Berlin: Stalling, 1926), pp.59-67, 93-95, & 120-122.

171 General der Artillerie Konrad Krafft von Dellmensingen, *Der Durchbruch am Isonzo, Teil 2: Die Verfolgung über den Tagliamento bis zum Piave* (Berlin: Stalling, 1926), pp.291-292.

drawing on Sprösser and Rommel's accounts of the events at Mount Matajur. Given Schittenhelm's connections with both these officers, the same caution may be necessary with his account, though he did make repeated references to the contribution of other German units to the overall success achieved, thereby indicating a more balanced perspective.[172]

Interestingly, Irving suggested Rommel acted in a similar fashion to Sprösser twenty years later in his account of 7th Panzer Division's exploits in France in 1940, downplaying the role of neighbouring units and on occasion claiming credit for their successes.[173] Indeed, Cyril Falls (author of several volumes in the British Official History of the war and a noted military historian) suggested, 'Rommel was even more inclined to be boastful as a young man in the First World War than as a senior commander in the Second'. That said, Falls conceded 'the facts which he [Rommel] presents in his narrative cannot be disputed and are as extraordinary an example of skill and daring as can be found in the annals of modern warfare.'[174]

Beyond these German sources, for many years Falls' account was the only study of Caporetto at an operational level available in English. Given his need to cover the whole campaign, Falls understandably gave only a few pages to the specific actions in which Rommel was involved and based his narrative largely on *Infantry Attacks*.[175] John and Eileen Wilks, however, have recently published an account of the wider battle, and Rommel's specific part in it. This draws especially on the extensive Italian literature,[176] thereby allowing the interaction between the opponents to be more fully understood. Finally, Mark Thompson's study of the Italian Front during the war as a whole provides a useful broader context,[177] while John Gooch's recent monograph on the Italian Army during the war offers valuable insights.[178]

Before considering the events of October 1917, however, brief mention should be made of the unusual character of the WMB. Expanded from a single company in October 1915 through drawing personnel (including Rommel) from across the small kingdom's army (which had remained to some extent distinct from the far larger forces of Prussia),[179] the WMB was a highly unusual unit. Despite its name, it was in fact little smaller than a regiment, possessing six infantry companies and six machine-gun platoons,[180] organised into three machine-gun companies. Rather than being assigned

172 For example, Schittenhelm, *Friaul*, pp.41-43.
173 Irving, *Trail of the Fox*, pp.51-52.
174 Captain Cyril Falls, *Caporetto, 1917* (London: Weidenfeld & Nicholson, 1966), p.52.
175 Falls, *Caporetto*, pp.40-53.
176 John Wilks and Eileen Wilks, *Rommel and Caporetto* (Barnsley: Cooper, 2001).
177 Mark Thompson, *The White War: Life and Death on the Italian Front, 1915-1919* (London: Faber & Faber, 2008).
178 John Gooch, *The Italian Army and the First World War* (Cambridge: Cambridge University Press, 2014).
179 Hermann Cron, *Imperial German Army 1914-18: Organisation, Structure, Orders-of-Battle*, trans. by C.F. Colton (Solihull: Helion, 2001), p.13.
180 Sprösser, *Gebirgsschützen*, p.43.

permanently to a single division, as was the norm for line infantry units, the battalion was used as a specialist unit, deployed at key points, often under command of the Alpenkorps, the Kaiserheer's only other mountain formation.

By October 1917, it had become the norm for Sprösser to divide the WMB into two or three *Abteilungen* (detachments) of varying size and composition, dependent upon the nature of the mission.[181] As *Infantry Attacks* and the unit history both make clear, although Rommel was formally only a company commander, he usually had responsibility for one of these detachments – in effect, a small battalion. In his account, Rommel referred to this *ad hoc* unit as the *Abteilung Rommel* (the Rommel Detachment). Caddick-Adams interpreted this as displaying an element of self-promotion.[182] However, Sprösser consistently used the same terminology in his history of the battalion, showing this was no quirk of Rommel's.[183] In fact, the naming of units after their commander was a longstanding and universal German military practice.[184] For example, corps commands were in practice named after their commander or the area where they were deployed, rather than their formal designation:[185] two of Fourteenth Army's corps at Caporetto, *General Kommando* (General Command) (GenKdo) 51 and III Bavarian Corps (which included the WMB), were referred to as Gruppe Berrer, after Generalleutnant Albert von Berrer, and Gruppe Stein, after General der Artillerie Hermann von Stein, their respective commanders.[186]

As has been noted, the capture of Mount Matajur represented the pinnacle of Rommel's war record: as an instructor between the wars, he was to recount his part in it more than three hundred times.[187] The broad course of the events in which Rommel and the WMB were involved, from 24 to 26 October, is simply outlined:[188]

- 24 October: Advancing in the first wave of the attack, the Rommel Detachment found the Italian front line shattered by the artillery bombardment. Advancing silently into the defensive zone, Rommel repeatedly manoeuvred around Italian posts, until he reached the summit of Mount Hlevnik. Coming under artillery fire, Rommel advanced yet further, penetrating more than a mile into the Italian position, halting only as night fell.
- 25 October: Moving off before dawn, the Rommel Detachment crept along the northern slopes of the Kolovrat ridge. After a mile and a half, Rommel launched a surprise assault, causing the defenders to surrender immediately. Advancing still further, Rommel forced an entire battalion of the Italian 213th

181 Wilks, *Caporetto*, pp.19-20.
182 Caddick-Adams, *Monty and Rommel*, p.98.
183 Sprösser, *Gebirgsschützen*, p.275.
184 *Rommel Papers*, p.10n1.
185 Cron, *Imperial German Army*, pp.87-89.
186 Sprösser, *Gebirgsschützen*, p.258 and Wilks, *Caporetto*, p.47.
187 Hesse, Wandlung, Irving Collection, img.321.
188 Sprösser, *Gebirgsschützen*, p.271-285 and Wilks, *Caporetto*, pp.91-116.

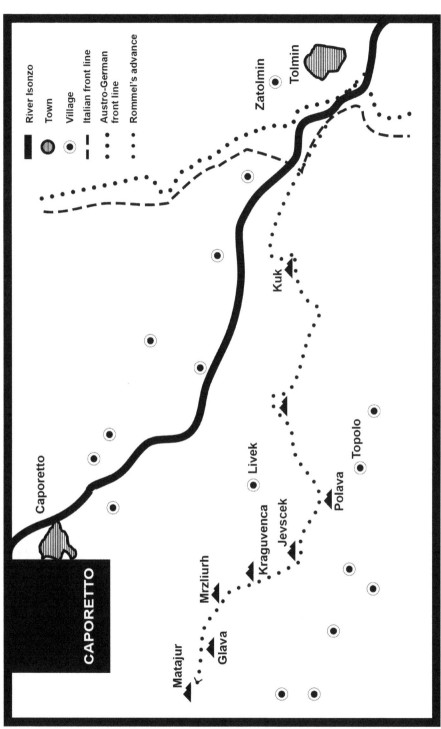

Map 3:2: Rommel's Capture of Mount Matajur, 24-26 October 1917

Regiment on Mount Nagnoj to yield by manoeuvring one of his companies to its rear. Now well behind the Italian lines, Rommel's men moved at a run to block the road to the village of Luico. Here, they surprised a complete brigade (14th and 20th *Bersaglieri* Regiments) on the march, taking two thousand men prisoner.

- 26 October: Moving through the night, Rommel led his men towards Mount Cragonza, which he seized through a sudden assault. Maintaining his rapid tempo, he surprised the Italian defenders of Mount Mrzli and, armed only with a white handkerchief, persuaded three battalions of the 89th Regiment to surrender. Although ordered to withdraw, due to a misunderstanding of the situation by Sprösser, Rommel pressed on with just a hundred men towards the ultimate prize of Mount Matajur, the lynchpin of the entire Italian position. Making good use of his trusty handkerchief, Rommel persuaded its garrison, twelve hundred men of the 90th Regiment, to lay down their arms. This brought his total haul of prisoners in those three days to over nine thousand, along with eighty-one guns, at the cost of just six dead and thirty men wounded.

Having achieved such an astonishing feat of arms, Rommel (and Sprösser's) frustration was understandable at discovering that, due to an error in map reading, Leutnant Schneider of Infanterie-Regiment 63 was credited with the capture of Mount Matajur and so secured the *Pour le Mérite*[189] that Rommel so coveted. Schittenhelm noted how the men of the WMB found the news impossible to comprehend, and Rommel personally took it particularly hard.[190] Fortunately, the Wurttembergers continued their efforts in a similar vein over the rest of the campaign, such that both Rommel and Sprösser received the famous medal in December, causing the former to note, with evident satisfaction, 'Two awards was a hitherto unheard-of honour for one battalion.'[191]

Before exploring the extent to which Rommel displayed the same characteristics in his approach at Mount Matajur as he was to do in 1940, it is worth pausing to consider Krafft's comments about his achievements. Immediately following the section describing the award to Schneider, where his text implicitly conceded an error had been made in giving the former the credit for seizing the key position, Rommel was described as an 'excellent and energetic leader'. Krafft went on to record that the actions of the Rommel Detachment were 'shining brightly in terms of their perseverance, cheerful application, skill and self-reliance'.[192] These words would hardly seem to justify the fury so publicly expressed by Sprösser.

189 Wilks, *Caporetto*, pp.114-116.
190 Schittenhelm, *Friaul*, pp.42-43.
191 Rommel, *Infantry Attacks*, pp.263-264.
192 Krafft, *Isonzo*, vol. 1, pp.120-121.

The first characteristic of Rommel's approach in May 1940 was his continual personal presence and intervention at the key point of the engagement. Given that, at Mount Matajur, he was commanding a force never larger than seven companies and at one point comprising only a hundred men,[193] all moving by foot over very rough mountain terrain, the scope for Rommel to move between different areas of the battlefield was limited. It would in any case be expected that an officer in these circumstances would be close to the action.

Nonetheless, although Rommel repeatedly led the way personally, it is clear this was done through calculated intent, rather than mere bravado. On the morning of 24 October, he reconnoitred at the head of his column as it advanced towards Mount Hlevnik, in order to ensure full advantage was taken of the available cover to outflank the Italian position.[194] At other times, Rommel placed himself behind the point platoon, in order to be in a position to respond quickly as the situation became clear.[195] In combat, Rommel's personal presence in securing a successful result was vital. On 25 October, when blocking the road to Luico, Rommel stood at the front of his positions and waved his handkerchief to convince the surprised Italian marching column to surrender, though a fierce firefight was required before two thousand men of the 4th Bersaglieri Brigade capitulated.[196] The following day, on Mount Mrzli, Rommel again led his men, handkerchief in hand, against fifteen hundred Italians. This time, the defenders panicked and surrendered without a shot.[197] Finally, later the same day, the handkerchief yet again proved decisive, when Rommel used it to capture the stunned men of the Salerno Brigade, twelve hundred strong.[198]

At each stage of the battle, therefore, Rommel carefully determined where he should position himself – sometimes a little way back, in order to be able to make a quick assessment of the changing situation, at other times right at the front of his men, in order to impose his personality and determination onto the action. This was not without personal danger. During the initial advance, a falling stone crushed Rommel's right foot so badly that for some time he needed the help of two men to carry on.[199] Later the same day, Rommel noted that, while he undertook a visual reconnaissance, an Italian machine-gun 'frequently obliged me to abandon my observations and dive for cover.'[200] The risks Rommel took when using his handkerchief to precipitate repeated Italian surrenders were, of course, extreme. His physical bravery and willingness to lead from the front were hardly in doubt.

193 Rommel, *Infantry Attacks*, pp.208 & 223.
194 Rommel, *Infantry Attacks*, pp.178-179, Wilks, *Caporetto*, p.94, & Schittenhelm, *Friaul*, pp.27-28.
195 Rommel, *Infantry Attacks*, pp.173-175.
196 Rommel, *Infantry Attacks*, pp.202-204, & Schittenhelm, *Friaul*, p.35.
197 Rommel, *Infantry Attacks*, pp.220-221, & Schittenhelm, *Friaul*, p.39.
198 Rommel, *Infantry Attacks*, pp.223-224.
199 Rommel, *Infantry Attacks*, p.175.
200 Rommel, *Infantry Attacks*, p.180.

The second characteristic of Rommel's approach in 1940 was his insistence on speed and the maintenance of tempo. This was repeatedly displayed during the fighting around Mount Matajur. As darkness fell on 24 October, Rommel ordered his men, who had been in action since shortly after daybreak,[201] to undertake combat reconnaissance during the night, while he himself worked out how to continue the attack the following day. Presenting his plan to Sprösser as soon as the latter reached the position at 0500 hours, Rommel was on the move again before dawn.[202]

During the intense fighting over the following two days, Rommel repeatedly emphasised the importance of speed and of making good use of time: tempo. On Mount Nagnoj and the Kolovrat ridge, he noted, 'A second's delay might have snatched away the victory which lay in our grasp. [...] Seconds separated us from our fate.'[203] Later that day, he noted the importance of giving the Italians as little time as possible to dig in, while ensuring the time available was used by his own men for a thorough preparation of the planned attack.[204] Schittenhelm noted, 'What drove them forward was the tried and tested experience that a wavering enemy should be given no time in which to recover their balance.'[205] Rommel sought to inspire his troops by urging them, 'Never give in. Never go back. Always straight towards the foe!'[206]

Perhaps the most striking example of Rommel's emphasis on tempo was when he cut the road to Luico, well behind the Italian lines. Rommel recorded how he 'tore down the road with the head of my detachment. [... The Italians] were all paralyzed by our sudden appearance. We rushed on [..., causing the garrison of Ravna to flee.] We followed right on their heels. [...] I did not wish to lose momentum [...] but wanted to act rapidly and in a decisive direction. There was no time for lengthy deliberations. [...] We moved on at the double!'[207] Nightfall offered no respite to the frenetic pace. Although the detachment bivouacked sometime after dark, a report from a patrol at 2230 hours that a key village ahead was undefended caused Rommel to set off again immediately.[208]

A sense of the consequences of this focus on maintaining pace emerges from the fact Rommel kept his men moving for fifty-two hours. During this time they marched 12 miles on the map, yet much further in practice, given the need in the process to ascend 8000 feet and descend 3000 feet, all the while carrying heavy equipment and engaging in often intense fighting.[209]

201 Rommel, *Infantry Attacks*, p.173.
202 Rommel, *Infantry Attacks*, pp.180-182 & 185.
203 Rommel, *Infantry Attacks*, pp.187-188.
204 Rommel, *Infantry Attacks*, p.194.
205 Schittenhelm, *Friaul*, p.40.
206 Schittenhelm, *Friaul*, p.39.
207 Rommel, *Infantry Attacks*, pp.198-201.
208 Rommel, *Infantry Attacks*, pp.208-210.
209 Rommel, *Infantry Attacks*, p.225.

Rommel's third characteristic in 1940 was his calmness and decisiveness in the face of the chaos and opportunity of battle. Again, this was foreshadowed in 1917. Early in the morning of 25 October, Rommel sought to surprise the Italian garrison of the Kolovrat ridge, silently infiltrating their positions. After making initial gains, the Italians began to respond: 'A few minutes had sufficed to change the situation completely in our disfavour and to make it very serious.' Far from becoming disconcerted or simply seeking to extricate his forces, however, Rommel's 'instinctive' appreciation of the situation[210] convinced him he could manoeuvre his forces in order to launch an attack against the rear of the Italian units threatening his men. After a brief fight, an entire enemy battalion of five hundred soldiers surrendered.[211]

Later that same day, having broken into the Italian position at Ravna, Rommel reached a knoll giving a splendid view into the depths of the enemy zone: 'I did not wish to lose momentum in Ravna but wanted to act rapidly and in a decisive direction. There was no time for lengthy deliberations. I rapidly weighed the three lines of action open to me.' These options were to: broaden the gap in the Italian line by attacking Mount Kuk to Rommel's right, seize the Luico Pass in order to open the way for the German 12th Division, or cut off the Italian forces in Luico itself. Coolly assessing the situation,[212] he quickly rejected the first option as unnecessary, since Mount Kuk would soon fall anyway. He discounted the second as well, as it would leave the enemy in Luico able to withdraw. Rommel therefore settled upon the third, and riskiest, option, as it would create a situation in which 'the encircled enemy could not have avoided annihilation or capture.' Despite concerns his force was already dangerously dispersed, Rommel did not hesitate but immediately set off at the double into the depths of the Italian position[213] – an action one historian assessed as moving 'beyond bold into the brash, and possibly slightly crazy'.[214]

The following day, Rommel's awareness of the need to seize opportunities was shown yet again at Mount Mrzli. Faced by three Italian battalions, yet accompanied by only a handful of his own men, Rommel would have been forgiven for hesitating, or even for deciding withdrawal was the most sensible course of action. Instead, he felt 'forced to act before the adversary decided to do something […]. I had the impression that I must not stand still or we were lost.' Advancing to within 150 yards of the silently watching enemy, Rommel's boldness caused panic amongst the defenders, with the entire formation throwing away its weapons and even shooting one of its own officers who hesitated to surrender.[215]

The final example of Rommel's boldness came at Mount Matajur itself. Advancing from Mount Mrzli, Rommel was suddenly ordered to pull back by Spösser, who had

210 Schittenhelm, *Friaul*, p.32.
211 Rommel, *Infantry Attacks*, pp.188-191.
212 Schittenhelm, *Friaul*, p.34.
213 Rommel, *Infantry Attacks*, pp.199-201.
214 Butler, *Field Marshal*, p.71.
215 Rommel, *Infantry Attacks*, pp.220-221.

assumed the mass of prisoners taken by the detachment meant the objective had already been taken. For once, Rommel took a few moments to ponder the situation, during which time all but one hundred of his men withdrew. Then he reached a decision: 'No! The battalion order was given without knowledge of the situation [...]. Unfinished business remained.' Vigorous action by his small remaining force allowed him to seize the key objective, taking a further twelve hundred prisoners in the process.[216]

In summary, therefore, it may be seen the characteristics Rommel displayed as a Generalmajor commanding a panzer division in May 1940 – his personal presence and intervention at the key points of the engagement, his emphasis on speed and tempo, and his calmness and decisiveness in the face of the chaos and opportunity of battle – were indeed equally apparent when he was an Oberleutnant commanding a group of mountain infantry companies in October 1917.

Effect on the Italians

What was the effect of Rommel's approach on the Italians? We have seen it was decisive and shattering, evidenced by the vast haul of prisoners taken, and the tiny number of casualties suffered, by the WMB. But units do not surrender for no reason, even when faced by soldiers of Rommel's ilk.

Rommel himself found the collapse of the Italian regiments facing him 'incomprehensible'. He put it down to two factors. First, he believed the Italians were not prepared for the 'supple' tactics employed by the Germans. As a result, when these unexpectedly appeared in their flanks or rear, the defenders 'regarded their situation as hopeless and gave up fighting prematurely'. Second, Rommel believed the war had become very unpopular with the ordinary Italian soldiers, such that they had limited resolve in the fight. In combination, the result was fatal: 'Perplexity and inactivity have frequently led to catastrophes. The councils of the mass undermined the authority of the leaders.' As the Italian officers hesitated in the face of unexpected German tactics, their limited hold over their unwilling troops evaporated, allowing these to surrender before the officers could react.[217]

The German accounts of Rommel's actions were all written without the benefit of access to Italian sources. Although many of the senior Italian commanders published memoirs soon after the war, these were frequently self-justifying in the face of disaster. It was not until 1967 that the Italian official history was released – the last of all the major powers' accounts to appear – though perhaps this distance was beneficial, in that its 'comprehensive and critical account of events [...] remains the one essential Italian' source.[218] For historians without a grasp of the Italian language, John and

216 Rommel, *Infantry Attacks*, pp.223-225.
217 Rommel, *Infantry Attacks*, pp.225-226.
218 Wilks, *Caporetto*, p.2.

Eileen Wilks have done a great service through their drawing on these sources for an anglophone audience.

The Italian *Comando Supremo*, General Luigi Cadorna was immediately in no doubt the defeat was due to the defending troops, who had 'retreated without fighting or had ignominiously surrendered unharmed to the enemy'. [219] Even before it was issued, his staff officers recognised the statement would damage his public reputation severely.[220] Cadorna followed this up, even while the retreat was still in full flood, with instructions to his field commanders to undertake detailed enquiries to identify and punish 'the traitors, the cowards, the slackers' responsible for the disaster.[221]

By contrast, John and Eileen Wilks suggested a more balanced explanation, arguing that 'so many different circumstances coalesced against the Italians that both chance and fortune seem to have deserted them altogether.'[222] Their explanation brought together the impact of the fierce winter storm that affected the battlefield on the opening day of the offensive, the confusion and distance of the senior Italian commanders, the ineffective response of the defensive artillery, and the already poor morale of the Italian infantry.[223] John Gooch equally highlighted how the Italian 'command arrangements and strategy were both in a state of some confusion' immediately before the offensive was launched.[224] But, although these factors undoubtedly all contributed to the collapse witnessed by Rommel, they do not provide sufficient answer to the question why so many men surrendered at that point, yet others were to fight with fierce bravery elsewhere and on subsequent days.

Understanding the reasons for the Italian collapse, and the contribution to this made by Rommel's specific approach to command, must start with an assessment of the defensive positions.[225] The Italian defensive model was based on a series of three lines. The first of these simply marked the limit of the previous offensive advance. Almost by definition, this line would be unsuited to an effective defence. In recognition of this fact, the second line was positioned some distance to the rear, along more propitious ground, and was intended to provide the main zone of resistance. Behind this, a third line had been marked as the rearward boundary for the defence, placed along the very strongest terrain.

While this model was not fundamentally different from that employed on the Western Front, often to great effect, its potential strength was undermined by four critical factors. First, despite the weakness of the first line, Cadorna had made clear his expectation every foot of the ground captured from the Austrians during the painful advances undertaken over the previous thirty months must be held, without

---

219 Quoted in Wilks, *Caporetto*, p.66.
220 Gooch, *Italian Army*, p.244.
221 Quoted in Gooch, *Italian Army*, p.245.
222 Wilks, *Caporetto*, p.67.
223 Wilks, *Caporetto*, pp.67-90.
224 Gooch, *Italian Army*, p.229.
225 Falls, *Caporetto*, pp.36-37, and Wilks, *Caporetto*, pp.33-37

hint of withdrawal. Although Cadorna ended up having a shouting match with the commander of Second Army, General Luigi Capello, when he discovered how far forward the troops were, yet he himself had approved the plans.[226] As a result, the majority of the defending forces were deployed here, placing them at risk of being overwhelmed by the initial German artillery bombardment and infantry assault.

Second, the mountainous nature of the terrain meant talk of defensive 'lines' was illusory, with troops instead deployed in a multitude of separate locations, which often failed to provide mutual support and left numerous gaps through which the Germans could infiltrate into the depths of the defensive system. The parallels are strong with the 'bird' cages' occupied by the men of the British Fifth Army when it collapsed in the face of German infiltration attacks in March 1918.[227]

Third, the reserves retained by Cadorna were very limited, both in number and quality, as well as being too far behind the front. The likelihood of these forces being able to react in sufficient time and strength to crush any German penetration through the first defensive line was low. Coupled with this, Second Army was huge and ramshackle, with twenty-five divisions spread between nine corps: far too large for nimble command. Moreover, Capello was in poor health and at times had handed over command to one of his corps commanders,[228] such that his ability to control the impending battle was questionable and there was a degree of confusion over who was actually in command at the moment the Germans and Austrians attacked. The defence would therefore be largely passive.

Finally, the Italian artillery was notoriously poor at ensuring coordination with the infantry, such that the troops in the front line could not rely upon receiving effective support from that quarter. Further, Cadorna, expecting a prolonged battle, had ordered his subordinates to be parsimonious with their ammunition, firing only when absolutely necessary.[229] Even that little which might have been expected from the artillery was effectively eliminated on the front of XXVII Corps, facing the Alpenkorps: its commander, General Pietro Badoglio, insisted that his guns should open fire only on his personal instruction, an instruction that did not come until well after the German offensive had started.[230] Indeed, both Rommel and Schittenhelm made almost no mention of Italian artillery fire in their accounts.

Turning to the men deployed into the defensive positions, they were in a fragile state even before Rommel launched his attacks. Due to failings in the preparations by senior commanders, many of the troops were deployed into their defensive positions only on the eve of the battle.[231] As Krafft noted, the action began during a fierce winter storm, which made it necessary to yell to be heard and soaked the troops,

226 Gooch, *Italian Army*, pp.229 & 233.
227 Samuels, *Command or Control?*, pp.207-214.
228 Wilks, *Caporetto*, pp.68-73.
229 Gooch, *Italian Army*, pp.239-240.
230 Falls, *Caporetto*, p.4, and Wilks, *Caporetto*, pp.85-87
231 Wilks, *Caporetto*, p.68.

who were left shivering with the cold.[232] Since the Italian defence was based on the high ground, while the Germans advanced through the valleys,[233] the weather may have affected the defenders more severely than the attackers. Quite apart from these physical impacts, the thick mist meant the newly deployed troops were often unable to get their bearings and so remained unfamiliar with the terrain around them.

To this sense of physical discomfort and spatial disorientation must be added the poor relationship between officers and men in the Italian Army. Schittenhelm recorded the Italian troops used to sing, 'While General Cadorna eats juicy sausages, the soldiers have dry chestnuts'.[234] Not only were the officers notoriously 'lazy and remote from their men',[235] but control was officially to be maintained through coercion and threat of violence. While the numbers of courts martial and executions in the Italian Army were comparable to (though still somewhat higher than) in the British Army, it was well known Cadorna favoured the decisive application of summary justice, and even literal decimation of units that had performed badly.[236] The sense of the army's 'right to command' was therefore already weak before Rommel launched his attacks.[237]

Notwithstanding these many factors, which certainly made the Italian defence fragile, something was required to push the troops over the edge, from passive discontent to active surrender. The only factor that provides a convincing explanation for events is shock, taking David Rowland's definition of this as: 'Morale conditions causing stunning, paralysis or debilitating effect [...] on an organisation in combat'.[238] This paralysis was evident in the passive behaviour of many of the Italian troops, who simply watched and waited as Rommel advanced, waving his trusty handkerchief, even though determined action by even a single machine-gun crew might well have been sufficient to hold off the small numbers of the WMB.

Leo Murray has termed this behaviour 'freezing', where the brain suffers 'cognitive blink' as it focuses only on the threat and stops processing other information. Although this can enable men to make better decisions more quickly, 'once a man is doing nothing, he is that bit more likely to carry on doing nothing'. Such paralysis is highly contagious: 'The way men fight and whether they fight is dominated by what they see their mates doing: the more comrades a soldier can see, the stronger the effect.' As a consequence, 'once a tactic convinces half of the enemy to stop fighting, nearly everyone else follows them.' Murray summarised the effect: 'If the conditions are right

232 Krafft, *Isonzo*, vol. 1, p.66.
233 Wilks, *Caporetto*, pp.67-68.
234 Schittenhelm, *Friaul*, p.44.
235 Falls, *Caporetto*, p.4.
236 Wilks, *Caporetto*, pp.27-28
237 Thompson, *White War*, p.317.
238 David Rowland, *The Stress of Battle: Quantifying Human Performance in Combat* (London: TSO, 2006), p.178.

then almost any man will fight, but change those conditions and almost everybody will stop fighting.'[239]

Analysis of one hundred and seventy-four infantry actions by David Rowland and his colleagues at the Defence Operational Analysis Establishment indicated surprise was the dominant factor in causing shock.[240] The essence of surprise was found to be 'when an act or development has taken place contrary to expectations, thus proving assumptions to be ill founded. [...] The degree of surprise achieved is dependent not only on the victim's mistaken assumptions, but also on his lack of advance warning of the attack, and his lack of preparation to deal with the unexpected. [...] The effect is to deny the victim the time and space in which to [...] react'.[241]

In the case of the events around Mount Matajur, Rommel's characteristic approach was almost perfectly designed to inflict the maximum surprise on the Italians. His personal presence and intervention at the key points of the engagement, his emphasis on maintaining tempo, and his calmness in the face of the chaos and opportunity of battle together combined to increase the likelihood of the men of the WMB appearing at places, deep within the defensive zone, where they were least expected, and then acting with a speed and decisiveness that both increased the threat posed by his attack and denied the defenders time in which to develop an effective response.

But it is important to note this surprise would probably not have been sufficient in itself to cause the dramatic collapse experienced by the Italians. Rowland's analysis found surprise alone led to shock in only 15% of cases. It was in combination with other factors, notably low defence morale, that the probability of shock increased to 50%.[242] In short, while Rommel's approach was highly likely to lead to the enemy being surprised, it was his good fortune to be facing Italian forces already at a very low ebb of morale. It was this combination that led to the spectacular haul of prisoners secured.

Cadorna was therefore partially correct in his statement that many of the troops had surrendered without fighting. What he failed to recognise was his own actions had undermined the morale of the Italian forces and had therefore made them especially vulnerable to the speed and flexibility of Rommel's attack.

Response of Rommel's Superiors

As with the crossing of the Meuse in 1940, it is necessary to consider the response of Rommel's superiors to his bold actions.

239 Leo Murray, *Brains & Bullets: How Psychology Wins Wars* (London: Biteback, 2013), pp.91, 125, 130, 34.
240 Rowland, *Stress of Battle*, p.200.
241 Rowland, *Stress of Battle*, p.169.
242 Rowland, *Stress of Battle*, p.200.

First, it is very clear that, rather than acting on his own, with little regard for his superiors, Rommel in fact sought to maintain close contact with Sprösser throughout the battle. A recurring theme in both *Infantry Attacks* and Schittenhelm's account is Rommel's constant attention to communications, with his assigned detachment from the battalion's signals company often making extraordinary efforts to lay telephone wires during even the boldest of penetrations.

One incident may stand as an example for his approach. During the night of 24/25 October, the signals company (which, at that time included an energetic young Austrian volunteer, Wolf Hauler, who was to be severely gassed in January 1918, whereupon it was discovered 'he' was actually May Senta von Hauler, the daughter of a fallen Austrian colonel!)[243] was for once unable to maintain the connection.[244] Rommel, smarting at an attempt by Major Count Bothmer, commander of the neighbouring Bavarian III Bataillon, Infanterie-Leib-Regiment (Life Guards), to issue orders to his detachment, nonetheless waited until Sprösser arrived. Rommel then immediately sought his superior's approval for the manoeuvre plan he had hatched during the night.[245] In his history of the WMB, Sprösser detailed the subsequent exchange between himself and Rommel, an account highly revealing of their relationship. Having been briefed as to the current situation, Sprösser asked Rommel what he suggested should happen next. He then challenged his subordinate to explain his reasoning – exactly the technique used at the Reichswehr Infantry School when Rommel was an instructor in Dresden a decade later. Satisfied with the response, Sprösser instructed Rommel to proceed, twice telling him to 'try his luck'. When Rommel raised the issue of Bothmer's orders, Sprösser simply told the young lieutenant to let him worry about that.[246] Rommel noted Sprösser and Bothmer 'reached an understanding'.[247] As he moved out, Rommel 'as always' took pains to ensure a telephone cable was laid behind him, maintaining communications with Sprösser's command post.[248]

The one occasion when Rommel acted directly contrary to his orders was immediately prior to the capture of Mount Matajur. Ordered by Sprösser to withdraw, Rommel disobeyed on the basis the order had been given without knowledge of the situation, and hence obedience would threaten the prescribed mission.[249] In the history of the WMB, Sprösser made clear his assessment of Rommel's actions: 'A tremendous effort by the commander and his troops, outstanding in its dedication and effort, in its exceptional initiative and nerve!'[250] As has been noted, this assessment

---

243 Sprösser, *Gebirgsschützen*, p.264, and Otto Riebicke, *Was brauchte der Weltkrieg? Tatsachen und Zahlen aus dem deutschen Ringen 1914/18* (Leipzig: Hase & Köhler, 1936), p.61.
244 Sprösser, *Gebirgsschützen*, p.275.
245 Rommel, *Infantry Attacks*, pp.180-182.
246 Sprösser, *Gebirgsschützen*, p.276.
247 Rommel, *Infantry Attacks*, p.182.
248 Rommel, *Infantry Attacks*, p.185 and Sprösser, *Gebirgsschützen*, p.277.
249 Rommel, *Infantry Attacks*, p.223.
250 Sprösser, *Gebirgsschützen*, p.284.

was also reflected by Krafft in his account of the battle: 'The achievement of the Rommel Detachment shines out brightly in its perseverance, cheerful impetus, skill and initiative'.[251] As was to be the case in 1940, success clearly wrote its own rules.

In short, not only was Rommel in close contact with his superiors throughout most of the battle, seeking their approval for his next actions, Sprösser explicitly instructed him to 'try his luck' in the unfolding situation, and, even when he did disobey orders, his initiative received strong approval from his superiors. Again, these statements give no support to the suggestion Rommel was behaving outside the army's acceptable limits.

Rommel and German Doctrine

Having considered the nature of Rommel's approach to combat and demonstrated the continuity between his practice in 1917 and 1940, it is necessary to consider the relationship between that practice and the doctrine set out in the army's military regulations. Of course, we have already considered the development of German doctrine during this period earlier, in Chapter Two. There, the focus was on an assessment of the German perspective on the three key factors identified at the end of Chapter One as determining the relative effectiveness of the different command approaches:

- Whether an army expects the problems encountered in warfare to be wicked, such that it is unlikely that senior commanders will be able to predict the local situation within which their subordinates operate (making approaches that emphasise subordinates' initiative liable to be more effective), or whether they are expected to be tame, such that senior commanders can determine local situations in advance (making approaches that use detailed orders more effective);
- Whether commanders can rely on their subordinates to interpret general directives within their local situation, in order to achieve the overall intent (enabling approaches that maximise low-level initiative), or whether deficiencies in capability or motivation mean commanders cannot trust their subordinates to act independently (requiring reliance on rigid adherence to orders); and
- Whether commanders seek to achieve certainty through extensive collection and collation of intelligence about the situation and detailed analysis of all the available options, in order to identify the 'correct' solution to a tame problem, or whether they emphasise speed of decision-making, even in the absence of a large part of the picture, in order to implement quickly 'good enough' decisions to wicked problems, thereby achieving tempo and inflicting surprise and shock on the enemy.

251 Krafft, *Durchbruch*, vol.1, p.121.

Clearly, there are some parallels between these factors and the three aspects that characterised Rommel's behaviour at Caporetto and when crossing the Meuse. The aim here, however, is to provide an examination of the doctrine from, as it were, the opposite direction. Chapter Two sought to understand the stance of the German doctrine on key aspects of warfare, in order to determine which of the theoretical command approaches described in Chapter One most closely aligned with that set out in the official manuals. By contrast, the focus here is on the extent to which the actual practice of a highly successful and respected individual commander was in accordance with that doctrine.

Amongst the last of Rommel's writings, produced while recovering from wounds suffered in July 1944, were four pages of reflections on 'modern military leadership'.[252] Here, he argued:

> Because of the great variety of tactical possibilities which motorisation offers it will in future be impossible to make more than a rough forecast of the course of a battle. This being so, the issue will be decided by flexibility of mind, eager acceptance of responsibility, a fitting mixture of caution and audacity, and the greater control over the fighting troops.[253]

The similarity of these characteristics with those Rommel had shown in his own practice at Dinant and Mount Matajur is striking, though perhaps not surprising.

He went on to make a number of suggestions for the future training of officers, a subject in which he was, as has been demonstrated above, highly experienced:

a. [...] The object of this instruction will be to induce a certain independence of mind [...]

b. Mental conception must be followed by immediate execution. This is a matter of energy and initiative. [...]

c. [...] By skilful psychological handling, in which personal example plays the principal part, the performance of troops can be increased enormously. [...]

d. [...] Only rarely in history has a battle gone completely according to the plan of either side [. ...] it is extremely important for the commander to know his opponent and be capable of assessing his psychological reactions [. ... and] to turn this knowledge to advantage.

e. [...] Anything which may deflect from unity of purpose, from the will to pull together, must be utterly eradicated.[254]

---

252 *Rommel Papers*, pp.516-519.
253 *Rommel Papers,* p.517.
254 *Rommel Papers*, pp.518-519.

These statements provide a further clear exposition of Rommel's military views, which reinforce the characteristics extrapolated from his tactical practice.

As has been noted, while recent historians reject the orthodoxy of the earlier post-war literature, that Rommel was a maverick operating far outside German doctrine, there remains significant disagreement over whether his approach was well within the mainstream or else at its furthest margins.[255]

On 27 January 1912, the twenty-year-old Rommel received his commission as a Leutnant (Second Lieutenant) in Infanterie-Regiment 124.[256] As a newly-minted officer, two of the key guides to the practice expected of him by the army would have been the *Exerzier-Reglement für die Infanterie* (*ExRfdI*) (Infantry Drill Regulations)[257] and the *Felddienst-Ordnung* (*FO*) (Field Service Regulations).[258]

The *ExRfdI* (1906) represented a decisive step forward from the previous edition, the *ExRfdI* (1888),[259] which had represented the culmination of the lessons from Moltke's Wars of German Unification (1864-1871). The new regulations reflected developments in modern weapons technology and observation of recent wars,[260] notably the Russo-Japanese War of 1905-1906. Central to the new manual's approach was a strong emphasis on the need for commanders to ensure that orders expressed their intent (*Absicht*) clearly, while leaving the choice of means by which this was to be achieved as open as possible to the initiative of their subordinates, down to company level. In this way, the concept of *Auftragstaktik* (equivalent to the command approach termed Directive Command in Chapter One above) became explicitly embedded within the German doctrinal manuals.[261]

Taking the first of the three characteristics displayed by Rommel, his personal presence at the critical point, the *ExRfdI* (1906) was clear the place of the officer (implied as being up to battalion commander level) was in or close behind the front line. This was based on the need for him to exert his direct influence on the troops and to have a personal knowledge of the terrain and enemy situation.[262] Although

---

255 For example, Sigg, *Unterführer*, p.89n360.
256 Caddick-Adams, *Rommel*, p.581.
257 DVE 130: Exerzier Reglement für die Infanterie vom 29. Mai 1906 (Neuabdruck) (Berlin: Mittler, 1909).
258 DVE 267: Felddienst-Ordnung (Berlin: Mittler, 1908) and *Field Service Regulations (Felddienst Ordnung, 1908) of the German Army*, trans. by General Staff, War Office (London: HMSO, 1908).
259 *Exerzir Reglement für die Infanterie* (Berlin: Mittler, 1888) and *The New German Field Exercise*, trans. by G.J.R. Glünicke (Bedford: Hockliffe, 1888).
260 Ralf Raths, *Vom Massensturm zur Stoßtrupptaktik: Die deutsche Landkriegtaktik im Spiegel von Dienstvorschriften und Publizistik 1906 bis 1918* (Freiburg: Rombach, 2009), p.28.
261 Stephan Leistenschneider, *Auftragstaktik im preussisch-deutschen Heer 1871 bis 1914* (Hamburg: Mittler, 2002), pp.134-136, and see also Martin Samuels, *Command or Control? Command, Training and Tactics in the British and German Armies, 1888-1918* (London: Cass, 1995), pp.68-77.
262 *ExRfdI* (1906), paras.277-278, & 281.

there was little specific reference in either the *ExRfdI* or the *FO* to Rommel's second characteristic (the need for commanders to maintain a rapid tempo of operations), the emphasis on the need for field officers to position themselves close behind the troops would have facilitated quicker reaction times and hence a high tempo.[263]

Rommel's third characteristic, his calmness and decisiveness in the face of the chaos and opportunity of battle, aligned closely with the doctrine. Both the *FO* and the *ExRfdI* were clear the inherent nature of warfare was such that unexpected situations would inevitably arise. This meant fixed rules could not be given and the orders received by officers would often be no longer relevant by the time they came to be implemented. To counter this friction, the manuals stated higher commanders should restrict themselves to setting out in their orders only so much detail as was absolutely required by their subordinates, while making their overall intent completely clear. Equally, those subordinates were expected to use their own initiative and knowledge of the situation to select the most appropriate means by which to carry out those orders, including disregarding their orders if events had made these no longer suited to the situation.[264]

The doctrine was alive to the associated risks and tensions. Both manuals stated explicitly, 'omission and neglect is a greater fault than a mistake in the choice of means'. Both also underlined the need for commanders to promote in their subordinates a spirit of independence and a willingness to take on responsibility, deemed 'the most important characteristic of command'.[265] Conversely, the *ExRfdI* immediately emphasised 'the independence of subordinates must not become arbitrariness' or the replacement of obedience by a sense of 'knowing better'.[266] Nonetheless, the regulations gave a clear support for what Robert Citino has argued was the central core of the German approach to command from the time of Frederick the Great: 'the German officer who acted aggressively would be confident that he was acting in the best traditions of the service'.[267]

As was noted earlier, in Chapter Two, although the conditions of trench warfare experienced in the First World War, especially on the Western Front, differed from pre-war expectations, the German high command (OHL – *Oberste Heeresleitung*) under Erich von Falkenhayn did little to revise the formal training regulations. It was only after his replacement in August 1916 by Paul von Hindenburg, supported by Erich Ludendorff, that an extensive series of new manuals for position warfare was developed.[268]

263 *ExRfdI* (1906), para.296.
264 *FO* (1908), paras.37 & 49-50, and *ExRfdI* (1906), paras.250, 272-275, & 304.
265 *FO* (1908), paras.4, 12, 25, & 37-38, and *ExRfdI* (1906), paras.251, 276, & 304.
266 *ExRfdI* (1906), paras.276 & 304.
267 Robert M. Citino, *The German Way of War: From the Thirty Years' War to the Third Reich* (Lawrence, KS: University Press of Kansas, 2005), p.141, see also pp.302-303.
268 Hermann Cron, *Imperial German Army 1914-18: Organisation, Structure, Orders-of-Battle*, trans. by C.F. Colton (Solihull: Helion, 2001), pp.29-32. See also General Erich Ludendorff,

One of the new manuals was the *Ausbildungsvorschrift für die Fußtruppen im Kriege* (*AVF*) (Training Regulations for the Foot Troops in War), first published in January 1917 and revised in January 1918.[269] Since the pre-war regulations were believed to remain relevant for situations of mobile warfare, few changes were required in this area. The new manual therefore primarily replaced Part I of the *ExRfdI* (1906), which set out the method of training, rather than address the command of troops in combat.[270] Although there was a section on the duties of leaders at various levels, this primarily focused on their roles as trainers of their troops, rather than as commanders, though the 1918 edition did repeat the pre-war emphasis on the purpose of training being to develop independently-thinking and -acting leaders and men.[271]

Since the WMB was primarily employed during 1917 on the Rumanian and Italian Fronts, in situations where position warfare was the exception, the impact on Rommel's practice of this manual, as well as those publications more explicitly focused on techniques for position warfare, may have been limited. Similarly, although the pace and extent of doctrinal development with regard to position warfare was very significant,[272] the very different context of the operations on the Romanian and Italian Fronts in which Rommel was engaged meant these changes may well have passed him by. Although the WMB was deployed to the Western Front in January 1918 and took part in the great offensives in the spring of that year, by then Rommel was no longer with the unit. He was instead kicking his heals in frustration in a junior staff role with Genkdo 64, a corps-level headquarters[273] responsible for a lengthy stretch of quiet front in the Vosges mountains.

The next major step in German doctrinal development came shortly after the end of the First World War, when Hans von Seeckt sought to re-establish the foundations of the new Reichsheer. As was noted earlier, the new doctrine emerged from extensive analysis of the German Army's experiences during the First World War: eighty-six committees, involving more than five hundred officers.[274] For Rommel, who was from 1 January 1921 a company commander in Infanterie-Regiment 13,[275] the two key manuals that emerged from this process were *HDv 487: Führung und Gefecht der verbundenen Waffen* (*Das FuG*) (Command and Combat of the Combined Arms) of

Urkunden der Obersten Heeresleitunq über ihre Tätigkeit, 1916-18 (Berlin: Mittler, 1920), pp.592-594.

269 *Ausbildungsvorschrift für die Fußtruppen im Kriege* (n.p.: Reichsdruckerei, January 1917), *Ausbildungsvorschrift für die Fußtruppen im Kriege*, 2nd ed. (n.p.: Reichsdruckerei, January 1918).

270 Lieutenant General Wilhelm Balck, *Development of Tactics – World War*, trans. by Harry Bell (Fort Leavenworth, KS: General Service Schools, 1922), pp.42-46 and *AVF* (1917), para.1.

271 *AVF* (1917), paras.7-12, & *AVF* (1918), paras.2, & 5-10.

272 Samuels, *Command or Control?*, pp.178-197 & 231-245.

273 Fraser, *Knight's Cross*, p.77.

274 James S. Corum, *The Roots of Blitzkrieg: Hans von Seeckt and German Military Reform* (Lawrence, 1992), pp.37-39.

275 Caddick-Adams, *Monty and Rommel*, p.583.

1921,[276] which replaced the pre-war *FO*, and *HDv 130: Ausbildungsvorschrift für die Infanterie (AVI)*[277] (Training Regulations for the Infantry) of 1922, which replaced both the *AVF* (1918) and the *ExRfdI* (1906).[278] Compared to the pre-war regulations, the interdependence and consistency between *Das FuG* and the *AVI* (1922) was much clearer, with the latter noting explicitly that the general principles of combat were laid out in the former and every commander should therefore have regard to that manual.[279]

Taking the first characteristic of Rommel's approach, his personal presence at the critical point, the post-war doctrine was clear this was an essential requirement of success. *Das FuG* stated, 'It is of the greatest importance that commanders at all levels constantly maintain personal touch with the troops placed under them. This enables them to make a correct assessment, through first-hand knowledge, of the needs and combat capabilities of their soldiers.'[280] This was reinforced in the section on The Position of the Commander,[281] which was referenced by both the main *AVI* (1922)[282] and its later supplement on command at battalion and regimental level.[283] Here, *Das FuG* stated even divisional commanders should be constantly amongst their troops, placing themselves far forward. Again, this close positioning of commanders with their troops also related to Rommel's second characteristic – his emphasis on speed and momentum, and hence tempo. The *AVI* (1922) was clear, 'Every military action must be based on surprise. Without surprise, great results are hard to secure.'[284]

The third characteristic of Rommel's approach – his calmness and decisiveness in the face of the chaos and opportunity of battle – was also clearly expressed in the new regulations. *Das FuG* stated, 'a formulaic approach [...] would be counter to the many-faceted nature of war', and 'The situation will rarely be so clear as to give an exact insight into the situation of the enemy. Uncertainty in war is the norm', such that results might well be gained at a different point of the line from where it was intended.[285] As a consequence, the *AVI* (1922) placed repeated emphasis on the need for commanders at all levels to remain calm and recognise the importance of their providing a role model to their troops.[286] This was linked with a requirement

276 *HDv 487/1: Führung und Gefecht der verbundenen Waffen* (Berlin, 1921), see also *Command and Combat Use of Combined Arms (German Field Service Regulations), September 1, 1921*, trans. by Captain P.B. Harm (np: Army War College, 1925).
277 *HDv 130: Ausbildungsvorschrift für die Infanterie* (Berlin: Mittler, 1922).
278 *AVI* (1922), pp.6-7.
279 *AVI* (1922), p.6.
280 *Das FuG* (1921), para.5.
281 *Das FuG* (1921), paras.61-65.
282 *AVI* (1922), para.102.
283 *HDv 130: Ausbildungsvorschrift für die Infanterie: Heft V*, unaltered reprint (Berlin: Reichsdruckerei, 1934), para.2.
284 *AVI* (1922), para.75.
285 *Das FuG* (1921), paras.5, 8 & 10.
286 *AVI* (1922), paras.4-5, 42 &101.

for commanders to be 'trained to a willingness to take on responsibility, as well as independently thinking and acting subordinates, [...]. Everywhere, every spiritual and physical resource must be expressed through independence.'[287] Ultimately, *Das FuG* included the famous sentence: 'Willingness to accept responsibility remains the most important quality of a leader. All leaders must constantly bear in mind, and emphasise to their subordinates, that neglect and carelessness will weigh more heavily against them than error in the choice of means.'[288] As in the pre-war manuals, the risks inherent in this approach were recognised. The *AVI* (1922) affirmed, 'Spontaneity and a willingness to accept responsibility must not lead to arbitrary decisions being taken without reference to the wider picture or to a sense of knowing better replacing obedience. Applied within the proper boundaries, these provide the basis for great success in war.'[289]

At Seeckt's insistence, the doctrine set out in *Das FuG* and the *AVI* (1922) remained current for more than a decade,[290] covering the whole of Rommel's time at the Infantry School in Dresden. *Das FuG* was replaced only in 1933 by *HDv 300: Truppenführung* (*TF*) (Unit Command),[291] while a new edition of the *AVI* was issued in a series of volumes from 1935 onwards.

The new manuals continued the shift, seen in *Das FuG* and the *AVI* (1922), whereby the focus of the *AVI* (1935) was on the practicalities of training and combat, while *TF* was more concerned with the approach and philosophy through which these were to be undertaken.

The *AVI* (1935) repeated a number of the points made in earlier editions. For example, the volume on the rifle company underlined commanders should position themselves where they could ensure personal influence over their men, often through their personal behaviour, as well as obtain good observation of the battlefield. The approach was maintained that the orders received by commanders at this level should lay down the mission to be achieved, while leaving the choice of means open.[292] The emphasis on the need for commanders to gain personal observation of the ground

---

287 *AVI* (1922), para.3.
288 *Das FuG* (1921), para.5.
289 *AVI* (1922), para.3.
290 Matthias Strohn, *The German Army and the Defence of the Reich: Military Doctrine and the Conduct of the Defensive Battle, 1918-1939* (Cambridge: Cambridge University, 2011), p.185.
291 *HDv 300/1: Truppenführung* (Berlin: Mittler, 1933). See also *On the German Art of War: Truppenführung*, ed. and trans. by Bruce Condell and David T. Zabecki (London, 2001). See also the analysis of the manual in Strohn, *Defence of the Reich*, pp.185-202, and Robert M. Citino, *The Path to Blitzkrieg: Doctrine and Training in the German Army, 1920-39* (Mechanicsburg, PA: Stackpole, 2008), pp.223-229.
292 *HDv130/2b: Ausbildungsvorschrift für die Infanterie, Heft 2: Die Schützenkompagnie, Teil b: Der Schützenzug und die Schützenkompagnie* (Berlin: Offene Worte, 1936), paras.377-379.

to be fought over was retained in the volume on the infantry battalion.[293] This was combined with instructions commanders should place themselves at the critical points of the battle, often far to the front, and thereby rapidly secure advantages through personal intervention.[294] The importance of securing surprise was also highlighted.[295] All these elements of the revised *AVI* (1935) were fully consistent with Rommel's characteristic presence in the front line, his emphasis on speed to secure surprise and tempo, and his focus on seizing the opportunities presented by the chaos of battle.

By contrast, the approach taken by *TF* was at times 'highly philosophical',[296] more concerned with the way in which commanders should exercise their role and secure dominance over the enemy.

Rommel's preference for being personally present at the critical point of the battle was again fully in accordance with the doctrine laid down by *TF*. In the section on the position of the commander and his staff, the manual repeatedly underlined this must be far to the front, with the troops and often with the advanced guard. In this way, the commander would be able to exercise his personal influence on the troops and maintain a sound understanding of the situation. That this was not merely an exhortation to officers of field rank was made clear by reference to commanders at corps and (especially) divisional level.[297]

The second characteristic of Rommel's approach – his emphasis on surprise, momentum, and hence tempo – was also expressed clearly in the doctrine. *TF* noted, 'Favourable situations must be quickly recognised and decisively exploited. Every advantage over the enemy increases one's own freedom of action.'[298] To this end, 'Surprise is a decisive factor in success. Actions based on surprise are only successful if the enemy is given no time to take effective counter measures.'[299] Commanders were therefore urged not to wait for clarification of an uncertain situation and to make decisions quickly.[300]

Finally, Rommel's calmness and decisiveness in the face of the chaos and opportunity of battle exactly matched the spirit desired by the new doctrine. *TF* was clear warfare was inherently chaotic, with friction and errors occurring constantly, producing 'combat situations [...] of an unlimited variety [. ... that] change frequently and suddenly and can seldom be assessed in advance.'[301] Orders were therefore to set

---

293 *HDv 130/9: Ausbildungsvorschrift für die Infanterie, Heft 9: Führung und Kampf der Infanterie. Das Infanterie-Bataillon* (Berlin: Offene Worte, 1940), para.32.

294 *HDv 130/9* (1940), paras.177, 197 & 145.

295 *HDv 130/9* (1940), paras.182 & 188.

296 Bruce Condell and David T. Zabecki, 'Editors' Introduction', in *German Art of War*, p.3.

297 *TF* (1933), paras.109-119, and *German Art of War*, pp.36-38.

298 *TF* (1933), para.29, and *German Art of War*, p.22.

299 *TF* (1933), para.32, and *German Art of War*, p.22.

300 *TF* (1933), paras.36, 59, 63 & 113, and *German Art of War*, pp.23, 28-29 & 37.

301 *TF* (1933), paras.1 & 3, and *German Art of War*, p.17.

out the mission, but leave the choice of means open.[302] To deal with these demands, 'leaders must be impervious to the changes in the fortunes of war'. This required officers who could 'think and act independently, who [could] make calculated, decisive, and daring use of every situation, and who [could] understand that victory depends on each individual.'[303] Orders were therefore to set out the mission, but should leave the choice of means open.[304]

The manual then repeated the mantra expressed in almost every edition of German doctrine since before Rommel was first commissioned:

> Willingness to accept responsibility is the most important quality of a leader. It should not, however, be based upon individualism without consideration of the whole, nor used as a justification for failing to carry out orders where seeming to know better may affect obedience. Independence of spirit must not become arbitrariness. By contrast, independence of action within acceptable boundaries is the key to great success. [...] Everyone, from the highest commander down to the youngest soldier, must constantly be aware that inaction and neglect incriminate him more severely than any error in the choice of means.[305]

Conclusions

The literature on Rommel is vast. He has been the subject of at least a dozen biographies, perhaps more than any other officer in German military history, and his actions provide the central thread for a great many accounts of events during the world wars. For the first three decades after 1945, this literature was characterised by two largely unquestioned assumptions. First, that Rommel's success was a consequence of his innate military genius, expressed through his famous *Fingerspitzengefühl*. An outsider to the German military establishment, he escaped the deadening constraints of its doctrine and, instead, operated with a boldness and flexibility that bewildered and overwhelmed his enemies, while at the same time leaving his superiors infuriated at his wilfulness and disobedience. Second, that his lack of experience of armoured forces meant his success with 7th Panzer Division in May 1940 was the result of his applying tactics he had used twenty years earlier, as a subaltern in the elite Wurttemberg Mountain Battalion, rather than from understanding the nature of armoured warfare or applying accepted German doctrine.

First challenged by David Irving in 1977, this picture has subsequently been significantly revised, especially with regard to the extent to which Rommel was a

302 *TF* (1933), paras.73 & 76, and *German Art of War*, p.30.
303 *TF* (1933), para.10, and *German Art of War*, p.18.
304 *TF* (1933), paras.73 & 76, and *German Art of War*, p.30.
305 *TF* (1933), paras.9 & 15, and *German Art of War*, pp.18-19.

maverick outsider to the German military establishment. There remains debate, however, over whether his approach to command was consistent with the army's doctrine or whether he operated only at its fringes at best. In addition, while the continuity between his approach in Italy in 1917 and in France in 1940 is generally accepted, this has been subjected to only limited analysis.

This chapter has shown that, throughout the 1930s, Rommel occupied a series of ever more senior positions at the centre of the army's officer candidate education system: first as an instructor at the Infantry School in Dresden, then at the War School in Potsdam, and subsequently as commandant of the War School at Wiener-Neustadt. In these roles, he was a key figure in the basic leadership and tactical training of a very significant proportion of the young officers who would lead the army during the first years of the Second World War. While his charisma and ability as a teacher are clear, the popularity of his lectures and the success within the German military establishment of his books on tactics, especially his seminal *Infantry Attacks*, were only possible because the views he expressed and the approaches he taught were fully consistent with the army's doctrine and so enjoyed official support.

Turning to Rommel's command practice, detailed examination of his experiences at Caporetto in October 1917 and in the crossing of the Meuse in May 1940 suggests there were indeed strong continuities. These can be encapsulated in three characteristics: his personal presence at the key points of the battle, his insistence on speed, both of action and movement, in order to achieve tempo, and his coolness in the face of unexpected and changing situations. In both battles, Rommel's behaviour repeatedly demonstrated these defining features, features that align closely with the command approach termed 'Directive Control' described in Chapter One. In this approach, the Knowledge Gap is closed through the personal observation by the commander of the situation at the key point of the battle, and his intent is then expressed through subordinates who are expected to use their own initiative to the very fullest.

The impact this approach had on his enemies was shattering. Stunned by the speed with which his troops manoeuvred and their sudden appearance in the most unexpected of places, shocked by the boldness of his actions and the determination of his assaults, the Italians in 1917 and the French in 1940 found themselves frozen into passive inaction. As a result, they allowed time and opportunity to slip through their fingers until the only possible response was surrender.

It should be noted, however, that in both cases Rommel was operating against troops who were already on the verge of being demoralised and were led by commanders of exceptional inflexibility. Whether his approach would have been as successful against more organised forces, or might indeed have led to disaster, can only be surmised. The obvious concern of his superiors at times during the second stage of the May 1940 campaign, a subject considered further in Chapter Five below, may reflect their lack of appreciation of the true fragility of the French forces and hence their reasonable fears Rommel's extreme boldness would lead him to fall into a trap.

But while there were strong continuities in Rommel's practice between the two world wars, it is simplistic to suggest these merely reflected his attempts to deal with an unknown situation by applying tactics with which he was more familiar.

Apart from the fact that Rommel would have been required to include situations involving armoured vehicles in his tactical exercises in his various instructor roles, examination of the official doctrine in the German Army's key field and infantry training manuals shows the features of his practice, as displayed in both battles, were entirely consistent with their expectations. Throughout successive iterations of the doctrine, from the *ExRfdI* (1906) and the *FO* (1908), through the *AVF* (1917) and (1918), the *AVI* (1922) and *Das FuG* of 1921, until the *AVI* (1935) and *TF* in 1933, the core characteristics of Rommel's approach aligned with the manuals' teachings. As was demonstrated in Chapter Two, the central field manuals of the German Army during this period showed a continual reliance on what has here been termed the Directive Command approach, with a noticeable shift towards a preference for Directive Control after the First World War. Far from struggling to escape the doctrine, it pushed him further along the route he had already chosen, and may have encouraged him down that route in the first place – we should perhaps see Rommel as the most perfect product of the doctrine, rather than as seeking to escape its deadening rigidity.

Finally, however, Rommel's clear adherence to the German Army's doctrine serves to highlight the great paradox that lay at its heart: the tension between commanders displaying independence, within the context of the whole, or descending into wilfulness, disregarding the wider context. It has been noted how Rommel's behaviour in 1940 was characterised by Sigg as representing 'überbietende Eigenmächtigkeiten' ('surpassing wilfulness'), breaking out completely from the scope of his orders.[306] Yet, as Citino has shown, this was fully consistent with the German military culture as it had developed over the previous three centuries, where 'even getting [a commander] to follow the mission was difficult enough'.[307] As Gross argued, Rommel was by no means alone in his behaviour during that campaign, with all of the armoured commanders pushed the concept of *Auftragstaktik* to the limit.[308] Against enemies as fragile and inflexible as the Italians in 1917 and the French in 1940, the risks (personal and tactical) this involved were justified and brought success. But against a more resilient foe, this emphasis on independence at the expense of the wider plan might not have been sound.

Accordingly, if Rommel's command approach throughout his career up to May 1940 represents a near perfect example of the German Army's command doctrine in practice, his behaviour thereafter may provide a case study of the limits of that

---

306 Sigg, *Unterführer*, pp.244-246.
307 Citino, *German Way of War*, p.302.
308 Gerhard P. Gross, *The Myth and Reality of German Warfare: Operational Thinking from Moltke the Elder to Heusinger*, ed. by Major-General David T. Zabecki (Lexington, KY: University Press of Kentucky, 2016), pp.203-204.

doctrine, perhaps especially of Directive Control as an approach, in contexts larger than a single army on a single front. As has been noted, even some of his closest associates suggested Rommel forever remained at heart the decisive lieutenant of 1917.[309] Appointed to command the *Deutsches Afrika Korps* in February 1941, Rommel fundamentally misunderstood the strategic purpose of his mission, assuming it to be actively offensive rather than merely intended to hold back the British advances. Rather than seek clarity, he instead repeatedly and deliberately ignored explicit instructions from the German higher command, descending into what Reuth termed 'wishful thinking [rather] than realistic consideration' of the situation.[310] While his brilliance at first secured repeated victories against the British, his limited understanding of the operational level of war meant those very characteristics that made him such an effective independent tactical commander caused him to place his own interpretation of the situation above that of his superiors and, ultimately, lead his army to destruction.[311]

Even within the official manuals, there had long been evidence of a concern the accepted culture might have its limits. As *TF* noted, repeating a mantra repeated in almost every iteration of the German doctrine since before Rommel was first commissioned:

> Willingness to accept responsibility is the most important quality of a leader. It should not, however, be based upon individualism without consideration of the whole, nor used as a justification for failing to carry out orders where seeming to know better may affect obedience. Independence of spirit must not become arbitrariness. By contrast, independence of action within acceptable boundaries is the key to great success.[312]

The conclusion Rommel was no maverick outsider, relying on his innate genius to defeat his enemies, leads to a final question: why armies construct such myths about their opponents.

A recurring theme in the history of warfare is the claim one's own defeat was an entirely understandable consequence of some characteristic of the enemy that gave them an overwhelming superiority. As in the case of Rommel, this may be that the opposing commander was claimed to be a genius. That this was no isolated occurrence may be illustrated by the fact that, when the German offensives in the spring of 1918 against first the British and then the French smashed the deadlock of the trenches, the defeats were attributed to revolutionary new tactics designed by General Oskar von

---

309 Hesse, Wandlung, img.320.
310 Reuth, *Rommel*, pp.83-92.
311 Niall Barr, 'Rommel in the Desert, 1942', in Beckett, *Rommel*, pp.81-112 (109-110).
312 *TF* (1933), para.9, and *German Art of War*, p.18.

Hutier against the Russians.[313] In fact, the tactics were the result of an extended period of development that had involved many senior commanders.[314] Conversely, it may be argued the enemy enjoyed a large numerical superiority and a decisive advantage in the quality of their equipment. For example, in May 1940, the French argued the Allied tanks were 'all along inferior in number and size' to the German panzers.[315] In reality, numbers were about equal, and the French SOMUA S-35 was probably the best tank deployed by either side.[316] The simplest explanation of this tendency is that being defeated in such circumstances has the effect of avoiding questions of blame and removing the need for any critical examination of one's own performance. As the *Daily Mail* suggested on 14 February 1942, 'if all else fails, it is always possible to minimise our failures and blunders by exalting the enemy's daring and foresight'.[317]

Yet such a response carries with it a range of all-too-obvious risks. Quite apart from the fact that overlooking potential weaknesses in one's own performance inevitably increases the probability of defeat in the future, presenting one's opponent as being superior in capability can have a negative impact on the morale of one's own forces. A classic example of this occurred some two years after the events around Dinant, when, on 1 February 1942,[318] General Claude Auchinleck, commander of the British Middle East Command, issued a highly unfortunate Order of the Day:

> There exists a real danger that our friend Rommel is becoming a kind of magician or bogey-man to our troops, who are talking far too much about him. He is by no means a superman, although he is undoubtedly very energetic and able. Even if he were a superman, it would still be highly undesirable that our men should credit him with supernatural powers.[319]

The thinking behind this order was clearly naïve, in that it can only have served to underline across the whole formation that Rommel was a fearsome foe. Basic psychology suggests using words such as 'magician' and 'superman' about one's opponent, even in the context of denying them, may be expected to have had the effect

---

313 Laszlo M. Alfoldi, 'The Hutier Legend', *Parameters*, 5 (1976), 69-74 (pp.70-71).
314 For the development of those tactics, see Gruss, H., 'Aufbau und Verwendung der deutschen Sturmbataillone im Weltkrieg' (unpublished doctoral thesis, Berlin University, 1939), Bruce Ivar Gudmundsonn, *Stormtroop Tactics: Innovation in the German Army, 1914-1918* (New York: Praeger, 1989), Martin Samuels, *Doctrine and Dogma: German and British Infantry Tactics in the First World War* (Westport, CT: Greenwood, 1992), and Samuels, *Command or Control?*, pp.231-245.
315 General Joseph Marie Eon, *The Battle of Flanders: Sedan - The Operations, and the Lessons to be Learned from Them* (London: Hachette, 1943), p.16.
316 Robert Allan Doughty, *The Breaking Point: Sedan and the Fall of France, 1940* (Hamden, CT: Archon, 1990), p.3.
317 Quoted in Connelly, 'Rommel as Icon', p.161.
318 Caddick-Adams, *Rommel*, pp.260-261.
319 Quoted in Young, *Rommel*, p.23.

of reinforcing those very fears in the minds of the British forces, the opposite from what was intended. Against a genius, one has no chance of victory, so self-preservation becomes an understandable priority instead.

It is perhaps unsurprising that, although Desmond Young clearly recalled having been a recipient of the Order himself, he was subsequently unable to track down a copy in any of the official British sources – the only surviving example proved to be a translation retained in Rommel's own papers.[320]

320 Young, *Rommel*, p.23n.

4

The British Tank Assault at Amiens, 8 August 1918

We are at the limit of our capabilities. The war must be ended.

Kaiser Wilhelm II[1]

Writing of the opening day of the Allied offensive at Amiens, the German Army's leading defence expert in the First World War, Fritz von Lossberg[2] noted, 'It was probably the greatest defeat suffered by a German army during the war.'[3] Reflecting this, the Reichsarchiv's monograph was simply entitled *The Catastrophe of 8 August 1918*.[4] Erich Ludendorff famously described it as 'the black day of the German Army',[5] a phrase subsequently taken as the title of another German account of the battle: *Der schwarze Tag*.[6] As Charles Messenger has suggested, it was 'the day we won the war'.[7]

Since the battle was so clearly a turning point, it provides an excellent case study for the exploration of the operation in practice of the British and German doctrines at that stage of the First World War, and especially of the interactions resulting from the different approaches and perspectives that lay at the root of those doctrines. While Chapter Two provided an analysis of the respective doctrines in theory, and Chapter

---

1   Oberstleutnant a.D. Alfred Niemann, *Kaiser und Revolution: Die entscheidenden Ereignisse im Grossen Hauptquartier* (Berlin: Scherl, 1922), p. 43.
2   Captain T.T. Lupfer, *The Dynamics of Doctrine: The Changes in German Tactical Doctrine During the First World War* (Fort Leavenworth, KS: Combat Studies Institute, 1981), p. 10.
3   General der Infanterie Fritz von Lossberg, *Meine Tätigkeit im Weltkriege 1914-1918* (Berlin: Mittler, 1939), p.354.
4   Major Thilo von Bose, *Die Katastrophe des 8.August 1918* (Schlachten des Weltkrieges, vol. 36) (Berlin: Stalling, 1930).
5   General Erich Ludendorff, *My War Memories 1914-1918* (London: Hutchinson, 1920), vol.2, p.679.
6   Generalleutnant Ernst Kabisch, *Der schwarze Tag: Die Nebelschlacht vor Amiens (8./9. August 1918)* (Berlin: Schlegel, 1933).
7   Charles Messenger, *The Day We Won the War: Turning Point at Amiens, 8th August 1918* (London: Phoenix, 2009).

Three considered the application of the German doctrine by a single officer, both this chapter and Chapter Five examine the doctrines at a more operational level. These two case studies are intended to bring out their practical consequences for the behaviour and approach of commanders in both armies. In addition, the case studies are designed especially to develop a deeper understanding of the fundamental nature of warfare, and hence the of relative effectiveness of the different command approaches described in Chapter One.

Explanations for the Disaster

Immediately after the battle, senior German commanders attributed the disaster to the combination of the thick fog that had blanketed the battlefield during the first hours of the attack and the massed use of tanks by the British.[8] This interpretation became the orthodoxy in subsequent German accounts.[9] Heinz Guderian, admittedly not an impartial commentator, argued these special factors had rendered the German infantry 'defenceless in the face of certain destruction'[10] and hence led to a collapse of their morale.[11] These explanations echo descriptions of the German attack on 21 March 1918, which suggested 'mist and masses' had overcome the British.[12]

Basil Liddell Hart, another tank enthusiast, accepted the German interpretation, stating the battle 'proved the supreme fulfilment of the tank [...] in the war'.[13] Perhaps surprisingly, J.F.C. Fuller, Chief of Staff of the Tank Corps during the battle, wrote immediately after the war that it was simplistic to attribute success solely to the use of tanks. Instead, he suggested it was a result of the combination of 'surprise, the moral effect of the tanks, the high moral [sic] of our own infantry, the rapid advance of our guns, and the good roads for supplies.'[14] Fuller, however, subsequently became a close associate of Liddell Hart and his later writings displayed a very different interpretation of the battle, more closely following his friend's line. In his memoirs,

---

8   General von der Marwitz, *Weltkriegsbriefe*, ed. by General der Infanterie a.D. von Tschischwitz (Berlin: Reimar Hobbing, 1940), p.306, and Kronprinz Rupprecht von Bayern, *Mein Kriegstagebuch* (Munich: Deutscher National, 1929), vol.3, p.346.

9   For example, General der Infanterie Hans von Zwehl, *Die Schlachten im Sommer 1918 an der Westfront* (Berlin: Mittler, 1921), pp.22-23, and Kabisch, *schwarze Tag*, p.196.

10   Heinz Guderian, *Achtung-Panzer! The Development of Tank Warfare*, trans. by Christopher Duffy (London: Cassell, 1992), pp.111-114.

11   Generaloberst Heinz Guderian, *Die Panzertruppen und ihre Zusammenwirken mit den anderen Waffen*, 3rd ed. (Berlin: Mittler, 1940), p. 9.

12   See Timothy H.E. Travers, *The Killing Ground: The British Army, The Western Front and The Emergence of Modern Warfare, 1900-1918* (London: Allen & Unwin, 1987), p. 231.

13   Captain B.H. Liddell Hart, *The Tanks: The History of the Royal Tank Regiment and its predecessors, Heavy Branch Machine-Gun Corps, Tank Corps and Royal Tank Corps, 1914-1945*, vol.1 (London: Cassell, 1959), p.177.

14   Brevet-Colonel J.F.C. Fuller, *Tanks in the Great War, 1914-1918* (New York, NY: Dutton, 1920), pp.227-228.

published in 1936, Fuller used striking language to emphasise the central role of the tanks: 'Iron fashioned into the tank had crushed out [the enemy's] fighting spirit and had paralysed his will to endure. Morally the tank disarmed him and cashiered him from the ranks of the brave.'[15] Twenty-five years later, he was even more definite: 'Without the tank there would have been no surprise commensurate with the one achieved, and it was the suddenness of the assault which detonated the panic. [...] the tank was a psychological, more so than a material weapon.'[16]

Liddell Hart and Fuller, however, were lone voices in the anglophone historiography. The British Official History rejected the explanations they and the Germans had put forward, arguing these were designed by the latter 'to save their self-esteem'. It suggested instead, 'The action of the tanks [...] did not come up to expectation. [...] Even the moral effect was not so great as claimed [...]. Actually the infantry with machine guns was the instrument of success; but its vital assistant was the artillery'.[17]

Subsequent scholars have largely followed the Official History and Fuller's original views. Gregory Blaxland argued, 'The Germans had first been stunned by the unexpected fury of the opening blow and then knocked flat, morally and physically, by the speed with which succeeding waves had passed through.'[18] Tim Travers emphasised 'tactical surprise, the opening barrage, the heavy mist or smoke, and the rapid infantry advance with rifles and Lewis guns', though he conceded 'the tanks were very valuable at critical moments' and noted the moral effect on the German defenders when tanks emerged from the mist.[19] Paul Harris focused on the total surprise achieved by the British, artillery superiority and the counter-battery effort, a two-to-one advantage in manpower, and the sheer skill of the attacking infantry.[20] This range of factors suggests these historians believed no single aspect of the attack was of central importance in securing victory, in contrast to the German focus on the combination of tanks and fog. Robin Prior and Trevor Wilson summed up this view, arguing, 'The Germans [...] were defeated by superior firepower tactics, which even their best troops could not withstand.'[21] Amiens might therefore be taken as

15 Major-General J.F.C. Fuller, *Memoirs of an Unconventional Soldier* (London: Nicholson & Watson, 1936), pp.316-317.
16 Major-General J.F.C. Fuller, *The Conduct of War, 1789-1961* (1961, reprinted London: Methuen, 1972), p.176.
17 Brigadier-General James E. Edmonds, *The Official History of the Great War: Military Operations: France & Belgium, 1918*, vol.4: *8 August to 26 September – The Franco-British Offensive* (London: HMSO, 1947) (hereafter BOH 1918(4)), pp.156-157.
18 Gregory Blaxland, *Amiens: 1918* (London: Star, 1981), pp.182-183.
19 Timothy Travers, *How the War Was Won: Factors that Led to Victory in World War One* (Barnsley: Pen & Sword, 2005), pp.121-123.
20 J.P. Harris, *Amiens to the Armistice: The BEF in the Hundred Days' Campaign, 8 August–11 November 1918* (London: Brassey's, 1998), pp.104-107.
21 Robin Prior and Trevor Wilson, *Command on the Western Front: The Military Career of Sir Henry Rawlinson, 1914-1918* (Barnsley: Pen & Sword, 2004), p.320.

representing the British Army at the peak of the 'learning curve' Gary Sheffield and others have argued characterised its experience during the First World War.[22]

It is striking, however, that in all these explanations the defenders appear as little more than passive victims of the British Army's expertise, almost on a par with the weather or the terrain. They imply the attack ran to plan and no army could have withstood the form of assault employed: victory was inevitable.

Treating the Germans as almost irrelevant was understandable in the memoirs of the senior officers who had commanded the British offensive, as most appeared before information was available concerning their opponents' actions.[23] This was not a trap into which the Official Histories fell, at least not directly. The British,[24] Australian,[25] and Canadian[26] accounts (all published two decades and more after the events) demonstrated a considerable familiarity with the German sources. In addition, articles in the *Army Quarterly*, the British Army's unofficial in-house journal between the wars, reviewed key German publications that presented the battle from the defenders' perspective.[27] Nonetheless, the British Official History for one aimed to provide a learning opportunity for officers, while avoiding unreasonable criticism of commanders on the spot. In order to avoid a 'wise after the event' impression, discussion of the enemy was relegated either to sections in a smaller font at the end of chapters, or to footnotes.[28] This had the effect of downplaying the German role in determining the course of the battle.

Curiously, more recent scholars have displayed rather less attention to the German side of events than did the Official Histories. Although Shane Schreiber drew out

22   See especially Gary Sheffield, *Forgotten Victory: The First World War: Myths and Realities* (London: Headline, 2001), though note Prior and Wilson, *Command*, pp. 394-397.
23   For example: Lieutenant-General Sir Arthur W. Currie, *Canadian Corps Operations During the Year 1918* (Ottawa: Department of Militia and Defence, 1919), Lieutenant-General Sir John Monash, *The Australian Victories in France in 1918* (London: Hutchinson, 1920), Major-General Sir Archibald Montgomery, *The Story of the Fourth Army in the Battles of the Hundred Days, August 8th to November 11th, 1918* (London: Hodder and Stoughton, 1920), and Fuller, *Tanks*.
24   BOH 1918(4), pp.1-162.
25   Charles Edwin Woodrow Bean, *Official History of Australia in the War of 1914-1918: vol. VI: The Australian Imperial Force in France During the Allied Offensive, 1918* (Sydney: Angus and Robertson, 1942) (hereafter AOH 6), pp.526-616.
26   Colonel G.W.L. Nicholson, *Official History of the Canadian Army in the First World War: Canadian Expeditionary Force, 1914-1919* (Ottawa: Duhamel, 1962) (hereafter COH), pp.386-421.
27   Historical Section (Military Branch) CID, 'A German Account of the British Offensive of August, 1918', *Army Quarterly*, 6 (April 1923), 11-16, which summarised Zwehl, *Schlachten*, and 'The German Catastrophe of the 8th of August 1918', *Army Quarterly*, 25 (October 1933), 65-71, which summarised Bose, *Katastrophe*.
28   Andrew Green, *Writing the Great War: Sir James Edmonds and the Official Histories, 1915-1948* (London: Cass, 2003), pp.52-55.

certain elements from those official accounts,[29] Harris's only German reference was to Ludendorff's famous quote,[30] James McWilliams and James Steel listed just two German sources, both in translation,[31] while Charles Messenger included five, just three in the original language.[32] Jack Sheldon, whose magisterial volumes have done so much to elucidate the German experience of the Western Front for an anglophone audience, has unfortunately yet to cover the battle.

The focus on 'this side of the hill', as it were, perhaps reflects a broader tendency. As Jim Storr has argued, 'there is little if anything in British military practice which suggests that combat is adversarial [. ...], with very little to suggest what the impact of enemy action on a procedure undertaken in war might be.'[33] Yet it was highlighted in Chapter One above that Clausewitz had emphasised on the very first page of *On War*, 'War is nothing but a duel on a larger scale. [... A] picture of it as a whole can be formed by imagining a pair of wrestlers. Each tries through physical force to compel the other to do his will; [...] in order to make him incapable of further resistance.'[34] Clausewitz's frequent return to the wrestling metaphor[35] made clear his belief the course of events makes sense only through consideration of both sides, and especially their interaction.

Focusing on events on the Canadian Corps' section of the offensive, which its commander, Lieutenant-General Sir Arthur Currie, described as 'the spearhead of the attack',[36] this chapter draws especially on German sources to understand how the interaction between the two armies led to the day's outcome. The focus is on the *psychological* aspects of friction (that is to say, shock) and the consequences for how the troops fought. In particular, this allows the issue of the impact of the combination of tanks and fog to be reassessed, and hence the command approaches of the two armies to be understood more deeply.

Two contrasting features of the battle illustrate the central importance of friction and shock. The British and French forces took more than eighteen thousand prisoners on 8 August.[37] These amounted to *two-thirds* of the total German losses of around twenty-seven thousand men for the day.[38] To put this in context, more prisoners

---

29   Shane B. Schreiber, *Shock Army of the British Empire: The Canadian Corps in the Last 100 Days of the Great War* (Westport, CT: Praeger, 1997), pp.33-69.

30   Harris, *Amiens to Armistice*, p.103.

31   James McWilliams and R. James Steel, *Amiens 1918: The Last Great Battle* (Stroud: History, 2008), pp.302-305.

32   Messenger, *Day We Won*, pp.249-254.

33   Colonel Jim Storr, *The Human Face of War* (London: Continuum, 2009), p.37.

34   Carl von Clausewitz, *On War*, ed. and trans. by Michael Howard and Peter Paret (Princeton, NJ: Princeton University Press, 1976), p.75.

35   I am grateful to Bruce Gudmundsson for bringing these to my attention.

36   Currie, *Canadian Corps Operations*, p.37.

37   Harris, *Amiens to Armistice*, p.103.

38   Bose, *Katastrophe*, pp. 196-197. Edmonds argued for a lower ratio of prisoners, but seems to have omitted those taken by the French from his total of fifteen thousand. BOH 1918(4), p.

were taken on that one day than by the entire BEF during the last *three months* of Passchendaele.[39] Whereas Lieutenant-General Sir Herbert Plumer's methodical 'bite and hold' technique during that battle sought to kill the defenders, who often fought on despite hopeless circumstances, at Amiens something caused the German defence to collapse psychologically. Yet, although the British suffered fewer than nine thousand casualties during the first day at Amiens,[40] the attack bogged down during the afternoon and made only limited, costly progress thereafter. The poor quality reserve divisions of those same corps whose men had surrendered in droves in the morning successfully sealed the gash in the German defensive line later that day. After four days, it was clear the front had stabilised and the offensive was closed down. This contrast demands an explanation that goes beyond simply the superiority of British tactics or the exhaustion of the German defenders.

In considering shock, this chapter again draws especially on the work of David Rowland and his colleagues at the former Defence Operational Analysis Establishment. As has been noted in earlier chapters, Rowland explored the reasons why troops are normally far *less* effective in combat than on peacetime firing ranges,[41] a phenomenon famously described by S.L.A. Marshall.[42] This research generated a model showing the impact of speed, surprise, threat and bombardment in generating individual and organisational shock.[43] Rowland's mathematical approach, based on extensive 'historical analysis'[44] of combat and training situations, which provided numerical assessment of the impact of each factor, makes his work challenging for non-mathematicians.[45]

This chapter therefore also draws on the work of Leo Murray, one of Rowland's associates, who recently provided a colloquial presentation of the main issues revealed through the DOAE's work.[46] Putting these two concepts of friction and shock together, Murray noted, 'The real trick, the heart of combat, is to do those things that make the enemy fight less. [...] If the conditions are right then almost any man will fight but change those conditions and almost everybody will stop fighting.'[47]

89n2.

39   16,212 prisoners between 21 August and 19 November 1917. *Statistics of the British Military Effort During the Great War, 1914-1920* (London: HMSO, 1922), p.632.

40   BOH 1918(4), pp.158-159.

41   David Rowland, *The Stress of Battle: Quantifying Human Performance in Combat* (London: TSO, 2006), p.56.

42   Colonel S.L.A. Marshall, *Men Against Fire: The Problem of Battle Command* (Norman, OK: University of Oklahoma Press, 2000).

43   Rowland, *Stress*, p.192.

44   Rowland, *Stress*, pp.19-20.

45   For example, Rowland, *Stress*, p.174, fig.7.2.

46   Leo Murray, *Brains & Bullets: How Psychology Wins Wars* (London: Biteback, 2013).

47   Murray, *Brains & Bullets*, p. 34.

Preparation and Deployment

By the end of 1917, the Entente Powers were at a military low: the British Army had expended itself at Passchendaele and Haig no longer had the manpower required for further offensive operations; the French Army was weakened by mutiny; the Italian Army had collapsed at Caporetto; and both Russia and Romania had sought peace terms. The Americans might be coming, but they had yet to arrive in any great strength, and Pershing's insistence they fight as a single unified national force, whatever its undoubted political merits, meant they could not reinforce the formations of their experienced, but exhausted, allies. By contrast, Germany was able to redeploy more than sixty divisions to the Western Front,[48] and refresh its combat divisions with younger men. For the first time since 1914, the Germans enjoyed numerical superiority on the Western Front - 192 divisions compared to 140.[49] Combining these numbers with the widespread application of the flexible tactics developed by the *Sturmbataillone* (Assault Battalions),[50] Ludendorff inflicted a series of hammer blows on the British and French Armies during the spring and early summer of 1918, in an effort to restore mobility to the Western Front and win the war.[51]

The attempt failed. Despite advancing tens of miles and threatening Paris, no breakout was achieved. The 917,000 casualties inflicted on the Entente forces were 'staggering' and represented an attrition rate double that experienced during Passchendaele,[52] but the German Army could not sustain the momentum as it too suffered 778,000 casualties.[53] During the spring, the Class of 1920 was called up, seventeen-year-olds conscripted more than two years earlier than normal.[54] That the tide had reached its peak was demonstrated on 18 July, when General Charles Mangin's French Tenth Army pushed the Germans back six miles and captured fifteen thousand prisoners in just two days.[55] That battle convinced Crown Prince Rupprecht, commanding the army group facing the British, that Germany's ability to launch offensive operations had ended and her forces would henceforth have to stand

---

48   Giordan Fong, 'The Movement of German Divisions to the Western Front: Winter 1917-1918', *War in History*, 7(2) (2000), 225-235 (p. 234).

49   Martin Samuels, *Command or Control? Command, Training and Tactics in the British and German Armies, 1888-1918* (London: Cass, 1995), p. 198.

50   See Bruce I. Gudmundsonn, *Stormtroop Tactics: Innovation in the German Army, 1914-1918* (New York: Praeger, 1989), and Samuels, *Command or Control?*, pp. 231-245.

51   For a masterful analysis of the offensives, and especially the decay in Ludendorff's command style, see Major-General David T. Zabecki, *The German 1918 Offensives: A Case Study in the Operational Level of War* (London: Routledge, 2006).

52   John Terraine, *To Win a War: 1918, The Year of Victory* (London: Papermac, 1986), p. 75n21.

53   McGrandle, 'German Casualties', p. 693.

54   Messenger, *Day We Won*, p. 5.

55   Terraine, *To Win a War*, pp. 95-100.

on the defensive.[56] Ludendorff had lost the initiative. The question was whether the Entente could seize it.

A few days earlier, on 13 July, Haig had instructed Lieutenant-General Sir Henry Rawlinson to revive earlier plans for an attack by his Fourth Army to the east of Amiens. Soon after, Haig informed Rawlinson he intended to reinforce Fourth Army with the Canadian Corps, allowing him to combine it with the Australian Corps and thereby employ the BEF's two most powerful formations in a single assault (the only time this ever happened).[57]

In preparing his scheme, Rawlinson was influenced by the Australian success on 4 July at Hamel. There, the support of sixty tanks from 5th Tank Brigade made possible a surprise attack that inflicted almost four thousand casualties on the Germans, half of them prisoners, for the loss of fewer than nine hundred men.[58] As a result, his initial plan for Amiens called for the use of 400 tanks, translated by the eve of the assault to 534 machines – effectively the entire Tank Corps, apart from 1st Tank Brigade.[59]

Surprise was central to the success of the operation – every man in Fourth Army had a notice headed 'KEEP YOUR MOUTH SHUT' pasted into his 'small book'.[60] In particular, the Canadian Corps had to redeploy from elsewhere in the line in complete secrecy, since the appearance opposite Amiens of this almost-untouched formation would be a clear signal to the Germans of an impending offensive. Elaborate steps were taken to ensure the Germans were given the impression the Canadians were to be used for an attack near Arras and so gained no inkling of their actual move to Amiens.[61] Two battalions, along with casualty clearing stations and a wireless station, were briefly moved to Flanders, and other units were given fictitious orders. The secrecy went to the highest levels of the formation: the divisional commanders and the senior administrative staff officer were kept in the dark until the day before the redeployment began on 30 July. Battalions found themselves entraining with sealed orders, 'not knowing whether they were going north, south, east or west.'[62] These measures had the desired effect. The Germans quickly identified the Canadian forces deployed to Flanders, but although they noted the disappearance of the main body of

56 Zabecki, *German 1918 Offensives*, p.269.
57 Brigadier-General Sir James E. Edmonds, *The Official History of the Great War: Military Operations: France & Belgium, 1918, vol. 3: May-July – The German Diversion Offensives and the First Allied Counter-Offensive* (London: HMSO, 1939) (hereafter *BOH 1918(3)*), pp. 311-313.
58 *BOH 1918(3)*, pp. 197-208 and Messenger, *Day We Won*, p. 11-22.
59 *BOH 1918(4)*), pp. 10 & 24.
60 *BOH 1918(4)*, p. 16 and WO95/437, War Diary, General Staff, Fourth Army: 1st to 31st August 1918.
61 See COH, pp. 389-391, BOH 1918(4), pp. 20-21, and J.F.B. Livesay, *Canada's Hundred Days: With the Canadian Corps from Amiens to Mons, Aug. 8 – Nov. 11, 1918* (Toronto: Allen, 1919), pp. 16-22.
62 Livesay, *Canada's Hundred Days*, p. 20.

the corps, they remained in the dark as to its destination. They could only surmise it might appear in the sector of the British Fourth Army.[63]

The way in which this major redeployment was handled allows an insight into the command approach being used by the British Army at that point in the war, and an assessment to be made of its effectiveness in reducing friction. It is clear commanders at corps level and above had more information about the situation than did their subordinates (and, indeed, regarded it as essential those subordinates had the minimum of information, in order to maintain secrecy from the Germans), resulting in a narrow Knowledge Gap. That the hundred-thousand-strong Canadian Corps, three cavalry divisions, and a dozen tank battalions, as well as the vast quantities of ammunition and other supplies required for the offensive, could be secretly redeployed in little more than a week speaks volumes for the efficiency and expertise of the BEF's logistics.[64] In these circumstances, there was every reason to believe the most effective means by which friction could be minimised was for orders to focus on detail, leaving no requirement for subordinates to exercise initiative (thereby narrowing the Alignment Gap): the troops would be shipped across the theatre like so much freight. The nature of such a large-scale logistical move, in which the efficient movement of many scores of trains required close control over timings and loads, meant local initiative could only serve to increase the level of friction experienced. The approach adopted may therefore be considered as reflecting the application of Logistic Control, and in the circumstances this would appear to have been the most appropriate command approach for the situation.

Yet this assessment overlooks the fact that, even in the most controlled of situations, friction can still emerge, as the Logistic Control approach may not effectively address the Effects Gap. As Clausewitz noted, 'Countless minor incidents – the kind you can never really foresee – combine to lower the general level of performance'.[65]

This was demonstrated by the experience of 1st Canadian Division. The divisional war diary recorded that, on 1 August, fewer than ten officers 'knew of the destination of the Division and of the operation to be carried out.'[66] The war diary and the division's after action report on the administrative arrangements for the battle[67] reveal the consequences of the formation being expected to follow almost blindly the detailed orders issued by higher headquarters.

---

63   Bose, *Katastrophe*, pp. 19-20.
64   See Ian Malcolm Brown, *British Logistics on the Western Front, 1914-1919* (Westport, CT: Praeger, 1998), pp. 234-237.
65   Clausewitz, *On War*, p. 119.
66   Libraries & Archives of Canada (hereafter LAC), RG9, III-D-3, Vol. 4840, Reel T-1923: War Diaries – 1st Canadian Division - Administrative Branches of the Staff (http://www.collectionscanada.gc.ca/archivianet/02015202_e.html) [accessed 24 September 2011].
67   LAC, RG9, III-D-3, Vol. 4840, Reel T-1923: Appendix V - 1st Canadian Division: Report on Administrative Arrangements for Operations East of Amiens, August 8th to 22nd, 1918.

Although it might be expected army and corps headquarters would have better knowledge of the local situation than did their subordinates, and so could treat them as passive objects, the reality of a complex environment meant this was not always the case in practice. There were therefore errors in the orders issued to the division. On 30 July, the divisional staff realised corps headquarters had set aside a concentration area too small to accommodate the whole formation, and several battalions had been allocated to the same village. Later, the buses transporting 1st Canadian Infantry Brigade Group discovered the road assigned for their route by army headquarters was much narrower than indicated on the map: blind obedience resulted in 'many of the buses running off the road and blocking off the column'. Similarly, the orders for part of the divisional ammunition column gave the wrong destination for entrainment (Ligny-sur-Canche rather than Ligny-St-Flochel). Once this had been realised, the troops had to march a further ten miles to the correct railhead, causing a delay of nearly four hours. The orders also overlooked key elements of the move: on 2 August, the divisional AA&QMG 'found the ammunition and trench munitions situation, owing to the secrecy of the move and lack of time, was in a precarious state'. In addition, a second aspect of friction was experienced when units did not correctly follow the orders given to them: some of the troops already in the division's assigned concentration area failed to move away to make space for the Canadians. The Alignment Gap was clearly not closed.

Although the other divisions in the Canadian Corps did not highlight such matters as clearly in their own after action reports, it seems highly unlikely the experience of 1st Canadian Division was unique. The nature of friction was such, therefore, that a host of minor errors served to hinder the smooth fulfilment of the plan.

While none of these outbreaks of friction resulted in serious setback for the planned offensive, it is clear the potential for major disruption was real. This was mitigated only by the dedication of the staff in resolving situations as they arose – an example of the troops on the ground using their initiative to ensure achievement of senior commanders' intent. The administrative staff of 1st Canadian Division were clear in their assessment of the lesson to be learned: 'Secrecy. Administrative Staff Officers must have all information early and it should be left to their discretion as to what they will communicate to Administrative Units.'[68] The Canadian Official History noted one brigade commander 'urged that in similar situations in the future battalion and company commanders be given a longer period in which to develop their plans and study their maps. He suggested that officers who could not be trusted to maintain secrecy were not fit to command battalions and companies.'[69] This was precisely the approach taken by the Australians: in contrast to the Canadians' fixation with secrecy, a series of briefing conferences gave details of the attack to all battalion officers several

68   RG9, III-D-3, Vol. 4840, Reel T-1923: 1st Canadian Division: Administrative Branch, p. 49.

69   COH, p. 390n.

days earlier their Canadian peers received this information.[70] While there were several subsequent incidents where the news could have reached the Germans, secrecy was maintained.[71]

In summary, therefore, it may be suggested that, even within the more predictable circumstances of a move behind friendly lines, the risk of friction remains. Even though a senior commander is likely to have greater knowledge of such situations than his subordinates, there will inevitably arise incidents where this is no longer the case, widening the Knowledge Gap. Similarly, troops cannot always be relied upon to follow orders, even when this is expected of them, increasing the Alignment Gap. As a consequence, Logistic Control can slide into Restrictive Control, where troops are expected to blindly follow orders, even if these are poorly suited to the actual position, and then have to wait for unexpected situations to be resolved through further orders. Even within the constraints of a complex logistical manoeuvre, this situation can be mitigated if junior officers feel empowered to use their initiative to take local decisions to achieve the broader intent, thereby ensuring a shift into Directive Command. Fortunately for Rawlinson, this is what appears to have happened during the redeployment of the Canadian Corps.

The Plan of Attack

By the morning of 8 August, reinforcements during the preceding fortnight had almost doubled Fourth Army's ration strength, bringing it to 441,588 men. It now consisted of fourteen divisions in three corps. From north to south: III Corps (Lieutenant-General Sir Richard Butler), the Australian Corps (Lieutenant-General Sir John Monash), and the Canadian Corps (Lieutenant-General Sir Arthur Currie). Supporting them were the three divisions of the Cavalry Corps (Lieutenant-General Sir Charles Kavanagh). Reflecting the industrialisation of the war, there were also 1386 pieces of field artillery and 684 heavy pieces, twelve battalions (in three brigades) of the Tank Corps, with 342 heavy tanks (Mark Vs), 72 light tanks (Whippets), 120 supply tanks, and 16 armoured cars, and also 800 RAF aeroplanes.[72]

This force, impressive though it was, did not represent the total available to the attack, since the front at Amiens marked the junction between the BEF and the French line. To the south of the Canadians lay the sector of the French First Army (General Eugene Debeney). Placed under Haig's command for the offensive, this formation deployed eleven divisions in three corps. Of these, two corps – XXXI Corps (General Paul-Louis Toulorge) on the left and IX Corps (General Noël Marie Amédée Garnier-Duplessix) on the right – were to make the initial assault. The infantry was supported by the three divisions of II Cavalry Corps (General Felix Robillot), but by only two

70   McWilliams, *Amiens 1918*, pp. 52-53 and 60.
71   AOH, pp. 513-514.
72   BOH 1918(4), pp.22-25 and 29.

battalions of light tanks.[73] This deficiency was perhaps outweighed by the allocation of fully 1104 aircraft, giving the Allies an overall superiority in the air of more than five to one.[74]

Rawlinson's plan for the attack was focused on the Australian and Canadian Corps. The Australians' left flank would be protected by a subsidiary operation by III Corps, while the Canadians' right flank would be covered by the French.

The first day's assault would comprise four phases (see Map 4.1). First, the infantry, supported by tanks, would seize the main German defensive position and, with it, much of the defenders' field artillery. This would involve an advance of 3500-4000 yards to a position designated the Green Line, to be reached within the first two hours. Since the infantry would then be beyond field artillery range, there would be a pause for two hours to allow selected batteries to move forward.

The second phase, led by the tanks and assisted by these mobile batteries and by RAF aircraft undertaking ground support, allowed a further two hours to extend the penetration by an additional 2000-5000 yards: the Red Line. This would overrun the German rear positions and place the attackers in a favourable position for consolidation against the expected German counterattack.[75]

This would complete the break-in phase of the battle and, in most previous offensives, would have marked the limit of the initial advance. A pause lasting days would have been required to bring forward artillery to support a second sequence of attacks, giving the defenders vital time in which to reconstruct their forces and positions. This 'bite and hold' system, while effective in securing slices of territory and holding them against even the fiercest counterattacks,[76] robbed the attack of its tempo.

In an important change of approach, however, Rawlinson sought to avoid this delay by using mobile forces, in the form of mixed formations of cavalry and light tanks, to lead a third phase. This would sweep forward a further 4000 yards and more, to the former Amiens Outer Defence Line: the Blue (Dotted Blue on the Canadian front) Line.

In a final, fourth, phase, the infantry would move up to consolidate this line, while the cavalry and light tanks pushed still deeper into the German rear areas, exploiting the chaos already created by armoured car detachments ranging far behind the defensive lines.[77] In this way, the break-in could be converted into a breakthrough and, perhaps, a breakout. This was clearly the intent of orders issued by GHQ on 5 August, expanded by a Fourth Army order the following day, which set a series of subsequent objectives well beyond the Blue Line.[78]

73 Messenger, *Day We Won*, pp.244-246.
74 BOH 1918(4), p.25.
75 Montgomery, *Fourth Army*, pp.22-25.
76 Ian M. Brown, 'Not Glamorous, But Effective: The Canadian Corps and the Set-Piece Attack, 1917-1918', *Journal of Military History*, 58(3) (July 1994), 421-444 (pp.426-427).
77 Montgomery, *Fourth Army*, pp.22-25.
78 BOH 1918(4), pp.30-31.

Map 4.1: Battle of Amiens, 8 August 1918

The Canadian Corps would attack on a 7000-yard front between the Amiens-Roye road on the right and the Amiens-Chaulnes railway on the left. The assault would be led by three divisions, from right to left, 3rd, 1st and 2nd. 3rd Cavalry Division, which included the Canadian Cavalry Brigade, was placed under Currie's command. 4th Canadian Division was held in reserve, to relieve the cavalry on the Blue Line in the fourth phase.

Supporting the Canadian infantry were 646 artillery pieces.[79] The average density of guns across the entire Fourth Army front was one field gun or howitzer for every 29 yards and one heavy piece for every 59 yards,[80] slightly *lower* than had been achieved for the preliminary bombardment for the Somme in July 1916.[81] However, the density achieved by the Canadian Corps on 8 August was almost twice as great, with one field gun for every 16 yards and a heavy piece for every 30 yards. The guns were to be used in an innovative manner. Unlike at the Somme, to ensure surprise there would be no preliminary bombardment: the guns would first open fire only when the infantry assaulted at 4:20 a.m.[82] Further, two-thirds of the artillery was assigned to counter-battery fire and interdiction of likely assembly places for reserves,[83] in order to cause friction for the defenders.

Several further innovations are of note:

- In an effort to deliver a combined arms approach, 4th Tank Brigade would support the initial Canadian attack with one battalion assigned to each of the first wave divisions (from right to left, 5th, 4th and 15th battalions, each with 36 fighting Mark V tanks), giving one tank for every 64 yards.[84]
- In order to place 'boots on the ground' quickly to protect the deep penetration against the inevitable German counterattack, 1st Tank Battalion, assigned to 4th Canadian Division, was equipped with 36 Mark V* tanks, primitive armoured personnel carriers, each capable of carrying the crews for two machine-guns and two Lewis guns. It would rush up to the Blue Line to stiffen the cavalry until the infantry arrived.[85]
- In order to protect the tanks and make up for the lack of artillery during the later stages of the advance, V Brigade, RAF, would provide ground support to

79   COH, pp. 396-397.
80   BOH 1918(4), p. 23.
81   Brigadier-General Sir James E. Edmonds, *The Official History of the Great War: Military Operations: France & Belgium, 1916*, vol. 1 (1932, repr. Woking: Shearer, 1986), p. 301.
82   All times from the British perspective. German time was one hour ahead, making the assault time 5:20 a.m. for the defenders.
83   BOH 1918(4), p. 34.
84   BOH 1918(4), p.34.
85   Fuller, *Tanks*, pp.219-221.

the corps with three squadrons, one each for the infantry, the cavalry and the tanks,[86] with a particular focus on spotting and destroying anti-tank guns.[87]

- Because the French had decided to compensate for their lack of tanks by retaining a brief preparatory bombardment, with their infantry not leaving the trenches until 5:05 a.m., forty-five minutes later than Fourth Army, the Canadian flank would be exposed until the French caught up.[88] The Canadian Independent Force, a mixed unit of armoured cars, Lewis guns and truck-mounted mortars, was therefore deployed to secure the right flank of the attack.[89]

In terms of the friction likely to be experienced by the opposing forces, Rawlinson's plan was designed to maximise the friction, and especially shock, imposed on the Germans, while minimising that affecting his own forces. Dispensing with a preliminary bombardment, and deploying large numbers of aircraft in a ground support role, would increase the surprise achieved by the attack. The effect would be both physical, catching German gun crews and infantry in the open, and psychological, denying the defenders time to respond mentally to the attack before it was upon them. In addition, artillery and air interdiction would prevent the German commanders from deploying reserves to support the troops in the main defensive zone, an effect amplified by armoured cars ranging deep beyond the front line. Again, the impact would be both physical, through telephone lines cut, headquarters destroyed, and bridges wrecked, and psychological, through distracting and confusing commanders. Finally, the use of cavalry, Whippets and Mark V* tanks to seize the Blue Line ahead of the infantry would disrupt German preparations for the inevitable counterattack.

Conversely, the two-hour pause on the Green Line to allow some field artillery batteries to move forward had the subsidiary benefit of building in extra time in case the initial advance was delayed. The second two-hour pause on the Red Line, designed in part to ensure the attackers were not caught off-balance by a German counterattack,[90] would serve a similar purpose. Further, the deployment of mobile forces onto the Blue Line would protect the British infantry in its final advance, despite being far beyond the range of most of its artillery.

---

86   BOH 1918(4), p.43.
87   Simon Coningham, 'The Battle of Amiens: Air-Ground Co-operation and its Implications for Imperial Policing', in *Changing War: The British Army, the Hundred Days Campaign and the Birth of the Royal Air Force, 1918*, ed. by Gary Sheffield and Peter Gray (London: Continuum, 2014), pp.207-229 (213-214).
88   COH, pp.396-398.
89   Bruce Ivar Gudmundsson, *On Armor* (Westport, CT: Praeger, 2006), pp.11-16.
90   Montgomery, *Fourth Army*, pp.22-25.

From the perspective of command, the orders for the attacking troops were detailed, laying down the timing of each phase of the battle and the lines to be reached.[91] The initial assault was carefully programmed and nothing was to be left to chance. Given the need to coordinate the artillery barrage with the advance of the tanks and infantry, at a time when communication with the advancing troops was almost impossible, such reliance on Logistic Control had repeatedly been proven the most effective means to ensure an ordered advance and a secure consolidation against German counterattacks. The assault was therefore to be commanded along the lines of what had become the standard British model: the 'set-piece'. In Monash's famous description,

> [T]he stage is elaborately set, parts are written for all the performers, and carefully rehearsed by many of them. The whole performance is controlled by a time-table, and, so long as all goes according to plan, there is no likelihood of unexpected happenings, or of interesting developments. [...] It will be obvious, therefore, that the more nearly such a battle proceeds according to plan, the more free it is from any incidents awakening any human interest. Only the externals and only the large aspects of such battles can be successfully recorded. [...] The story of what did take place on the day of battle would be a mere paraphrase of the battle orders prescribing all that was to take place.[92]

It is noteworthy, however, Monash then immediately emphasised that the second phase of 8 August, where the focus shifted away from the infantry and heavy tanks and onto the cavalry and Whippets, was *not* a set-piece operation. As a consequence, 'the developments from hour to hour, and even from moment to moment, are full of intense human interest, and replete with tales of individual courage and initiative.'[93] Clearly, the use of Logistic Control would not be suitable in such a context.

By contrast, Rawlinson appears to have sought to render irrelevant whatever command approach the Germans sought to employ. Their commanders at every level would be overwhelmed by the surprise of the attack, and rendered incapable of taking effective action by the suppression of their artillery and interdiction of their infantry movements. They would therefore be unable to exert any real influence over the course of the battle, regardless of whether they sought to retain tight control over their forces or decentralise. Whether this would be effective in practice, given the German command system was shown in Chapter Two to have been one of Directive Command, where troops were expected to function even in the absence of detailed orders, was to be seen.

From the perspective of tempo, Rawlinson was seeking to ensure the British attack operated at a much faster rhythm than could the German defence. Taking

91   For example, see the Canadian Corps orders at the National Archives in WO95/1053.
92   Monash, *Australian Victories*, pp. 226-227.
93   Monash, *Australian Victories*, p. 227.

the four stages of the Boyd Loop, described in Chapter One, as a guide, the German commanders would be unable to *observe* the situation, due to the destruction of telephone lines by artillery fire and the disruption of communications by the armoured cars. This, coupled with threats to their personal safety from ground-attack aircraft, would make them unable to *orientate* themselves, and hence would undermine the validity of their *decisions*. Finally, the capacity of their forces to *act* on those decisions would be minimised by interdiction of assembly places and roads. A key question, however, was whether the two two-hour pauses, first on the Green Line and then on the Red Line, would give the defenders time to recover their equilibrium and bring up sufficient reserves to blunt the British advance.

The Defence

Rawlinson's desire to include pauses to allow his infantry to consolidate their positions against the risk of counterattack was based on bitter experience. By the end of 1917, the German Army had developed a sophisticated system of defence, designed to absorb the force of an enemy offensive in a deep battle zone. At the heart of this doctrine was an emphasis on counterattack at every level.[94] The defensive zone was held in depth by 'position' divisions (*Stellungsdivisionen*), which kept the attackers off-balance through continual small-scale counterthrusts (*Gegenstösse*). Behind the position, beyond field artillery range, were 'intervention' divisions (*Eingreifdivisionen*). These launched large-scale counterthrusts, designed to push the enemy back out of the defensive zone. In order to ensure sufficient forces, position divisions should hold fronts of 2500-3000 metres, with intervention divisions behind. Should these immediate counterthrusts fail to recover the original front line, deliberate counterattacks (*Gegenangriffe*) would be made once further reserves had arrived, but only if the ground to be recovered was considered valuable enough to warrant the resulting losses.[95]

---

94 This fits with Clausewitz's insistence that 'defense is a stronger form of war than attack', in part because of the defender's ability 'to surprise his opponent constantly throughout the engagement by the strength and direction of his counterattacks.' Clausewitz, *On War*, pp. 357-369.

95 Die Abwehr im Stellungskrieg, 4th edn (20 September 1918), para. 9-10, in Erich Ludendorff, *Urkunden der Obersten Heeresleitung über ihre Tätigkeit 1916/18* (Berlin: Mittler, 1920), pp. 608-609. For the evolution of the doctrine, see Samuels, *Command or Control?*, pp. 158-197.

On 8 August, the German defenders facing the Canadians were from Generalkommando (Genkdo) 51[96] (Generalleutnant Eberhard von Hofacker), part of General der Kavallerie Georg von der Marwitz's Second Army. Hofacker, who had been given command of the corps in November 1917, following his successful leadership of 26th (1st Württemberg) Division at Caporetto, had placed four of his five divisions in the line: 117th and 225th Divisions faced the Canadians, while 14th Bavarian Division and 192nd Division lay south of the Amiens-Roye road, in the French sector. Only 109th Division was in reserve.[97] The 7000 metres of front held by the two divisions opposite the Canadians was somewhat wider than laid down in the regulations. Moreover, the availability of only one intervention division for the whole corps was much less than recommended: towards the end of the great battles of 1917, it had become the norm for there to be a intervention division behind each position division.[98]

Whether the defending forces were spread too thinly was underlined by concerns regarding their quality. The thirteen divisions under Marwitz's command were generally in poor shape, averaging only 3000 men each,[99] but this disguised a wide variation. On 3 August, he had assessed their individual combat-readiness, identifying four categories: fully combat ready (two divisions, including 117th), combat ready for position warfare (five divisions, including 225th and 14th Bavarian), suitable only for defensive operations on a quiet front (three divisions, including 192nd), or ready to be dissolved (three divisions, including 109th).[100]

A sense of the relative state of these divisions can be gained from their rifle strength (excluding machine-gunners) shortly before the British attack. One of the divisions in Marwitz's second category (41st) averaged just 315 riflemen in each of its nine battalions, a division in the third category (13th) averaged only 284,[101] while a division in the fourth category (43rd Reserve) averaged a mere 168 riflemen per battalion.[102] At that time, the official combat strength of a battalion was 650 men.[103] 117th Division, however, was a different story: under its new commander, the one-armed Generalmajor Karl Höfer, it had distinguished itself during the Battle of the Lys in April 1918, but

---

96 Effectively a corps headquarters, but (like all sixteen such headquarters created after September 1916) given a designation in Arabic, rather than Roman, numerals to underline the shift from command of a fixed corps to a varied range of divisions, dependent upon the task at hand. Hermann Cron, *Imperial German Army 1914-18: Organisation, Structure, Orders-of-Battle*, trans. by C.F. Colton (Solihull: Helion, 2001), pp. 87-89.

97 Bose, *Katastrophe*, map.

98 Ludendorff, *War Memories*, p.489.

99 Liddell Hart, *Tanks*, vol.1, p.178.

100 Bose, *Katastrophe*, pp.26-27.

101 Although six hundred replacements reached the division a week before the battle, it was felt these could not be assigned to units until the formation was withdrawn into reserve.

102 Bose, *Katastrophe*, pp. 26-36.

103 Cron, *Imperial German Army*, p, 112. The figures are not entirely comparable, as Cron's figure includes machine-gunners.

had been out of the line since early May (apart from a three-week defensive stint in June). At the beginning of August, it was therefore fresh, well trained and up to strength.[104] Even so, on the Canadian Corps front at least, the attackers outnumbered the defenders by perhaps five to one.

The risks resulting from the limited number of defenders were increased by their sense of complacency. The physical defences had been constructed to only the most limited extent. Units seem to have been more concerned with ensuring their reports on the development of positions were accepted by the higher command than with actually building the positions – a task they considered impossible due to lack of manpower.[105] Reports suggesting the possibility of an attack by Rawlinson's forces,[106] including one sighting of a hundred tanks, were not taken seriously. One German staff officer complained of Second Army headquarters' indifference, arguing that no-one deployed such a powerful force just for a 'joyride'.[107] In fact, as Liddell Hart noted, there were no tanks near the front line on the dates of these reports.[108]

In summary, Hofacker's front facing the Canadians was held by two sound divisions, though on somewhat extended fronts, but with reserves wholly inadequate in both numbers and quality, in positions far from being the deep zone of obstacles imagined by higher commanders. In addition to these physical factors, the senior commanders had little inkling of the impending attack, while the frontline troops were 'jumpy' and fearful of facing tanks. Furthermore, 8 August brought two of the coincidences so typical of the role of chance in producing friction in warfare. First, a thick blanket of fog shrouded the battlefield, blinding the defence,[109] though Wise refers to this heavy ground mist as 'inevitable',[110] implying it may not have been as unexpected as has traditionally been assumed. Second, 117th Division was in the midst of relieving 109th Division, with neither division fully in place or familiar with their new positions. Consequently, both formations[111] were 'in a state of disintegration'.[112]

104 Bose, *Katastrophe*, p. 135 and Anlage 2.
105 Oberkommando des Heeres, *Der Weltkrieg, 1914 bis 1918: Die militärischen Operationen zu Lande*, vol.14 (Berlin: Mittler, 1944) (hereafter GOH), p.549.
106 For example Hauptmann Hubert Hofmiller, *Das k.B.4.Infanterie-Regiment "König Wilhelm von Württemberg" im Weltkriege 1914-1918* (Munich: n.p., 1921), p.26 and Cyril Falls, 'An Aspect of the Battle of Amiens, 1918', *Army Quarterly*, 6 (Jul 1923), 298-306 (p.299).
107 Bose, *Katastrophe*, pp.18-19 and BOH 1918(4), p.37.
108 GOH, p.551 and Liddell Hart, *Tanks*, vol.1, p.178.
109 Kabisch, *Schwarze Tag*, p. 124. Fog was one of the key factors in creating friction noted by Clausewitz, see Clausewitz, *On War*, p. 120.
110 Wise, *Canadian Airmen*, p.525.
111 Bose, *Katastrophe*, p.136.
112 Montgomery, *Fourth Army*, p.37n1.

To the Green Line and on to the Red

On the other side of the trenches, the front of 1st Canadian Division, led by 3rd Canadian Infantry Brigade (Brig-Gen G. S. Tuxford), almost exactly coincided with that of 117th Division,[113] with only the northernmost section of the German defences falling in the sector of 2nd Canadian Division's 4th Canadian Infantry Brigade (Brig-Gen R. Rennie).[114] Combining the war diaries and after action reports of these two formations[115] with Bose's account[116] and the relevant German regimental histories gives a clear sense of the challenges faced with regard to friction and shock.

Although the German artillery bombarded the positions occupied by 4th Canadian Brigade shortly before the start of the attack, causing numerous casualties in one battalion, this fire rapidly faded once the British barrage began and the infantry moved off. Both brigades found the fog reduced visibility to just ten yards. As a result, one officer of 3rd Canadian Brigade found himself unintentionally leading his unit towards the rear before correcting himself with his compass. The battalion commanders mitigated this source of friction by personally moving into the front waves and placing compass-bearing parties on the flanks of their units. The fog was a particular problem for the tanks, with 4th Tank Battalion reporting 'Tanks could not see one another neither could they see any Targets except the flash of Machine Guns': several tanks accidentally slid into small trenches.[117] As a result, only twelve of the battalion's twenty-two tanks reached the Green Line. The fog also hindered the RAF, which was barely able to operate, though a few bold pilots were able to provide some limited ground support.[118]

In 3rd Canadian Brigade, 16th (Canadian Scottish) Battalion largely faced Infanterie-Regiment 157, the left hand regiment of 117th Division.[119] This unit had placed II Battalion/157 in the front line and III/157 in the battle zone. The Canadians faced little opposition at first – the fog made it almost impossible for the German officers to exert any influence over the defence and the anti-tank guns were overrun before they could open fire. Indeed, the sound of fighting was so limited the commander of II/157, Major Mende, assumed the attack had been easily repulsed. The first

---

113 BOH 1918(4), pp.48n1.
114 Bose, *Katastrophe*, map 2.
115 RG9/III-D-3/4878/T-10676: War Diaries – 3rd Canadian Infantry Brigade, August 1918, War Diary and Appendix 10a, and RG9/III-D-3/4883/T-10680: 4th Canadian Infantry Brigade, August 1918, War Diary and Appendix 10.
116 Bose, *Katastrophe*, pp.138-142.
117 WO95/110: 4th Tank Battalion, August 1916 to September 1919: Report on Operations with 1st Canadian Division, Luce Valley, August 8th, 1918, s.10.
118 S. F. Wise, *Canadian Airmen and the First World Wa: The Official History of the Royal Canadian Air Force*, vol. 1 (Toronto: University of Toronto, 1980), p.526.
119 Generalleutnant Tiede, Hauptmann Himer and Oberleutnant Röhricht, *Das 4.Schlesische Infanterie-Regiment Nr.157*, Erinnerungsblätter deutscher Regimenter, vol.14 (Berlin: Stalling, 1922), pp.59-60.

Canadian hand grenade exploded in his dugout only moments after a runner reached him with news of the true situation. The Canadian advance continued smoothly, despite growing resistance (an attempted counterthrust by III/157 in Aubercourt was overwhelmed moments after it was ordered), and the German regimental commander and his entire staff were soon captured. The Canadians then surprised a large number of German guns, whose crews put up a vigorous fight but were unable to prevent the attackers reaching the Green Line only slightly behind schedule.

Despite being hit by their own barrage, 13th (Royal Highlanders of Canada) Battalion also made rapid progress. Their opponents, Grenadier-Regiment 11, had placed both combat battalions, Fusilier/Gren11 and II/Gren11, in the front line. Both were shattered by the British barrage and the advancing tanks. Only remnants escaped to the rear, where they were rallied by the regimental commander, Major von Fehrentheil und Gruppenberg. They held back the advance until he was killed by fire from two trench mortars brought forward by the Canadians, and then retreated.

Reserve-Infanterie-Regiment 22 held the northern portion of 117th Division's front, with I/Res22 in the front line and II/Res22 in the main position. Due to the ongoing relief, these troops were still under the command of Major Graf von Brockdorff, commander of Grenadier-Regiment 2 of 109th Division. 14th (Royal Montreal) Battalion, along with 18th (Western Ontario) Battalion of 4th Canadian Brigade, rapidly overran I/Res22, but were held back by determined resistance around Marcelcave, rapidly organised by Brockdorff. The Canadian war diaries report determined infantry attacks, supported by tanks, finally overcame the defence, with no prisoners taken after men advancing in response to white flags were fired upon. The resistance would have been stronger, had not two companies of II/Res22 been suppressed in their shelters by the British bombardment. These, along with the regimental staff, were captured as soon as this lifted, since the Canadians followed close behind the barrage.

Having reached the Green Line around the intended time of 8:00 a.m., 3rd and 4th Canadian Brigades consolidated and the advance was resumed by 1st and 5th Brigades. The reserve battalions of 117th Division's three regiments held the key to whether or not the attackers would reach their second objective: the Red Line. The official German monograph noted, 'A simultaneous counterthrust of these three battalions under a united command might perhaps have achieved results, even if only temporary, given the lack of sufficient artillery.'[120] These hopes were in vain. As expected, the longer range meant the British artillery barrage was less effective in disrupting the German communications system behind the battle zone. However, aircraft undertaking ground attacks as well as artillery interdiction fire imposed significant delay and loss on the reserve battalions as they moved forward to hold back the Canadians until the counterattack forces (109th Division) could arrive. As a result, they deployed late

---

120 Bose, *Katastrophe*, p.142.

and piecemeal and, despite determined resistance, the three battalions were unable to impose significant delay on the Canadian advance.[121] Although the Canadians had experienced varying degrees of disorder in their advance to the Green Line, delaying the attack of 3rd (Toronto) Battalion by forty minutes, the combined support of tanks, aircraft and artillery allowed them to overcome this friction and reach the Red Line virtually on schedule.[122]

Rawlinson's surprise attack was as just successful on other parts of the front in imposing an overwhelming level of friction on the German defence, as shown by the experience of two of the other defending divisions: 13th Division (von Borries), part of XI Corps (Kühne) facing the Australians, and 14th Bavarian Division (von Kleinhenz) facing the French.

The history of Infanterie-Regiment 13[123] of 13th Division recorded the fog, mixed with smoke from the bombardment, reduced visibility to no more than ten paces. The forward battalion, III/13, was quickly overwhelmed. Since all communication with the frontline had been immediately lost, the first II/13, holding the battle zone, knew of the attack was when the Australians were already behind both flanks. The battalion commander attempted to deploy his reserve, but to little avail. The regimental headquarters was quickly outflanked and the commander, Major Neumann, wounded. Only a few stragglers reached the positions of the reserve battalion, I/13. The experience of Infanterie-Regiment 15 was similar.[124] Despite the thick fog and minimal artillery support, the forward battalion held on for an hour before being overwhelmed. Just as the regimental commander, Major von Bila, was trying to organise a counterthrust by the reserve battalion, III/15, he and his adjutant were severely wounded by a British shell that destroyed his headquarters. Recognising relief by III/15 was a remote hope, given its position 8000 metres to the rear, the remnants of the regiment attempted to withdraw, but were swiftly captured by the Australians. Infanterie-Regiment 55[125] was equally unable to rest the onslaught. The forward battalion, III/55, was quickly eliminated. II/55, in the battle zone, managed to put up some resistance, especially around Cerisy, but the odds were too great and only a few men escaped.

In 14th Bavarian Division, at the southern end of the battlefield, the history of the Bavarian 4th Infantry Regiment[126] records the French attack forced the defenders back, only for them to find the Canadians had already broken through to the

121 Bose, *Katastrophe*, pp.142-144.
122 McWilliams, *Amiens 1918*, pp.141-144.
123 Generalmajor Carl Groos and Hauptmann Werner von Rudloff, *Infanterie-Regiment Herwarth von Bittenfeld (1. Westfälisches) Nr. 13 im Weltkriege 1914-1918*, Erinnerungsblätter deutscher Regimenter, vol. 222 (Berlin: Stalling, 1927), pp. 309-311.
124 Kabisch, *Der schwarze Tag*, pp. 150-153.
125 Oberstleutnant Schulz, *Infanterie-Regiment Graf Bülow von Dennewitz (6. Westfälisches) Nr. 55 im Weltkriege* (Detmold: Meyerschen, 1928), pp. 233-234.
126 Hofmiller, *k.B. 4. Infanterie-Regiment*, p. 26.

north and seized positions to their rear. As if to prove the scale of the disaster, the account notes not even the brigadier's car was able to escape! Similarly, the history of the Bavarian 8th Infantry Regiment[127] notes simply the fight of the two forward battalions ended quickly, with little information available due to the rapid cutting of telephone communications. The reserve battalion came forward, but it too was overrun. From a regimental strength of 1059 officers and men at the end of May, fully 945 were lost on 8 August. The history of the third regiment in the division, the Bavarian 25th Infantry Regiment,[128] reported its two forward battalions (I/25 and III/25) maintained a fierce resistance for almost four hours. As had been the case with their colleagues in the Bavarian 4th Infantry Regiment, when the survivors of the two battalions retreated to avoid encirclement, they discovered the French were already behind them. Few reached the safety of Infanterie-Regiment 183 to the south. Finally, the forward observation detachments of the divisional artillery, the Bavarian 23rd Field Artillery Regiment,[129] were helpless, as communication with the guns was lost almost immediately. Further back, the crews found themselves having to defend their positions with close range direct fire, finally spiking the guns when the French were almost upon them.

These accounts demonstrate the British and French had clearly succeeded in their aim of suppressing and overwhelming the defence, while resisting friction themselves. Sheer numbers, supported by tanks and fog, had been sufficient to overwhelm the defenders, despite their fierce resistance. 117th Division was left 'nearly quite shrink to nothing, barely any infantry left'.[130] By contrast, 3rd Canadian Brigade, for example, suffered only 192 officers and other ranks killed or missing, and 535 officers and other ranks wounded.[131]

Looking at the command approaches employed by the two armies, it is notable how their accounts presented rather different pictures. For the Canadians, the emphasis was on the actions of junior officers and other ranks, such as the lone bravery of Private John Bernard Croak and Corporal James Herman Good, both of 13th Royal Highlanders of Canada.[132] Although Lieutenant-Colonel Elmer W. Jones, commander of 21st Canadian Battalion, was killed leading his men,[133] the only other reference to actions by field officers during the attack was to the incident when the battalion commanders

127 Major August Göz, *Das k.B. 8. Infanterie-Regiment Grossherzog Friedrich II von Baden*, Erinnerungsblätter deutscher Regimenter, Bayerische Armee, vol. 43 (Munich: Bayerisches Kriegsarchiv, 1926), pp. 40-41.

128 Major Heinrich Braun, *Das k.B. 25. Infanterie-Regiment*, Erinnerungsblätter deutscher Regimenter, Bayerische Armee, vol. 44 (Munich: Bayerisches Kriegsarchiv, 1926), pp. 52-53.

129 *Das k.B. 23. Feldartillerie-Regiment*, Erinnerungsblätter deutscher Regimenter, Bayerische Armee, vol. 23 (Munich: Bayerisches Kriegsarchiv, 1923), pp. 63-65.

130 OH1918(4) p.89 quoting Bose, *Katastrophe*, p.147.

131 RG9/III-D-3/4878/T-10676: War Diary - 3rd Canadian Brigade, 8 August 1918, pp.4-5.

132 Livesay, *Canada's Hundred Days*, p. 47.

133 Livesay, *Canada's Hundred Days*, p. 49.

of 3rd Canadian Brigade joined the front wave at the start of the assault, in order to ensure their men advanced in the correct direction despite the fog.[134] The brigade's war diary made no reference to any orders being issued by Brigadier Tuxford during the day.[135] Similarly, 4th Canadian Brigade recorded only regular reporting to divisional headquarters of the attack's progress.[136] Reflecting this lack of active engagement in the battle, neither brigade headquarters moved forward until some hours after the attack.[137] The implication must be this phase of the battle ran according to plan (the Effects Gap was narrow), thereby making further intervention by senior commanders unnecessary. Where minor issues did arise, these were resolved by the subalterns without the need for further intervention. In effect, an approach akin to Logistic Control operated and was effective.

By contrast, German accounts made frequent reference to attempts by battalion and regimental commanders to rally their troops, organise counterthrusts and call forward the reserve battalions for their sectors.[138] In addition to the incidents already noted, the commander of 233rd Infantry Brigade of 117th Division rushed to the headquarters of I/157 as soon as the seriousness of the attack was appreciated. His aim was to make a personal assessment of the situation, and he consequently organised a counterthrust by the remnants of three battalions[139] – a command approach equivalent to Directive Control.

Surprise, Shock and Panic

Yet examination of the casualty lists included in several of the German unit histories suggests problems with this presentation of events. Although the narrative sections of all those volumes recorded the forward two battalions of each regiment were destroyed following a determined resistance, and the third battalions were then involved in fierce fighting, the number of fatalities suffered by those regiments was surprisingly low:

---

134 RG9/III-D-3/4878/T-10676: 3rd Canadian Bde War Diary, 8 August 1918, Appendix 10a, p. 2.
135 RG9/III-D-3/4878/T-10676: 3rd Canadian Bde War Diary, 8 August 1918, p. 4.
136 RG9/III-D-3/4883/T-10680: 4th Canadian Bde War Diary, 8 August 1918, pp. 4-6.
137 RG9/III-D-3/4878/T-10676: 3rd Canadian Bde HQ moved forward at 2:10 pm (War Diary, 8 August 1918, p. 4), while RG9/III-D-3/4883/T-10680: 4th Canadian Bde HQ moved at 7:15 am (War Diary, 8 August 1918, p. 5).
138 See Bose, *Katastrophe*, pp. 139-143.
139 Bose, *Katastrophe*, p. 143.

Unit	Division	Officer Fatalities	Other Rank Fatalities	Facing
Infanterie Regiment 13[140]	13th	2	38	Australians
Infanterie Regiment 15[141]	13th	7	150	Australians
Infanterie Regiment 55[142]	13th	2	-	Australians
Infanterie Regiment 18[143]	41st	4	9	Australians
2nd Grenadier Regiment[144]	109th	1	18	Canadians
Bavarian 8th Infanterie Regiment[145]	14th (Bavarian)	8	94	French
Bavarian 25th Infanterie Regiment[146]	14th (Bavarian)	7	90	French
Infanterie Regiment 183[147]	192nd	2	11	French

The small numbers of men killed contrasts with the large numbers of prisoners. War diaries show some 1800 men and 42 guns were captured by 3rd Canadian Brigade,[148] and 1000 men and 19 guns by 4th Canadian Brigade,[149] figures that tally closely with subsequent analysis that showed 117th Division as a whole lost 48 officers and 1810 other ranks as prisoners, while 109th Division gave up 25 officers and 869 men.[150]

The contrast is clearest with the Bavarian 8th Infantry Regiment (14th Bavarian Division), where the regimental history recorded 945 casualties were suffered (almost the entire strength of the unit),[151] yet just 102 of these were dead: most of the men simply surrendered. A similar picture emerges from the history of Infanterie Regiment

140 Groos, *Infanterie-Regiment 13*, Ehrentafel.
141 Generalleutnant Gustav Riebensahm, *Infanterie-Regiment Prinz Friedrich der Niederlande (2. Westfälisches) Nr.15 im Weltkriege 1914-18* (Minden: Self-Published, 1931), Ehrentafel, pp.397-499.
142 Schulz, *Infanterie-Regiment 55*, pp.313-315.
143 Oberleutnant Werner Meyer, *Das Infenterie-Regiment von Grolman (1.Posensches) Nr.18 im Weltkriege*, Erinnerungsblätter deutscher Regimenter, vol.285 (Berlin: Stalling, 1929), p.381.
144 Generalmajor Döring von Gottberg, *Das Grenadier-Regiment König Friedrich Wilhelm IV (1.Pommersches) Nr.2 im Weltkriege*, Erinnerungsblätter deutscher Regimenter, vol.256 (Berlin: Kolk, 1928), pp.497-523.
145 Göz, *k.B.8.Infanterie-Regiment*, pp.88-91.
146 Braun, *k.B.25.Infanterie-Regiment*, pp.90-92.
147 Major Dr Armin Hase, *Das 17. Königliches Sächsisches Infanterie-Regiment Nr.183*, Erinnerungsblätter deutscher Regimenter, Sächsische Armee, vol.5 (Dresden: Baensch, 1922), pp.118 & 120.
148 3rd Canadian Bde War Diary, 8 August 1918, p. 4.
149 4th Canadian Bde War Diary, 8 August 1918, Appendix 10, p. 3.
150 Montgomery, *Fourth Army*, p.37n1.
151 Göz, *k.B.8.Infanterie-Regiment*, pp.40-41 and 88-91.

18, facing the Australians, which unit suffered only 11 fatalities, but 6 officers (mainly company commanders) were captured, along with most of their men.[152] The same was found with the artillery: 79th Field Artillery Regiment, also with 41st Infantry Division, suffered 15 fatalities, but 10 officers and 133 men surrendered.[153]

A further disparity emerges from calculating the fatalities suffered at Amiens as a proportion of the total for the war by individual regiments. For Infanterie-Regiment 13, the 38 other rank dead represented less than one percent of the 4038 lost during the war as a whole,[154] while for the Bavarian 8th Infanterie Regiment, the 94 other rank deaths represented just over four percent of the 2306 total.[155] The 157 deaths in Infanterie Regiment 15 also represented around five percent of its 3181 total wartime fatalities.[156] By contrast, the 21 dead suffered by the Bavarian 23rd Field Artillery Regiment was more than ten percent of that regiment's wartime losses of 200 men,[157] showing how unusual it was for artillery units to be overrun by the enemy.

Something had clearly gone very wrong indeed for the defenders, such that, notwithstanding the fine words of their post-war regimental histories, most of the soldiers in the forward regiments had simply given up and surrendered. What had caused the mighty German Army to collapse in such spectacular fashion?

As has been noted, Rawlinson had gone to considerable efforts to ensure his attack came as a surprise to the Germans, and in this he had largely succeeded. But what do we mean by 'surprise' and is this sufficient explanation? As noted in Chapter One, Rowland offered a useful definition: 'The achievement of the unexpected in timing, place or direction of an initiative [...]. It can also include the effect of [...] weapon type, their combined use, strength, numbers or speed.'[158]

In these first two phases of the battle, up to the Red Line, Rawlinson had 'achieved the unexpected' in both the timing and place of the offensive. The sheer number of tanks and aircraft involved – more than had ever been deployed by any army – was also unexpected, and hence surprising. However, the Germans were well aware of the potential impact of tanks (Marwitz had faced the previous British tank attack at Cambrai) and the duration of preliminary bombardments had been steadily reducing over the past year, so neither would have been surprising of themselves.

Rowland noted the effect of surprise is 'soldiers cannot perform', due to lack of time and space. Based on extensive historical analysis, he was able to demonstrate surprise on average reduced the effectiveness of the defence by around sixty per cent and hence

152 Meyer, *Infanterie-Regiment 18*, p.381.
153 Fritz   Heidrich,   *Geschichte   des   3.Ostpreußischen   Feldartillerie-Regiments   Nr.79*, Erinnerungsblätter deutscher Regimenter, vol.17 (Berlin: Stalling, 1921), pp.127-133.
154 Groos and von Rudloff, *Infanterie-Regiment 13*, Ehrentafel.
155 Göz, *k.B.8.Infanterie-Regiment*, p.101.
156 Riebensahm, *Infanterie-Regiment 15*, pp.397-499.
157 *k.B.23.Feldartillerie-Regiment*, Ehrentafel.
158 Rowland, *Stress*, p.169.

the attacker's casualties by two thirds.[159] While these are significant figures, the huge disparity in casualties between the British and Germans during this phase of the battle suggests this is not sufficient explanation. For that, it is necessary to consider shock.

As has been seen, Rowland defined shock as 'morale conditions causing stunning, paralysis or debilitating effect'.[160] Whereas surprised troops 'cannot' react (due to lack of time or capability), shocked troops could, but do not.[161] This led to a further connection, between shock and panic, where panic is the instant reaction to a fear-inducing event, while shock follows when no effective reaction (such as flight) is possible.[162] His analysis of armoured attacks indicated whether shock and/or panic occurred depended on four main factors: surprise, 'invulnerable' tanks, poor visibility, and the speed of the attack. Where all four were present, there was a ninety-five per cent probability of shock.[163] This was clearly the case during the opening stages of the attack at Amiens. Faced with an unexpected assault by tanks, against which they had little or no counter due to the blinding of their anti-tank guns, looming suddenly from the impenetrable fog, there can be little doubt, notwithstanding the colourful accounts of the regimental histories, most of the German defenders, already exhausted and demoralised after the failure of Ludendorff's spring offensives, succumbed to panic and fled to the rear, or became shocked and surrendered en masse.

Rowland's analysis also allows the tanks' contribution to be isolated. Analysis of *infantry* attacks shows the combination of surprise, low defence morale and poor visibility gave a probability of shock greater than fifty per cent.[164] Comparing these figures, it is immediately clear the presence of the tanks almost doubled the likelihood of the Germans being shocked, shifting this from even odds to a near certainty. It seems likely the intensity of that shock, and hence the probability of panic, was also much greater.

In summary, therefore, the intensity of the British interdiction fire, supplemented after 9:00 a.m. by aircraft undertaking ground support, cut the communications of German commanders in the battle zone. Attempts to organise local counterthrusts were stifled almost as soon as they were ordered and regimental commanders' efforts to rally their troops gained only limited time. The British advance was too fast for the defenders to be able to implement the German doctrine of maintaining an ongoing level of resistance throughout the battle zone, supported by larger-scale counterthrusts by the reserve battalions, designed to keep the attacker off-balance until the main reserves arrived and launched a substantial counterthrust designed to recover the whole of the battle zone. Although Montgomery noted 'fighting was at one time going

159 Rowland, *Stress*, pp.169-174.
160 Rowland, *Stress*, p.178.
161 Rowland, *Stress*, p.169.
162 Rowland, *Stress*, pp.189-191.
163 Rowland, *Stress*, pp.195-198.
164 Rowland, *Stress*, pp.199-200.

on simultaneously between Morgemont Wood and Aubercourt, an area more than 2,000 yards in depth',[165] the strength of the attack, the hundreds of tanks, and the second fresh brigade of infantry behind each assaulting brigade, meant this resistance could not be maintained beyond noon. This fits with the causes of success highlighted by most recent historians.

But deeper analysis of the German experience suggests, in fact, the critical factor at this stage of the battle was the *combination* of tanks and fog – precisely as was argued by every subsequent German source and echoed by Liddell Hart and Fuller. The fog blinded Marwitz's anti-tank guns, leaving his infantry helpless against 'the awesome rumble of the invisible tanks [which] made the defenders ripe for surrender'.[166] The result was panic and the rapid collapse of the defence, expressed in the large haul of prisoners and the limited casualties suffered by the attacking infantry. It is perhaps unsurprising the German regimental histories preferred to paint a rather more valiant picture in their accounts of the battle.

Through to the (Dotted) Blue Line

The Canadians reached the Red Line at about 11:00 a.m.,[167] the Australians a few minutes earlier.[168] The main German defences had been seized and the position divisions holding them effectively obliterated. Only scattered remnants of their reserve battalions and the low quality units of 109th Division, disordered after being caught in the midst of relief by 117th Division, stood in the way of the attack. Although, as will be seen, Marwitz was actively gathering reserves from far and wide in a desperate attempt to plug the breach, there was a window of opportunity for Rawlinson to convert his break-in into a breakthrough, and possibly even a breakout, with potentially decisive results. But the British had been in this situation often during 1917, lured into advancing, exhausted and disorganised, beyond the reach of their field artillery, only to be swept back to their starting positions by the powerful counterthrusts of the German reserve divisions. Rawlinson's orders therefore called for the attacking infantry to consolidate.[169] Yet this time the situation was different:

> [A]t this stage there was more noise of movement than of firing, [... Currie] was able to feel assured that, except at isolated places, there seemed to be little resistance; some parties of Germans were merely waiting under cover to surrender at the first opportunity, others were showing white flags [...]. No enemy guns

165 Montgomery, *Fourth Army*, p.36.
166 Liddell Hart, *Tanks*, vol.1, p.178.
167 BOH 1918(4), p.51
168 McWilliams, *Amiens 1918*, p.148.
169 Montgomery, *Fourth Army*, pp.22-25.

seemed to be firing and no co-ordinated defence was apparent; many officers thought that armoured vehicles could have gone anywhere.[170]

And armoured vehicles were available, in the form of two battalions, each of forty-eight Whippet light tanks, and a further two battalions, each equipped with some thirty-six Mark V* tanks, carrying in total more than two hundred and fifty machine-gun teams. In addition, while the main body of the attacking infantry consolidated their positions on the Red Line against any potential counterthrust, fresh forces were deployed for the third phase of the assault, in the form of two cavalry divisions and parts of three infantry divisions. Furthermore, in order to avoid the delays resulting from the overly centralised command arrangements that had bedevilled the cavalry exploitation at Cambrai,[171] the commanders of the cavalry divisions at Amiens were given authority to make their own decisions over when to advance, without the need to await orders from corps headquarters.[172]

On the fronts of both the Australian and Canadian corps, the advance was in three waves. In the lead was a cavalry division, supported by a battalion of Whippets, which would move rapidly to seize the (Dotted) Blue Line. Next, a battalion of Mark V* tanks would strengthen the position with their cargo of machine-gun teams. Finally, fresh infantry formations would consolidate the line. On the left, these forces were 1st Cavalry Division with 6th Tank Battalion (Whippets), 15th Tank Battalion (Mark V*), and parts of 4th and 5th Australian Divisions. On the right were 3rd Cavalry Division with 3rd Tank Battalion (Whippets), 1st Tank Battalion (Mark V*), and 4th Canadian Division.[173]

From the perspective of command and friction, this innovative plan of attack was intended to maintain a high level of tempo in the British operation. This would keep the Germans off balance through a combination of the rapidity of the advance (denying their commanders sufficient time to orientate themselves to the developing situation and rendering their responses out of date even before they could be implemented) and the disruption of the defending forces through engaging them in combat before they were ready (imposing friction on the operation of those forces). In the event, both innovations proved almost complete failures.

The Mark V* tanks failed to live up to expectations as primitive armoured personnel carriers. As the dense fog cleared, the German field guns were able to take a deadly toll on the slow-moving tanks: only six of 1st Tank Battalion's thirty-four Mark V*s reached the Dotted Blue Line. And even when the vehicles did reach their objective, their passengers were in no state to deploy their machine guns: 'the infantry

---

170 BOH 1918(4), pp.51-52.
171 Stephen Badsey, *Doctrine and Reform in the British Cavalry, 1880-1918* (Aldershot: Ashgate, 2008), p.289.
172 David Kenyon, *Horsemen in No Man's Land: British Cavalry and Trench Warfare, 1914-1918* (Barnsley: Pen & Sword, 2011), pp.202-204.
173 Fuller, *Tanks*, pp.219-222.

detachments in these tanks suffered severely. Unaccustomed to the heat and fumes, the men became sick; some of them fainting. Detachments of 16 tanks were obliged to seek the fresh air and follow the infantry on foot. [...] The infantry obtained no advantage from the tanks which moved independently away ahead of them.'[174] Nor were the aircraft of the RAF able to provide the intended support: although the disappearance of the fog allowed the tempo of flying operations to be raised, the aircrew found it unexpectedly difficult to spot the German anti-tank guns, though smoke screens were of some benefit.[175]

Meanwhile, the combination of cavalry and light tanks did not lead to a partnership built on their respective strengths. Wherever there was minimal enemy resistance, the Whippets could not keep up with the fast-moving horsemen, but these were in turn unable to operate against machine guns.[176] The after action report of 4th Canadian Division was scathing: 'cavalry are of little use against machine gun positions or woods. In fact, they are a detriment [...]. Their charges at many times against woods and machine gun positions, were exceedingly gallant but futile.'[177] Fuller was scornful of the concept of linking the Whippets with cavalry,[178] though the evidence is clear it was his own idea originally and was taken up by Rawlinson on his advice.[179]

Stephen Badsey has suggested these judgements are too harsh and blame the cavalry for difficulties in what were in fact two highly complex manoeuvres:

> trying to move an exploitation force as large as a division or larger rapidly through a slower moving force, against enemy opposition in the middle of a battle [. ... and] how to fight and co-ordinate an all-arms battle that was also mobile. That the cavalry and Whippets moved at different speeds, and had different levels of protection, was a problem to be solved by proper tactics, not an insuperable objection to their being used together.[180]

Once again, however, these explanations overlook the possibility the *Germans* may have played a role in the course of events. In exploring this aspect of the battle, it is necessary to focus on the actions of commanders in seeking to minimise the friction experienced by their own troops, and the impact of shock in reducing the effectiveness of those efforts.

174 RG9/III-D-3/4861/T-1939: 4th Canadian Division, Narrative of Operations, Battle of Amiens, pp.8 & 20.
175 Wise, *Canadian Airmen*, p.527.
176 BOH 1918(4), p.53.
177 RG9/III-D-3/4861/T-1939: 4th Canadian Division, Narrative, pp.16-17.
178 Fuller, *Tanks*, p.228.
179 J.P. Harris, *Men, Ideas and Tanks: British Military Thought and Armoured Forces, 1903-1939* (Manchester: Manchester University Press, 1995), pp.176-177.
180 Badsey, *British Cavalry*, pp.291 & 296.

Whereas the infantry's advance through the Green Line and to the Red Line ran almost entirely to plan, with only limited friction experienced by the attacking troops, the movement to the Blue Line was undertaken in a situation of considerable friction – the technological innovations largely failed to deliver the desired results and so units were unable to rely on their existing orders. Two factors appear to have been of critical importance here: the morning fog had now largely dispersed, and the German defenders were no longer surprised by the attack.

As has been noted, during the initial phases of the attack, the thick fog had blinded the German anti-tank gunners, so they were unable to engage the advancing tanks until these were almost upon them – 4th Tank Battalion, for example, reported only two tanks lost from enemy field gun fire during the advance to the Red Line.[181] Now, the clearing fog produced a very different experience – 1st Tank Battalion suffered nine losses from the eleven tanks of A Company to a single field battery firing over open sights from Le Quesnel.[182] Similarly, an anti-tank battery of Field Artillery Regiment 79 in 41st Division succeeded in destroying six British tanks, in large part due to the efforts of Vizefeldwebel (Sergeant-Major) Schwesig of 2/FAR79.[183] This may have been the unit seen by Fuller, when he visited the battlefield later in the day: 'Near Bayonvillers I came across a tragic row of Mark V One Star tanks, all of which as they had topped a slight rise had been hit by a battery of field guns'.[184] That these were not isolated events may be demonstrated by the fact Marwitz recorded a similar incident occurring two weeks later, when a German artillery lieutenant singlehandedly destroyed fourteen British tanks.[185]

These references to the effectiveness of individual gun commanders highlights a key, and surprising, finding from Rowland's analysis – the impact on anti-tank effectiveness of what he termed 'heroes'. He discovered guns operating under the supervision of officers or senior NCOs performed at their full potential capability. By contrast, 'approximately one third of weapons [not directly under an officer of senior NCO] made no effective contribution to the battle at all. [...] The remaining two thirds operated at an effectiveness level of roughly 0.3 [30%]'.[186]

As the fog lifted, the officers and senior NCOs of the German anti-tank guns could at last start to influence the defence and generate significant execution amongst the slowly advancing. Faced with this sudden devastating fire, the slow-moving Mark V* tanks advanced still more cautiously. This meant their engines spewed out even more fumes to disable their machine-gunner passengers, while the reduction in

---

181 WO95/110 – 4th Battalion, Tank Corps (August 1916 to September 1919), History of the Fourth Tank Battalion, p.20.
182 WO95/109 – War History of the 1st Tank Battalion, 1916-1919, The War Histories & War Experiences of the 1st Tank Battalion, Tank Corps, France, January 1919, p.37.
183 Heidrich, Feldartillerie-Regiment 79, pp. 114-117.
184 Fuller, Unconventional Soldier, p.311.
185 Marwitz, Weltkriegsbriefe, p.307.
186 Rowland, Stress, pp.118 & 146.

pace allowed the supporting infantry to overtake them. Often overlooked by British armoured enthusiasts, this was a salutary reminder of how vulnerable the tanks still were to determined anti-tank guns. The sight of the Mark V* tanks being destroyed in significant numbers by the defending guns may also have reduced the shock experienced by the remaining German infantry, which was no longer confronted by an invulnerable enemy emerging suddenly from thick fog. This may have contributed to the line stabilising in front of the British cavalry.

Next, we must turn to the effectiveness of the cavalry. The far greater level of uncertainty within which this phase of the attack was undertaken, compared with the certainties of the earlier infantry advance to the Green and Red Lines, was reflected in the war diaries of the two cavalry divisions. These made repeated reference to commanders moving forward, with the divisional headquarters keeping no more than 2000-3000 yards behind the leading units, and issuing frequent orders in response to the changing situation.[187]

The left flank of the mounted force was formed by 1st Cavalry Brigade of 1st Cavalry Division (Maj-Gen Mullins), supporting 5th Australian Division. On the left, 5th Dragoon Guards (Lt-Col Terrot) had been ordered to seize the Blue Line 'if not too strongly resisted'. In the event, the position was unoccupied, so the regiment advanced deeper into the German position, where it surprised and captured a train full of men returning from leave, which had been disabled by a bomb dropped by an RAF plane. The horsemen were forced to dismount when they reached the Framerville-Vauvillers road, 1000 yards beyond the Blue Line, due to growing resistance from III/376 of 109th Division.[188] After Colonel Terrot's horse was hit and requests for reinforcements were unanswered, the regiment withdrew to the Blue Line, having captured 20 officers and 740 men. Twenty-nine awards for gallantry were made to men of the regiment for their actions that day.[189]

On their right, 2nd Dragoon Guards (Lt-Col Ing) were informed by Brigade Headquarters at 9:15 a.m. that 'the Bosch Defence was reported to be weakening, and to push through our Infantry'. Although Colonel Ing's orders were delayed reaching B Squadron, its commander understood the situation and advanced on his own initiative. Over the following hour or so, Ing manoeuvred his squadrons onto and a little beyond the Blue Line, adjusting his plans to the circumstances, until the growing strength of the German opposition[190] forced the regiment to dismount on the Blue Line itself, in order to bolster the few Australian infantrymen who had reached the position.[191]

187 RG9/III-D-3/5072/T-11350: 1st Cav Div, Appx 25 p. 1 for distance behind line.
188 Bose, *Katastrophe*, p. 176.
189 WO95/1109 – War Diaries 1st Cavalry Division, 1st Cavalry Brigade, 5th Dragoon Guards, 8 August 1918 and Report on Operations.
190 Gottberg, *Grenadier-Regiment 2*, pp. 435-436.
191 WO95/1109 – War Diaries 1st Cavalry Division, 1st Cavalry Brigade, 2nd Dragoon Guards (Queen's Bays), 8 August 1918.

Supporting the Canadians were 9th and 2nd Cavalry Brigades of 1st Cavalry Division and the whole of 3rd Cavalry Division (Maj-Gen Harman). The level of resistance here was significantly greater than experienced by 1st Cavalry Brigade. Moving forward from Guillaucourt at 11:15 a.m., 9th Cavalry Brigade immediately came under heavy machine-gun fire, which largely halted the advance until 2nd Cavalry Brigade was deployed to their right, allowing both formations to reach the Dotted Blue Line around 1:00 p.m. Further to the right, 3rd Cavalry Division had found itself involved in action around Cayeux Wood, just beyond the Red Line. Since the Canadian Cavalry Brigade, on the right, was held up at Beaucourt, General Harman at 1:40 p.m. revised his plans in order to deliver an outflanking manoeuvre by 6th and 7th Cavalry Brigades from the left.[192] Kabisch reported their appearance in the rear of the German defenders was 'especially confusing' (*ganz besonders verwirrend*), as this demonstrated without doubt the front had been broken. The presence of the horsemen behind the defensive line also severely disrupted the process of ammunition resupply.[193]

Despite orders stating, 'It must be borne in mind that the task of the Tanks is to assist the Cavalry, and the closest co-operation and touch must be maintained throughout the action',[194] the after action report of 3rd Tank Battalion revealed the Whippets were normally either well ahead of or behind the cavalry, often completely losing touch with them.[195] Where there was no enemy, the cavalry moved far faster than the tanks, but when German machine-gunners were encountered, the cavalry was forced to change direction or wait for the tanks.[196] However, the battalion's account also noted incidents when the two forces *did* cooperate successfully, the tanks suppressing machine-guns and thereby allowing the cavalry to penetrate the defences. The intensity of the action is indicated by the battalion firing 18,410 rounds from its Hotchkiss machine-guns[197] – an average of 500 rounds per tank.

Yet, even without armoured support, the cavalry could be effective against machine guns. As Kenyon noted, where it delivered a rapid charge, casualties were often light and the defenders surrendered as soon as the horsemen reached their positions. The moral effect on the Germans could clearly be significant.[198] Again, this is consistent with Rowland's findings from historical analysis. Cavalry attacks securing surprise in conditions of poor visibility inflicted shock on the defenders in ninety-five percent of cases – the same as tanks. But by the time the British cavalry moved to the Blue Line,

192 RG9/III-D-3/5072/T-11350: 1st Cavalry Division, War Diary.
193 Kabisch, *schwarze Tag*, p. 184.
194 WO95/106: 3rd Battalion, Tank Corps, May 1917 to March 1919, Operation Order No. 3, p.3.
195 WO95/106: Preliminary Report on Operations with the Cavalry Corps and Canadian Corps on 8th, 9th, and 10th, August, 1918, pp.2-4.
196 Liddell Hart, *Tanks*, vol.1, p.181.
197 WO95/106: Preliminary Report, p. 8.
198 Kenyon, *Horsemen*, pp.205-206.

the fog had cleared and the defenders were well aware of the attack and hence unlikely to be surprised. In such circumstances, Rowland found the key factor was the speed at which the cavalry charged. Charges delivered at the gallop over distances under two hundred metres achieved shock in just over half the situations examined: slower charges never did.[199] The accounts from Amiens reveal the cavalry was sometimes able to charge at the gallop and, when it did so, could defeat the German machine-gunners, as when 1st Cavalry Division overwhelmed two battalions of Infanterie-Regiment 376 around Cayeux.[200] But the terrain meant the defenders often had a field of fire far greater than two hundred metres, or rough ground prevented a full gallop. In such circumstances, the cavalry was helpless and dependent upon the supporting Whippets. Yet, in their turn, these were vulnerable to the German anti-tank guns.

In the final phase of the advance, 4th Canadian Division (Maj-Gen Watson) began its advance beyond the Red Line at 12:10 p.m., one and a half hours after being informed the position had been seized by 3rd Canadian Division. On the left, 12th Canadian Brigade eliminated a determined resistance from woods northeast of Beaucourt with the assistance of several tanks, mobile field guns and a trench mortar. Little opposition was then met until the infantry reached the Dotted Blue Line. The relative ease of this part of the advance may have been due to 7th Cavalry Brigade having crossed the ground several hours earlier and then holding the Germans back behind the Dotted Blue Line, though there was no reference to the cavalry in the infantry's account of this phase of the battle. On the right, 11th Canadian Brigade faced heavy machine-gun fire from Beaucourt Wood. A charge by the cavalry 'with great dash and gallantry' had seized the village, but could make no progress against the wood, while an attack by tanks also failed. Slow progress continued to be made, at heavy cost, with the need for officers to understand the situation through personal assessment being demonstrated through the commanders of both 54th and 75th Battalions going forward 'under the most perilous conditions' to see for themselves. This resulted in a decision at 7:00 p.m. not to attempt an assault on Le Quesnel until the following day.[201]

This brief account suggests the cavalry and Canadian infantry sought to deal with the friction experienced in the advance to the Dotted Blue Line through active command by senior officers, who placed themselves at or close behind the front line in order to ensure they understood the situation as it developed and then issued orders designed to respond to that situation. This implies a system of Directive Control, where formation commanders set objectives and tasks for their subordinates, but left them sufficient flexibility in which to exercise initiative over the precise means by which these were to be achieved.

199 Rowland, *Stress*, pp.198-199.
200 Bose, *Katastrophe*, p.178.
201 RG9/III-D-3/4883/T-10680: Report on Operations, 4th Canadian Division, pp. 4-7.

What the war diaries failed to note, however, were the opportunities lost. 5th Dragoon Guards in 1st Cavalry Brigade withdrew to the Blue Line because its squadrons were 'much depleted', yet it had suffered only sixty-three casualties from a strength of over five hundred.[202] Further, as the German accounts make clear, the hastily formed defensive line consisted only of two battalions (III/376 and II/Gren2), both weakened through the loss of their machine-gun and mortar companies.[203] But the Germans made good use of the pause in the assault and plugged the gap, bringing order to their shattered troops and establishing a coherent defence, before the cavalry sought to resume its advance.[204]

Similarly, although 6th and 7th Cavalry Brigades reached the Dotted Blue Line east of Caix by 2:30 p.m. and found the way ahead deserted, 'silent except for the droning of flies and the distant popping of guns', no significant attempt was made to advance beyond the objective.[205] This situation was replicated to the north as 2nd Canadian Brigade relieved 2nd Cavalry Brigade on the Dotted Blue Line between 1:15 p.m. and 2:35 p.m.[206] Only at 3:15 p.m. was 7th Cavalry Brigade finally ordered to press on towards Beaufort, but by then it faced heavy machine-gun fire that halted the advance. Thus, although the cavalry was in fact capable of advancing, even in the face of a solidifying defence, in the event it chose not to do so.

Fuller was scathing in his criticism, noting with particular frustration, 'when, long before dusk, the cavalry retired and in some cases almost to our original front line to water their horses, orders were sent to the Whippet tanks to retire with them!'[207] The Canadian Official History was similarly critical of the cavalry's performance, noting due to 'an apparent reluctance by Cavalry Corps Headquarters to act without instruction from the Fourth Army a great opportunity was lost.'[208] The British Official History reported, 'although Fourth Army orders clearly directed that the cavalry should push forward [...] with the least possible delay', they failed to do so in the absence of explicit orders from the Cavalry Corps.[209] Indeed, the Cavalry Corps appears to have ordered 3rd Cavalry Division to remain on the Dotted Blue Line and allow 2nd Cavalry Division to pass through and pick up the advance[210] – by the time 4th Cavalry Brigade began to advance, two hours later, the defences were too strong and no progress could be made.[211] Even when Montgomery explicitly ordered

202 WO95/1109 – War Diaries 1st Cavalry Division, 1st Cavalry Brigade, 5th Dragoon Guards, 8 August 1918.
203 Bose, *Katastrophe*, p.176.
204 Bose, *Katastrophe*, p.181.
205 McWilliams, *Amiens 1918*, p.167.
206 McWilliams, *Amiens 1918*, p.169.
207 Fuller, *Unconventional Soldier*, p.308.
208 COH, p.407.
209 BOH 1918(4), p.55.
210 RG9/III-D-3/5072/T-11350: War Diary, 3rd Cavalry Division, 8 August 1918.
211 Messenger, *Day We Won*, p.126.

Kavanagh to ensure that the cavalry did not stop on the Dotted Blue Line, but should press deeper into the German positions, communications difficulties meant this instruction took almost four hours to reach 1st Cavalry Division headquarters,[212] by which time the defence had hardened.

The Germans too noted the road was largely open for a deeper penetration.[213] The history of Grenadier-Regiment 2 of 109th Division recorded with surprise the British troops halted for much of the afternoon, apparently waiting for fresh reserves and guns to move forward, ready to renew the assault the next day, despite the weak forces opposing them.[214] That the regiment suffered only twenty men dead and missing during the day,[215] despite holding the front line for several hours, is further evidence the attack beyond the Blue Line was not pressed home with vigour. Kabisch suggested a less timetabled and cautious advance by the British would have led to significantly greater success.[216]

This seems to indicate elements of Restrictive Control were operating within the cavalry at more senior levels. Regimental and brigade commanders clearly felt able to exercise initiative in how they secured the objectives set out in the orders issued by divisional and corps commanders, in some respects employing Directive Control, but they were unwilling to go beyond these when unexpected opportunities arose, even if this would have delivered the intentions of senior commanders at division and corps level. These criticisms mirror the apparent lack of drive evident during the failed exploitation at Cambrai[217] and suggest the problems facing the cavalry were less around technology than command approach.

The German Higher Command

Once the guns had opened fire, the nature of battle in the First World War was such commanders at corps and army level normally had only limited ability to influence the immediate course of events. Their physical distance from the battlefield and inadequate means of communication with the front line meant they focused on deploying reserves and planning for the subsequent days of the battle.[218] It is this dimension of command that must now be examined, starting with the Germans.

As has been noted, the German forces facing Rawlinson's offensive fell almost entirely within the zone of Marwitz's Second Army. In many respects a typical senior

212 WO95/575 – Cavalry Corps, 24th March 1916 to 8th October 1918. Narrative of Operations, August 8th to 12th, 1918, p. 2.
213 GOH, p.557.
214 Gottberg, *Grenadier-Regiment 2*, p.437.
215 Gottberg *Grenadier-Regiment 2*, pp.497-523.
216 Kabisch, *schwarze Tag*, p.187.
217 Badsey, *British Cavalry*, pp.291-292.
218 Prior and Wilson, *Command on the Western Front*, pp. 318-319.

German commander, Marwitz was the son of a noble officer from Brandenburg.[219] A graduate of the famous War Academy, he had spent the subsequent twenty years alternating between staff and line command roles, becoming Inspector-General of Cavalry in 1912. Appointed to command a cavalry corps on mobilisation in August 1914, his successful leadership of an infantry corps during the Brusilov Offensive was rewarded by a return to the West in December 1916 to take up command of Second Army.[220] Nicknamed the 'automatic boiler' by his troops, for his ability to work himself up into a fury, Marwitz was well suited to the task of encouraging the best motivation from his troops, though perhaps less inclined to the quiet reflection of difficulties and their solutions. Fortunately, his chief of staff, Oberst Erich von Tschischwitz, combined a notable tactical awareness with a profound calmness – characteristics displayed to great effect when he played a central role in planning Second Army's surprise counterattack at Cambrai – making him a perfect balance for Marwitz.[221]

Despite the confusion resulting from the combination of the unexpected British assault, the loss of communication with the front line due to the destruction of telephone wires, and the thick fog, Marwitz quickly perceived his troops were facing a major assault. In contrast to the panic gripping his forward units, he and his senior commanders kept their heads.

At 5:00 a.m., just thirty-five minutes after the attack began, he alerted 107th Division in his reserve to be ready to reinforce XI Corps, holding the northern section of the line against the British III Corps. At 5:30 a.m., he released 109th Division to Genkdo 51 opposite the Canadians. At 6:30 a.m., he redeployed 243rd Division (the counterattack division of Genkdo 54) to support the troops facing the Australians. Recognising the British offensive was a major operation and required more than the reserves already directly under his command, Marwitz also obtained 26th Reserve Division from Seventeenth Army on his right and 119th Division from Eighteenth Army on his left.[222] Within two hours, therefore, and before the British had even reached the Green Line, Marwitz had committed five reserve divisions – a force equal to that originally holding the front line.

In the event, none of these divisions reached the battle zone on 8 August. Prior to the offensive, the commander of the RAF in France, Major-General John Salmond, had identified the movement of German forces during the latter part of the day as a critical factor.[223] His planning, however, became focused on preventing the forces facing the Allied attack from being able to withdraw, rather than on hindering the arrival of fresh forces. As a consequence, attention was concentrated on the eleven road and rail bridges across the Somme, rather than on other rail choke points.

219 Marwitz, *Weltkriegsbriefe*, p. 9.
220 'Obituary of General v.d. Marwitz', *Army Quarterly*, 19(2) (January 1930), 238-241 (pp. 239-240).
221 Kabisch, *schwarze Tag*, pp. 33-34.
222 Bose, *Katastrophe*, pp.130-131 & 171-172.
223 Wise, *Canadian Airmen*, pp.523-524.

Throughout the afternoon, Salmond hurled the aircraft of IX Brigade against the bridges: 205 sorties.[224] Casualties were heavy, with some thirty machines lost and a slightly larger number severely damaged (the overall wastage rate for low-flying aircraft was an unsustainable 33%),[225] but only two of the bridges were hit, neither being destroyed.[226] Echoing comments made at the time,[227] the RAF Official History subsequently emphasised bridges were 'a most difficult kind of bombing target ... [such that even u]nder the most favourable conditions for aiming, therefore, there would have been much uncertainty over success'.[228] As a result, the RAF's impact on the movement of the German reserves appears to have been very limited. Marwitz made no mention of these attacks in his diary and his efforts to seal the hole smashed in his lines ran largely to plan

On the battlefield itself, however, the effect of the aircraft providing ground support was devastating:[229] 'vehicles and men fled eastwards in headless confusion. In places, individual teams of horses, having left their wagons standing, galloped back in complete panic'.[230] Later in the battle, Marwitz himself was forced to hide in a shell hole as an 'army of planes [...] whizzed up in the blinking of an eye' to bomb the convoy he was driving with.[231] In one extraordinary incident, a single aircraft maintained such continuous fire on a hundred German troops massed for a counterattack they surrendered as soon as the Canadian infantry arrived.[232] Perhaps inevitably, the cost in aircraft was high, with three-quarters of losses being to ground fire.[233]

The chaos poured from the air was increased on the ground by the sixteen armoured cars of 17th Tank Battalion. Towed across the trenches by tanks after the initial assault, they sped ahead of the advancing infantry just before these reached the Blue Line. Ranging freely behind the German lines, 'there were [...] several cases of armoured cars following German transport vehicles, without anything unusual being suspected, until fire was opened at point-blank range.'[234] This threw the German supplies organisation around Proyart and Framerville into utter disorder.[235] Yet, despite operating deep inside the defensive system, the battalion suffered not

224 H.A. Jones, *The War in the Air: Being the Story of the Part Played by the Royal Air Force*, vol. VI (Oxford: Clarendon, 1937), p.442.
225 Jones, *War in the Air*, p.446.
226 Wise, *Canadian Airmen*, pp. 531-534.
227 Wise, *Canadian Airmen*, p.540.
228 Jones, *War in the Air*, p.457.
229 Zwehl, *Schlachten*, p.22.
230 Bose, *Katastrophe*, p.131.
231 Marwitz, *Weltkriegsbriefe*, pp.304-305.
232 Wise, *Canadian Airmen*, p.527, for other examples see also Jones, *War in the Air*, pp.437-440.
233 Coningham, 'Battle of Amiens, p. 214.
234 Fuller, *Tanks*, pp.290-292.
235 Kabisch, *schwarze Tag*, p.186.

a single fatality.[236] Through these means, the British dramatically increased the friction affecting the Germans, hindering Marwitz's ability to launch the massive counterthrusts from behind the battle zone that often devastated British advances during 1917.

Despite this chaos, however, senior German commanders continued to function effectively. The commander of Genkdo 51, Hofacker, persuaded III Corps to his left to deploy three assault detachments from 1st Reserve Division into the area east of Le Quesnel, providing his defence with much needed depth.[237] While these forces moved into position, at 10:45 a.m. he placed 109th Division, released from Marwitz's reserve, astride the Chaulnes railway in order to halt the British advance around Harbonnieres and Caix.

Following the near total destruction of 117th Division, its commander, the one-armed Generalmajor Karl Höfer, was given responsibility for the zone south of the railway line, facing the main attack by the Canadian Corps and 3rd Cavalry Division. Despite the heavy weight of air attack and artillery fire, Höfer immediately drove his staff car right up to the front line around Caix. Here, he found a gap in the line 800 metres wide, with men from four divisions fleeing eastwards in utter confusion. Höfer's personal intervention steadied the troops in this area, re-establishing the defence along the heights to the east of Caix, which marked the Blue Line.[238]

A similar story was played out a short distance to the north, where the attack of 1st Cavalry Brigade was halted by 'considerable opposition, apparently organised by a Divisional General who is thought to have been an Austrian'.[239] In fact, this second incident probably involved one of the four Austrian staff officers who, along with Höfer, had breakfasted with Marwitz a few days earlier. They had just completed a fortnight's training with one of the Assault Battalions and were about to start attachments to divisions for further instruction.[240] In deciphering prisoners' accounts, the British seem to have conflated the two incidents, perhaps revealing an expectation such events must be an exceptional and unusual occurrence. In reality, these episodes demonstrated the increasing willingness of senior German officers to become personally involved in resolving crises at the key points of the battle, employing Directive Control.

At about the same time as Höfer and the Austrian staff officer were starting to plug the gap in the lines in the area around Caix, this weakness in the defences had become apparent to Marwitz. He immediately transferred 119th Division (now arrived from Eighteenth Army) to the command of Genkdo 51. In so doing, Marwitz issued not

---

236 WO95/116 – 17th Battalion, Tank Corps, April to December 1918. Report on Operations of 17th (Armoured Car) Tank Battalion, 8th August, 1918, p.2.
237 Bose, *Katastrophe*, pp.171-172.
238 Bose, *Katastrophe*, pp.178-179.
239 WO/95/1109, 5th Dragoon Guards, war diary 8 August 1918, and 1st Cavalry Division, Appx 25, p.2.
240 Marwitz, *Weltkriegsbriefe*, pp.302-303.

an order (*Befehl*), but an intention (*Weisung*), regarding how Hofacker should use the formation. In German military terminology, a *Weisung* was the weakest level of instruction, designed to leave the greatest scope for the subordinate to use their initiative and knowledge of the situation.[241] Despite being 'nailed to the telephone',[242] Marwitz recognised his knowledge of the situation was likely to be less complete than that of the commander on the spot. He therefore restricted himself to 'advising' Hofacker to deploy the division to the east of Vrely in order to launch a counterthrust against the Canadians advancing either from Caix or to the north, but left the final decision to his subordinate.[243]

By the time night fell, the five German divisions holding the front attacked by the British had been obliterated, losing over 600 officers and 26,000 men, as well as more than 400 guns.[244] The British believed there were 'few hostile reserves immediately available',[245] which would have meant Rawlinson was on the verge of a potentially war-winning fracture of the German front.

In truth, Marwitz had drawn reserves from near and far. Seven additional divisions, sufficient to re-establish a continuous defensive line, would be in place by the time the offensive entered its second day. But the troops grimly manning the new defences, in places six miles to the east of the old front line, were already combat weary, with many units at the limits of their fighting capacity, while their artillery was depleted or still en route. Germany's prospects for the coming day were grim.[246] The key question was whether the British would be able to maintain the tempo of their assault.

In the event, only a few score tanks remained operational, surprise had passed, and the fog was long gone. Added to this, a significant level of command confusion within Fourth Army meant the assaults on the succeeding days lacked power. It was hardly surprising, therefore, no further incidents of massed surrender were recorded, even though the German divisions hastily shifted to the battlefield were of no better quality than those that had collapsed so spectacularly on the first day of the battle. As a result, 9 August proved to be 'a day of wasted opportunities'.[247] Although Rawlinson still made progress, it was very limited in comparison, and at much heavier cost, than the heady successes of 8 August.

241 Stephan Leistenschneider, *Auftragstaktik im preussisch-deutschen Heer 1871 bis 1914* (Hamburg: Mittler, 2002), p. 60.
242 Marwitz, *Weltkriegsbriefe*, p. 303.
243 Bose, *Katastrophe*, p. 192.
244 Bose, *Katastrophe*, p. 196.
245 Montgomery, *Fourth Army*, p.51.
246 Bose, *Katastrophe*, pp. 196–197.
247 BOH 1918(4), p. 93.

Order, Counter-Order, Disorder

One Canadian commentator wrote the attack at Amiens 'merely applied successfully' the plan originally developed for Cambrai, where it had proven impossible to exploit the initial successes achieved due to the absence of sufficient reserves.[248] Rawlinson had already identified this as a critical factor and had therefore retained three divisions in Fourth Army reserve: 17th, 32nd and 63rd. Having spent the morning of 8 August at his headquarters, monitoring events and discussing with Haig the action to be taken to exploit the successes being achieved, Rawlinson ordered these reserves to move forward in readiness to maintain the momentum of the attack the following day. Then, accompanied only by an ADC, he drove to the advanced headquarters of the Canadian Corps at Gentelles, arriving around 4:00 p.m. Currie was absent, visiting his divisions, so Rawlinson considered the situation with Currie's BGGS, Brigadier General N.W. Webber. He agreed to release 32nd Division to reinforce the Canadian effort the following day,[249] a decision subsequently confirmed by telegram from Fourth Army headquarters.[250]

Currie was given discretion to fix the time at which his assault would be renewed, with the Australians conforming to this: he decided on 5:00 a.m.[251] Given the fragile nature of the German defences, attacking so early offered a good chance of shattering the enemy position before Marwitz had time to solidify his forces. However, as Montgomery subsequently noted, 'difficulties of communication and other causes' meant the attack was in the event disjointed, with individual brigades and divisions starting their operations at a variety of times between late morning and early afternoon, with coordination between the different arms haphazard at best.[252] This dramatic increase in the level of friction experienced by the British was especially unfortunate, as the Germans remained disorganised and incapable of mounting serious counterattacks. But what Montgomery failed to make clear was those 'difficulties of communication and other causes' were in large part the consequences of his own actions.

At 6:30 p.m., just as Currie was about to issue the orders for the next day's attack, a telegram was received from Montgomery. This cancelled the release of 32nd Division and, ominously, instructed Webber to travel back to the corps' main headquarters at Dury 'for telephone conversation'. The roads were clogged with the units of 32nd Division moving forward, lorries trying to carry supplies to the advanced troops, and columns of prisoners trudging to the rear, so it took Webber fully two hours to reach Dury. Upon finally reaching the telephone, he found the sole purpose of his

248 Livesay, *Canada's Hundred Days*, p. 91.
249 WO95/1053 – Letter from N.W. Webber to J.E. Edmonds, 8 May 1939, p. 1.
250 BOH 1918(4), pp. 85-86.
251 BOH 1918(4), p. 86.
252 Montgomery, *Fourth Army*, pp. 51-52.

journey appeared to be for Montgomery to express how 'very irate [he was] with Army Comdr [sic] for daring to give away 32nd Divn [sic] and with [Webber] for aiding and abetting'.[253]

The consequences of Montgomery's actions, both in countermanding the army commander's direct orders (especially when Rawlinson's original release of 32nd Division to Currie was reconfirmed by telephone at 7.00 p.m.,[254] half an hour *after* Montgomery had withdrawn it) and in summoning Webber back from his position simply for a dressing down, were very significant. Instead of being able to issue orders for the next phase of the attack at 6:30 p.m., giving the troops more than ten hours to prepare, the orders had to be entirely rewritten, losing valuable time. Furthermore, due to the confusion on the roads, these new instructions did not reach the divisions until after 4:00 a.m., by which time zero hour had been postponed until 10:00 a.m.[255] This loss of five hours was a directly consequence of Montgomery's actions.

Compounding the resulting case of 'order, counter-order, disorder', while Webber was motoring to and from his unpleasant telephone conversation and the staff at Canadian Corps headquarters were recasting their plans for the battle, the troops of 32nd Division continued to march towards the front line, while those of 3rd Canadian Division continued to settle down in the rear, following their relief on the Red Line. Both divisions were therefore badly out of position when the new orders arrived and had to march past each other, moving in opposite directions on clogged roads, to reach the places now assigned to them.[256]

The friction caused by Montgomery's actions was therefore very significant. In addition, he had directly contradicted an order given personally by Rawlinson when he was at Canadian Corps advanced headquarters, and so might have been expected to have had a clearer understanding of how the battle was unfolding than did Montgomery, back at Fourth Army headquarters. Before concluding Montgomery was acting in a manner consistent with Restrictive Control, however, the question must be considered whether in fact he did have a better understanding of the situation than Rawlinson.

Although 32nd Division was originally intended to be used to support the renewal of the Canadian advance on 9 August, its deployment from Flanders did not go smoothly. A five-hour delay meant the last of its infantry did not reach their concentration point at Gentelles Wood, ten miles behind the new front line, until midnight on 8 August and the artillery did not arrive until early the following afternoon. Responding to this friction, it had been agreed late on 7 August the division should not be employed until

253 WO95/1053 – Webber to Edmonds, 8 May 1939, p. 2, BOH 1918(4), pp. 86-87, and COH, pp. 410-411.
254 WO95/1053 – Message slip, 7 p.m., 8 August 1918.
255 COH, p. 410.
256 McWilliams, *Amiens 1918*, pp. 192-193.

the third day of the battle.[257] In the event, 32nd Division was finally released to the Canadian Corps at 8:15 p.m. on 9 August.[258]

The situation in the late afternoon of 8 August, therefore, was Montgomery, behind the lines at Fourth Army headquarters, was aware 32nd Division was not fully detrained and therefore could not reach the Blue Line in time to renew the attack the next morning, as had originally been planned. But Rawlinson, at Canadian Corps advanced headquarters, was aware the German defences were perilously weak and that a determined attack might cause them to collapse. By coincidence, this headquarters was very close to 32nd Division's concentration point and it is possible that Rawlinson may have felt the troops were sufficiently ready as to justify the risk of using them before the formation was fully deployed. Indeed, the battalions of 96th Brigade reached Domart, just behind the old front line, at midnight and could have been used to renew the attack late the next morning, even if this might have required reliance on the Canadian artillery. In the event, all they did that day was to march the five miles to Beaucourt, in preparation to attack on 10 August.[259]

It appears Montgomery displayed a strong reluctance to depart from the agreed plan for the battle, even though the advance had been even more successful than expected and the senior commander was on the spot issuing orders. This stance might have been justified, given the frequency during 1917 with which German counterthrusts by reserve forces had swept away impetuous advances by British troops. Yet the result of Montgomery's countermanding of Rawlinson's orders was in fact to create at least as much disorder as he had been seeking to avoid. By forcing the exhausted units of 3rd Canadian Division to turn about and march back where they had come, Montgomery may well have created a situation where the renewed attack on 9 August was even more delayed and less organised than had he allowed Currie to use 32nd Division. It may therefore be suggested Montgomery's action was indeed representative of Restrictive Control, leading to an increase in friction and a loss of tempo. The result was the Germans were given vital hours in which to consolidate their new line and launch counterthrusts sufficient to reduce the British advance to a crawl and cause the battle to be closed down on 11 August.[260]

Impact on the German Supreme Command

We have seen how the British attack had inflicted shock on the defenders of the German front line, causing them to surrender in droves, but the effect had been limited in time and space. The rear battalions trying to plug the gap torn in the

---

257 WO95/2372 – 32nd Division, War Diary, August 1918. Report on Operations of 32nd Division, August 10th & 11th, 1918, p. 2.

258 WO95/2372 – 32nd Division. Report on Operations, p. 4.

259 WO95/2397: war diaries of 2/Manchester, 15/Lancashire Fusiliers and 16/Lancashire Fusiliers.

260 Messenger, *Day We Won*, pp. 211-212 & 219.

German line had proven far more able to resist the advancing tanks and cavalry as the fog cleared. Similarly, Marwitz and his senior commanders had faced the surprise of the offensive with a decisive calmness all the more remarkable given the chaos and confusion generated by the massive RAF ground-attack effort and the rampaging armoured cars of 17th Tank Battalion ranging far behind the defensive zone. But what of the German supreme command?

In a lecture delivered shortly before the Second World War, General Sir Archibald Wavell argued 'the first essential of a general [is] the quality of robustness, the ability to stand the shocks of war'.[261] Marwitz and his subordinates had responded well. What of Ludendorff?

On 4 August, Ludendorff had written to Rupprecht, stating his belief the deployment of German forces in depth in strong positions meant 'we can look forward to every enemy attack with the greatest confidence'.[262] The psychological impact of the Rawlinson's successful attack was therefore significant.[263]

Ludendorff was already in a weakened mental state, following his failed offensives over the previous four months. As Gerhard Gross noted, those operations had shown he was out of his depth in the operational-strategic level of such offensives. Linked to this, his 'all or nothing' approach, believing in decisive military victory as the only means to end the war,[264] meant their failure left him, as Correlli Barnett described it, 'like a beetle on its back, waving and wriggling furiously to no effect. At the head of the German army during these critical days was violent rage, indiscriminate blame, fundamental panic, paralysis of command'.[265]

That Ludendorff experienced a nervous breakdown has been convincingly disputed by Franz Uhle-Wettler:[266] rather, his behaviour following 8 August indicates he was suffering from shock. Ludendorff certainly recorded Amiens was 'the worst experience that I had to go through, except for the events that, from September 15th onwards, took place on the Bulgarian Front and sealed the fate of the Quadruple Alliance'.[267]

Rowland identified three characteristics of soldiers in a state of shock:[268]

261 General Sir Archibald Wavell, *Generals and Generalship: The Lees Knowles Lectures Delivered at Trinity College, Cambridge in 1939* (Harmondsworth: Penguin, 1941), p.15.
262 Rupprecht, *Kriegstagebuch*, vol.3, pp.345-346.
263 Major Friedrich Altrichter, *Die seelischen Kräfte des Deutschen Heeres im Frieden und im Weltkriege* (Berlin: Mittler, 1933), p.158.
264 Gerhard P. Gross, *The Myth and Reality of German Warfare: Operational Thinking from Moltke the Elder to Heusinger*, ed. by Major-General David T. Zabecki (Lexington, KY: University Press of Kentucky, 2016), pp.126-129.
265 Corelli Barnett, *The Swordbearers: Supreme Command in the First World War* (London: Cassell, 2000), p.342.
266 Franz Uhle-Wettler, *Erich Ludendorff in seiner Zeit: Soldat – Stratege – Revolutionär: Eine Neubewertung* (Berg: Vowinckel, 1995), p.348.
267 Ludendorff, *War Memories*, vol.2, p.679. The Quadruple Alliance comprised Germany, Austria-Hungary, the Ottoman Empire, and Bulgaria.
268 Rowland, *Stress*, p.184.

- behavioural, where individuals become restless;
- emotional, where individuals vary between a flattening of mood and an intense anxiety; and
- cognitive, where powers of concentration and ability to reason logically are impaired

Considering each of these in turn, as soon as the British offensive had begun, Ludendorff immediately began to bombard Rupprecht with telephone calls and telegrams.[269] He also spoke personally to Rupprecht's chief of staff, Generalleutnant Herman von Kuhl, then also to the chiefs of staff not only of each of his armies but even every one of his corps.[270] Further, Ludendorff sent Oberstleutnant von Klewitz from his personal staff to replace Tschischwitz as Marwitz's chief of staff – a decision regretted by Marwitz[271] and criticised by Lossberg.[272] In addition, the Chief of the OHL Operations Staff (Oberstleutnant Georg Wetzell) maintained a constant telephone contact with the operations staff officers of the army group and also each of its armies.[273] These calls by Ludendorff and his staff went far beyond the information-gathering activities expected from a national military headquarters, especially given the German tradition of decentralised command. Nor can they be considered akin to the active assumption of on-the-spot command by Höfer and the other senior German commanders at Amiens, where their personal example and observation of the situation were vital to restoring the defence. However, as Zabecki and Uhle-Wettler have shown, the calls did reflect Ludendorff's growing tendency to bypass the chain of command.[274] The effect of this restlessness was utterly discouraging to senior commanders, who felt excluded from discussions between OHL and their formations – one army commander reported to Rupprecht, 'I do not really know anymore why I am here, as everything has been decided before I am even asked'.[275]

In terms of his emotional state, Ludendorff had already shown signs of 'nervous excitement',[276] yet Lossberg thought he seemed very depressed,[277] suggesting significant mood swings. Kuhl noted Ludendorff, taken completely by surprise by the British offensive, responded to that devastating psychological blow by losing all hope of a strategic solution to Germany's situation.[278] The collapse at Amiens traumatised him, as he 'saw suddenly yawning before [him], as if revealed by a flash of lightening,

---

269 Rupprecht, *Kriegstagebuch*, vol.3, p.348.
270 Rupprecht, *Kriegstagebuch*, vol.2, p.435.
271 Marwitz, *Weltkriegsbriefe*, p.303.
272 Lossberg, *Meine Tätigkeit*, p.354.
273 Rupprecht, *Kriegstagebuch*, vol.2, p.435.
274 Zabecki, *German 1918 Offensives*, p.327 and Uhle-Wettler, *Ludendorff*, p.348.
275 Rupprecht, *Kriegstagebuch*, vol.2, p.435.
276 Zabecki, *German 1918 Offensives*, p.288.
277 Lossberg, *Meine Tätigkeit*, p.352.
278 Zabecki, *German 1918 Offensives*, p.319.

the abyss of inevitable defeat'.[279] Yet, in themselves, the British advances at Amiens were hardly decisive:[280] the German armies had themselves recently achieved greater successes,[281] yet these had not ended the war. Ludendorff however was convinced, 'Our war machine was no longer efficient. Our fighting power had suffered, even though the great majority of divisions still fought heroically. The 8th of August put the decline of that fighting power beyond all doubt and in such a situation as regards reserves, I had no hope of finding a strategic expedient whereby to turn the situation to our advantage. On the contrary, I became convinced that we were now without that safe foundation'.[282]

The calls, and Ludendorff's perhaps over-dramatic conclusions, may also reflect a loss of cognitive 'grip'. Ludendorff's assumption the defeat was decisive brought with it the conclusion the entire philosophy underpinning German military thought since Moltke had failed. For someone as steeped in that tradition as was Ludendorff, this would have been a shattering realisation. As General der Infanterie Mertz von Quirnheim, postwar head of the *Reichsarchiv*, reported, people must *want* to comprehend a situation before they *can* comprehend it.[283] A separation from reality in Ludendorff's thinking processes would have been understandable.

Murray noted the tendency, which he termed 'fussing', 'for people under pressure to focus on what is manageable rather than what is important'.[284] Rupprecht recorded his amazement at Kuhl's calmness when Ludendorff rang to discuss individual battalions of the Alpine Corps[285] - a case of a commander operating 'six down'! As an experienced commander, Ludendorff surely knew this level of involvement was inappropriate, yet he did not stop. His loss of perspective and descent into fussing may reflect an unconscious attempt to counteract the disturbing sense of having utterly lost control of the strategic situation by taking tight control of tactical matters that (apparently) remained completely within his power.

Ludendorff's dismal conclusion regarding the combat capability of his formations was understandable, given he believed the formations facing the British attack were fresh and in strong positions. Yet, as has been seen, much of the collapse at Amiens may have been due to shock from the combination of a surprise attack by seemingly invulnerable tanks across a battlefield shrouded in thick fog. Once these special factors had passed, the performance even of the poor quality reserve formations had been creditable. Ludendorff, and subsequent historians such as Alexander Watson, may

279 'The British Campaign in the West, Part I: August – November 1918', *Army Quarterly*, 5 (January 1923), 314-330 (p.317).
280 GOH, p.567.
281 Uhle-Wettler, *Ludendorff*, p.347.
282 Ludendorff, *War Memories*, vol.2, p.684.
283 Bucholz, *Hans Delbrück*, p.135n7.
284 Murray, *Bullets and Brains*, p.105.
285 Rupprecht, *Kriegstagebuch*, vol.2, p.435.

therefore have been overly pessimistic in attributing defeat to a significant collapse in the troops' combat motivation.[286]

Based on Ludendorff's gloomy presentation of the situation on 10 August, it is perhaps hardly surprising the Kaiser concluded, 'We are at the limit of our capabilities. The war must be ended.'[287] Although Hindenburg presented a more balanced assessment of the situation at a conference on 14 August,[288] attended by the Kaiser, Hindenburg, Ludendorff, the Chancellor Georg von Hertling and the recently appointed Foreign Secretary, Paul von Hintze, Ludendorff's dismay was infectious and the unavoidable need for immediate peace negotiations was confirmed.[289] Acceptance of defeat then spread rapidly through the upper reaches of the German Government, with Rupprecht recording, on 15 August, he could only reinforce the similar assessment reached by the leaders of the Bavarian Government.[290] Eighty-eight days later, Germany signed the armistice.

Conclusions

German and British explanations for the scale of the defeat on 8 August 1918 were very different. The former stressed the combination of thick fog and massed tanks, the latter emphasised the superior British firepower tactics. Both, however, treated the German defenders as passive victims.

When considered from the perspective of command, certain conclusions can be drawn with respect to the preferences displayed by the two armies and the consequences for the level of friction experienced and the tempo of operations achieved.

Despite the dramatic loss of ground and manpower suffered since March, Haig had maintained his forces in a state where they were now able to combine a suite of technological and tactical innovations into a system capable of obliterating the German defences.

In so doing, the British displayed a strong tendency towards close control by senior officers. The move of the Canadian Corps from Flanders to Amiens was undertaken in the greatest secrecy. While this was understandable and represented the application of Logistic Control, the reluctance to let even fairly senior officers and, perhaps more importantly, their logistics staffs into the secret meant there were a number of instances where the plans went awry, resulting in the approach in practice

286 Alexander Watson, *Enduring the Great War: Combat, Morale and Collapse in the German and British Armies, 1914-1918* (Cambridge: Cambridge University, 2008), p.195. This is not to suggest that Watson's basic thesis is unsound.

287 Oberstleutnant a.D. Alfred Niemann, *Kaiser und Revolution: Die entscheidenden Ereignisse im Grossen Hauptquartier* (Berlin: Scherl, 1922), p. 43.

288 Marshal Paul von Hindenburg, *Out of My Life*, trans. by F.A. Holt (London: Cassell, 1920), pp. 395-396.

289 Barnett, *Swordbearers*, pp. 354-355.

290 Rupprecht, *Kriegstagebuch*, vol. 2, p. 438.

being more akin to Restrictive Control. Only prompt initiative by relatively junior officers mitigated this friction and avoided significant delays building up. Similarly, Montgomery's countermanding of Rawlinson's attempt to respond to the unexpected collapse of the German defences by deploying 32nd Division sooner than planned, on the grounds the formation was not yet fully deployed, may also be taken as an example of Restrictive Control. The resulting increase in friction and drop in the tempo of operations demonstrate the weaknesses of this approach.

Conversely, the reluctance of British forces to take advantage of the gap in the German lines created by the destruction of the forward defences and the rapid advance of the cavalry to the Blue Line before the available reserves could be deployed, may provide an example of Umpiring. Rawlinson had made clear in his orders the attack was to be undertaken with vigour, with the aim of achieving a deep penetration of the German position, but none of the commanders at divisional level and above seem to have taken significant active steps to push the troops forward once it became clear they were digging in on the Blue Line despite the limited resistance beyond. Indeed on the contrary, there is evidence to suggest they held them back, even though the commanders on the ground could see there was little in front of them and a deeper advance could have been made. While this reliance on the original battle plan reduced the level of friction experienced by the British forces on the ground, it also led to a decline in the tempo of the offensive, giving Marwitz vital time in which to restore his position, and hence generated friction that prevented achievement of the broader British objectives.

Looking at the German experience, it is notable officers at all levels sought to move forward in order to influence the battle effectively through personal observation, Höfer's rallying of fleeing troops around Caix being only the most explicit example. Conversely, commanders behind the lines seem to have seen their role as being primarily focused on deploying reserves to support the most threatened sectors of the line, and providing guidance to their subordinates over how these forces might be employed in order to achieve the overall intent, but leaving the final decision to the man on the spot, given his better knowledge of the local situation, as when Marwitz gave 119th Division to Hofacker. Taken together, these characteristics may be considered representative of Directive Command at the most senior level, and Directive Control at more junior levels.

But this contrast between the command approaches of the two armies provides only a partial explanation of events. Far more important appears to have been the impact of shock. Surprised by the appearance of hundreds of tanks, against which they were helpless due to the blinding of their anti-tank artillery by thick fog, the German defenders surrendered in their thousands. Drawing on Rowland's models, it seems unlikely this was a rational decision by demoralised troops. Rather, they were psychologically overwhelmed and became incapable of effective response, fleeing in panic or surrendering with barely a fight, as shown by the very low rates of fatalities suffered by the regiments in the front line and the limited casualties inflicted on the attackers.

Once the initial surprise wore off and the fog lifted, however, decisive action by German commanders from Marwitz downwards mitigated the psychological impact of the attack.[291] The weak reserve divisions successfully held off the somewhat half-hearted attempts by the British cavalry and Whippets to push beyond the Blue Line, despite a massive counter-battery and interdiction effort by Rawlinson's artillery, a major ground support commitment by the RAF, and the rampaging armoured cars of 17th Tank Battalion.

But perhaps the most important facet of the battle was its psychological impact on Ludendorff personally: he was stunned by the British attack and the successes gained. The shock convinced him the German Army had suffered a fundamental loss of combat motivation – a conviction with limited foundation.

Clausewitz argued victory was achieved through putting the enemy's forces 'in such condition that they can no longer carry on the fight'. In this context, he noted, rather than such a result being a question primarily of physical destruction, 'the loss of morale has proved the major decisive factor.'[292] We have previously noted the comment of Marshal Foch, quoting Joseph de Maistre: 'A battle lost is a battle one thinks one has lost; for a battle cannot be lost physically'.[293] When considering the course of the Battle of Amiens from the German perspective, one is driven to conclude the psychological shock of the initial British armoured thrust, greatly magnified through the combination of surprise and fog, proved the key factor, not only for the immediate behaviour of the defending troops in the front line, but also for Ludendorff, scores of miles away at OHL.

---

291 Altrichter, *seelischen Kräfte*, p.155-157.
292 Clausewitz, *On War*, pp.230-231.
293 Marshal Ferdinand Foch, *The Principles of War*, trans. by Hilaire Belloc (New York, NY: Holt, 1920), p. 286.

5

The British Armoured Counterattack at Arras, 21 May 1940

[A]fter those first great battles it was only the spectacular about them that received much emphasis. This distorted the picture so badly that even today enthusiasm for one modern aspect of war or another leads some of us into a disregard [...] of the extremely valuable lessons [...] of the world's most remarkable battle.

Infantry Journal[1]

At 1400 hours on Tuesday, 21 May 1940, the tanks of 4th and 7th Battalions,[2] Royal Tank Regiment (4/RTR and 7/RTR) moved forward to the southwest of Arras for what was to be the first time either unit had been in combat since 1918.[3] Indeed, this was to be the first engagement of the Second World War between British heavy tanks and a German enemy.[4] Their supporting infantry, 6th and 8th Battalions, Durham Light Infantry (6/DLI and 8/DLI), as well as the motorcycles and scout cars of 4th Battalion, Royal Northumberland Fusiliers (4/RNF), were somewhere behind them.[5] By the end of the day, all five units were back behind their starting positions, very much the worse for wear: they had unexpectedly encountered significant German forces from Erwin Rommel's 7th Panzer Division and from the SS Totenkopf (Death's Head) Division.

1   'Army and Super-Army', *Infantry Journal*, 49(2) (August 1941), 2-15 (p.2).
2   At this time, infantry tank units retained the terms 'battalion' and 'company' in preference to 'regiment' and 'squadron', Captain Basil H. Liddell Hart, *The Tanks: The History of the Royal Tank Regiment, Vol. 2: 1939-1945* (London: Cassell, 1959), p.11n.
3   The National Archives, Kew: WO167/460: War Diary, 7th Royal Tank Regiment, May 1940, entry for 21 May 1940.
4   Major Paul W. Thompson, *Modern Battle: Units in Action in the Second World War* (Harmondsworth: Penguin, 1942), p.63.
5   WO167/459: War Diary, 4th Royal Tank Regiment, May 1940, Appendix 23.

The British Official History went to some pains to play down the scale and intent of the operation, describing it as merely 'a large-scale mopping-up operation'.[6] Nonetheless, it was 'the only true manoeuvre the BEF was able to make during the campaign'.[7] Although long overshadowed by the later, much larger and more dramatic, tank battles in the Western Desert and in Normandy, in the mid-1980s the counterattack caught the imagination of military planners, leading the British Army to commission a series of studies of the battle.[8] Their intent was clear: 'the hasty improvisation, errors and confusion which characterised so much of British planning and execution [of the Arras operation] may provide useful lessons to the contemporary strategist concerned with the possibility of a counter-stroke by I British Corps in the 1980s.'[9] An encounter battle involving weak NATO forces against rapidly advancing Soviet forces was a likely scenario at that time, and the potential to learn lessons from a parallel operation in 1940 in order to facilitate a decisive 'manoeuvrist' response seemed clear: 'history reveals that those who have won against the odds have managed to seize the initiative [... and t]he key [...] is to use manoeuvre to concentrate force at the critical point',[10] 'at Arras in 1940 it was brilliant'.[11]

This may have been especially the case, as will be seen below, given the undoubted impact on the Germans of even so flawed an operation as this unquestionably was. After the war, the commander of Army Group A, Generaloberst Gerd von Rundstedt, told Basil Liddell Hart, 'A critical moment in the drive [to the sea ...] was caused by a British counter-stroke southward from Arras [...]. None of the French counter-attacks carried any serious threat as this one did.'[12] Similarly, General der Panzertruppen Heinz Guderian, commanding XIX Panzer Corps to the south of the attack, noted in his memoirs, 'The English did not succeed in breaking through, but they did make

---

6   Major L.F. Ellis, *History of the Second World War: United Kingdom Military Series: The War in France and Flanders* (1953, reprinted Uckfield: Naval & Military, 2004), pp.88-89.

7   David Fraser, *And We Shall Shock Them: The British Army in the Second World War* (London: Book Club Associates, 1983), p.63.

8   Former Tactical Doctrine Retrieval Cell, Staff College, Camberley: TDRC-7030A: Brian Bond, Arras 21 May 1940: A Case Study in the Counteroffensive (1984) (published in Correlli Barnett and others, *Old Battles and New Defences: Can We Learn from Military History?* (London: Brassey's, 1985), pp.61-84), TDRC-7148: HQ 20 Armoured Brigade, 4 Armoured Division Study Period, Arras – 21 May 40 (1985), TDRC-7778B: Battlefield Guide, Arras, 21 May 1940 (1986), and TDRC-8666: Captain R.J. Edmondson-Jones, Arras and the Modern Counter-Stroke (1988).

9   Bond, 'Arras', p.61.

10   Colonel R.A. Oliver, 'Training for the Friction of War', in *The British Army and the Operational Level of War*, ed. by Major-General J.J.G. Mackenzie and Brian Holden Reid (London: Tri-Service, 1989), pp.166-191 (p.167).

11   Colonel P.A.J. Cordingley, 'Armoured Forces and the Counter Stroke', in Mackenzie, *British Army*, pp.94-107 (p.99).

12   Quoted in Basil H. Liddell Hart, *The Other Side of the Hill: Germany's Generals, Their Rise and Fall, with Their Own Account of Military Events 1939-1945*, 2nd ed (1951, reprinted London: Pan, 1978), p.184.

a considerable impression on the staff of Panzer Group von Kleist, which suddenly became remarkably nervous.'[13] Indeed, Kenneth Macksey argued, 'Because of the British army at Arras in 1940, the British [were able to come] back to that place in September 1944.'[14]

Brian Bond's analysis provided the basis for most subsequent studies by the British Army. While noting 'the military historian is not well-qualified to extract contemporary lessons from case studies', he drew several tentative conclusions: the potential for even a small counterstroke to achieve significant results against an over-extended enemy, the importance of good timing, the need for combined arms tactics, and the requirement for clarity over approach and actions with allies. But 'the most difficult problem of all' was how to exploit the dislocation caused by the success of such an attack.[15]

The British Official History was clear about the reasons why the attack was a failure: Rommel deployed a strong gun-line that finally halted the British tanks after they had overrun his forward elements. In addition, poor communication between the British infantry and armoured units, coupled with inexperience in combined arms operations, added to the losses suffered by the attackers.[16] The recent analysis by Karl-Heinz Frieser, the head of the German Army's historical research institute, broadly agreed. Noting the extraordinary bravery of the British tank crews, he too highlighted the poor coordination between armour and infantry.[17] Similarly, Gregory Blaxland suggested the consequential collapse of command arrangements meant it was 'virtually a case of attacking by instinct'.[18] Picking up the first element of the British Official History's explanation, Alistair Horne too emphasised the impact of Rommel's gun-line.[19] Again, though from an armoured perspective, Liddell Hart ascribed the defeat of the tanks to 'little infantry support, less artillery support, and no air support'.[20] In short, historians are broadly in agreement the attack failed because the British were unable to coordinate their forces, leaving unsupported tanks to be shattered by German gunners firing over open sights: 'it was indeed a haphazard affair, more a swipe in the dark than a deliberate attack'.[21]

Yet no account has sought to explore or understand exactly why the attack, organised by one of Britain's leading thinkers on the use of tanks and deploying

13   General Heinz Guderian, *Panzer Leader* (1952, reprinted London: Futura, 1974), p.114.
14   Major Kenneth Macksey, *The Shadow of Vimy Ridge* (London: Kimber, 1965), p.241.
15   Bond, 'Arras', pp.82-83.
16   Ellis, *France and Flanders*, pp.95-96.
17   Colonel Karl-Heinz Frieser, with John T. Greenwood, *The Blitzkrieg Legend: The 1940 Campaign in the West* (Annapolis, MD: Naval Institute Press, 2005), p.286.
18   Gregory Blaxland, *Destination Dunkirk: The Story of Gort's Army* (London: Kimber, 1973), p.143.
19   Alistair Horne, *To Lose A Battle: France 1940* (1969, republished Harmondsworth: Penguin, 1979), pp.568-569.
20   *The Rommel Papers*, ed. by B.H. Liddell Hart (London: Collins, 1953), p.33.
21   Blaxland, *Destination Dunkirk*, p.148.

professional armoured units, was so very significantly affected by friction. Nor have historians considered in any depth why the German troops, who had operated in such an agile manner over the previous week, fled in disorder and surrendered in their hundreds. Finally, consideration has been very limited of how and why Rommel, having successfully fought off the British attack, so exaggerated the forces facing him the German high command became convinced the long anticipated Allied counteroffensive was about to sweep them away.

The explanations offered by previous historians, recognising most have addressed the battle only in passing as a single incident within the wider campaign, seem at best partial and incomplete. The intention here, therefore, is to apply the model of command approaches developed in Chapter One as a means to secure a deeper understanding of why both sides experienced such high levels of friction.

Sources and Approach

In considering this operation as a case study for understanding friction, it is possible to draw upon significant source material. For the British, the starting point must be the official history[22] and the usual war diaries, after action reports[23] and unit histories prepared by the various British units.[24] In addition, the commanders of both British divisions involved, Major-General Harold Franklyn of 5th Division and Major-General Giffard Martel of 50th (Northumbrian) Division, subsequently published personal accounts.[25] Similarly, the events of the day were covered from the German

22   Ellis, *France and Flanders*, pp.87-97.
23   WO167/244: G Branch, 5th Division, January – June 1940, WO167/300: GS Branch, 50th Division, February – May 1940, WO167/404: 151st Infantry Brigade, WO167/729: 6th Durham Light Infantry, January to June 1940, WO167/730: 8th Durham Light Infantry, January to June 1940, WO167/414: 1st Army Tank Brigade, April to June 1940, WO167/459: 4/RTR, WO167/460: 7th Royal Tank Regiment, May 1940, and WO167/800: 4th Royal Northumberland Fusiliers, January to June 1940.
24   Major Ewart W. Clay, *The Path of the 50th: The Story of the 50th (Northumbrian) Division in the Second World War, 1939-1945* (Aldershot: Gale & Ploden, 1950), Captain B.H. Liddell Hart, *The Tanks: The History of the Royal Tank Regiment and its Predecessors, Heavy Branch Machine-Gun Corps, Tank Corps & Royal Tank Corps, 1914-1945*, vol.2 (1939-1945) (London: Cassell, 1959), D. Rissik, *The DLI at War: The History of the Durham Light Infantry, 1939-1945* (Durham: DLI, 1954), Harry Moses, *The Faithful Sixth* (Durham: County Durham, 1995), Major P.J. Lewis, *8th Battalion, The Durham Light Infantry, 1939-1945* (Newcastle upon Tyne: Bealls, 1949), and Brigadier C.N. Barclay, *The History of the Royal Northumberland Fusiliers in the Second World War* (London: Clowes, 1952).
25   Lieutenant-General Sir Giffard Le Quesnel Martel, *Our Armoured Forces* (London: Faber & Faber, 1945), Lieutenant-General Sir Giffard Le Quesnel Martel, *An Outspoken Soldier: His Views and Memoirs* (London: Praed, 1949), and General Sir Harold E. Franklyn, *The Story of One Green Howard in the Dunkirk Campaign* (Richmond: Green Howards' Gazette, 1966).

perspective in their recent monograph[26] and in the relevant unit histories,[27] both based on the contemporary war diaries. In addition, Rommel left his own account,[28] and his actions have been considered by his many biographers, even if generally only briefly.[29] Finally, the counterattack features, to a greater or lesser extent, in the many accounts of the overall campaign.[30]

Given this wealth of material, the importance of the counterattack as the only active step taken by the British and French to respond to the German penetration, and the fact it caused near panic within sections of the German high command and contributed to the famous 'halt order' that perhaps made the evacuation from Dunkirk possible, it is surprising that, apart from the studies commissioned by the British Army in the mid-1980s, the operation has not been the subject of any focused analysis

26 Frieser, *Blitzkrieg Legend*.
27 Alfred Tschimpke, *Die Gespenster-Division: Mit der Panzerwaffe durch Belgien und Frankreich*, 5th ed. (Munich: NSDAP, 1942), Horst Scheibert, *Die Gespenster-Division: Die Geschichte der 7. Panzer-Division* (Eggolsheim: Dörfler, 2006), Generalleutnant Anton Detlev von Plato, *Die Geschichte der 5. Panzerdivision, 1938 bis 1945* (Regensburg: 5. Panzerdivision, 1978), Chris Mann, *SS-Totenkopf: The History of the 'Death's Head' Division 1940-45* (Staplehurst: Spellmount, 2001), Charles W. Sydnor, *Soldiers of Destruction: The SS Death's Head Division, 1933-1945* (Princeton, NJ: Princeton University Press, 1990), Jack Holroyd, *Images of War: SS-Totenkopf France 1940: Rare Photographs from Wartime Archives* (Barnsley: Pen & Sword, 2012), Karl Ullrich, *Like a Cliff in the Ocean*, trans. by Jeffrey McMullen (Winnipeg: Fedorowicz, 2002), and Wolfgang Vopersal, *Soldaten, Kämpfer, Kameraden: Marsch und Kämpfe der SS Totenkopf-Division, Vol 1: Aufstellung, Frankreichfeldzug, Bereitstellung für Rußlandfeldzug* (Bielefeld: Truppenkameradschaft der 3. SS-Panzer-Division, 1983).
28 *Rommel Papers*, pp.29-34.
29 Desmond Young, *Rommel* (London: Collins, 1950), pp.69-71, Ronald Lewin, *Rommel as Military Commander* (New York, NY: Barnes & Noble, 1968), pp.19-22, David Irving, *The Trail of the Fox: The Life of Field-Marshal Erwin Rommel* (London: Weidenfeld and Nicolson, 1977), pp.46-47, David Fraser, *Knight's Cross: A Life of Field Marshal Erwin Rommel* (London: Harper Collins, 1994), pp.182-187, Maurice Philip Remy, *Mythos Rommel* (Munich: List, 2002), p.49, Ralf Georg Reuth, *Rommel: The End of a Legend*, trans. by Debra S. Marmor and Herbert A. Danner (London: Haus, 2005), p.43, Dennis Showalter, *Patton and Rommel: Men of War in the Twentieth Century* (New York, NY: Berkley Caliber, 2006), pp.186-191, Peter Caddick-Adams, *Monty and Rommel: Parallel Lives* (London: Arrow, 2012), pp.228-232, *Rommel: A Reappraisal*, ed. by Ian F.W. Beckett (Barnsley: Pen and Sword, 2013), pp.37-40, and Daniel Allen Butler, *Field Marshal: The Life and Death of Erwin Rommel* (Oxford: Casemate, 2015), pp.164-166.
30 For example, Macksey, *Vimy Ridge*, pp.190-241, John Williams, *The Ides of May: The Defeat of France, May-June 1940* (London: Constable, 1968), pp.227-228, Guy Chapman, *Why France Collapsed* (London: Cassell, 1968), pp.184-187, Horne, *To Lose a Battle*, pp.561-570, Blaxland, *Destination Dunkirk*, pp.132-148, Brian Bond, *France and Belgium, 1939-1940* (London: Purnell, 1975), pp.114-118, Nicholas Harman, *Dunkirk: The Necessary Myth* (London: Hodder and Stoughton, 1980), pp.92-102, Ronald Atkins, *Pillar of Fire: Dunkirk 1940* (London: Sidgwick and Jackson, 1990), pp.92-97, Major General Julian Thompson, *Dunkirk: Retreat to Victory* (London: Pan, 2009), pp.82-100, and Hugh Sebag-Montefiore, *Dunkirk: Fight to the Last Man*, rev. ed. (Harmondsworth: Penguin, 2015), pp.142-155.

in its own right. This chapter seeks to address that deficiency, within the context of the overall focus on the relationship between friction and command approaches.

Chapter Three examined how, between 12 and 15 May, Rommel led 7th Panzer Division in such a way as to burst across the defensive line of the River Meuse and deep into the French rear zones within days of crossing the frontier. Combined with the parallel penetration achieved to the south by Guderian's XIX Panzer Corps following its crossing of the river at Sedan, the effect had been to shatter the physical defences of the French forces and the psychological equilibrium of their senior commanders at every level:

- The French Supreme Headquarters was on 16 May in a state of 'panic', with the supreme commander, General Maurice Gamelin, showing such strong signs of unease one staff officer reported, 'No one dares to approach him';[31]
- General Alphonse Georges, commander of the North-Eastern Front, on 14 May 'flung himself into a chair and burst into tears';[32]
- General Gaston-Henri Billotte, commander of 1st Army Group, and General Georges-Marie-Jean Blanchard, commander of First Army, were on 20 May both 'in a state of complete depression. [...] Ready to be slaughtered';[33] and
- General Rene-Felix Altmayer, commander of V Corps under Blanchard, later that same day 'made an exhausted and beaten impression [...] and wept quietly'.[34]

The British, by contrast, having yet to face serious attacks by the Germans, remained in generally good spirits, despite having to pull back from their advanced positions in Belgium while under significant air attack. It is beyond the remit of this chapter to explore the debates between the British and French high commands, especially those on 20 May during the visit to France by General Sir Edmund Ironside, the Chief of the Imperial General Staff (CIGS). It will suffice to note Ironside's discussions with Lord Gort, commander of the BEF, and later with Billotte, led to a decision to launch a counterattack at Arras the following day, yet also created confusion over its scale and scope.[35]

Here, the focus is on six issues emerging from the battle that offer the potential to cast a wider light:

---

31   Colonel J. Minart, quoted in Williams, *Ides of May*, p.203.
32   Bond, *France and Belgium*, p.102.
33   General Sir Edmund Ironside, quoted in Horne, *To Lose A Battle*, p.560.
34   Major Vautrin, quoted in Frieser, *Blitzkrieg Legend*, p.283.
35   Ellis, *France and Flanders*, pp.83-87.

- The Knowledge Gap between the situation as presented in the orders issued to the attacking British forces and the reality on the ground, how this occurred and why, and the response of the British command system;
- The Alignment Gap between the task set out in those orders and ability of troops to perform as expected, how this occurred and why, and the response of the British command system;
- The Effects Gap between what could reasonably have been expected from the advance and the reality of its initial impact on the troops of 7th Panzer Division and the SS Totenkopf Division;
- The Alignment Gap in the German tactical response to the British attack, and what this reveals concerning that army's command approach;
- The command approach adopted by the British commanders during the operation itself, and their response to the loss of communications; and
- How such a small-scale operation, which failed to achieve its tactical objectives, still caused Rundstedt to experience shock, leading him to issue the 'halt order' and maintain the pause even after everyone around him was convinced the danger had passed.

Orders and Reality – The Knowledge Gap

The first theme for examination here concerns the Knowledge Gap, the gap between the knowledge of the situation held by commanders at different levels of an operation. As was shown in Chapter One, the nature of warfare means the knowledge held at different command levels is rarely the same and is frequently incomplete (or just plain wrong). How an army responds to this imbalance in knowledge is a central feature in determining the command approach employed.

The first incidence of the Knowledge Gap may be found when exploring the way in which the attacking forces were informed of the purpose of the counterattack.

The war diary of 50th Division recorded, during the night of 19/20 May, 'news was received that [...] 50 Div[ision] was to proceed [...] for offensive action near ARRAS'.[36] Martel was summoned to see Gort, who told him he was to deliver a counterattack against the narrow corridor the German armoured forces had punched through the French defences behind the Meuse and which had that day reached the sea at Abbeville. 1st Army Tank Brigade, the only heavy tanks within the BEF, would come under his command for the operation. Shortly afterwards, Gort decided to strengthen the forces in the area and assigned 5th Division, commanded by Franklyn. Since Franklyn was senior to Martel, Gort gave him responsibility for the operation as a whole,[37] the troops under him being termed Frankforce.

---

36 WO167/300: 50th Division, War Diary, 19 May 1940.
37 Martel, *Our Armoured Forces*, p.60.

At 0900 hours on 20 May, Franklyn therefore went to see Gort. In his memoirs, he recorded he was told the aim of the operation was simply 'to make Arras secure, gaining as much "elbow room" as possible south of the town. To the best of my memory he [Gort] used the term "mopping-up".' The written summary of these instructions, prepared shortly afterwards by the BEF's Deputy Chief of the General Staff, Brigadier Oliver Leese, stated Franklyn's role was 'to support the garrison in ARRAS and block the roads to the south of ARRAS cutting off the German communications from the East',[38] a mission consistent with Franklyn's account.

Later that same day, Franklyn visited GHQ for a second time, hoping to receive information about the enemy forces he would be facing and further guidance regarding the task he was to undertake: 'I got neither.' In fact, Gort did not even see Franklyn himself, but sent Leese, who 'merely hinted that Gort was hoping for a more serious drive South of Arras than indicated in the original instructions'.[39] Franklyn was therefore somewhat surprised when, encountering Ironside as he left Gort's headquarters, he found himself being wished the best of luck for the forthcoming operation by the CIGS. Although Ironside's words were hardly consistent with the minor mopping-up mission Franklyn thought he was meant to be undertaking, he appears not to have sought clarification from his superior.

Ironside had himself just returned from meeting Billotte, during which the Frankforce operation had been converted into the centrepiece of a major offensive to sever the German corridor. Yet neither Ironside nor Gort appear to have felt the need to inform Franklyn of this somewhat fundamental change of plan. It therefore remained no more than 'a paper scheme'.[40] Even more bizarrely, when Franklyn and Martel then drove to visit General René-Jacques-Adolphe Prioux, commander of the Cavalry Corps of light armoured divisions, and General Altmayer, whose forces were to link with Frankforce, they briefly encountered Billotte (whom neither had met previously), yet the French general left quickly, again without sharing any intelligence about the expanded aims of the operation. Although Prioux and Altmayer then explained the new intent, they too failed to explain this had been agreed by Ironside and Billotte only a few hours earlier. When Franklyn responded this plan went far beyond what Gort had instructed him to do, he noted Altmayer 'seemed relieved. It was clear that the French general had little faith in the project.'[41]

Still further opportunities to clarify the position arose. Not only did Leese himself visit Franklyn's headquarters later that afternoon, 'exuding charm and the desire to be helpful',[42] expressing his satisfaction with the latter's plan for the attack,[43] but he

38   WO167/244: 5th Division, Report on Operations of Frankforce, 20th May to 24th May 1940, p.9.
39   Franklyn, *One Green Howard*, pp.14-16.
40   Chapman, *France Collapsed*, p.184.
41   Franklyn, *One Green Howard*, pp.14-15 and Ellis, *France and Flanders*, pp.87-88.
42   Blaxland, *Destination Dunkirk*, p.136.
43   Franklyn, *One Green Howard*, p.17.

returned again, early in the morning of 21 May, to observe Franklyn issue his orders.[44] Intriguingly, neither of these meetings were mentioned by Leese's biographer.[45]

One factor that seems striking in retrospect is Franklyn's apparent lack of curiosity in following up these indications there was more to the operation than had been indicated. Although he did try to see Gort for a second time, and spoke to Leese on four separate occasions, gaining the impression from the latter that something more was being hinted to him, his actions appear to have been passive, rather than actively seeking clarification from his superiors. He did not ask Ironside to explain why he was offering him best wishes for such a minor attack, nor did he contact Gort's headquarters after Prioux and Altmayer had indicated a more extensive aim for the operation. Franklyn was therefore largely reactive in response to his orders, not attempting to put himself into the mind of his commander and understand the broader aim.

Equally, the fact Leese failed to take steps to inform Franklyn of Gort's broader intention, even though he clearly had concerns about how the attack was being planned, is almost inexplicable, unless he too had been kept in the dark by Gort. However, this seems unlikely, given Franklyn's comments Leese had hinted there might be more to the attack than had been stated in his notes of the meeting with Gort. The only credible alternative explanation is Leese felt restrained from doing more than make intimations, given Franklyn was his senior in rank, possibly indicating a reversion (unconsciously) to the command approach of Umpiring, where a superior with greater knowledge of the local situation still hesitates to intervene, despite seeing his subordinate making errors.

A clue to Franklyn's behaviour may be found in the very honest description of his own state of mind during the orders conference held at 5th Division headquarters at 0600 hours on 21 May:

> It is not easy to face up to one's first independent command in war. I had never commanded even a company in battle. [... I] had had a great deal of experience during the First World War as [a] staff officer [...], but without responsibility. [... I] had been [an] instructor [...] at the Staff College and consequently [my] theoretical knowledge was sufficient. [... O]ne was not feeling as calm and collected as one would have wished. [...] A general who is unable to control his feelings, is apt to fuss and so upset his staff [...]. Besides, any display of anxiety from above soon spreads rapidly and shakes the confidence of subordinates. I do not pretend that I was entirely successful in this respect myself. Try as I would

---

44   Ronald Lewin, *Man of Armour: A Study of Lieut-General Vyvyan Pope and the Development of Armoured Warfare* (London: Cooper, 1976), p.116.
45   Rowland Ryder, *Oliver Leese* (London: Hamilton, 1987), pp.74-75.

I could not prevent my voice cracking from time to time. This made me feel annoyed and ashamed.[46]

Franklyn noted he was convinced orders should be given in person wherever possible, as written orders 'should not take the place of what is of special value, that is a commander impressing personally and with confidence what he himself, and not merely his staff, wants to be done.'[47] Equally, it is clear from his own account such confidence, and a clear understanding of what needed to be achieved, were both somewhat absent when he issued his orders that morning.

Taken as a whole, this incident may suggest Franklyn assumed he simply had to follow the orders given to him: if no further explanation was forthcoming, there was nothing further he could do. The baleful influence of Field Service Regulations, Part II (Operations) (1935), examined in Chapter Two, remained powerful: '14(5) i: A formal order will never be departed from either in letter or spirit so long as the officer who issued it is present, or there is time to report to him and await a reply without losing an opportunity or endangering the force concerned.' This wording had been repeated, unaltered, only a few months before the battle, in Military Training Pamphlet No.23,[48] which effectively replaced FSR II (1935).[49] Franklyn had had sufficient time in which to seek an update from his superior and had done so, but without any benefit. He was therefore bound to obey: FSR II (1935) and MTP 23 allowed no other course. He was therefore operating under the command approach of Restrictive Control.

As a consequence, the war diary of 50th Division noted Franklyn's verbal orders were the attack 'was intended to destroy all enemy forces in area south of R[iver] SCARPE as far as R[iver] SENNE [actually the River Sensée].'[50] The force would therefore sweep anticlockwise around Arras from the north-west, with the aim of meeting up with 13th Brigade of 5th Division, which would attack from the east of the town.[51] This was very much in line with the original orders Franklyn had received from Gort,[52] but as such took no account of the expanded nature of the operation subsequently agreed with Ironside and Billotte. Given this breadth of the Knowledge Gap, with Franklyn not knowing what he was meant to be aiming to achieve, the potential for a decisive manoeuvre had already been lost at the first hurdle.

A second incidence of the Knowledge Gap is revealed through consideration of the information regarding the enemy that was shared down the British command chain.

---

46   Franklyn, *One Green Howard*, p.18.
47   Franklyn, *One Green Howard*, p.19.
48   Military Training Pamphlet No.23: Operations, Part III. Appreciations, Orders, Intercommunication and Movement (October 1939), sec.3(5)i.
49   Army Training Memorandum No.36 (War) (September 1940), pp.22-23.
50   WO167/300: 50th Division War Diary, 21 May 1940.
51   Martel, *Our Armoured Forces*, p.64.
52   WO167/244: 5th Division, Report on Operations, p.9.

The history of 50th Division commented Franklyn's orders gave 'very little detailed information about the location of the enemy'.[53] By contrast, the British Official History was at pains to point out the completeness of the information given in the Frankforce orders and hinted the gap in the information provided came at a lower level.[54]

Intriguingly, the orders issued by Martel have been lost: the relevant appendix of the 50th Division war diary at the National Archives is missing,[55] and surprisingly no copy survives in the war diaries of any of the other formations involved in the attack, even though copies would have been distributed to all concerned. The orders appear to have gone missing at an early date, as the initial account prepared from those war diaries as a factual basis for the narrative in the Official History made no reference to them, even though it referred to the other relevant sets of orders.[56]

A copy of the orders, however, does survive in Martel's personal papers. This shows twenty-three copies were made and distributed, which makes their disappearance from the various war diaries even more surprising. The orders stated simply the information about the enemy was 'As given at Conference',[57] referring to the session when Martel briefed his brigadiers. It therefore remains unclear how the information regarding the enemy provided by Franklyn was presented by Martel to those formations under his command. In addition, it must be noted that referring those who received the written orders to a briefing at which most had not been present was hardly an example of clarity.

Gort had told Franklyn he 'was only likely to encounter weak German detachments'.[58] In seeking to give his subordinate guidance as to the opposition he should expect to face, Gort was suffering from the severe disadvantage that the BEF's intelligence arrangements had largely broken down. In part, this was because changes to the German Enigma machines immediately before the start of operations meant the BEF had 'no intelligence to speak of' until the new codes were broken on 22 May. That said, Gort himself had significantly contributed to the lack of intelligence by breaking up his headquarters as soon as the campaign had begun. He himself, with only a small core staff, had moved to a small command post 50 miles away from GHQ, thereby upsetting the flow of information about the enemy between his new command post, the main intelligence unit at GHQ and the formations within the BEF. Gort's knowledge of the situation was therefore frequently limited and inaccurate.[59]

53   Clay, *Path of the 50th*, p.14.
54   Ellis, *France and Flanders*, p.89.
55   WO167/300: 50th Division, Appendix 35: Operation Order No.9 is missing.
56   CAB44/67: The BEF in France and Flanders, Part II, (a) and (b), pp.144-145.
57   Imperial War Museum: Private Papers of Lieutenant-General Sir Giffard le Quesnel Martel, Folder 3/1, Item 19.
58   Franklyn, *One Green Howard*, p.14.
59   F.H. Hinsley, with E.E. Thomas, C.F.G. Ransom and R.C. Knight, *British Intelligence in the Second World War: Its Influence on Strategy and Operations*, vol.1 (London: HMSO, 1979), pp.143-147.

Despite the limited basis for Gort's advice to Franklyn, that he would face only weak German forces, this was broadly reflected in the subsequent Frankforce orders issued at 0500 hours on 21 May: 'Enemy tanks seen West of ARRAS. [...] Tanks seen passing through AVESNES [...] evening 20 May and six tanks approaching ST. POL 2130 hours. Strong col[um]ns [of] inf[antry] with tanks on r[oa]d CAMBRAI – ARRAS.'[60] The reference to enemy armour to the west of Arras was important, but the main emphasis was on enemy forces to the southeast of Arras, towards the limits of the intended advance around the city. This was followed up at 1345 hours, just before the attack: 'Concentrations [of] enemy lorries and A[rmoured] F[ighting] V[ehicles] reported on r[oa]d ARRAS – ST. POL 1020 h[ou]rs today, also on r[oa]d ARRAS-FREVENT. Col[um]n enemy M[otor] T[ransport] reported moving N[orth] W[est] from DOULLENS. This report unconfirmed.'[61] This was a more worrying position, but reached the troops only after they had crossed the start line, and so was much too late for them to adapt their plans.

By contrast, the orders issued by 1st Army Tank Brigade stated, 'Enemy have light elements of Arm[oure]d cars and l[igh]t tanks, possibly some inf[antry]' in the area of the advance.[62] The orders of 151st Infantry Brigade similarly noted, 'Enemy infantry and tanks are known to be operating in the area South and S[outh] W[est] of ARRAS in numbers which are uncertain but not believed to be great.'[63] There was no reference to the German armour on the road to St Pol and this was therefore a rather less threatening picture than presented in Franklyn's orders. In both cases, this assessment of the enemy situation was presumably based on Martel's briefing to his brigadiers.

Yet this comparative lack of information about the Germans in the orders issued by Frankforce and by the attacking brigades may be contrasted with the knowledge of the situation held by both Martel and Franklyn. The former noted that on 20 May, 'Much valuable information was obtained from the 12th Lancers who had established posts along this front and did such splendid work during all this difficult time.'[64] Later that day, as he was preparing his plan, Franklyn was visited by Herbert Lumsden, the Lancers' commander: 'He painted a very different picture of the opposition that I was likely to encounter south of Arras. He left no doubt in my mind that the problem now was far more difficult than one of "mopping up".'[65]

60   WO167/244: 5th Division, Frankforce Operation Instruction No.1, para.1.
61   WO167/300: 50th Division, Frankforce Operation Instruction No.2, para.1.
62   WO167/414: 1st Army Tank Brigade War Diary, Appx A, Operation Order No.6, para.1.
63   WO167/404: 151st Infantry Brigade War Diary, Appx 13, Operation Order No.10, para.1(a).
64   Martel, *Our Armoured Forces*, p.60.
65   Franklyn, *One Green Howard*, p.16.

Quite how difficult is indicated by the details presented in the Lancers' war diary[66] and regimental history.[67] These recorded Lumsden had been summoned to GHQ at 1930 hours on 19 May. The briefing he received was not recorded, but must have been fairly specific, as the first entry in the war diary for the morning of 20 May noted, 'It seemed certain that [...] only [German] mechanised formation[s], and those in small packets, could have penetrated into the area [south of Arras], and that a determined drive southwards especially if the French could be induced to make their long promised counter-attack northwards, would produce far reaching results.'[68] This picture of limited forces facing Frankforce was in accordance with the picture painted by Gort to Franklyn later that morning.

The remainder of the entry in the war diary for 20 May described the results of the regiment's reconnaissance efforts in the area Arras, Bapaume, Peronne, Amiens and Doullens. A large column of enemy tanks was reported approaching Arras from Cambrai. Next, tanks were spotted south of Arras, seeking to outflank the British position. A considerable number of enemy tanks were then seen moving north from Baeumetz, with further heavy tanks noted in Wanquetin and Avesnes. Finally, a large column of enemy was reported moving towards St Pol.[69] This number of enemy tanks, operating over the whole area into which Martel was about to advance, indicated Gort's suggestion to Franklyn he would face only weak German detachments was far wide of the mark. Lumsden clearly passed on this information to both Franklyn and Martel when he met each of them later that day, yet the orders issued by both generals hardly reflected the threatening picture painted by the Lancers' findings – the Frankforce orders, for example, referred to just six tanks approaching St Pol.[70]

The following morning, Franklyn ordered the Lancers to reconnoitre the area to the north-west and west of Arras, across which Martel's forces were due to advance that afternoon. At 0940 hours, it was reported there were tanks and a considerable quantity of enemy vehicles in Avesnes. Then, at 1012 hours, a column of German artillery, stragglers from 8th Panzer Division,[71] drove unsuspecting into the Lancers' positions on the Arras – St Pol road, three miles from Arras, only to be destroyed by their sudden fire. All morning, the regiment reported bumping into German forces.[72] Yet this picture was barely represented in Frankforce Operation Order No.2, issued immediately before the attack began.[73]

66   WO167/452: 12th Lancers War Diary.
67   Captain Patrick Findlater Stewart, *The History of the XII Royal Lancers (Prince of Wales's)* (London: Oxford University, 1950), pp.358-361.
68   WO167/452: 12th Lancers, 19-20 May 1940.
69   WO167/452: 12th Lancers, 20 May 1940, and Stewart, *XII Lancers*, p.359.
70   WO167/244: 5th Division, Frankforce Operation Instruction No.1, para.1.
71   Macksey, *Vimy Ridge*, p.217.
72   WO167/452: 12th Lancers, 21 May 1940, and Stewart, *XII Lancers*, pp.360-361.
73   WO167/300: Frankforce Operation Instruction No.2, para.1.

Once again, senior British commanders seem to have either decided to ignore information incompatible with their orders or else felt it was not necessary for them to pass it to their subordinates, simply requiring them to follow their orders regardless of the changed circumstances. The impact on the operation was significant: Brigadier Jack Churchill, commander of 151st Brigade, commented in his after action report on 'the inaccuracy of the information on which the attack was based'.[74] Again, this suggests a reliance on Restrictive Control as a command approach.

Quite why neither Franklyn nor Martel chose to include in their orders the picture of a strong enemy force increasingly apparent from the information provided by the Lancers is unclear. One possibility is both officers were already uncertain about the purpose of the operation and may have been struggling with a sense the forces available to them were insufficient for the more expansive objectives being hinted at by Leese and the French commanders, especially given the growing evidence that the German forces in the area were far stronger than had been stated by Gort. Consciously accepting there was a contradiction between forces and objectives would have required them to accept their orders were no longer practical. Since implementing orders known to be inappropriate would stretch the loyalty even of officers brought up to rigid obedience, it may be hypothesised both Franklyn and Martel found it easier instead to disregard the reconnaissance reports. They may have rationalised this through assuming that Gort, as their senior commander, 'must' have been correct in his appreciation of the situation and that, therefore, any evidence that they received that contradicted his assessment 'must' be either wrong or incomplete. In a situation of a conflict between orders and reality, a subordinate brought up within the Restrictive Control approach to command may find it simpler to adjust reality than to question his orders.

Weight is given to this being the correct explanation by a comment in Franklyn's memoirs. Having noted Martel had been criticised for playing down the strength of the enemy in his orders, no doubt a coded reference to the statements in the Official History noted earlier,[75] he commented, 'To my mind, such criticism is wholly unjustified, for surely the nearer the front the less one should suggest the horrors awaiting an attack.'[76] In other words, if an attack is doomed, the commander should not trouble his subordinates with that knowledge!

Orders and Doctrine – The Alignment Gap

The attack was therefore already experiencing significant friction even before the troops started to move, due to the width of the Knowledge Gap around both the purpose of the operation and the strength of the German forces that might be encountered. The level of friction was about to be increased further by the development of a wide

---

74   WO167/404: 151st Infantry Brigade, Notes on Operations 16 May to 2 June 1940, p.3.
75   Ellis, *France and Flanders*, p.89.
76   Franklyn, *One Green Howard*, p.20. See also Blaxland, *Destination Dunkirk*, p.139.

Alignment Gap, as the British units were tasked with operating in a manner which bore only limited relationship to the army's doctrine and for which they had little training.

By one of those workings of chance that so typify warfare, in planning for Britain's first armoured action against the Germans since 1918, Franklyn had in Martel 'perhaps the greatest tank expert in the British Army.'[77] Martel had served as J.F.C. Fuller's deputy on the staff of the Tank Corps during the First World War, and had played a key role in planning the offensive at Amiens in August 1918.[78] He remained a central figure in the further development of armoured forces between the wars, even going so far as to design a two-man 'tankette' himself.[79]

In addition, the GHQ Adviser on Armoured Fighting Vehicles, Brigadier Vyvyan Pope, was also present during the operation. Pope, as an infantry battalion commander, had lost his right arm in the defeat of 21 March 1918, but had clung to his commission, in due course becoming a leading player in the development of armoured doctrine. He had coupled this with valuable experience as a staff officer, serving directly under Alan Brooke from 1936 until 1939, first in the Directorate of Military Training at the War Office, and then as chief of staff in II Corps.[80] Pope discussed the forthcoming battle with Franklyn on 20 May as the latter was preparing his plan and then attended (with Leese) the conference the next morning where Franklyn issued his orders.[81] It seems probable he also discussed the forthcoming battle with Martel.

Martel recorded Franklyn ('a very experienced officer') 'delegated the actual attack [...] to myself, and gave me a free hand in doing so.'[82] Given Franklyn's high regard for Martel's expertise with armoured forces, this was perhaps to be expected, though it suggests a comfort with Directive Command not previously seen in the BEF's preparations for the battle, such that this might be considered on the verge of Umpiring.

The history of 50th Division noted, however, that at Arras, 'it was not easy to decide the best tactics. If the main threat was the enemy tanks, then our tanks should lead, supported closely by infantry and guns. If, on the other hand, a defensive position or strong defended localities were met, then a combined plan of attack, employing all arms, would be necessary.'[83] This uncertainty over how to proceed could be taken as suggesting, in preparing his plan for the attack, Martel had little in the way of official doctrine to guide him.

77   Franklyn, *One Green Howard*, p.16.
78   Martel, *Outspoken Soldier*, pp.15-17.
79   A.J. Smithers, *A New Excalibur: The Development of the Tank, 1909-1939* (London: Grafton, 1988), pp.238-267.
80   Lewin, *Man of Armour*, pp.24-26 and 93-103.
81   Lewin, *Man of Armour*, pp.114 & 116.
82   Martel, *Our Armoured Forces*, p.62.
83   Clay, *Path of the 50th*, p.14.

In fact, there was a clear doctrine, set out in *MTP 22: Tactical Handling of Army Tank Battalions*, issued in September 1939.[84] MTP 22 was explicit how infantry tanks should be used:

- 'Army Tank Battalions are [...] organized, equipped and trained for employment with formations of all arms. [...] they are not designed to act independently but in co-operation with infantry and artillery.'[85]
- 'An army tank unit is only one member of the team [... .] Infantry tanks are a supporting weapon, and though they will usually provide the leading wave in an attack, their object is to assist the infantry to gain and hold the objective.'[86]
- 'The components of the attack should fall upon the defence in rapid succession; the artillery covering fire should be closely followed by tanks which, in their turn, should be closely followed by the infantry.'[87]

The previous (August 1938) edition of the doctrine, set out in *MTP 8: Notes on the Tactical Handling of Army Tank Battalions*,[88] had also been clear over the deployment of the "I" tank battalions in an attack. It had laid down the attack should be led by a small number of tanks, with a further echelon following in a second wave in close cooperation with the infantry. The remaining tanks should be held in reserve.[89] Only in the case of a highly organised defence should the bulk of the tanks be used in the initial operation.[90]

Although there was therefore a clear doctrine to guide Martel, there was a major problem: the doctrine had been developed on the assumption the "I" tanks would be used in an attack against a defended position, such as encountered by Rawlinson at Amiens in August 1918. As such, the doctrine suggested each battalion should seek to neutralise an area no larger than 1000 yards square, while noting the Germans favoured the use of tanks in masses, with five hundred tanks on a two-mile front[91] (equivalent to perhaps 600 yards per battalion). By contrast, at Arras in May 1940, Martel was tasked with clearing a zone 4 miles wide and 10 miles deep,[92] some *eighty times* the area recommended by MTP 8 for the two battalions available to him. Conversely, the information given by Franklyn regarding the enemy gave no

---

84 *Military Training Pamphlet No.22: Tactical Handling of Army Tank Battalions, Part III: Employment* (September 1939).
85 MTP 22(III), sec.1(1).
86 MTP 22(III), sec.2(1).
87 MTP 22(III), sec.5(1).
88 *Military Training Pamphlet No.8: Notes on the Tactical Handling of Army Tank Battalions* (August 1938).
89 MTP 8, sec.8.
90 MTP 8, sec.5.
91 MTP 8, sec.4.
92 Ellis, *France and Flanders*, p.90.

suggestion there were any organised defensive positions in the area to be cleared.[93] In effect, tank units intended for breaching a gap in a strong entrenched position were to be employed in their first battle in mopping up dispersed enemy forces over a wide area. Given that the mission given to Martel was significantly different from that envisaged for infantry tank battalions, he was therefore forced to operate some distance outside the doctrine.

Rather than advance across the whole of the 4-mile front, which would have left his forces seriously over-extended,[94] Martel resolved to divide his force into two columns, each comprising a tank battalion and an infantry battalion, supported by a battery of field artillery and another of anti-tank guns, along with scout cars from 4/RNF.[95] He was himself acutely aware of the novelty of his approach, noting, 'This was the first time that any division had advanced through the enemy lines in mobile columns with tanks. [… However, a]lthough it was new at the time, this method of advancing in mobile columns of all arms became an accepted practice during the war.'[96]

Although the use of mobile columns was an innovation, the deployment of the forces in all-arms teams was broadly in line with the doctrine: the tanks leading the assault, supported by infantry and artillery. However, the small number of vehicles available meant they were all placed in the leading wave, rather than some being assigned to a second echelon, intended to support the infantry more closely. Martel was clear, should a robust defence be encountered, the tanks would pause for the infantry to catch up, and then launch a combined attack.[97]

Given Martel had devised a plan that required the forces implementing it to operate outside the army's doctrine, it is necessary to consider whether they were capable of doing so – a second way in which the Alignment Gap might be wide. This requires an exploration of both their prior training and their capacity on the day of the attack itself.

The history of 50th Division noted, 'The troops had never had any previous training in working in a mobile column with tanks, and this was their first serious encounter with the Germans. The test was therefore a high one for a Territorial division.'[98] While they may not have had previous experience in mobile columns (unsurprising, given Martel underlined this was an innovation), this should not of itself be taken to imply the troops had no prior experience of preparing for armoured operations. In fact, Martel had ensured that, once mobilised on 1 September 1939,

> Technique for movement and acting in co-operation with armoured forces was studied and practised in every detail. The Division had visions of forming part

---

93   Clay, *Path of the 50th*, p.14.
94   Martel, *Our Armoured Forces*, p.64.
95   Ellis, *France and Flanders*, p.90.
96   Martel, *Outspoken Soldier*, p.157.
97   Martel, *Our Armoured Forces*, pp.64-65.
98   Clay, *Path of the 50th*, p.14.

of a great mechanised striking force in France, driving deep into the enemy positions, cutting his communications and carrying out the type of mobile armoured warfare which many of those in the division had cherished for a long time.[99]

This training, however, was cut short by the division's deployment to France in January 1940, where the near absence of any British tanks with which they could test the techniques developed during the previous autumn hindered the achievement of any advanced standard of expertise. As a consequence, the DLI regimental history noted, 'no one had any previous experience' of cooperating with tanks,[100] a point reinforced by the history of 6/DLI.[101] Moreover, since its arrival in France, the division had been used primarily for labouring duties: constructing defences and reserve positions.[102] Such employment was understandable, given most of the men were miners and shipbuilders, well used to heavy manual work, and most of their junior officers and NCOs were either fresh-faced recruits or aging veterans of the First World War.[103] In short, while Martel may have believed his infantry had a sound understanding of the principles of armoured warfare, and so had the potential to operate as a fast-moving mobile exploitation force, the reality was rather different.

The position of the two RTR battalions of 1st Army Tank Brigade was broadly similar to that of the infantry of 50th Division. Only 4/RTR had been in France for long, having sailed on 19 September 1939. Brigade Headquarters and the other two battalions (7/RTR and 8/RTR) had remained in England, until transported across to Dunkirk early in May 1940, and even then 8/RTR had been left behind.[104] Since active operations started within hours of 7/RTR's arrival in France, not only had the two battalions had no opportunity for joint training during the previous eight months, but there also appears to have been minimal training with infantry during that period. The war diary of 4/RTR recorded that, immediately after Brigade HQ arrived in France and took command of the battalion on 3 May, the formation undertook five days of intensive training, but this was entirely devoted to schemes within the battalion, other than a single one-day exercise, without any external units involved.[105] As a consequence, while the tank crews may have been familiar with the doctrine set out in MTP 22, this seems to have been primarily theoretical, at least in terms of its application in practice with other arms.

In addition to these factors of doctrine and training, a further factor leading to the potential for a wide Alignment Gap between the expectations of senior commanders

---

99   Clay, *Path of the 50th*, p.6.
100   Rissik, *DLI at War*, p.25.
101   Moses, *Faithful Sixth*, p.131.
102   Clay, *Path of the 50th*, pp.7-8.
103   Harman, *Dunkirk*, p.94.
104   Liddell Hart, *Tanks*, vol.2, pp.6-7.
105   WO167/459: 4/RTR.

and their actual performance was the practical ability of the troops involved to carry out their instructions.

The friction resulting from the absence of both doctrine and training for the sort of attack they were about to be called upon to conduct was exacerbated by the fact all of the British units started the operation in a state of near exhaustion. During the ten days preceding the attack, 1st Army Tank Brigade had driven almost 300 miles, with no time available for maintenance.[106] This reflected considerable confusion on the part of senior British commanders as to the proper role of the "I" tanks, and the fact the brigade had available only three Scammell trucks for towing tanks. Given 'the bulk of [this distance had been spent] moving at 3 m.p.h. on roads blocked by refugees and the results of constant air attacks', 12 tanks had already been lost through mechanical breakdown.[107] The remainder were reaching the limits of their endurance, with the tracks worn, constantly breaking and no spares available.[108] Similarly, the motorised infantry of the two DLI battalions, who had therefore had very little training in route marches,[109] had found themselves having to travel on foot for more than 50 miles during the previous three days, 'in very warm weather and often over roads crowded with refugees. The men were extremely tired and footsore [… yet t]here was little rest for the Battalion[s].'[110]

Recognising the implications of this weariness for the fighting potential of his forces, Martel 'issued strict orders that all these troops were to rest at once on arrival and obtain as much sleep as possible. No plans were to be discussed about impending operations, as that might easily result in commanders and staff not taking the necessary rest.' As a consequence, he noted, 'the commanders arrived at my headquarters at 7.30 a.m. [on 21 May] quite fresh and able to absorb their instructions and the troops were rested and ready for the hard day which was in front of them. Ordering rest in this way is one of the most important duties of a commander.'[111] Martel may have been overstating the impact of the few hours of rest on the troops: the history of 6/DLI commented the men remained 'very tired' and 'had not had sufficient rest to overcome their weariness',[112] and there were still a further 8 miles to march that morning before the units reached their start line.[113]

Although Martel's instructions that the attacking units not be informed of the impending operation had granted them at least a few hours of rest, it may have increased the Alignment Gap in other ways. Reflecting the doctrine set out in

106 WO167/459: 4/RTR, appx.23, p.3.
107 Liddell Hart, *Tanks*, vol.2, p.12.
108 Clay, *Path of the 50th*, p.14.
109 Thompson, *Dunkirk*, p.87.
110 Moses, *Faithful Sixth*, p.128. See also Lewis, *8th DLI*, pp.13-14.
111 Martel, *Armoured Forces*, p.62.
112 Moses, *Faithful Sixth*, pp130 & 132.
113 Rissik, *DLI at War*, p.25.

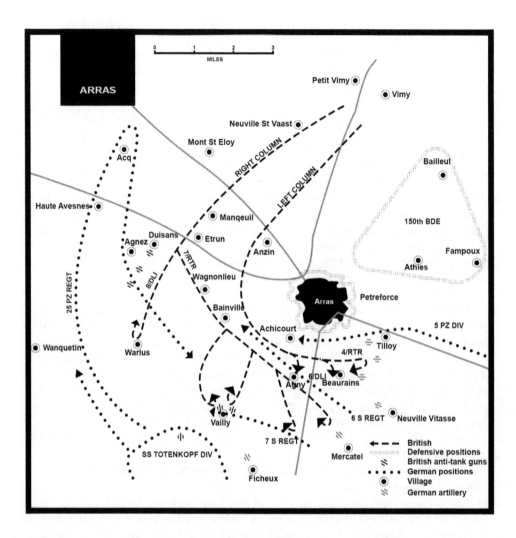

Map 5.1: The Arras Counterattack

MTP22, which emphasised the role of the tanks was to assist the infantry,[114] Martel placed each column under the command of the infantry battalion commander.[115]

Given the attack was to be made by only a handful of battalions, it might well have made sense for Martel to have held a single briefing with his brigadiers and lieutenant-colonels. In the event, however, he stuck to the usual 'chain of command' approach[116] and issued his orders to his brigadiers alone, leaving them to brief their own battalion commanders separately, at their respective brigade headquarters, around 1000 hours.[117] The impression made by Brigadier Pratt's orders on one unknown officer in 7/RTR may be judged by the comment scribbled in pencil at the top of the copy retained in the battalion's war diary: 'About as much use as a sick headache!'[118] Although Martel intended the infantry and tank battalion commanders to meet and make detailed plans once they had reached the assembly areas behind the start line,[119] this would have left precious little time for any effective coordination.

In the event, even this limited coordination failed to materialise. In a classic example of the Alignment Gap in practice, friction intervened. First, Martel's orders were not explicit over the command arrangements: although stating each column was to be commanded by the infantry colonel, the orders did not include the tank battalions within the paragraph setting out the composition of those columns. Instead, they simply noted that the 'advance will be carried out in two columns [...] with the tanks preceding each col[um]n'.[120] While the proposed meeting of battalion commanders would have allowed this potential confusion to be resolved, this did not happen in practice. Although the war diary of 8/DLI recorded its commander, Lt-Col Beart, did indeed meet with the commander of 7/RTR, Lt-Col Heyland, at 1245 hours, all contact with the tanks was lost at 1330 hours and the 'Tank Liaison Officer was unable to get in touch at any period.'[121] The connection between the two arms was so limited the war diary of 7/RTR did not mention the meeting.[122] Nonetheless, the two commanders had at least met, which was more than was achieved by their counterparts in the other column, Lt-Col Miller of 6/DLI and Lt-Col Fitzmaurice of 4/RTR. The war diary of 4/RTR recorded Fitzmaurice had gone to the designated point to make contact with the infantry, but 'No trace of the infantry could be found and information was finally received that the infantry would be an hour late in crossing the

114 MTP 22(III), sec.5(1).
115 Martel, *Armoured Forces*, p.65.
116 Blaxland, *Destination Dunkirk*, p.138.
117 WO167/729: 6/DLI War Diary, 21 May 1940; WO167/730: 8/DLI, War Diary, 21 May 1940; WO167/414: 1st Army Tank Bde, Notes on Events, 21 May 1940.
118 WO167/460: Appendix 25, p1.
119 Clay, *Path of the 50th*, p.16.
120 Martel Papers, 3/1, 19, paras.6-7.
121 WO167/730: 8/DLI, War Diary, 21 May 1940.
122 WO167/460: 7/RTR War Diary.

start line.' Brigadier Pratt ordered the tanks to advance at the allotted hour,[123] despite no contact having been made with the infantry. As a result, there was in practice no cooperation between the infantry and tanks in either column. As far as the infantry were concerned, the tanks had 'moved off too soon and disappeared in the distance'.[124]

Not only were the tanks unable to establish communications with the infantry, they also struggled to do so within their own units and with 1st Army Tank Brigade HQ. The war diaries of the brigade and both battalions commented on the fact wireless control collapsed almost immediately, due to a combination of 'the lack of time for netting, very bad atmospherics, and casualties to commanders tanks'. In addition, 4/RTR's rear link set shorted just before the start line was crossed. Control within the units was consequently extremely difficult and communication between them and brigade headquarters non-existent.[125]

Closer examination of this breakdown in communications suggests it may have been exacerbated by the command approach adopted by Brigadier Pratt. Both battalions had been ordered to maintain strict radio silence throughout the period from the beginning of operations, including during the 130-mile road march through Belgium. This was only broken when the tanks went into action on 21 May. Yet, according to 4/RTR's Battalion Reconnaissance Officer, Second Lieutenant Peter Vaux, the radio sets of the Matildas tended to drift off frequency, especially if the vehicles drove over rough ground, and were notoriously awkward to tune. The absence of any opportunity to check whether they were properly tuned meant it was hardly surprising only one or two vehicles remained on the correct frequency at the start of the operation, by which time it was too late to retune them. As Vaux noted, 'I suppose the fault was really that of HQ 1st Tank Brigade, who hung on to wireless silence so long [... .] Certainly there was nothing wrong with the sets themselves'.[126]

In short, through requiring his units to follow his orders precisely, and constraining their ability to prepare for the next phase of battle, Pratt had reduced his formation into a swarm of individual bees, each with a powerful sting, but able only to act on its own. MTP22 had recognised, 'occasions will frequently arise when [sub-unit commanders] will be called on to exercise great initiative and make important decisions when reference to higher authority is impractical',[127] such that 'a junior commander will often be faced with situations requiring a quick decision even sometimes involving deviation from his original orders'.[128] While this favouring of Directive Command, in contrast to the emphasis on Restrictive Control in FSR II (1935),[129] is notable,

---

123 WO167/459: 4/RTR, appx.23, p.1.
124 Rissik, *DLI at War*, p.26. See also Moses, *Faithful Sixth*, p.132 and Lewis, *8th DLI*, p.15.
125 WO167/414: 1st Army Tank Bde, Notes, p.4; WO167/459: 4/RTR, appx.23, p.4; and WO167/460: 7/RTR, Appx.31, p.4.
126 Bryan Perrett, *The Matilda* (London: Allan, 1972), p.15.
127 MTP 22(III), sec.1(5).
128 MTP 22(III), sec.2(3).
129 FSR II (1935), para.14(5)i.

this was hardly a situation to be generated through internal failings. MTP22 had gone on to note, 'To enable him to arrive at a correct solution with rapidity, [the junior commander] must understand clearly the object of the operation and the needs of the infantry with whom he is working'.[130] As has been demonstrated above, this understanding was almost completely lacking at Arras.

Auspices for the Attack

In summary, as the tanks of 4/RTR and 7/RTR roared off into their first battle, with the infantry struggling to catch up, the level of friction being experienced even before the first enemy had been encountered was already very high indeed.

The Knowledge Gap was wide, with both Franklyn and Martel believing the aim of the operation was merely to mop up any enemy on the outskirts of Arras, whereas Ironside and Gort imagined it as part of a decisive thrust to cut off the head of the German armoured thrust and so turn the tables on the over-bold enemy. In addition, although both divisional commanders had received intelligence from 12th Lancers regarding the strength of the enemy forces facing them, suggesting this was far greater than had been suggested by GHQ, this information was not passed to the attacking troops. In both cases, these gaps may have been widened by a reliance on Restrictive Control by the British commanders.

The Alignment Gap was also wide, with Martel having to order tactics that bore little relation to the army's doctrine, since the task assigned to him was so different from that envisaged by MTP22's authors. The troops would therefore have to manoeuvre in ways for which the doctrine gave them little guidance. The likelihood of their being able to respond flexibly to this novel situation was low, however, given the training in combined arms operations of all of the units involved was minimal. Furthermore, all of the units about to launch the attack were already exhausted from lengthy route marches, and breakdowns in liaison and radio communications meant there would be little scope for commanders to manoeuvre their forces as part of a larger whole. Sub-units would simply have to work on their own initiative, based on the very limited guidance in their orders and their own sense of the tactical situation immediately around them.

Even before the first shots had been fired, therefore, it is clear the auspices were not favourable for what was probably the Allies last chance to halt the German advance and turn the tide of the campaign.

---

130 MTP 22(III), sec.2(3).

The Other Side of the Hill – The Effects Gap

In order to understand the extent to which the effectiveness of the British forces corresponded to that expected by their commanders, it is necessary to start by considering the position on 'the other side of the hill'.

It has been seen the German forces around Arras were in significantly greater strength than had been suggested by Gort when he briefed first Martel and then Franklyn during the night of 19/20 May. Lumsden's 12th Lancers subsequently reported there were several enemy columns in the area, including numerous tanks. In fact, this gives an indication of the rapid pace of the German advance, since Gort was broadly correct about the position when he spoke to Franklyn, but this assessment of the situation quickly became out of date as 7th Panzer Division penetrated a full 40 km during the single day of 20 May.[131] The picture of the enemy forces now being painted by the Lancers revealed the situation as it had been understood by the British was being transformed, and the risks associated with the operation assigned to Martel were consequently significantly increased.

In the week since Rommel's crossing of the Meuse on 13 May and his subsequent penetration of the French defences (see Chapter Three), the Ghost Division had maintained its breakneck advance. On 16 May, it found itself 45 km ahead of its supporting infantry. Early the next morning, Rommel reached the River Sambre at Landrecies, almost 100 km from the Meuse. The French were taken completely by surprise: some ten thousand men, along with a hundred tanks, gave themselves up to the weak German forces that suddenly appeared at this critical crossing point.[132] By nightfall on 18 May, Rommel was 52 km ahead of the nearest infantry division, and 29 km to the west of 5th Panzer Division, the other armoured division now under XXXIX Motorised Corps. The following day, while Gort and Ironside planned their attempt to cut off the head of the German advance, 7th Panzer Division consolidated its positions, taking a second bridgehead across the L'Escaut Canal south of Cambrai, 20 km to the east of Arras, in readiness for a further advance.[133]

During the morning of 20 May, as Franklyn was being briefed by Gort for his 'mopping up' operation around Arras, 25th Panzer Regiment, accompanied by Rommel acting as an 'escort', reached Beaurains, 3 km south of Arras. Rommel was well aware of how exposed his northern flank was, as the division experienced a day of intermittent fighting as French forces attempted to press south.[134] As a result of these moves, instead of the weak forces indicated by Gort, Martel was about to advance

---

131 Russel H. Stolfi, *A Bias for Action: The German 7th Panzer Division in France & Russia, 1940- 41* (Quantico, VA: Command & Staff College Foundation, 1991), p.35.
132 Stolfi, *Bias for Action*, pp.21-24.
133 Stolfi, *Bias for Action*, p.28.
134 Stolfi, *Bias for Action*, pp.29-30.

against an entire panzer division operating at full throttle, forces significantly more numerous than his own.

In the event, on the morning of 21 May, Rommel inadvertently played into the hands of the British. Despite the ongoing pressure against his exposed right (northern) flank, he sent Rothenberg and his tanks rushing yet further ahead, moving round to the north west of Arras, while his infantry followed behind. Again, the Ghost Division was almost unsupported, with only the untested infantry of the SS Totenkopf Division to its left, south of Arras, and 5th Panzer Division somewhere to its rear, to the south east of the city.[135] As Rommel plunged his iron-tipped spear yet deeper into the Allied position, Martel's tanks accidentally ploughed into the wooden shaft, taking both sides completely by surprise.

The first Rommel was aware of the British attack was shortly after 1500 hours. Following close behind 25th Panzer Regiment, which was already to the west of Arras, he realised the infantry of Schützen-Regiment 7 (SR7) were coming up much more slowly than intended. Driving back, he finally found them in the vicinity of Wailly, where a fierce engagement was underway against the tanks of 7/RTR in Martel's right column. Given the division had easily resisted French attacks the previous day, he was not unduly troubled: 'I ran on [...] towards the [anti-tank] battery position. It did not look as though the battery would have much difficulty in dealing with the enemy tanks, for the gunners were calmly hurling round after round into them in complete disregard of the return fire.'[136]

In fact, the first instance of the Effects Gap was being experienced. 7/RTR reported being fired upon by an armoured car and by several 37mm anti-tank guns (from Rommel's Panzer-Jäger-Abteilung 42 (PzJgAbt42)), but 'against the heavy British tanks, our anti-tank guns, even at close range, were insufficiently effective'.[137] The RTR crews found their thick armour gave them near total protection against the German anti-tank guns.

On 21 May, 7/RTR deployed thirty-five Matilda I (A11) tanks, along with six larger Matilda II (A12) tanks.[138] The Matilda I's 60 mm of frontal armour, and especially the Matilda II's 78 mm,[139] was far thicker than the meagre 25 mm of Rommel's Czech-built Panzer 38(t) tanks[140] or even the 40-60mm of the French Char B tanks[141] 7th Panzer Division had previously encountered. The PAK35/36 guns of PzJgAbt42 could penetrate just 38 mm of armour.[142] 'The defensive front formed by [the anti-tank

135 Stolfi, *Bias for Action*, pp.35-36 and *Rommel Papers*, pp.29-30.
136 *Rommel Papers*, p.30.
137 IWM: Enemy Documents Section: AL596, 7th Panzer Division, Kriegstagebuch, 21 May 1940.
138 Martel, *Our Armoured Forces*, p.65.
139 Perrett, *Matilda*, pp.95 & 97.
140 Forty, *Armies of Rommel*, p.41.
141 Frieser, *Blitzkrieg Legend*, p.39.
142 Mann, *SS-Totenkopf*, pp.171-172.

battalion] was therefore quickly penetrated by the enemy, the guns destroyed by fire or overrun, the crews largely obliterated.[143] Given their thicker armour, the Matilda IIs were especially effective: the two vehicles commanded by Major King and Sergeant Doyle overran two batteries of anti-tank guns, destroyed four German tanks, and even dealt with an 88mm anti-aircraft gun, enabling them to thrust right into the heart of the enemy position.[144]

A little to the north of Rommel's position, events were taking a similar course. The twenty-three Matilda Is and ten Matilda IIs of 4/RTR in Martel's left column[145] had encountered elements of I Bataillon, Schützen-Regiment 6 (I/SR6), supported by further anti-tank guns from PzJgAbt42, near the village of Achicourt. Here too, the German gunners calmly operated their weapons, their company commander later reported, 'yet the shots from our 3.7 cm anti-tank guns bounced off, even at short range.'[146] Staff Sergeant-Major Armit of 4/RTR in a Matilda I noted, '[in] the space of a minute, they hit my tank about ten times, but none of the hits did any real damage.'[147] The battalion's after action report noted, 'One tank showed as many as 14 direct hits and the only indication the crew had of being hit was a red glow for a few seconds on the inside of the armour plate.'[148]

When considering the impact of tank attacks on the morale of the defenders during the battle of Amiens in August 1918 (Chapter Four), reference was made to the historical analysis undertaken by David Rowland and his colleagues at the Defence Operational Analysis Establishment. Their research allowed them to calculate the relative importance of four factors in determining whether an armoured assault resulted in the enemy experiencing shock: the achievement of surprise, the presence of 'invulnerable' tanks, poor visibility, and the speed of the attack.[149]

At Arras in May 1940, it is clear the British attack came as a complete surprise to the Germans. Although they had been under pressure from their northern flank throughout the past few days, there had been no coordinated attack such as that now being delivered by 1st Army Tank Brigade. In addition, the Matildas of both types were clearly invulnerable to the standard anti-tank guns deployed by 7th Panzer Division. Conversely, although the battlefield was crossed by a number of railway embankments and was studded with villages and woods, the visibility enjoyed by both sides appears to have been good. In addition, the limited speed of the tanks (8 mph

143 IWM: 7th Panzer, KTB, 21 May 1940.
144 Perrett, *Matilda*, pp.26–27.
145 Martel, *Our Armoured Forces*, p.65.
146 Quoted in Scheibert, *Gespenster-Division*, p.35.
147 Perrett, *Matilda*, p.23.
148 WO167/459, appx 23, p.3.
149 David Rowland, *The Stress of Battle: Quantifying Human Performance in Combat* (London: Stationery Office, 2006), p.195.

for the Matilda I, 15 mph for the Matilda II)[150] meant there was plenty of time for the defenders to react.

Rowland's analysis suggested, where an attack featured invulnerable tanks alone, the likelihood of the defenders suffering shock was roughly fifty percent. If attackers with invulnerable tanks also secured surprise, as was the case at Arras, the probability rose to eighty-five percent.[151]

The after action report of 4/RTR noted the vulnerability of the German anti-tank guns: 'A burst of well directed .303 M.G. fire at the flash invariably silenced the guns even up to ranges of 800 yards.' The report also commented on, 'The poor fighting qualities of the German troops encountered. [...] large numbers were observed lying on the ground face downwards feigning dead, others ran up to the tanks surrendering.'[152] The men of 6/DLI, following behind 4/RTR, found, 'The morale of the German infantry was low and they seemed always to be quite ready to be taken prisoner.'[153] Similarly, 7/RTR noted, 'A large number of casualties [were] inflicted, columns of enemy lorries [...] destroyed, armoured cars burned and a large number of anti-tank guns put out of action. At one time the enemy were completely demoralized and were running away [...] a large number of prisoners were taken'.[154] 1st Army Tank Brigade highlighted how the Germans were 'shaken by the [British] tanks' ability to withstand considerable 2 p[ounde]r [37mm anti-tank gun] fire at close quarters.'[155] A number of anti-tank gun crews fled in the face of the inexorable advance of the Matildas.[156] Rommel himself admitted, 'The enemy tank fire had created chaos and confusion among our troops [...] and they were jamming up the roads [...] with their vehicles, instead of going into action with every available weapon to fight off the oncoming enemy.'[157]

It is clear Martel's tanks had been successful in inflicting shock on the Germans they encountered, as predicted by Rowland's analysis. His own analysis made this clear: 'When a tank can advance and ignore the fire of the main enemy anti-tank guns, a great moral effect is produced. Such a tank dominates the battlefield. In this case the German infantry often ran into long grass or other cover and, as our infantry advanced, they waved their hands in the air and surrendered. ... the moral effect when the attack was first launched was very great.'[158]

The chaos and collapse of morale suffered by 7th Panzer Division is underlined by the fact the formation suffered 173 men missing on 21 May. Not only was this by

150 Perrett, *Matilda*, pp.95 & 97.
151 Rowland, *Stress*, pp.195-197.
152 WO167/459, appx 23, p.3.
153 Quoted by Macksey, *Vimy Ridge*, p.213.
154 WO167/460, appx.31, p.4.
155 WO1567/414, appx.7.
156 Macksey, *Vimy Ridge*, p.212, & Perrett, *Matilda*, p.20.
157 *Rommel Papers*, pp.30-32.
158 Martel, *Armoured Forces*, p.69.

far the largest number recorded for a single day, it was almost two-thirds of the total (264) for the entire campaign.[159] However, this should not be taken as necessarily suggesting the troops were of poor quality. After all, in the past few days they had successfully undertaken an opposed river crossing and had destroyed a series of French formations. Hardly the achievements of flaky troops. Instead, it seems more likely many of Rommel's anti-tank gunners and infantrymen simply panicked at the sight of the invulnerable British tanks unexpectedly appearing on their flank and rolling inexorably through their positions. Based on Rowland's historical analysis, such a reaction would be likely on the part of almost any troops in these circumstances. This interpretation may be reinforced by the truly exceptional number of men reported missing – never again were Rommel's men to be subject to an attack so likely to result in shock.

That this was indeed a temporary panic, rather than a genuine collapse of morale or a sign of poor quality troops, is indicated by the fact 90 of the men initially listed as casualties found their way back to their units within the next few days.[160] It seems fair to assume most of these men had been among the 173 men declared missing, rather than included with the 116 men wounded. The implication is they had become detached from their units in the fluid confusion of the engagement, quite possibly through their own flight in panic, rather than surrendering. The actual number of men from the division captured by the British was therefore probably fewer than one hundred.

Rommel's situation was clearly serious. For the first time in the campaign, the British and French had launched a determined attack. Taking the Germans completely by surprise, their invulnerable tanks had swept aside the anti-tank screen, destroyed numerous vehicles, and caused panic among the men of the Ghost Division. If the panic spread and the British penetration extended only a few miles deeper to the south, then the five panzer divisions of Panzergruppe Kleist might be cut off. Isolated from their supporting infantry and without logistic support, they could then surely expect to be destroyed by the large number of fresh French formations still available. This was perhaps the decisive moment of the entire campaign.

The decisive moment found a decisive commander. Rommel was at the key point, facing the tanks of 7/RTR at Wailly. He later recorded,[161]

> We tried to create order. [...] we found a light A.A. troop and several anti-tank guns [... .] With [my aide, Leutnant] Most's help, I brought every available gun into action at top speed against the tanks. Every gun, both anti-tank and anti-aircraft, was ordered to open rapid fire immediately and I personally gave each gun its target. [...] We ran from gun to gun. [...] All I cared about was to halt the

159 Stolfi, *Bias for Action*, p.22.
160 Scheibert, *Gespenster-Division*, p.36.
161 *Rommel Papers*, p.32.

leading enemy tanks by heavy gunfire. Soon we succeeded in putting the leading enemy tanks out of action. [...] Although we were under very heavy fire from the tanks during this action, the gun crews worked magnificently.

The severe personal danger into which Rommel yet again placed himself at this time was readily apparent. Not only was Most mortally wounded at his side, but at one point he was cornered in a shell-hole by a British tank, only for the crew to bail out of the vehicle and surrender to him![162]

Although Rommel noted the crew of one howitzer battery, some distance ahead of him, did leave their guns, swept along in the general panic,[163] most of the German artillerymen appear to have reacted with considerable calmness. The somewhat excitable account of the division, published under Rommel's personal direction soon after the campaign, recorded how the gunners welcomed their new targets and put the British tanks under heavy fire.[164] Rather than join the anti-tank gunners and infantry in flight, therefore, most of the batteries fought on, even to the point where their howitzers were destroyed and their crews killed.[165] The gunners of Artillerie-Regiment 78 (AR78) suffered especially heavy casualties, the most of any battalion in the division.[166] This suggests the German field gunners did not suffer from shock.

The contrast between the panic that affected the infantry (and at least some of the anti-tank gunners) and the calm of the artillerymen may again be explained by reference to Rowland's analysis. The former had unexpectedly found themselves facing tanks that were, to them, invulnerable. The probability of them suffering shock was therefore around eighty-five percent. By contrast, although the field gunners may still have felt surprised by the British attack, their heavier artillery pieces meant the Matildas were not invulnerable. Rowland found, in cases where defenders faced tanks that enjoyed surprise alone, but were neither invulnerable, nor appearing out of poor visibility, nor moving at high speed, the probability of them experiencing shock was much reduced, at around sixty percent.[167] Nonetheless, sixty percent remains a high figure. The fact that, with few exceptions, the field gunners did not experience shock suggests a further explanation for their steadfastness is required.

This further explanation may perhaps be found in another aspect of Rowland's analysis (noted in Chapter Four), which highlighted the impact on the effectiveness of anti-tank crews of what he termed 'heroes'. He discovered guns manned by crews operating under the direct supervision of officers or senior NCOs performed at their full potential capability. By contrast, 'approximately one third of weapons [not directly under an officer of senior NCO] made no effective contribution to the battle at all. [...]

162 Sebag-Montefiore, *Dunkirk*, p.148.
163 *Rommel Papers*, p.32.
164 Tschimpke, *Gespenster-Division*, p.116.
165 Scheibert, *Gespenster-Division*, p.35.
166 Stolfi, *Bias for Action*, p.36.
167 Rowland, *Stress*, pp.195-197.

The remaining two thirds operated at an effectiveness level of roughly 0.3'.[168] In other words, unless under the immediate control of a senior commander, most anti-tank gun crews took only minimal active participation in an action.

It was perhaps here that Rommel's very personal and immediate style of command, a clear demonstration of the Directive Control command approach, most proved its worth. It has been noted how, when facing the tanks of 7/RTR, Rommel 'personally gave each gun its target. [...] The objections of gun commander [...] were overruled.'[169] Prior to the start of the offensive, less than two weeks earlier, Rommel had never experienced active operations with artillery under his direct command. Yet, at Arras, whether consciously or not, he had adopted a command approach that meant every one of his guns operated under the supervision of an officer (i.e. himself), and hence performed at their full potential. The effect was to increase the fighting power of his guns by perhaps a factor of five.[170]

The effect of this personal intervention by the divisional commander was decisive: as Frieser noted, 'Because the division commander personally exposed himself to this danger, his men could only do likewise.'[171] Rommel recorded, across the two engagements, the artillery destroyed thirty-six tanks.[172] This represented two-thirds of the forty-three Matildas lost during the battle as a whole.[173]

This action is of particular interest, as it was the very first occasion when the 88mm weapons were used in an anti-tank role against British tanks.[174] Several historians have suggested the intervention of these guns decisively shifted the balance: 'The gun which finally did the damage was the 88mm, soon to become a legend in its own right and scourge of Allied tank commanders.'[175] This, however, was not the German view. Indeed, the impact of the 88mm guns appears to have been limited: Rommel recorded they accounted for just one heavy tank and seven light tanks, whereas the field guns of AR78 knocked out twenty-eight tanks.[176]

The legend the 88mm anti-aircraft guns did the damage, weapons being used in an innovative manner by a brilliant commander, may simply be yet another example of the common tendency of armies to ascribe their defeats to the genius of the enemy, against which they could not be expected to be successful. In fact, the FLAK36 gun had been designed from the start with the intention it should be used in a dual role

---

168 Rowland, *Stress*, pp.118 & 146.
169 *Rommel Papers*, p.32.
170 Rowland, *Stress*, p.145.
171 Frieser, *Blitzkrieg Legend*, pp.276-277.
172 *Rommel Papers*, pp.32-33.
173 Only thirty-one of the original seventy-four Matildas remained operational on 22 May. WO167/460: Appx xxxi, p.4.
174 Perrett, *Matilda*, p.26.
175 Forty, *Armies of Rommel*, p.63. See also Blaxland, *Destination Dunkirk*, p.143, and Harman, *Dunkirk*, pp.99-100.
176 *Rommel Papers*, pp.32-33.

and this was described in the army's doctrine. To underline Rommel was hardly being innovative in this situation, 5th Panzer Division also used its 88mm guns in an anti-tank role.[177] Indeed, the use of anti-aircraft guns in an anti-tank role had been included in *British* doctrine since 1929,[178] and more explicitly since 1935, though this was considered something that would occur only 'in special circumstances'.[179]

In fact, many of the tanks of 7/RTR seem to have been destroyed when lighter gunfire caused kit stored on the outside of the vehicles to catch fire,[180] though it was also suggested some of the fires were caused by tracer rounds penetrating the front louvers of the tanks.[181] This again confirmed Rommel's longstanding tactic, noted in Chapter Three, of emphasising sheer weight of fire, regardless of its practical effectiveness,[182] as a decisive factor in undermining the enemy's will to fight.

Despite their success against the Matildas, Rommel's guns, firing over open sights as they were, were utterly vulnerable to enemy counter-battery fire. But this required forward observation officers, and the problem of how to provide such a function in an armoured engagement had yet to be solved by the British.[183] As a result, the guns of 92nd Field Regiment, Royal Artillery, deployed in support of the attack, 'were not called upon to fire until late in [the] day'.[184] Most of the surviving British tanks turned away. The main armoured attack was over.

Flight or Fight – The Alignment Gap

Despite this barrage of anti-tank fire, however, some of the Matildas of 7/RTR did penetrate Rommel's anti-tank screen. Advancing deeper, they ploughed into the SS Totenkopf Division, which was covering 7th Panzer Division's southern (left) flank. Rommel noted the SS 'had to fall back [...] before the weight of the tank attack.'[185]

177   Claus Telp, 'Rommel and 1940', in *Rommel: A Reappraisal*, ed. by Ian F.W. Beckett (Barnsley: Pen and Sword, 2013), 30-59 (p.51), *Heeresdienstvorschrift (HDv) 300/1: Truppenführung* (1933), paras. 758 and 812, and Plato, *5. Panzerdivision*, p.78.
178   *Field Service Regulations: Vol.II: Operations* (1929), sect.81(2)iv.
179   *Field Service Regulations: Vol.II: Operations* (1935), sect.39(1).
180   Macksey, *Vimy Ridge*, pp.222-223.
181   US Army, Special Bulletin No.11: British Tank Operations in the Vicinity of Arras, May 19-23, 1940 (22 August 1940) <http://cgsc.contentdm.oclc.org/cdm/singleitem/collection/p4013coll8/id/2739/rec/17> [accessed 23 December 2016], p.14. Most of this bulletin was a verbatim copy of Martel's own report on the battle, IWM: Martel Papers, 3/1, item 19.
182   *Rommel Papers*, p.32.
183   Caddick-Adams, *Monty and Rommel*, p.231.
184   IWM: 92nd Field Regiment, RA, War diary, 21 May 1940.
185   *Rommel Papers*, p.33.

Guderian was rather less polite about the troops' reaction: 'the SS Division Totenkopf, which had not been in action before [...,] showed signs of panic.'[186]

Like most army officers writing their memoirs after the war, Guderian had every reason to distance himself from the SS, but his account would initially seem substantiated by the number of prisoners given up by the formation. British accounts state they captured almost four hundred enemy troops on 21 May.[187] Since, as was noted earlier, 7th Panzer Division reported 173 men missing, it has been suggested that the remainder of the British haul, over two hundred, must have come from the Totenkopf Division,[188] the only other formation significantly involved in the battle. Given the limited part played by the division in the engagement, this would appear to indicate there had indeed been a significant collapse of its morale. Yet these figures for prisoners do not stand closer inspection: the number of men missing following the action, as detailed in the division's war diary, was precisely ... two.[189] Nor were the numbers made up by loses from other German units: the only other formation in the area was 5th Panzer Division, which reported just two dead and seventeen injured, with not one listed as missing.[190]

The response of the British Official History to this disparity between the number of prisoners claimed by the British (almost 400) and the number of missing recorded by the Germans (175) was to suggest the latter's casualty figures must have been under-reported.[191] In this, it was perhaps subconsciously following the parallel assumptions adopted by James Edmonds in his official history of the First World War. Edmonds had argued German casualty figures during that conflict were understated by some thirty percent,[192] a claim conclusively disproven by James McRandle and James Quirk.[193] However, there is no evidence whatsoever to suggest the German formations in 1940 underestimated their casualties, and indeed no reason for them to have done so. The fact the casualty figures were stated on a daily basis in the war diaries and these were not corrected to account for the large number of men reported as missing who subsequently returned to their units provides evidence of their accuracy.

Conversely, historian Nicholas Harman suggested the British had indeed taken large numbers of prisoners, especially from the SS, but these were subsequently

---

186 General Heinz Guderian, *Panzer Leader*, trans. by Constantine Fitzgibbon (London: Futura, 1974), p.114.

187 IWM: Martel Papers, 3/1, Item 19: Report on Operations of Frankforce, 20th May – 24th May 1940 [by Major-General Harold Franklyn], p.2.

188 Thompson, *Dunkirk*, p.99.

189 Charles Trang, *Totenkopf* (Bayeux: Heimdal, 2006), p. 43.

190 Plato, *5. Panzerdivision*, p.71.

191 Ellis, *France and Flanders*, pp.94-95.

192 Brigadier-General James E. Edmonds, *The Official History of the Great War: Military Operations: France & Belgium, 1916*, vol.1 (1932, repr. Woking: Shearer, 1986), pp.496-497.

193 James McRandle and James Quirk, 'The Blood Test Revisited: A New Look at German Casualty Counts in World War I', *Journal of Military History*, 70(3) (July 2006), 667-701 (pp.686-688).

massacred by the DLI – he noted one officer of 7/RTR recorded, 'The [DLI] troops displayed great animosity towards the prisoner, and I was compelled to draw my revolver and order them off'.[194] There is no direct evidence to support this hypothesis, and the number of German fatalities is not consistent with it. Instead, it seems much more likely, although the British may indeed have taken some 400 prisoners during the operation, the confused and chaotic nature of the retreat back to their start line that evening meant the majority were able to escape and report back to their units during the following days.

Returning to the response of the Totenkopf Division to their unexpected engagement with the Matildas, Charles Sydnor suggested, although the men of one supply column 'abandoned their vehicles and fled pell-mell', most of the formation 'performed commendably'. This interpretation is perhaps supported by the division's overall casualty figures for the day: in addition to the two men reported as missing, there were 39 dead and 66 wounded.[195] By contrast, almost half of 7th Panzer Division's 378 casualties that day were accounted as missing.[196] This picture of a spirited defence is reinforced by Chris Mann's comment most of the casualties came from the divisional anti-tank battalion, whose crews fought on desperately until the guns were destroyed, many being crushed by the Matildas.[197] Similarly, the division's medical unit noted most of the casualties treated had been hit in the lungs and stomach, indicating they had been wounded while running *towards* the enemy.[198]

There is therefore some evidence to suggest Rommel and Guderian were unfairly negative in their dismissive accounts of the Totenkopf's performance during the battle and the reality was actually more in line with the picture painted in the division's euphoric account of its actions. Published soon after the campaign's end, this highlighted the Arras counterattack as 'the first great success' achieved by the formation:

> With humming motors, smashing every attempt at resistance, the SS Totenkopf Division rolled unstopping along the narrow roads south of Arras through the enemy territory. As the enemy finally realised their situation, it was already too late. Nothing could halt our storming advance any longer. The enemy's last card, their last trump, the armoured breakthrough attempt at Arras, shattered itself against the heroic resistance of the Death's Headers. Those were 'the days' of the heavy weapons of our division. The enemy's last hope smashed against the steel

194 Harman, *Dunkirk*, pp.97-99.
195 Sydnor, *Soldiers of Destruction*, p.96.
196 Scheibert, *Gespenster-Division*, p.36.
197 Mann, *SS-Totenkopf*, p.79.
198 Sydnor, *Soldiers of Destruction*, p.96n10.

ring formed by the anti-tank guns, artillery and pioneers of the SS Totenkopf Division.[199]

Far from the SS fleeing in panic, these accounts suggest they fought fiercely, perhaps playing a key role in stabilising the situation and even rescuing Rommel and 7th Panzer Division.[200] So what was the reality? Did the Totenkopf Division stand and fight, as its commanders would have expected, or did it flee in panic, thereby creating a wide Alignment Gap?

The SS Totenkopf Division was one of three divisions formed in October 1939, after Hitler approved Himmler's proposal to create an armed wing of the SS, the Waffen SS, to fight alongside the army in the projected campaign in the west.[201] The core of the division was drawn from the existing three regiments of the *Totenkopfverbände* (Death's Head Units). These had been established the previous month by bringing together various units of concentration camp guards and were intended for 'police and security' measures behind the German lines during the invasion of Poland.[202] Their commander, SS-Gruppenführer Theodor Eicke, was present at the meeting where Hitler announced the creation of the SS divisions, so it was perhaps inevitable he was appointed to lead the new formation.[203]

Born in German-controlled Alsace on 17 October 1892, Eicke left school early and joined the army. He served throughout the First World War, though his practical military experience was limited, as he worked as a paymaster. Eicke joined the Nazi party in December 1928, rising with great rapidity through the ranks, reaching the level of SS *Standartenführer* (colonel) by the time he became a fulltime SS official early in 1932. In June 1933, Himmler personally selected him to become the commandant of the first concentration camp, established at Dachau on the outskirts of Munich, perhaps on account of his experience as a security officer for IG Farben during the 1920s. Eicke proved highly successful in his new role, leading to his promotion in July 1934 to the rank of SS *Gruppenführer* (lieutenant-general) and appointment as inspector of all concentration camps nationwide and leader of their guards, the *Totenkopfverbände*. This promotion may well have been in part a reward for Eicke's role during the 'night of the long knives' a few days before, when he had personally shot Ernst Röhm, leader of the SA.[204]

199 SS Totenkopf-Division, *Damals: Erinnerungen an Grosse Tage der SS Totenkopf-Division im Französischen Feldzug 1940* (Stuttgart: Belser, 1941), p.11.
200 Sydnor, *Soldiers of Destruction*, p.96.
201 Sydnor, *Soldiers of Destruction*, pp.43-45.
202 Sydnor, *Soldiers of Destruction*, pp.34-35.
203 Vopersal, *Soldaten*, pp.13-14.
204 For Eicke's history and the establishment of the *Totenkopfverbände*, see Sydnor, *Soldiers of Destruction*, pp.3-36, Mann, *SS-Totenkopf*, pp.20-33, Vopersal, *Soldaten*, pp.13-37, Holroyd, *SS-Totenkopf France*, pp.7-13, and Ullrich, *Like a Cliff*, pp.4-7.

Eicke was clear he wanted no military formalities in his concentration camp guard units, practices he considered outdated and useless. Instead, he emphasised the need for comradeship between all ranks, combined with toughness and what Sydnor termed 'harsh and often brutal punishments' for even the smallest breach of his rules. This led to a curious mixture of close camaraderie and an insistence on instinctive obedience and conformity.[205] These characteristics carried forward when the *Totenkopfverbände* were selected to form the core of the Totenkopf Division. Eicke's own command approach was focused on blind obedience and rigid discipline, underlined by his announcement any officer who disobeyed specific orders would be relieved of his command.[206] This reliance on Restrictive Control was at significant variance from the philosophy of Directive Command, complemented by Directive Control, preached by the army.

Following the creation of the Totenkopf Division, this deliberate distancing from the army was reflected in Eicke's approach to military operations. This was perhaps reinforced by the fact, although most of his divisional staff had seen service during the First World War and with the *Freicorps*, none had served in the Reichswehr as a commissioned officer.[207] In training his division, he therefore consciously departed from the army's operational manuals. As Sydnor put it, 'In the more complex and sophisticated theories of motorized operations, Eicke had neither learning nor the slightest interest. In his blunt and impatient mind the rules were plain enough: concentrate every available soldier, weapon, and vehicle in the front line, then smash away at the enemy with relentless fury until he crumbled.'[208] This could hardly have been more different from the philosophy of encirclement as a means to undermine the enemy's will to resist, which characterised the army's approach.

It is perhaps not surprising Eicke expressed a determination to distance himself from the army. The army hardly welcomed the establishment of the Waffen SS: Generaloberst Walther von Brauschitsch, the army's commander-in-chief, and General Friedrich Fromm, commander of the replacement army, who were also present in October 1939 when Hitler announced its creation, were reportedly furious at the decision.[209] Himmler had to intervene personally before the army was willing to release weapons and equipment to the new formations, or to admit SS men to the army technical schools, moves essential if the Totenkopf Division was to be properly established as a motorised infantry formation. Even then, the supply of heavy weapons was slow.[210] Nonetheless, Generaloberst Maximilien von Weichs, to whose Second Army the Totenkopf Division was assigned, was significantly impressed by

205 Sydnor, *Soldiers of Destruction*, pp.26-30.
206 Sydnor, *Soldiers of Destruction*, pp.53 & 60-61.
207 Sydnor, *Soldiers of Destruction*, pp.47-53.
208 Sydnor, *Soldiers of Destruction*, p.65.
209 Vopersal, *Soldaten*, p.13.
210 Sydnor, *Soldiers of Destruction*, pp.64, 68, 70 & 80.

the standard of training achieved by the end of April 1940. As a direct result, Eicke finally received the first four 150mm heavy guns he had so long coveted.[211]

Although the Totenkopf was one of just seven fully motorised infantry divisions in the army, Franz Halder and the OKH (Army High Command) remained deeply suspicious of Eicke. At the start of operations in May 1940, therefore, the formation was assigned to the strategic reserve. Having kicked his heels in frustration for a week, Eicke finally received orders to move on 17 May. With a strength of 408 officers, 1542 NCOs, and 10,014 men, the Totenkopf Division began its first campaign.[212] It entered combat two days later, in an operation to support 7th Panzer Division in dealing with French Moroccan troops defending the line of the River Sambre near Cambrai. After fierce fighting that lasted throughout the night, during which the SS suffered their first casualties (16 dead and 53 wounded), the French positions were cleared and 1600 prisoners taken.[213]

The troops that faced the Matildas of 7/RTR the following day therefore had minimal combat experience, but were imbued with a ferocious offensive spirit, coupled with a brutal insistence on rigid obedience to orders – Restrictive Control.

On the evening of 20 May, the division had been ordered to fill the gap between 7th Panzer Division and 8th Panzer Division, which was advancing on a parallel track to the south. Since the British were expected to launch attacks from Arras against the rear of Rommel's formation, Eicke deployed his men in a strongpoint system of defence almost 50km long, facing north towards the city. The next morning, he was ordered to continue the march westwards, supporting 7th Panzer Division's intended sweep to the north-west, bypassing Arras.[214]

Eicke was with the advanced elements of his division when he learned British tanks had engaged his men near Mercatel. In contrast with Rommel's direct and personal intervention in the desperate battle happening nearby around the village of Vailly, the Totenkopf 'had to organise its defences with local commanders'[215] – there is no reference in any account to Eicke having taken part in the action. There are suggestions this may have been due to the British fortuitously coming close to overrunning his divisional command echelon.[216] Writing to Rommel some months later, the commander of Fourth Army, Generaloberst Hans-Günther von Kluge, defended the performance of the SS, noting the Totenkopf Division 'had it particularly hard on 21 May, as it was reported the enemy tank attack hit the divisional staff directly and shattered

211 Sydnor, *Soldiers of Destruction*, pp.82-84.
212 Vopersal, *Soldaten*, p.89.
213 Sydnor, *Soldiers of Destruction*, pp.92-93. Mann, *SS-Totenkopf*, pp.76-77, incorrectly gives the number of prisoners as 16,000.
214 Ullrich, *Like a Cliff*, pp.16-17, and Vopersal, *Soldaten*, p.115.
215 Ullrich, *Like a Cliff*, p.17.
216 Hans-Adolf Jacobsen, 'Dunkirk 1940', in *Decisive Battles of World War II: the German View*, ed. by Hans-Adolf Jacobsen and Jürgen Rohwer (London: Deutsch, 1965), pp.29-69 (p.50).

it. As a result, its leadership was temporarily hobbled'.[217] This would explain Eicke's absence from the action. No such incident, however, is recorded in any of the detailed histories of the Totenkopf Division. This might perhaps indicate it was actually an excuse invented after the event, to disguise Eicke's lack of action.

Although there is no reference in the German sources to one of their senior commanders being overrun, the after action account of 50th Division noted a German general was reported to have been killed.[218] In addition, the war diary of the 12th Lancers noted, 'The occupants of a Staff Car [...] caught in [a] skirmish were reported to include a General who had commanded German mechanised forces in Poland with great success and his staff, but they could not be found.'[219] Although no senior German commander became a casualty, and Eicke had not commanded mechanised forces in Poland, it is possible these reports referred to him. Conversely, it seems more likely the staff car was from 8th Panzer Division, which provided the troops ambushed by the Lancers.[220] The commander of that division, Generalleutnant Adolf-Friedrich Kuntzen, had led the formation, in its previous incarnation as the 3rd Light Division, in Poland. However, he certainly survived the battle unharmed.

SS-Totenkopf-Infanterie-Regiment 3 (SSTIR3) had been deployed with the mission of guarding against any British attack from Arras, and had been reinforced for this purpose by a company of the SS-Totenkopf-Abwehr-Abteilung (Anti-tank Battalion). Nonetheless, the unit was taken by surprise when the attack actually came: the men appear to have assumed nothing would reach them from that quarter, since elements of 7th Panzer Division were advancing between them and the city. As a result, I/SSTIR3 was 'ripped apart' when the Matildas appeared, and II/SSTIR3 drove off 'at an elevated speed' in the direction of Wanquetin, its rear company (5/SSTIR3) being destroyed by the British tanks.[221] This rapid movement away from the enemy was hardly consistent with the division's emphasis on aggressive action and fits with Rommel's account of the SS falling back. Elsewhere, similar scenes of panic and flight took place, as the British tanks rolled into the SS division's supply columns.[222]

The British tanks were, however, actively engaged by six 'Skoda' PzKpfw 35(t) tanks (a slightly older and lighter variant of the PzKpfw 38(t) tanks that were the mainstay of Rommel's Panzer Regiment 25)[223] from SS-Totenkopf-Aufklärungs-Abteilung

217 Letter from von Kluge to Rommel, 30 November 1940, in David Irving's Private Research Collection, Selected Documents on the Life and Campaigns of Field-Marshal Erwin Rommel (hereafter Irving Collection), Rommel 1917-1941 <http://www.britishonlinearchives.co.uk/group.php?cat=&sid=&cid=9781851172511&date_option=equal&page=&pid=72511f> [accessed 24 August 2015], imgs.109-112
218 WO167/300: Appreciation of the Effects of Bringing in T Tank and Infantry Reinforcements into Battle of Arras.
219 WO167/452: War diary, p.17.
220 Macksey, *Vimy Ridge*, p.217.
221 Ullrich, *Like a Cliff*, p.17, and Vopersal, *Soldaten*, pp.115 & 118.
222 Vopersal, *Soldaten*, p.127.
223 George Forty, *The Armies of Rommel* (London: Arms & Armour, 1997, p.39).

(SSTAkA)[224] (Reconnaisance Battalion).[225] Their fire disabled three British tanks and so allowed elements of 7th Panzer's Nachrichten-Abteilung 83 (Communications Battalion), pinned by the enemy attack, to move away to safety.[226] In the same area, Totenkopf anti-tank guns and artillery fired over open sights. As had been the case with their army colleagues to the north, the crews of the 37mm anti-tank guns found their shells simply bounced off the Matildas' thick armour, leading the men to give their weapons the disparaging nickname of *Türklopfer* (doorknockers)![227] The heavier 105mm guns of the artillery regiment, however, proved more effective, destroying three tanks. It is of note, again, the most effective fire appears to have come from guns, which were under the immediate command of officers.[228]

Still the British continued their advance: 'Tiny beings are the men in front of the brown steel colossuses, which unperturbed, as if guided by invisible forces, roll towards them, their rattling tracks more wearing on the nerves and their droning motors more stunning to the senses than the crashing and banging of guns.' It was hardly surprising at least some of the SS men fled for their lives, the British shooting after them like 'startled rabbits'. Others, however, led by their officers, attacked the tanks at short range, trying to shoot through the vision slits with their side arms and with the obsolescent *Panzerbüchse* anti-tank rifle. The result of this foolhardy bravery was as inevitable as the casualties were high. Two PzKpfw 35(t) light tanks were also destroyed.[229]

Further British tanks rolled forward from Agny towards Ficheux, which was defended by nine anti-tank guns. Yet again, these proved ineffective, their shells bouncing off the Matildas' thick armour and ricocheting into the air, like signal flares. 'Calmly and surely', the anti-tank gunners adjusted their sights and aimed at the tracks of the British tanks, soon disabling eight.[230]

During this action, a curious incident occurred. An armoured command vehicle drove up to the SS men and an army officer poked out his head, asking to be directed to the Totenkopf divisional headquarters. An SS corporal responded by merely gesturing towards the rear with his thumb, at which the army officer leaped from his vehicle and berated him, 'Soldier, don't you know who I am?', before climbing back on board and roaring off in the direction of Wailly. The officer? Rommel.[231] Given such treatment, it is surprising he was not even less complimentary about the performance of the SS in his account of the battle.

224 Vopersal, *Soldaten*, 120.
225 Trang, *Totenkopf*, p.42.
226 Vopersal, *Soldaten*, p.119.
227 Holroyd, *SS-Totenkopf*, p.51.
228 Vopersal, *Soldaten*, p.120.
229 Vopersal, *Soldaten*, pp.121-122.
230 Vopersal, *Soldaten*, pp.124-125.
231 Vopersal, *Soldaten*, p.124.

The SS Totenkopf division claimed to have destroyed twenty-three British tanks around Mercatel alone, while the anti-tank battalion claimed to have destroyed thirty-seven tanks during the day as a whole.[232] However, the British lost only forty-three Matildas in total on 21 May,[233] of which 7th Panzer reported it had accounted for twenty-nine.[234] There can therefore be little doubt the SS men were guilty of exaggeration. 7/RTR had begun the engagement with twenty-three Matilda Is and nine Matilda IIs. Since the battalion had already had to fight its way through Rommel's gun line before it reached the positions occupied by the Totenkopf division, it seems highly unlikely it was at full strength by that point in the battle. The SS therefore probably faced perhaps two dozen tanks at most. Of 7/RTR's total losses of ten Matilda Is and ten Matilda IIs (some of these last were lost while attached to 4/RTR),[235] it may be suggested the SS accounted for no more than six or seven, along with some light tanks.

Given they were, in effect, facing little more than a quarter of the strength of the British forces committed to the attack, the SS losses of 105 men killed and wounded[236] compare unfavourably with the 205 killed and wounded suffered by 7th Panzer Division,[237] which bore the brunt of the offensive. Although the Totenkopf division appears to have fought with more bravery than suggested in some accounts, there certainly were incidents of panic and flight. As with the similar instances in 7th Panzer Division, however, these may be ascribed as much to the shock resulting from the surprise assault by 'invulnerable' tanks as to any lack of experience or moral fibre on the part of the men. The proportionately heavy casualties suffered by the division might indeed suggest these episodes of panic were comparatively isolated, with most soldiers fighting with foolhardy boldness, rather than fleeing.

It is therefore the total absence of Eicke from the accounts of the battle that becomes noteworthy. This is especially the case, given his insistence the troops should follow his every order to the letter. Eicke appears to have neither issued any orders of relevance, nor gone himself to the epicentre of the engagement. This contrasts with Rommel's instinctive ability to be wherever the fighting was fiercest. Given Eicke's reliance on Restrictive Control, this silence on the part of the divisional commander might well have left the SS men uncertain of what to do, potentially remaining passive. Instead, the emphasis on aggressive action seems to have led most of them to engage the nearest enemy forces, thereby keeping the Alignment Gap narrower than might otherwise have been the case. However, this same emphasis may have resulted in the proportionately high casualties, widening the Effects Gap, where the impact of troops' actions were less than might have been forecast.

232 Ullrich, *Like a Cliff*, pp.19 & 23.
233 WO167/460: Appx xxxi, p.4.
234 *Rommel Papers*, pp.32-33.
235 Sebag-Montefiore, *Dunkirk*, p152.
236 Sydnor, *Soldiers of Destruction*, p.96.
237 Scheibert, *Gespenster-Division*, p.36.

Forward Command (Or Not)

It might be expected the first reaction to the blunting of the British armoured attack would have come from the commanders of the two tank battalions: but both were already dead, their deaths highlighting deficiencies in the army's doctrine.

Liddell Hart noted the Matilda I was 'no good to a C.O.'[238] Having only a two-man crew meant the commander was 'a very busy man indeed, having to direct the driver, talk on the radio, [as well as] fire and maintain the gun'.[239] This was clearly impractical for a battalion commander. Instead, both colonels were mounted in Mark VIB light tanks. Although these vehicles were fast, with a top speed of 35mph (five times that of the Matilda I and twice as fast as the Matilda II), their armour was just 14mm thick at the front and a mere 4mm elsewhere.[240] In October 1936, the General Staff had considered the Mark VI 'superior to any light tank produced by other nations',[241] but by 1940 its thin armour and reliance (like the Matilda I) on machine-guns alone, meant it was 'useless' against the German panzers.[242] Yet it remained the mainstay of both the divisional cavalry regiments, which provided the BEF's reconnaissance capacity, and the cavalry light tank regiments in 1st Armoured Division,[243] which was deployed to France after the Germans had attacked. Nonetheless, its three-man crew meant the battalion commander had some hope of staying above the immediacy of what was happening around him, while its relatively high speed allowed him to move quickly around the battlefield.

But expecting the battalion commander to operate from a light tank while in the midst of heavy infantry tanks involved an obvious risk. This was demonstrated near Beaurains, when Lt-Col Fitzmaurice of 4/RTR was killed by a direct hit on his tank from a field battery near Mercatel, in a zone where heavy German anti-tank fire had already reduced the battalion to just ten widely separated vehicles.[244] Liddell Hart stated Lt-Col Heyland of 7/RTR was hit by machine-gun fire, while trying to direct the attack on Wailly from outside his tank.[245] Martel, by contrast, recorded he was killed in his tank.[246] This seems to be supported by the after action report written by one of the battalion's company commanders, which noted that 'wireless control broke down due to casualties in command tanks & to other factors in the stress of battle'.[247]

---

238 Liddell Hart, *Tanks*, vol.2, p.15.
239 Perrett, *Matilda*, p.12.
240 Perrett, *Matilda*, p.13.
241 Quoted by J.P. Harris, *Men, Ideas and Tanks: British Military Thought and Armoured Forces, 1903-1939* (Manchester: Manchester University Press, 1995), p.275.
242 Sebag-Montefiore, *Dunkirk*, p.8.
243 Ellis, *France and Flanders*, pp.369-370.
244 WO167/459: Appendix 23, p.1.
245 Liddell Hart, *Tanks*, vol.2, p.15.
246 Martel, *Armoured Forces*, p.66.
247 WO167/460: Appendix 33, p.2.

In short, the battalion commanders were unable to fulfil their function effectively from a Mark VI light tank, being too vulnerable to enemy anti-tank fire and too susceptible to failures of the radio net.

Higher up the chain of command, Brigadier Jack Churchill of 151st Brigade spent much of the battle forward, with his troops. Although his headquarters was in Ecurie, two miles north of Arras and as such well behind the fighting line, the brigadier himself was rather nearer events. At 1600 hours, he visited the headquarters of 6/DLI in Achicourt, then about a mile behind the forward troops, who were clearing Achy. Churchill ordered the battalion to halt once it had taken Beaurains, which it did at 1700 hours, and await 8/DLI coming up on its right. He seems to have remained with the battalion during its difficult withdrawal, as he was next recorded at 2330 hours, visiting the headquarters of his reserve battalion, 9/DLI, in Maroeuil. Finally, at 0400 hours the next morning, he went to 6/DLI on the Vimy Ridge.[248] In short, Churchill went forward and connected with his units, seeking to influence the battle as events unfolded. That said, his orders in each case were to hold fast or to withdraw, and his influence on the brigade as a whole, as opposed to just the battalion he was with at the time, may have been limited.

Further still up the chain of command, Martel spent the battle 'mov[ing] in a car from one column to the other and tr[ying] to assist them as far as possible'.[249] Churchill may have visited 6/DLI at Achicourt at 1600 hours, but his war diary failed to mention Martel had been there half an hour before, ordering Lt-Col Harry Miller to secure Beaurains and turn it into a 'tank-proof locality'. By the time Churchill arrived, Martel had already moved off for 8/DLI, near Warlus. There, he emphasised to Lt-Col Beart 'the necessity to press hard and obtain further information so that the necessary forces or artillery support could be brought to bear to clear a way through' the village. Recognising the attack had been halted, Martel then returned to see Franklyn in his headquarters, to agree with him how the ground gained should be held against the Germans.[250]

Franklyn appears to have remained with his headquarters throughout the day. At first, he received the very positive reports of the Matildas' early successes: 'By [1600 hours] I began to get news that the German Tanks were no match for ours which were much more heavily armoured, and when their infantry saw that their anti-tank guns were useless, those that were not killed or captured began to run, throwing away their weapons.' By 2000 hours, however, the reports were much grimmer. Franklyn noted 'the infantry was collected into the captured villages and the tanks withdrawn and re-organised', but there is no suggestion this was done on his order.[251] His influence

248 WO167/404: 151st Bde, War Diary 21/22 May 1940.
249 Martel, *Outspoken Soldier*, p.157.
250 Martel, *Armoured Forces*, pp.66-67.
251 Franklyn, *Green Howard*, p.22.

during the battle appears to have been minimal. Given he was operating, in effect, as a corps commander, this may not have been unreasonable.

One other officer should be mentioned. It has already been noted Brigadier Pope, the GHQ Adviser on Armoured Fighting Vehicles, had been present when Franklyn issued his original orders. Once the attack began, he climbed up to the Arras racecourse, from where he had an excellent view of the battlefield: 'it did my heart good to see the resolute manner in which the [1st Army Tank] Brigade went into action. There was a good deal of machine-gun and anti-tank fire, more than I expected, but the tanks pushed on without faltering and as they passed the fire was subdued.' In a scene parallel to the incident at Amiens in August 1918, when the similarly one-armed German Generalmajor Höfer of 117th Division had personally gone to the frontline in a bid to steady his wavering troops, Pope, unable to find Martel, went forward into the battlefield. Moving on foot, he found one of the tank battalion commanders (probably Heyland of 7/RTR) 'in a state of some excitement, having completely lost himself. [...] I formed the impression that he was not in control of his unit at all.' Heyland was killed soon afterwards. Pope then went to find the infantry colonel (probably Beart of 8/DLI) and urged him to catch up with the tanks.
252

Churchill, Martel and Pope, therefore, were all operating from forward positions. They may not have been in the very heart of the fighting, as was Rommel, but they were fairly close behind the troops and were seeking to respond to events as they unfolded. Like Rommel, therefore, they were adopting a command approach akin to Directive Control. It noteworthy, however, the two officers with a background in tank operations, Martel and Pope, appear to have been more active in this way than were the two infantrymen, Churchill and Franklyn. Indeed, while Franklyn had not been impressed by Churchill prior to the attack and had wished one of the brigadiers in 5th Division could have led the operation instead, after the operation, he recorded he was 'convinced that no one could have done more than Churchill [...], partly *owing to Martel's inspiration*'.253

It is therefore all the more noticeable none of the accounts makes any reference to the actions of the commander of 1st Army Tank Brigade, Brigadier Pratt, after he had issued his orders at 1000 hours. The brigade's war diary merely noted its headquarters moved during the battle to Ecurie, alongside that of 151st Infantry Brigade, and remained there throughout the rest of the day. Although wireless communications within the formation had broken down,254 Pratt appears to have stayed with his headquarters. In contrast to Churchill, let alone Pope and Martel, there is no suggestion Pratt moved forward from his command post to reconnect with his troops. This is all the more remarkable, given Pope explicitly ordered him to do just that. Indeed, it

252 Quoted in Lewin, *Man of Armour*, p.117.
253 Franklyn, *Green Howard*, p.20, emphasis added.
254 WO167/414: Notes on Events from May 12th, p.4

can only have been in reference to Pratt's failure to act, thereby adopting a command approach akin to Umpiring, that Pope recorded, 'I cannot but think that in this action the commanders generally were too far back. In an armoured action it is essential that commanders should be well up to take immediate advantage of fleeting opportunities and to deal with sudden changes in the situation.'[255] Nonetheless, the battle seems not to have done Pratt's career permanent harm. Although he never again commanded active forces, on returning from France, he was promoted to major-general and put in charge of the British mission to the US Army regarding tank use and design. Martel recorded in this role Pratt 'did very fine work for the Allied cause'.[256]

Having explored the actions of the various senior British commanders, it is necessary to examine the influence they had on the troops. Churchill, Martel and Pope may have been adopting a command approach akin to Directive Control, but what was the experience of their troops?

The war diary of 6/DLI made no reference to the visits by Martel and then Churchill.[257] The battalion history provided an explanation: Lt-Col Miller remained with his main headquarters throughout the action and rapidly lost contact with his companies. His second-in-command, Major Peter Jeffreys, who advanced with the forward headquarters, was left to fight the battle, reliant on his own initiative. Such was the breakdown of communications Miller completely misplaced his unit and, accompanied by only a small column of men, searched aimlessly for it for two days until, 'totally exhausted [, … i]t was thought best that he return to England'.[258] Miller's own account, extensively quoted by Macksey, suggests he was more actively involved than implied by the battalion history, but careful reading reveals his role was largely passive.[259] In short, although Churchill and Martel went forward to Miller's headquarters and issued orders to him, not only did these orders never reach Jeffreys and the companies engaged with the Germans, neither commander noticed Miller had no idea where his men were. The situation with the companies of 4/RNF was similar, the war diary providing very few details of the action during the day, noting simply, 'There were many casualties and many brave deeds'.[260]

The situation with 8/DLI was more positive. The war diary recorded Martel's visit at 1600 hours: 'G.O.C. Div. arrived DUISSANS. Learnt local situation. Gave situation on other parts of the front and ordered more push.'[261] Churchill's visit the following morning, at 0900 hours, was also recorded, by which time Lt-Col Beart had been wounded: Churchill 'sent for a doctor who ordered him to hospital'.[262] It

255 Quoted in Lewin, *Man of Armour*, p.117.
256 Martel, *Armoured Forces*, pp.155-156.
257 WO167/729: 6/DLI, War Diary, 21 May 1940.
258 Moses, *Faithful Sixth*, pp.132-139.
259 Macksey, *Vimy Ridge*, pp.213-216.
260 WO167/800: 4/RNF, War Diary, 21 May 1940.
261 WO167/730: 8/DLI, War Diary, 21 May 1940.
262 WO167/730: 8/DLI, War Diary, 21 May 1940.

is noteworthy the battalion history highlighted Beart's wound had come early in the action, 'but [he] had continued to direct operations with such calmness that he might have been on a training scheme. It was a great inspiration to see him, in spite of his wounds, moving about where the fire was heaviest.'[263] The detail given in the war diary indicates Beart was, throughout the engagement, in the thick of things. The impact on the unit's operations of the interventions by Martel and Churchill was less obvious.

Resolution and Doubt

The British knew their attempt to clear the enemy from the surrounds of Arras had reached its limit and the infantry were ordered to hold the captured villages, while the few remaining tanks were withdrawn.[264] The initiative had now passed to the Germans: as Martel noted, 'The enemy were [...] very incensed at the successful attack which had been launched against them.'[265]

In characteristic style, Rommel did not hesitate. He had already requested air support at around 1600 hours, very soon after he had become aware of the British armoured attack on his infantry. Around 1800 hours, the Luftwaffe began to arrive – aircraft of I and VIII Air Corps delivered some three hundred dive-bomber attacks during the following two and a half hours. Although these attacks did cause some casualties, 'the main effect on the Infantry was moral. An unfortunate result [...] was that a number of the Infantry left the cover of the villages and later suffered heavy casualties when the enemy developed a strong counter-attack with tanks'.[266] This attack came from 25th Panzer Regiment, which Rommel had ordered to pull back from Acq and attack the flank of the British, near Agnez and Duisans, in order to cut off their retreat.

As well as the shaken British infantry, Rothenburg's troops ran into a column of tanks. These were some sixty SOMUA S-35s, probably the best tank deployed in the campaign by either side,[267] from the French 3e *Division Légère Mécanique* (3e DLM) (Light Mechanised Division). In a confused engagement, Rothenburg first broke through the French position, destroying seven tanks, and then through the line formed behind them by 260th Battery, 65th Anti-Tank Regiment, Royal Artillery, eliminating six of its twelve guns. In the process, Rothenburg lost around a dozen of his own tanks,[268] though the British claimed to have destroyed more than twenty panzers.[269]

263 Lewis, *8th DLI*, p.19.
264 Franklyn, *Green Howard*, p.22.
265 Martel, *Armoured Forces*, p.67.
266 IWM: Martel Papers 3/1, Item 19: Report on Operations of Frankforce, p.3.
267 Robert Allan Doughty, *The Breaking Point: Sedan and the Fall of France, 1940* (Hamden, CT: Archon, 1990), p.3.
268 *Rommel Papers*, p.33 and Frieser, *Blitzkrieg Legend*, pp.277 & 284-285.
269 IWM: Martel Papers 3/1, Item 19: Offensive Operations Carried Out South of Arras, p.5.

Given the British tank attack earlier that afternoon had come to grief against the line of guns hastily deployed by Rommel, with dozens of armoured vehicles destroyed, it is noteworthy Rothenburg was able to penetrate the defensive position that faced him. He may have had twice as many tanks as Pratt, around 150 compared to 74, but most were Panzer IIs and 38(t)s, which had only 30mm and 25mm of frontal armour respectively.[270] These were far less powerful than the French SOMUA and were vulnerable to the 2-pounder (40mm) guns deployed by the British anti-tank battery.[271]

The war diary and divisional history of 7th Panzer Division both noted only that the engagement was a bitter tank-versus-tank skirmish, making no reference to infantry on either side, nor to any actions by the commanders.[272] Rothenburg's behaviour, however, can be inferred from his actions in other engagements during the campaign: his 'attitude in battle was entirely fatalistic: he simply did not fear death. [... He] habitually placed himself at the forefront of each advance.' This fearlessness had been demonstrated in the previous war, winning him a battlefield commission[273] and, like Rommel, he was one of the handful of junior officers awarded the coveted *Pour le Mérite*.[274] It seems likely, therefore, Rothenburg was in the thick of the fighting, controlling his regiment from his Panzer IV, and this exercise of Directive Control may have been a key factor in the ability of his tanks to defeat a determined anti-tank defence, in contrast to what Pratt's much more powerful Matildas had been able to achieve.

As the strength of the German forces became clear, Martel ordered a general retreat back to the starting line.[275] It was a chaotic withdrawal, with a number of close escapes. However, by the time dawn broke, the British force had 'drifted back to its starting-point on Vimy Ridge.'[276] The counter-attack was over, and with it, any hope of cutting off the German thrust to the Channel.

Although that mission had in fact always been beyond the capacity of the limited forces available to Franklyn, his attack had come as a complete surprise to the Germans. They may have been following good practice by having forces, notably the Totenkopf Division, deployed as anti-tank flank guards, but the shock the troops experienced when the British did actually attack indicates a degree of complacency had crept in. Faced with a surprise assault by 'invulnerable' tanks, many of the troops, both the SS and from 7th Panzer, had taken to their heels and fled. But the commanders on the

270 Forty, *Armies of Rommel*, pp.39-41
271 Macksey, *Vimy Ridge*, p.224.
272 IWM: 7th Panzer KTB, 21 May 1940 and Scheibert, *Gespenster-Division*, p.35.
273 Samuel W. Mitcham, *Rommel's Lieutenants: The Men Who Served the Desert Fox, France, 1940* (Mechanicsburg, PA: Stackpole, pp.21-25 and
274 Of the 534 awards made to officers in the land army, only 16 went to individuals at or below company level. Jürgen Brinkmann, *Die Ritter des Ordens "Pour le Merité" 1914-1918* (Bückeburg: self-published, 1982).
275 Martel, *Armoured Forces*, pp.67-68.
276 Macksey, *Vimy Ridge*, pp.226-227.

ground had not panicked. Demonstrating physical courage and command resolution, Rommel and (probably) Rothenburg had personally rallied their men and recovered the situation, driving the attackers back to their start line. Thus far, the situation represented, in some respects, a parallel to that at Amiens in August 1918: initial panic followed by stabilisation of the position under resolute forward leadership by commanders applying Directive Control. Would the response of the German high command also be similar to Ludendorff two decades earlier?

The starting point must be the reports Rommel sent up the chain of command, initially to his immediate superior, Generalleutnant Rudolf Schmidt of XXXIX Corps, which led him to issue the following status report:

> The enemy – mainly the English – switched on 21 May to the offensive for the first time on a larger scale; to the west of Arras, moving eastwards against the 7th Pz.Div. and the western wing of the 5th Pz.Div. Presumed intention of the enemy: either to pierce from Arras through Doullens to join the French army south of the Somme or else to delay the advance of the German armoured thrust to the canal, in order to gain time for embarkation to England.[277]

These reports formed the basis for further updates from those formations, to General der Infanterie Hermann Hoth's Panzer Group, through Kluge's Fourth Army, to Rundstedt at Army Group A, and finally to OKH itself.

Caddick-Adams suggested the British attack 'threw Rommel off balance for the first (and only) time' in the campaign.[278] Macksey, emphasising the shock and personal danger that had surrounded Rommel during the battle, commented 'his thoughts ran riot in his first report'.[279] This report, signed by Rommel personally, spoke of 'very heavy combat with hundreds of enemy tanks and following infantry', highlighted the ineffectiveness of the German anti-tank guns,[280] and included situation maps showing a force of five Allied divisions advancing from Arras.[281]

Historians are divided over whether these 'exaggerated disaster dispatches' were a deliberate ploy by Rommel, whose 'excessive ambition led him astray to the extent that he magnified the danger to make his achievement look even better than it already was',[282] or whether he was genuinely shaken by the unexpectedness and impact of the British attack.[283] There is, however, general agreement Rommel's report was

277 Quoted by Plato, *5. Panzerdivision*, p.71.
278 Caddick-Adams, *Monty and Rommel*, p.232.
279 Macksey, *Shadow of Vimy Ridge*, p.224.
280 Scheibert, *Gespenster-Division*, pp.36-37.
281 Maps reproduced in Richard Holmes, *Army Battlefield Guide: Belgium and Northern France* (London: HMSO, 1995), following pp.190 and 192.
282 Frieser, *Blitzkrieg*, p.289.
283 Horne, *Lose a Battle*, p.569.

indeed 'exaggerated'.[284] After all, the attack had actually involved only 74 tanks, not 'hundreds', and there had been only four battalions in Martel's two columns, not five divisions.

Gordon Corrigan, in his deliberately controversial *Blood, Sweat and Arrogance*, was scathing of this consensus: 'It has to be doubted whether the German army [...] could really interpret the very limited actions of seventy-four British tanks, plus some French Somuas off to the flank, as being ten times that number.' He concluded the shocking nature of the report was 'a simple clerical error': the Germans would have recognised the main force opposing them was the British 5th Division, and the clerk marking up the maps accidentally wrote 'divisions' rather than 'division'. In other words, the whole suggestion Rommel was claiming to be attacked by overwhelming forces is a myth.[285] Corrigan's argument, however, failed to account for the fact Rommel's report definitely spoke of 'hundreds of tanks', so the Germans clearly believed they had been attacked by a substantial force. In addition, there is no indication on the maps these were intending to identify specific British formations, such as the 5th Division. While a series of British positions were indicated on the maps, no other formations were named, yet it would be expected, had Rommel identified 5th Division, he would also have been aware of the other British formations in the area.

There can be little question Rommel had a flair for self-publicity, demonstrated not least by his creating the 'Rommel Album', recording the actions of 7th Panzer Division in heroic detail. This was presented to Hitler after the campaign and has been described as 'one of the most impressive documents on the campaign in the west'.[286] However, while Rommel was not averse to claiming credit for the successes of neighbouring troops,[287] there is no suggestion in any of the accounts of the campaign that he directly exaggerated the scale of the forces ranged against him – given the extent of his achievements, there was no need for him to do so.

Similarly, there is no evidence to suggest that Rommel was shaken or panicked by the British attack, unexpected and initially dangerous though it was. The calmness of his personal intervention, even when he was himself under fire, with his aide killed at his side, has been highlighted above. In the circumstances, it would have been quite understandable had Rommel decided to pause and regroup his formation the following day, yet he 'recovered his equilibrium almost immediately'[288] and 'kept attacking quite unconcernedly',[289] accompanying the attack in his usual forward style.[290] If the

284 Bond, *France and Belgium*, p.117.
285 Gordon Corrigan, *Blood, Sweat and Arrogance and the Myths of Churchill's War* (London: Phoenix, 2007), pp.244-246.
286 Frieser, *Blitzkrieg*, pp.289 & 421n145.
287 Irving, *Trail of the Fox*, pp.51-52.
288 Showalter, *Patton and Rommel*, p.191.
289 Frieser, *Blitzkrieg*, p.287.
290 IWM: 7th Panzer KTB, 22 May 1940.

alternative explanations for why Rommel's report referred to substantial enemy forces are unconvincing, the question arises whether it was in fact so 'exaggerated'.

Reference has been made earlier to the valuable scouting work of Lumsden's 12th Lancers. Similarly, 7th Panzer Division also deployed its own integral reconnaissance unit, Aufklärungs-Abteilung 37 (AA37), which included fifty armoured cars, along with mechanised infantry and motorcyclists.[291] Hans von Luck, commanding one of its companies at Arras, recorded, 'We had the feeling of being alone at the head of a division advancing tempestuously.' At the very tip of the German penetration, Luck commented his men frequently became intermingled with the floods of retreating French troops, which would have given much opportunity for identifying the forces ranged ahead of the division. Here again, Rommel's behaviour demonstrated his physical bravery. During the crossing of the La Bassée canal on 20 May, he 'stood like a target on the embankment and directed the fire, while next to him men were being wounded and even killed. Once again he spurred us on by his exemplary behaviour.'[292]

It seems reasonable to suggest Luck and his colleagues in AA37 would have been able to develop at least a partial picture of the forces facing 7th Panzer Division. Although historians tend to focus on the four battalions forming the core of Martel's two columns, these were far from being the only Allied forces in the Arras area. Examination of the British Official History demonstrates these included:

- Petreforce, under Major-General Roderick Petre, comprising:[293]
  - The garrison of Arras, drawn from GHQ troops, centred on 1st Battalion, Welsh Guards, along with a number of company-sized units of artillery, engineers and armoured reconnaissance
  - 23rd Division, with 69th and 70th Brigades (though the latter had been overrun by Rommel on 20 May)[294]
  - 36th Brigade of 12th Division
- Frankforce, under Major-General Franklyn, comprising:[295]
  - 50th Division, with 150th and 151st Brigades
  - 5th Division, with 13th and 17th Brigades
  - 1st Army Tank Brigade

In addition, as noted earlier though not mentioned by the Official History, the French 3e DLM was in the area of Arras and supported Martel's attack. In total, therefore, the Allied forces in the Arras area on 21 May were drawn from a total of five different

---

291 Scheibert, *Gespenster-Division*, p.24, and Forty, *Armies of Rommel*, p.43.
292 Hans von Luck, *Panzer Commander: The Memoirs of Colonel Hans von Luck* (London: Cassell, 2002), pp.39-40.
293 Ellis, *France and Flanders*, p.65.
294 Ellis, *France and Flanders*, p.79.
295 Ellis, *France and Flanders*, p.83.

divisions, along with an independent tank brigade and various other units: precisely the number of divisions reported by Rommel.

Turning to the 'hundreds of tanks' reported by Rommel, it has already been noted there were only 74 Matildas available to Pratt's brigade. However, the establishment of each tank battalion also included 7 Mark VI light tanks and 8 armoured carriers, while each of the two DLI infantry battalions had an allocation of 10 carriers. In addition, 4/RNF had 11 scout cars, while 12th Lancers had an establishment of 38 armoured cars.[296] Taken together, the forces deployed by Martel had an establishment of 199 armoured vehicles of all types, though perhaps only 150 of these were available for the operation. In addition, 3e DLM had an establishment of 88 SOMUA tanks and 151 Hotchkiss tanks, for a total of 239, though previous losses meant the actual numbers on 21 May were rather lower.[297] In total, however, the Allies deployed formations with an establishment of around 450 armoured vehicles, with perhaps rather more than 200 physically present during Martel's counter-attack. Again, these numbers are not inconsistent with Rommel's reports. In addition, 5th Panzer Division had spotted twenty enemy tanks in the vicinity of Sailly, to the east of Arras, though the expected attack had failed to materialise.[298]

In short, although Franklyn had managed to use only the equivalent of a single brigade and 74 tanks for his attack, the total forces available to the Allies in the area do indeed appear to have been broadly in the region of the five divisions and hundreds of armoured vehicles Rommel recorded in his reports. The inability of the British and French to concentrate these substantial forces into a powerful thrust to cut through the shaft of the German advance and so isolate the panzer spearhead becomes even more striking.

As Rommel's report moved up the chain of command, it was read with growing concern: the panzers were soon halted and the offensive was not resumed until 27 May, by which time the Allied position had been transformed and the evacuation from Dunkirk was well underway.

Much ink has been spilled on the origins of the famous Halt Order. In *The Other Side of the Hill*, first published in 1948, Liddell Hart was clear the responsibility for the order lay with Hitler personally, overriding the advice of his generals.[299] Writing in 1950, Rundstedt was equally clear: '*The blame* for this rests only on Hitler and *not on me*'.[300] Liddell Hart, who had formed a very positive view of Rundstedt when interviewing him as a prisoner of war, calling him 'a gentleman to the core', reflected

296 Ellis, *France and Flanders*, pp.369-371.
297 Frieser, *Blitzkrieg Legend*, pp.243 and 413n93.
298 Plato, *5. Panzerdivision*, p.71.
299 Captain Basil H. Liddell Hart, *The Other Side of the Hill* (London: Cassell, 1948), pp.139-140.
300 US Foreign Military Studies, C:053: Campaign in the West (1950), p.4, emphasis in original.

this perspective in the revised 1951 edition of his book, stating the miracle of Dunkirk was only possible 'due to Hitler's intervention'.[301]

The position was reinforced further in 1952, with the publication of two (auto) biographies. In the first, Guderian agreed the order had come from Hitler.[302] The second, an authorised biography of Rundstedt written by his former chief of staff, Günther Blumentritt, also emphasised responsibility for the halt order lay with Hitler alone. Blumentritt noted Rundstedt only issued the order following direct instructions from Hitler, and he and his chief of staff (i.e. Blumentritt himself) 'naturally raised an immediate protest against this order which, from a military standpoint, was utterly incomprehensible. But nevertheless Hitler insisted that it be carried out.' Despite accepting certain entries in the Army Group war diary might suggest the orders were issued in Rundstedt's name, Blumentritt argued, 'Never could a general have made such a fateful decision on his own responsibility and without Hitler's approval.'[303]

The British Official History, published in 1953, took a very different view. It noted how all the senior German commanders had subsequently 'assert[ed] that the decisions were solely Hitler's, they [thereby] excuse[d] themselves from failure to stop the evacuation and la[id] all the blame on him.' Based on detailed examination of the war diaries, the Official History concluded Hitler did *not* initiate the halt order, but instead merely endorsed Rundstedt's orders. Furthermore, it was Rundstedt himself, having been given freedom of action by Hitler, who then extended the initial pause.[304] Responding to this, historian Hans Meier-Welcker noted the order was certainly understood by Kluge at Fourth Army (and hence by his subordinates) and the staff at OKH to have been issued at Hitler's direct instruction. In addition, Hitler never cast any blame on Rundstedt for the unfortunate consequences of the order. Nonetheless, Meier-Welcker was equally clear that, throughout this incident, Hitler and Rundstedt were in complete agreement over the actions to be taken.[305] Frieser went further: the panzer advance was stopped by Rundstedt, acting on his own initiative, on 23 May. Hitler fully agreed with this stance and the subsequent orders, which were issued at his request, simply confirmed Rundstedt's existing instructions. Moreover, Hitler expressly left decisions on the duration of the halt to Rundstedt.[306]

While the decision to halt was therefore Rundstedt's, he was by no means alone in being shaken by the unexpected attack by the British and French at Arras.[307] Guderian

301 Captain Basil H. Liddell Hart, *The Other Side of the Hill* (1951, reprinted London: Pan, 1978), pp.103 and 184.
302 Guderian, *Panzer Leader*, p.117.
303 Guenther Blumentritt, *Von Rundstedt: The Soldier and the Man* (London: Odhams, 1952), pp.74-78.
304 Ellis, *France and Flanders*, pp.347-351.
305 Han Meier-Welcker, 'Der Entschluss zum Anhalten der Deutschen Panzertruppen in Flandern 1940', *Vierteljahrhefte für Zeitgeschichte*, 2(3) (1954), 274-290.
306 Frieser, *Blitzkrieg Legend*, pp.292-295.
307 Fraser, *Knight's Cross*, p.187.

noted the operation made 'a considerable impression on the staff of Panzer Group von Kleist, which suddenly became remarkably nervous'.[308] Kleist alerted OKH he 'feels he cannot tackle his task as long as the crisis at Arras remains unresolved'.[309] At Fourth Army, Kluge expressed similar concerns to Rundstedt[310] and ordered his panzers to halt and consolidate.[311] Rundstedt was therefore responding in concert with his senior subordinates when on 23 May he instructed the advance 'will not be resumed until the situation at Arras is clear'.[312] The halt order of 24 May, issued after Rundstedt and Hitler had discussed the position, therefore merely confirmed the existing situation, 'On the orders of the Führer, [...] the general line [...] will *not* be crossed northwest of Arras. On the western wing, instead, the important thing is to get all mobile units to close up'.[313]

What was different, however, was Rundstedt retained his concern regarding the situation and maintained the halt long after all the other generals had recovered from the effects of the British attack and were urging the panzers be let off the leash again. By 25 May, Kluge had regained his balance and protested at being ordered to hold back his armoured forces in order to allow the infantry to catch up.[314]

Others had doubted the need for the halt order in the first place. At OKH, Generaloberst Franz Halder, Chief of the General Staff, throughout maintained the attack at Arras was of minor importance only, noting on 23 May the crisis would be over within 48 hours. The following morning, his assessment of the situation was 'the enemy's fighting power probably does not amount to much more than local resistance'. On 26 May, he was noting with frustration, 'Our armoured and motorised forces have stopped as if paralysed [...] in compliance with top level orders, and must not attack. [...] these orders from the top just make no sense'.[315] Likewise, at corps level and below, the halt order was greeted with disbelief: Guderian (XIX Panzer Corps) was 'speechless',[316] while Reinhardt (XLI Panzer Corps) believed holding back the advance would only benefit the enemy.[317] Indeed, the latter appears to have played a central role in convincing Kleist the danger was less than he had feared, taking advantage of the latter visiting his forward headquarters to argue the forces facing him were weak and disorganised.[318]

308 Guderian, *Panzer Leader*, p.114.
309 Halder, *War Diary*, p.32 (1730 hours, 23 May 1940).
310 Charles Messenger, *The Last Prussian: A Biography of Field Marshal Gerd von Rundstedt, 1875-1953* (London: Brassey's, 1991), p.114.
311 Frieser, *Blitzkrieg Legend*, p.287.
312 Halder, *War Diary*, p. 25 (22 May 1940).
313 Quoted in Frieser, *Blitzkrieg Legend*, p.295, emphasis in original.
314 Messenger, *Last Prussian*, p.118.
315 Halder, *War Diary*, 23-26 May 1940, pp.30-37.
316 Guderian, *Panzer Leader*, p.117.
317 Frieser, *Blitzkrieg Legend*, p.293.
318 Blaxland, *Destination Dunkirk*, p.213.

In short, although the Allied attack at Arras appears to have unsettled a number of the senior German commanders, all except Rundstedt had recovered their composure within a day or so, yet he chose to continue the pause for an additional two days. Indeed, just after midnight on 25 May, when Halder issued orders from OKH that the advance should be resumed, Rundstedt, noting Hitler had 'expressly left the manner of handling the operations of Fourth Army' to him, simply refused to pass the instruction on to Kluge,[319] directly ignoring an explicit order from his superior.

Messenger argued Rundstedt's actions 'made sound tactical sense', given both the potential for the terrain ahead of the panzers to be unsuitable for armoured forces and the need to conserve their strength ready for the next phase of operations against France, moving south across the Somme.[320] Yet the fact every other German commander disagreed with Rundstedt's assessment suggests Messenger overstated the case and Rundstedt was indeed being overly cautious. That Rundstedt overreacted to the British attack, and maintained an excessive caution even in the face of strong and growing pressure from all quarters, indicates the events around Arras had made a significant psychological impact on him, perhaps leaving him in a state of shock.

In considering Ludendorff's behaviour following the British offensive at Amiens in August 1918 (Chapter Four), it was noted Rowland identified three characteristics of soldiers in a state of shock:[321]

- behavioural, where individuals become restless;
- emotional, where individuals vary between a flattening of mood and an intense anxiety; and
- cognitive, where powers of concentration and ability to reason logically are impaired.

Assessing Rundstedt's behaviour at this time is difficult, as he left no memoirs or diary,[322] and Blumentritt's biography aimed to protect him against criticism in this incident – it is revealing the book appeared only in English, with no German translation ever made.[323] There is therefore limited evidence available through which to enter into Rundstedt's state of mind. It is therefore necessary to put his behaviour during these days in May 1940 into the broader context of his experience and character.

Rundstedt's early career gave little hint he was to rise to the very pinnacle of his profession. Born in 1875 into an ancient noble family with a long military tradition, his education followed the standard path of cadet school and military college.

319 War Diary, Army Group A, 25 May 1940.
320 Messenger, *Last Prussian*, pp.117-118.
321 Rowland, *Stress*, p.184.
322 Blumentritt, *Rundstedt*, p.9.
323 Andreas Hillgruber, 'Field-Marshal Gerd von Rundstedt', in *The War Lords*, ed. by Field Marshal Sir Michael Carver (London: Weidenfeld and Nicolson, 1987), pp.188-201 (p.200).

Aspirations to join the cavalry or the field artillery could not be fulfilled, so in 1893 he was commissioned into Infanterie-Regiment 83. He passed the entrance examination for the prestigious *Kriegsakademie* in 1899, but was considered too junior, so was permitted to take up his place only in 1903. On graduation in 1906, he was graded as fitted to join the General Staff and was soon recommended for accelerated promotion, but he was again felt to be too young and advanced to the rank of captain only in March 1909. As was usual for members of the General Staff, he alternated staff and line postings, being recalled from his position as a company commander in late July 1914 to become the Ia (operations officer) of 22nd Reserve Division upon general mobilisation. On 6 September, the divisional commander, Generalleutnant Otto Riemann, was wounded, leaving Rundstedt (still only a captain) to run the battle, which he did very well. Despite two periods of serious ill health, Rundstedt was promoted to major and filled a succession of staff roles, ending the war as chief of staff of XV Corps.[324]

Despite an unspectacular war record, Rundstedt was marked out by Seeckt as one of the key officers who would take the Reichswehr forward. He was promoted to lieutenant colonel in October 1920, along with Blomberg, Bock, Hammerstein and Leeb. In 1923, he was the first of this group to be promoted to full colonel. During the period to 1933, Rundstedt filled a series of posts at divisional, corps (*Wehrkreis*) and army (*Gruppenkommando*) level, again alternating between staff and command roles, reaching the rank of General der Infanterie.[325] Unusually, Rundstedt remained in the role of commander-in-chief of Gruppenkommando 1, which covered Berlin, for six years, until finally permitted to retire in October 1938, after 45 years of service, with a last promotion to Generaloberst.[326] Recalled just months later, Rundstedt led Army Group South against Poland, with Manstein as his chief of staff.

Rundstedt was 'a comparatively complex character, not easy to understand. He was sometimes totally taciturn and sometimes apparently communicative; at times he was excitable and then again apparently imperturbable; he strove in vain for poise and harmony of mind. He was a restless being without enormous self-confidence, a sceptic without capability for enthusiasm or sense of his own superiority.' Rundstedt was modest and self-sufficient. As his career developed, however, he 'tended increasingly to avoid clear-cut positions and to vacillate.'[327] This was reflected in his command style, giving his subordinates the maximum possible independence, while guiding them with a firm hand.[328] Although therefore broadly adhering to the doctrine of Directive Command, there is some evidence Rundstedt could sometimes become too

---

324 Blumentritt, *Rundstedt*, pp.13-22, and Messenger, *Last Prussian*, pp.3-40.
325 Blumentritt, *Rundstedt*, p.26, and Messenger, *Last Prussian*, pp.42-57.
326 Blumentritt, *Rundstedt*, pp.32-33, and Messenger, *Last Prussian*, p.75.
327 Hillgruber, 'Rundstedt', p.189.
328 Messenger, *Last Prussian*, pp.47 & 82.

distant, slipping into Umpiring: Manstein noted how, on occasion, Rundstedt would become frustrated with his subordinates, yet would hesitate to intervene personally.[329]

On the question of the use of armoured forces, Rundstedt did not support the approach promoted by Guderian and others that the panzers should operate independently, ahead of the infantry. 'Rather, he was one of the more progressive leaders of the school that regarded tanks as useful servants, not as the future masters, of the battlefield' and, as such, he was highly focused on using tanks as a means to remove the 'machine-gun paralysis' that had affected the infantry in the First World War.[330] Although he acceded to the bold use of armour against France proposed by Manstein,[331] there is some suggestion he was not entirely comfortable with the plan, Guderian noting he gained the impression Rundstedt did not understand tanks at all.[332]

Contrary to his usual practice of 'commanding through his staff',[333] Rundstedt started the campaign by trying to keep close to his forces. On 9 May, the day before the offensive began, he went forward from his main headquarters in Coblenz to Bitburg, just 12 miles behind the front. As the panzers reached the Meuse in their headlong dash, he moved his headquarters still further forward, to Bastogne.[334] On 14 May, he visited Sedan, receiving a briefing on the situation from Guderian, who recorded they stood 'in the very middle of the bridge, while an air-raid was actually in progress. He [Rundstedt] asked dryly: "Is it always like this here?" I could reply with a clear conscience that it was.'[335] Following this incident, Rundstedt pushed his headquarters further forward still, to Charleville. But here his mood seems to have changed. Early on 16 May, he ordered a temporary halt to the advance,[336] and he was not to leave his headquarters[337] for more than ten days, losing personal contact with his subordinates.

Rundstedt and his peers, as Macksey noted, 'were men who had witnessed the foundering of the 1918 offensive on the very ground they were about to break into again. They respected the ability of their enemy [...]. Because of these deeply inborn views they were prey to fears of counter-action and wholesale failure.'[338] Blumentritt reflected this when he recorded the crossing of the Meuse was a 'miracle which Rundstedt could not understand'. He emphasised his chief 'rated the French High Command very highly'. It was therefore surely inevitable that the French would launch a powerful counterstroke against the Germans' vulnerable southern flank, seeking to

329 Mungo Melvin, *Manstein: Hitler's Greatest General* (London: Phoenix, 2011), p.143.
330 Liddell Hart, *Other Side of the Hill*, pp.104-105.
331 Blumentritt, *Rundstedt*, p.59.
332 Messenger, *Last Prussian*, pp.103-195.
333 Hillgruber, 'Rundstedt', p.198.
334 Blumentritt, *Rundstedt*, pp.67-68.
335 Guderian, *Panzer Leader*, p.105.
336 Messenger, *Last Prussian*, pp.103
337 Blumentritt, *Rundstedt*, p.70.
338 Mackey, *Vimy Ridge*, p.195.

seize the few bridges over the Meuse, across which had to cross all the supplies for the panzer divisions rushing headlong for the Channel. But the French did not attack – a second miracle. Yet despite these extraordinary events, Rundstedt 'had always to assume the most unpleasant things for the Germans on the part of the enemy'.[339]

Even prior to the British counterattack at Arras, therefore, Rundstedt was beginning to display Rowland's three characteristics of shock. In behavioural terms, his efforts to maintain close personal contact with his troops, even if this involved placing himself in significant physical danger, were replaced by a near monastic retreat in his headquarters, ever further behind the front. In emotional terms, his confidence in the success of the offensive was replaced by an ever-growing anxiety the French must surely take advantage of his stretched and vulnerable southern flank. And, on top of this strain, Rundstedt and Blumentritt were trying to control an 'unwieldy mass of 71 Div[ision]s'. Given the deliberately small number of staff officers in German headquarters, it was perhaps unsurprising Halder was starting to think Army Group A was 'experiencing considerable difficulties'. His suggestion the staff had 'not been energetic and active enough'[340] may be further evidence Rundstedt was suffering from the cognitive impact of shock, where powers of concentration and ability to reason logically are impaired.

It was in this fertile context news of Rommel's report was received. At last, the Allies had actually attacked, in considerable strength and clearly with the aim of cutting off the steel tip of Army Group A's scattered forces. While Rundstedt's initial decision to halt the advance was, as has been seen, in line with the views of many of his senior subordinates, his obstinate refusal to reassess the situation and recognise the French and British, against every logical expectation, were not going to launch any coordinated counterstroke, indicates a deeper paralysis. Perhaps the clearest evidence to suggest Rundstedt really was disorientated by events lies in Blumentritt's use of the word 'miracle' to describe the position – miracles are by definition beyond comprehension.

Yet it is also important to recognise shock is not a permanent state, but fades over time. On 26 May, Halder recorded Rundstedt 'could not stand it any longer and went up front to Hoth and Kleist, to get the lay of the land for the next moves of his armour.'[341] The Allies had failed to take advantage of their opponent's passivity as a result of shock and, as a result, had allowed the opportunity for a decisive counterstroke to pass. Nonetheless, Gort had used the time to arrange for the BEF to be evacuated from Dunkirk, decisively rescuing his defeated army to fight another day.

339 Blumentritt, *Rundstedt*, pp.68-71.
340 Halder, *War Diary*, 23 May 1940, p.31.
341 Halder, *War Diary*, 26 May 1940, p.37.

Conclusions

This chapter has sought to go beyond the first order explanations for the defeat of the British counterattack at Arras presented in most previous accounts of the operation. These largely focus on external factors, such as Rommel's ability to build a gun-line able to shatter the armour even of the heavy Matilda tanks, and the breakdown of communications within the British units, which meant those tanks advanced without the infantry support that might have overcome the German artillery. In doing so, the focus has been on six deeper issues emerging from the battle offering the potential to cast a wider light.

The British attack was, from the start, affected by a wide Knowledge Gap. Having issued his initial instructions to Franklyn, which envisaged little more than a mopping-up operation in the immediate vicinity of Arras, Gort then agreed with Ironside and Billotte the attack should be expanded into a decisive thrust southwards, designed the cut off the panzers and regain touch with the French forces to the south. Yet not only did Gort not inform Franklyn of this fundamental change of plan, Franklyn made only half-hearted attempts to obtain clarification, despite growing indications something had changed. In doing so, Franklyn may have felt restrained by the wording in FSR II (1935), which only allowed an officer to depart from his orders if there was no opportunity to consult with his commander. Whether intentionally or not, Gort and Franklyn therefore adopted a command approach equivalent to Restrictive Command. This led to friction as result of a wide Knowledge Gap: Franklyn issued orders inconsistent with the intent of his commander-in-chief.

The Knowledge Gap was then made wider still when neither Franklyn nor Martel included in their orders the picture of a strong enemy force increasingly apparent from the information provided by the British reconnaissance forces. Instead, they continued to refer only to the weak enemy forces known when Gort issued his original instructions a day and a half earlier. It is possible both officers were already uncertain regarding the purpose of the operation and may have been struggling with a sense the forces available to them were insufficient for the more expansive objectives being hinted at by Leese and the French commanders. Consciously accepting there was a contradiction between forces and objectives would have required them to accept their orders were no longer practical. Since implementing orders known to be inappropriate would stretch the loyalty even of officers brought up to rigid obedience, Franklyn and Martel may have found it easier instead to disregard the reconnaissance reports. In a situation of a conflict between orders and reality, a subordinate brought up within the Restrictive Control approach to command may find it simpler to adjust reality than to question his orders. As Franklyn commented, 'surely the nearer the front the less one should suggest the horrors awaiting an attack.'[342]

---

342 Franklyn, *One Green Howard*, p.20.

The level of friction experienced by the British was further increased as a result of a wide Alignment Gap. The task assigned to Martel's units was well outside what had been envisaged in the army's doctrine. Instead of the heavy "I" tanks working in close support of a dense infantry assault on a defended position, they were ordered to sweep a large area believed to contain only scattered enemy forces. Further, the units involved had no experience of working in combined infantry / tank columns. This was made worse by the fact the orders Martel issued were ambiguous as to the command arrangements for his two columns, and the rushed nature of the operation meant the battalion commanders had minimal opportunity to sort this out between themselves prior to the start of the counterattack. Finally, Pratt's insistence the tanks maintain radio silence in the days before the battle meant communications across his brigade broke down almost immediately, rendering both himself and his battalion and company commanders virtually irrelevant and leaving his subalterns to fight as best they could, a further instance of the negative impact of a reliance on Restrictive Control.

Despite the significant level of friction being experienced by the British attack, the surprise achieved by the initiative, coupled with the fact that the Matildas were proof against the German 37mm PAK guns, led to the defenders suffering a severe psychological jolt, pushing them into shock and, in many cases, flight. This could have led to a disastrous collapse of the German position, an event avoided in large measure through the personal intervention of Rommel. Demonstrating his usual mix of personal bravery and resolute decisiveness, he established a gun-line from his artillery, personally directing fire that brought the British tank advance to a halt. The absence of this Directive Control by a senior commander was all too apparent in the reaction of the SS Totenkopf Division, when it was engaged by the handful of tanks that managed to penetrate Rommel's gun-line. As had been the case with 7th Panzer Division, the SS men initially fled in panic, though perhaps not on the scale subsequently suggested. The divisional commander, Eicke, however, was notable by his absence. His reliance on strict obedience to orders, implying use of Restrictive Control, meant, lacking such direction, his men had to revert to the instinctive aggression he had inculcated into the formation. The limits of this as an approach to combat are indicated by the comparatively heavy casualties suffered by the SS men.

It is clear forward command by senior German commanders, especially Rommel himself, was central to the ability of 7th Panzer Division to recover from its initial shock. The picture on the British side was rather more mixed. On the one hand, Martel, Churchill and Pope all went forward from their headquarters and spent the day roaming across the battlefield, moving from one unit to another. This may be contrasted with the decision by Pratt to remain with his headquarters, despite the fact communication with his units broke down almost immediately, a situation made worse by the early deaths of both tank battalion commanders. Yet, whereas the German commanders went forward right to the front-line, exposing themselves to significant personal danger, none of the British commanders appear to have gone beyond the positions of the main battalion headquarters. Although both Martel and

Churchill visited Miller at 6/DLI during the afternoon, neither recognised he had completely lost control of his unit. The influence of these senior commanders on the course of the battle may therefore be questioned.

But perhaps the most important facet of the battle was its psychological impact on Rundstedt personally: even though the British counterattack was quickly defeated and Martel's forces driven back to their starting lines with heavy losses, he was convinced the French commanders, whom he respected greatly, were about to follow the obvious course and launch a powerful thrust against the lengthy and exposed flanks of the deep penetration created by the panzers in their headlong rush to the sea, cutting off the steel tip of the German spear.

Indeed, in this response, Rundstedt may have been influenced by the pervasive teaching of decades, reaching its peak under Alfred von Schlieffen, which argued penetration of the enemy line merely offered the defenders the chance to surround the attackers, whereas encirclement from the flanks was the only sure route to success.[343] The shock persuaded him the offensive was about to suffer a decisive counterstroke. This was a conviction with limited foundation, yet Rundstedt stuck to it for several days, hiding in his headquarters and ignoring the increasingly vocal complaints of his subordinates. Yet shock is only a temporary phenomenon. As the British and French made no attempt to take advantage of the German paralysis, Rundstedt recovered his nerve. The offensive restarted, the panzers rolled forward again, and the forces encircled in Belgium were crushed. But it was too late, and hundreds of thousands of men had been evacuated from Dunkirk, forming the core of the army that returned to the continent almost exactly four years later.

The events at Arras again demonstrated the correctness of Clausewitz's belief victory is achieved through putting the enemy's forces 'in such condition that they can no longer carry on the fight'. Once again, rather than such a result being a question primarily of physical destruction, 'the loss of morale has proved the major decisive factor.'[344] When considering the course of the British counterattack at Arras from the German perspective, it was the psychological shock of the initial British armoured thrust, apparently proving the high command's worst fears were about to be realised, that was decisive. It was not the troops on the ground, who knew they had won that battle, but rather Rundstedt, scores of miles away in his headquarters at Charleville, who convinced himself that he was defeated.

343 Jehuda Wallach, *The Dogma of the Battle of Annihilation: The Theories of Clausewitz and Schlieffen and Their Impact on the German Conduct of Two World Wars* (Westport, CT: Greenwood, 1986), pp. 41-46.
344 Clausewitz, *On War*, pp.230-231.

6

Epilogue

Everything depends on penetrating the uncertainty of veiled situations to evaluate the facts, to clarify the unknown, to make decisions rapidly, and then to carry them out with strength and constancy. [...] From the beginning of operations, everything in war is uncertain.

Moltke the Elder[1]

The study of military history in the English-speaking world has probably never been more popular than today. Many factors have contributed to raising the profile of the subject, including the re-emergence of active combat operations into the awareness of the British and American public following the 9/11 attacks, the sense the military experience of the Second World War will soon have slipped out of living memory, and the recent centenary of the First World War. Most libraries and bookshops devote substantial shelf-space to the flood of new and reprinted works on military topics published in response to this interest.

Yet, as was noted in the opening pages of this book, it is evident the bulk of this literature is characterised by straightforward narrative (*what happened*), or technical description (*what equipment was used*) rather than analysis (*why it happened*). There are many writers, whether popular or academic, engaged in the study of war, but the number focused on understanding warfare (*the undertaking of war*) is very small. Jim Storr has suggested in Britain probably fewer than two dozen individuals are so engaged, almost all of them directly employed by the army.[2]

At least in part, this may be a consequence of the natural tendency for writers and their readers to prefer to focus on the technical inventiveness, brave exploits and bold successes (or, especially in Britain, heroic failures) of one's own forces.

1 *Moltke on the Art of War: Selected Writings*, ed. by Daniel J. Hughes (New York, NY: Ballantine, 1993), p.46.
2 Jim Storr, *The Human Face of War* (London: Continuum, 2009), p.11.

This inward-looking perspective, however, results in (and may reflect) only limited awareness of the fact warfare is inherently a struggle between opposing forces – it is an interactive activity, like tennis, soccer, or wrestling, rather than a personal performance against the clock or the record book, like swimming, gymnastics, or rowing. Thus, most of the secondary works consulted in the preparation of this book (with a very few honourable exceptions) relied almost entirely on sources relating only to one or other army, with even the limited consideration of material regarding the enemy forces generally confined to a handful of publications available in translation. This approach affects the thinking of armies just as much as it does that of armchair military enthusiasts.

Even where there is an acknowledgement the enemy forces may play a role in determining the outcome of an engagement, explanations too often focus on simplistic factors, such as numbers, the 'genius' of individual commanders, or the characteristics of equipment (calibre of gun, thickness of armour, etc.). As Stephen Biddle has argued, 'Today, most analyses are either rigorous but narrow, or broad but unrigorous. Mathematical models of combat, for example, are rigorous but typically focus on material alone [... .] By contrast, holistic assessments consider issues such as strategy, tactics, morale, combat motivation, or leadership as well as just materiel but treat these variables much less systematically. Real progress demands rigor *and* breadth: a systematic treatment of both material and nonmaterial variables, backed up with a combination of empirical evidence and careful deductive reasoning.'[3] Yet even a cursory reading of the history of warfare demonstrates armies differ from each other in their practice in quite fundamental ways, responding to the same situations and challenges with strongly divergent behaviours. As Biddle has suggested, this suggests explanations for why one army defeated another need to look much deeper than the limited approaches usually adopted.

As was noted at the start of this book, since the 1980s, one major area of exploration for these differences in the ways armies respond to situations has been the field of command. In this sense, command is to be understood as the methodology and system of attitudes by which superiors seek to direct the actions of their subordinates. As such, it is distinct from the question of leadership, though there are naturally strong interlinkages between the two topics.

This process has both paralleled and drawn upon the similar debate in the German Army in the 1880s and 1890s between the *Normaltaktiker* ('normal tacticians') and the proponents of *Auftragstaktik* ('mission tactics').[4] The former emphasised the central importance of tight control by superior commanders, in order to retain overall coherence, while the latter argued it was necessary for subordinates to use

3   Stephen Biddle, *Military Power: Explaining Victory and Defeat in Modern Battle* (Princeton: Princeton University, 2004), p.2. Emphasis in original.
4   Antulio J. Echevarria, *After Clausewitz: German Military Thinkers Before the Great War* (Lawrence, KS: University Press of Kansas, 2000), pp. 32-42.

their initiative, in order to respond to changing local situations. Yet, even here, much of the recent discussion has focused on may be termed 'command techniques', the mechanics of how commanders seek to employ their forces, rather than their context or the reasons why particular armies adopt particular approaches to command. For example, Biddle argued 'a particular pattern of force employment', which he termed 'the modern system', was pivotal for understanding the results of engagements during the twentieth century. He noted, 'Not everyone can master it, however. The modern system is extremely complex and poses painful political and social tradeoffs. While some have been able to surmount these challenges and implement the modern system fully, others have not.'[5] Yet, having identified a vital factor, he did not explore the reasons why it arose, such that his examination remained essentially descriptive rather than analytical, despite its complex mathematical basis.

The purpose of this book, therefore, has been to take a series of steps towards establishing a conceptual foundation for the discussion of command, going beyond simple description, in order to provide an analytical basis for different command approaches. The resulting theoretical model has then been tested through an examination of the doctrine and practice of the British and German armies between 1918 and 1940. Although it has been necessary to take account of trends and developments prior to 1918, this period has been selected as it represents a key phase in the military thought and practice of both armies. By the summer of 1918, the British and German armies had each reached a peak of professional expertise. The experiences gained over the previous four years of fighting had been encapsulated into highly flexible tactics, equipment that enabled these, and focused training, as well as the associated command approaches. Taken together, these gave both armies a level of combat effectiveness far in advance of the formations deployed in 1914. The interwar years were broadly a period during which the British and the Germans each sought to capture the lasting lessons of the First World War and build these into their doctrine. This process was made more complicated by this being undertaken in a context of rapid technological change, which took armour, aircraft and communications into areas far beyond what had been possible in 1918. The battles of 1940, therefore, were largely fought according to the doctrine developed during that time. The Fall of France consequently represents the fulcrum for subsequent doctrinal development, as both armies then reflected upon the ways in which the theories built up during two decades of peace needed to be reassessed in the light of the practical evidence and experience gained during that campaign.

Model of Command Approaches

The central contention of this book has been that the starting point for any meaningful analysis of command approaches must be to see them, not simply as context-free

---

5   Biddle, *Military Power*, pp.2-3.

techniques, but as responses to a basic characteristic of the military environment: friction.

As was shown in Chapter One, Carl von Clausewitz was the first to understand how friction creates the gulf that so often exists between what commanders *intend* to happen and what *actually* happens.[6] As he noted in *On War*, 'This tremendous friction, which cannot, as in mechanics, be reduced to a few points, is everywhere in contact with chance, and brings about effects that cannot be measured, just because they are largely due to chance. [...] Friction [...] is the force that makes the apparently easy so difficult.'[7] Since friction is so central to determining the course of events on the battlefield, all armies need to address it as a matter of routine through their command approaches.

During the late 1980s and early 1990s, a small group of researchers at the University of Manchester, led by the late Michael Elliott-Bateman and including the current author, began to question the basis for the debates then occurring within the British and American armies, which led to the adoption of the command technique now known as Mission Command. In particular, we were concerned that the widespread perception Mission Command was 'just another' managerial concept, rather than being a response to friction, would result in significant misunderstanding of its key features and hence significant deviation from endorsed practice. The evidence of subsequent decades has indeed proven this to be the case.[8]

The group aimed to develop a more robust model than the simplistic centralised/decentralised dichotomy characterising the debate at the time. Central to our argument was the proposition different armies perceive the basic nature of combat in fundamentally different ways, with some seeing it as inherently structured, while others understand it as being essentially chaotic. We argued the perception of the nature of combat held by any given army is expressed in the command approach it generally employs. We proposed those armies understanding combat as inherently structured seek to reduce friction by imposing control of the battle from above through what we termed 'Restrictive Control'. Conversely, armies considering it to be chaotic endeavour to reduce friction by maximising the scope for subordinates to use their initiative to achieve the overall intent, an approach we termed 'Directive Command'. Our examination of a number of engagements, ranging from the First World War, through the North Africa campaign in the Second World War, to the Falklands War, led us to suggest the British Army generally demonstrated a preference for Restrictive Control, while the German Army leaned towards Directive Command. A variant approach, termed 'Umpiring', was also identified, thereby usefully serving to

6   Hew Strachan, *Clausewitz's On War: A Biography* (New York, NY: Atlantic Monthly, 2007) p.153.
7   Carl von Clausewitz, *On War*, ed. and trans. by Michael Howard and Peter Paret (Princeton, NJ: Princeton University Press, 1976), pp. 120-121.
8   Eitan Shamir, *Transforming Command, The Pursuit of Mission Command in the U.S., British and Israeli Armies* (Stanford, CA: Stanford University Press, 2010)

demonstrate the standard centralised/decentralised dichotomy was indeed simplistic, and a more sophisticated framework, with a larger number of possible approaches, was necessary. But the connections and basis of these hypotheses, in particular how the different understandings of the nature of war related to friction, and hence how the resulting command approaches sought to reduce friction, and whether they were effective in doing so, were not pursued. The model, therefore, was still largely descriptive and remained partial.[9]

The key to addressing these issues was more recently presented by Stephen Bungay and a group of likeminded researchers, of whom Storr was one. Analysing Clausewitz's description of the many factors that generate friction, Bungay developed a model of friction that suggested it arose through three 'gaps', which allow the alternative options open to commanders to be drawn out:[10]

- Knowledge Gap: plans are imperfect because there is a gap between what commanders would *like to know* about the local situation and what they *actually know*. Commanders may seek to close this gap either by demanding more information or by adapting their command approach to cope with less;
- Alignment Gap: actions are imperfect because there is a gap between what commanders *want* units to do and what they *actually* do. Commanders may seek to close this gap either by limiting themselves to orders setting out their general intent, leaving implementation to their subordinates' initiative, or they may require their subordinates to follow detailed orders precisely; and
- Effects Gap: outcomes are imperfect because the nature of war means an army's actions may produce *unexpected results*. Commanders may respond to this gap either by intervening or by allowing their subordinates to react to the changed situation.

The deeper model of friction developed by Bungay and his colleagues is therefore of particular importance, as it can be linked with the initial model of command approaches developed by the Manchester group. Combining the thinking of these two groups allows a new and more sophisticated typology of command approaches to be generated, based on these representing different approaches to reducing friction, as it is differently perceived by different armies.

In Chapter One, these three gaps were considered as three broadly 'either/or' axes, which produces a simple model comprising eight permutations, listed at Figure 6.1.

---

9   The framework was most clearly set out in Martin Samuels, *Command or Control? Command, Training and Tactics in the British and German Armies, 1888-1918* (London: Cass, 1995), pp. 3-5, and Spencer Fitz-Gibbon, *Not Mentioned in Despatches... The History and Mythology of the Battle of Goose Green* (Cambridge: Lutterworth, 1995), pp. xiv-xvi.

10   Stephen Bungay, *The Art of Action: How Leaders Close the Gaps between Plans, Actions and Results* (London: Brealey, 2011), pp. 30-35.

Figure 6.1: Command Approaches

Knowledge Gap	Alignment Gap	Effects Gap	Command Approach	Description
Superior knows less than subordinates	Subordinates should use initiative	Superiors will intervene	1: Enthusiastic Amateur	Superiors intervene, despite the fact they know less than their subordinates do and these will use their initiative.
		Superiors will not intervene	2: Directive Command	Superiors will not intervene, because they know less than their subordinates do and are confident these will use initiative.
	Subordinates should do as they are told	Superiors will intervene	3: Restrictive Control	Superiors know less than their subordinates, but issue definitive orders (in the expectation these will be adhered to), and intervene to ensure compliance. *In practice*, they act as if they know more than their subordinates do.
		Superiors will not intervene	4: Detached Control	Superiors know less than their subordinates know, but nevertheless issue definitive orders, and then leave their subordinates struggling to put these into effect. Subordinates actually know more than superiors, but are not allowed (or expected) to use initiative to resolve the problems arising from orders based on a poor understanding of the situation.

Superior knows more than subordinates	Subordinates should use initiative	Superiors will intervene	5: Directive Control	Superiors know more than their subordinates know, issue definitive orders and will intervene, but require their subordinates to use their initiative.
		Superiors will not intervene	6: Umpiring	Superiors will not intervene, even though they know more than their subordinates do, as they are confident subordinates will use initiative.
	Subordinates should do as they are told	Superiors will intervene	7: Logistic Control	Superiors know more than their subordinates and issue definitive orders, then intervene to ensure these are acted on, recognising (or believing) subordinates cannot be relied upon to use initiative safely.
		Superiors will not intervene	8: Neglected Control	Superiors know more than their subordinates and issue definitive orders, yet fail to intervene when events work out differently, since they are content to see subordinates fail (thereby strengthening their own position).

More detailed analysis of these command approaches showed four of them (Enthusiastic Amateur, Detached Control, Umpiring, and Neglected Control) are inherently self-contradictory, though of course that does not mean they have never been employed in practice by a particular army or commander, usually with very negative consequences.

Further consideration of the remaining four approaches showed each can be appropriate, under particular circumstances:

- Logistic Control – The superior has a better understanding of the situation than do his subordinates, and where he can be sure that, if they act in accordance to his instructions, the results can be predicted with some accuracy;
- Restrictive Control – Subordinates may be unable or unwilling to act effectively according to their own initiative;

- Directive Command – Superiors can be assured that their subordinates will apply their own initiative, and will do so in ways that are effective in furthering the higher intent; and
- Directive Control – Even though superiors have full confidence in the appropriate initiative of their subordinates, the commander's direct and personal intervention at the key point may prove decisive.

The key element noted in the previous paragraph was that the appropriateness, and hence effectiveness, of each of the four command approaches is dependent on the circumstances. It was argued the central factor in determining those circumstances is the basic nature of warfare. If warfare is linear, then Logistic Control and Restrictive Control are likely to be most effective, if chaotic, then Directive Command and Directive Control.

Examination of both management thinking and the analysis by Clausewitz clearly suggest that, on the whole, warfare is inherently chaotic, rather than linear. It was noted Scientific Management, which was the leading approach in many sectors of industry from the late nineteenth century, was based on the assumption the issues facing managers were linear, and hence predictable, with known or calculable solutions. Subsequent researchers[11] concluded, however, such 'tame' problems did not represent practical reality, especially outside the controlled world of the factory. Instead, many societal issues were 'wicked', being complex or chaotic, without an agreed solution, and dynamic. If such 'wicked' issues are prevalent in the world of management, where many organisations do not operate in a competitive market at all, while others function in a context of regulation, where strict controls are placed on direct intervention by one company against another, then surely this must be all the more true in the context of warfare. In passing, Martin van Creveld has argued this very aspect makes warfare such an attractive 'game', since it 'permits, even demands, the full mobilization of all the participants' intellectual, moral, and physical qualities; this is because in war there are few if any rules that would prevent whatever qualities the combatants have from being used to the full extent.'[12]

Turning to the thinking presented by Clausewitz, while analysts disagree over whether he saw warfare as completely chaotic or as inherently predictable, this may be to consider the issue from only unhelpful extremes. The two arguments may be brought together by drawing a distinction between systems that are completely unpredictable and those that cannot be predicted with certainty. Clausewitz appears to have regarded warfare as inherently chaotic, while still placing great weight on the importance of planning. As Helmuth von Moltke the Elder noted: 'No plan of operations extends with certainty beyond the first encounter with the main hostile

---

11   Horst W.J. Rittel and Melvin M. Webber, 'Dilemmas in a General Theory of Planning', *Policy Sciences* 4 (1973), 155-169.
12   Martin van Creveld, *The Culture of War* (Stroud: Spellmount, 2009), pp.66-67.

force. [...] Yet in spite of all this, the conduct of war has never degenerated into blind arbitrariness.'[13] This perhaps brings out a central feature of command approaches: the ability to bring together the knowledge of the broader context with that of the local situation, in order to recognise the most appropriate action to take at the tactical level in order to deliver the desired result at the higher level.[14]

Taken together, both modern management thinking and Clausewitz's analysis suggest warfare is indeed inherently chaotic. As a consequence, many of the problems facing commanders are likely to be 'wicked'. In such circumstances, Directive Command may be the most effective command approach for reducing the level of friction experienced by friendly forces, supplemented by Directive Control when commanders can position themselves personally at the decisive point. It should not be overlooked, however, that some of the problems arising in warfare will nonetheless be 'tame' such that Logistic Control, supplemented by Restrictive Control where the reliability of subordinates is questionable, may still be the appropriate approach.

The conclusion must therefore be none of the four command approaches is inherently superior to the others, as they are all dependent upon context. All should therefore be acceptable in practice. This conclusion stands in stark contrast to that reached by most military theorists, who have generally sought to demonstrate one approach or another is the 'correct' one for an army to follow.

The above discussion has focused on the relative effectiveness of the different command approaches at reducing the level of friction experienced by one's own forces. Yet it is here the interactive nature of warfare becomes key. Indeed, Alfred von Schlieffen, Chief of the German General Staff from 1889 to 1905, argued the history of warfare was nothing more than a catalogue of generals' mistakes, such that the role of the commander was primarily to take advantage of these in order to secure victory.[15] Two conclusions flow from this. First, not only should commanders seek to reduce the level of friction experienced by their own forces, but they should also aim to increase that affecting their opponent, for example by taking advantage of their errors. Second, it may be more important to consider the relative level of friction being experienced by the respective opponents, rather than the absolute level experienced by either. This fits closely with the point made at the start of this discussion, that the essence of warfare is it is a dynamic interplay between active opposing forces.

Here, the work of Colonel John Boyd, USAF, appears to be key. While there are certainly conceptual flaws in the OODA (Observation, Orientation, Decision, Action) Loop he developed, examination of the final version of the model, presented in 1995 shortly before his death, reveals a highly sophisticated double-loop learning process, which addressed many of the deficiencies of the basic version. Central to the

---

13 *Moltke on the Art of War*, pp. 92-93.
14 My thanks to Stephen Bungay for encapsulating the argument in these terms.
15 Wiegand Schmidt-Richberg, *Die Generalstäbe in Deutschland 1871-1945* (Stuttgart: MGFA, 1962), p. 18.

issues relevant to the analysis of command approaches that is the focus of this book, Boyd argued it was the speed with which commanders convert the information they receive (Observation) into orders (Decision), through the process of Orientation, that was central to the effectiveness of their operations. As Patton recognised, 'A good solution applied with vigour *now* is better than a perfect solution ten minutes later'.[16]

But the key to Patton's comment was that it had to be a 'good solution', not just a quick one. And here, two factors seem to be critical: the commander's knowledge of the situation and his ability to comprehend it – the Orientation phase of Boyd's model. As Clausewitz noted, 'War is the realm of uncertainty; three quarters of the factors on which action in war is based are wrapped in a fog of greater or lesser uncertainty. A sensitive and discriminating judgement is called for[,…] that, even in the darkest hour, retains some glimmerings of the inner light which leads to truth'.[17] He termed this form of intelligence 'genius'. Such was its impact, from the ability to grasp and comprehend situations more fully and more quickly than was possible for others, that he claimed it operated 'outside the rules'.[18] The essence, it is argued here, is that the ability to respond to the Knowledge Gap in this way is a powerful force-multiplier.

Through their reliance upon the commander's intent as a guide for subordinates, the speed of decision-making under both Directive Command and Directive Control is likely to be faster than under Logistic Control or Restrictive Control, since the time required to develop and issue high level directives will normally be much less than is needed to produce detailed orders. However, the quality of decision-making is likely to be lower in the case of Directive Command and Restrictive Control, as the commanders in those situations have a wider Knowledge Gap and hence their Orientation is likely to be less effective than under Logistic Control or Directive Control. As such, commanders employing Directive Control can expect to make good decisions (based on personal observation) rapidly, thereby getting inside their adversary's Loop. By contrast, those applying Restrictive Control are likely to make poor decisions (due to an incorrect assessment of the relative knowledge of commander and subordinates, or an inability to rely on subordinates' initiative) at a slow pace. The chances of getting inside the enemy's Loop in order to increase friction are therefore low.

Taking account of the model of the problems facing commanders in warfare as being 'wicked' or 'tame', and connecting it with the three 'gaps' and the different command approaches responding to these, Chapter One therefore concluded that three factors seem to be of greatest importance:

---

16   Charles M. Province, *The Unknown Patton* (New York, NY: Hippocrene, 1983), p. 165.
17   Clausewitz, *On War*, pp.101-102. My thanks to Aidan Walsh for bringing these quotes to my attention.
18   Clausewitz, *On War*, p.140.

- Whether an army expects the problems encountered in warfare to be 'wicked', such that it is unlikely senior commanders will be able to predict the local situation within which their subordinates operate (making approaches that emphasise subordinates' initiative liable to be more effective), or whether they are expected to be 'tame', such that senior commanders can determine local situations in advance (making approaches that use detailed orders more effective);
- Whether commanders can rely on their subordinates to interpret general directives within their local situation, in order to achieve the overall intent (enabling approaches that maximise low-level initiative), or whether deficiencies in capability or motivation mean commanders cannot trust their subordinates to act independently (requiring reliance on rigid adherence to orders); and
- Whether commanders seek to achieve certainty through extensive collection and collation of intelligence about the situation and detailed analysis of all the available options, in order to identify the 'correct' solution to a 'tame' problem, or whether they emphasise speed of decision-making, even in the absence of a large part of the picture, in order to implement quickly 'good enough' decisions to 'wicked' problems, thereby achieving tempo and inflicting surprise and shock on the enemy.

This theoretical analysis of the relationship between command approaches and friction, detailed in Chapter One, sought to test the contention a command system is not simply a neutral technique, but (whether consciously or not) is a response to the fundamental nature of warfare. As such, it concluded some approaches are more likely than others to deliver victory. Nonetheless, it should be recognised many factors affect the preference for, and application of, particular command approaches by different armies. These factors, which may include political expectations, cultural tunnel vision, and technology, merit further discussion. Presenting the typology here may encourage such deeper examination of the subject.

Command and Written Doctrine

Having developed a theoretical model of command approaches, this was used in Chapter Two as a tool to analyse the doctrine for command, as it developed in the British and German armies, with a particular emphasis on the period 1918 to 1940. Did the doctrines of command expressed by the two armies suggest they had different perceptions of the nature of warfare? If so, was that reflected in different command approaches being espoused? In essence, the key question was whether the model of command approaches, linking these to an army's perception of the causes of friction, provided a useful and robust means of understanding an army's doctrine.

The starting point for consideration of the doctrine espoused by the German Army during this period has to be *Heeresdienstvorschrift (HDv) 300: Truppenführung* (Army Service Regulation 300: Unit Command of Troops). First published in 1933, the manual remained in force throughout the Second World War. The manual has since been widely lauded as perhaps the finest expression of military doctrine ever written.

Using the three factors identified, at the end of Chapter One, as a means to guide analysis of the text, it is clear the authors of *Truppenführung* perceived warfare as being non-linear, not least as a consequence of the interaction of one's own forces with the independent will of the enemy, presenting commanders with 'wicked' issues to resolve. This was underlined by reference to the incompleteness of the information received, the lack of certainty that could be achieved, and the fact orders would often be overtaken by events. This led to a strong emphasis on the need for subordinates to be granted significant scope for the exercise of their initiative, encapsulated in two key statements:[19]

- *Everyone, from the highest commander down to the youngest soldier, must constantly be aware that inaction and neglect incriminate him more severely than any error in the choice of means.*
- An order should contain all that a subordinate needs to know to be able to execute his mission – and nothing more.

These statements were coupled with repeated emphasis on the importance for commanders at all levels to make decisions quickly. In order to make this possible, the manual required senior commanders to place themselves far forward, at the decisive point of the battle, thereby maximising both their knowledge of the situation and the speed with which their decisions could be communicated to the troops for implementation.

Truppenführung expressed a perception of warfare as being chaotic, and hence promulgated a doctrine of command most closely equating to Directive Command, though with strong leanings towards Directive Control at the critical point.

This doctrine, however, did not spring from nowhere. Examination of earlier German doctrinal manuals indicates much of the thinking expressed so concisely in *Truppenführung* in fact represented a logical development from statements made in manuals first published the mid-1880s, manuals produced under the direction (and sometimes via the pen) of the Elder Moltke.

Consideration of successive editions of the *Felddienst-Ordnung* (Field Service Regulations) from 1887 onwards reveals some of the statements considered central to the doctrine presented in *Truppenführung* were simply carried forward from manuals written forty years earlier. Nonetheless, although it was clear the authors of the *Felddienst-Ordnung* perceived warfare as being inherently chaotic, and hence placed great weight on the need for commanders to avoid constraining the scope for initiative of their subordinates, there was far less emphasis on surprise or the need

---

19   *Heeresdienstvorschrift (HDv) 300/1: Truppenführung* (1933), paras.14 and 73. Emphasis in original.

for rapid decision-making than in the later manual. This was also reflected in the various editions of the *Instructions for Large Unit Commanders* from 1869 onwards, which differed from *Truppenführung* principally in discouraging commanders from placing themselves too far forward, and hence running the risk of becoming lost in the local detail.

The manuals produced during the First World War, notably Ludendorff's famous *Grundsätze für die Abwehr im Stellungskriege* (Principles for the Defence in Position Warfare) and *Der Angriff im Stellungskriege* (The Attack in Position Warfare), also offered clearly continuity from those before 1914. Two developments, however, stand out. First, the need for initiative at every level, even down to the individual soldier, was still more strongly stated than before, reflecting the decentralisation forced by the overwhelming firepower of the Western Front. Second, whereas the importance of achieving surprise was almost entirely absent from the *Felddienst-Ordnung*, by 1918 it was a major feature of the army's doctrine, giving added impetus to the emerging principle that commanders should place themselves forward.

The German Army's first post-war field manual, published in 1921, was *HDv 487: Führung und Gefecht der verbundenen Waffen* (Command and Combat of the Combined Arms), colloquially known as *Das FuG*, and written under the personal supervision of the Reichswehr's commander-in-chief, Hans von Seeckt. As had the earlier manuals, *Das FuG* emphasised the chaotic nature of warfare and the consequent need for commanders to encourage initiative on the part of their subordinates. Unexpectedly, however, although repeating from the wartime manuals the importance of commanders placing themselves far forward, the new manual made no mention of seeking to achieve surprise as a key aim for commanders.

In summary, German manuals from the 1880s onwards stressed the nature of warfare as a clash between two independent wills meant it was characterised by rapidly changing and unpredictable situations. As a consequence, commanders could not see far into the future and often had to operate on the basis of partial and uncertain information, features characteristic of 'wicked' problems and reflecting the tendency for the Knowledge Gap to be wide. It was therefore essential to narrow the Effects Gap by relying upon the initiative of subordinates. In order to ensure the Alignment Gap did not become a major source of friction, the doctrine emphasised subordinates must ensure their actions were based on their commitment to, and understanding of, the higher commander's overall intent and their ability to interpret the best way in which to achieve this, drawing on their better knowledge of the local situation. This was most clearly expressed in two key rules: commanders were required to include in their orders 'all that a subordinate needs to know to be able to execute his mission – and nothing more'; and subordinates were sternly reminded 'inaction and neglect incriminate [them] more severely than any error in the choice of means'. These phrases were repeated in successive editions of the manuals over a period of fifty years, though *Truppenführung*'s simplicity and directness of language perhaps expressed these doctrines more succinctly and memorably than before. It is clear the command approach presented throughout the period, to 1933 and beyond, was equivalent to Directive Command.

Where *Truppenführung* broke new ground was in its focus on surprise as a key goal. This also led to an emphasis on the need to secure tempo over the enemy through rapid decision-making, based on senior commanders positioning themselves personally at the decisive point of the battle at its climax. While *Das FuG* started to point in that direction, its focus was still on the moral impact on the troops of seeing their commanders sharing in their joys and sorrows. By contrast, the emphasis in *Truppenführung* was on the ability of the commander to make better decisions faster. This doctrine, which had first emerged in the manuals of 1917 and 1918 but was overlooked in *Das FuG*, marked a vital new departure in German doctrine. It pushed commanders towards the command approach here termed Directive Control, though only in the limited circumstances of the decisive point.

Turning to the British Army, the main doctrinal manual throughout this period was the various editions of *Field Service Regulations* (FSR). The final edition issued prior to the Second World War was written by Archibald Wavell and published in 1935.

At first sight, FSR II (1935) shows a number of important similarities to *Truppenführung*. Like the German manual, the British doctrine noted warfare was an active contest between participants. Using the analogy of boxing, it emphasised this made battle unpredictable and subject to friction. It therefore noted commanders should avoid constraining the scope for initiative enjoyed by their subordinates. At this point, however, the parallel with *Truppenführung* stopped. Whereas the German manual, repeating a phrase used by successive editions of the doctrine since the 1880s, underlined failure to act was worse than errors in the choice of means, FSR II (1935) placed significant boundaries on the ability of subordinates to exercise their initiative. This was permitted only when subordinates were presented with information their superiors could not have known, and even then they were required to seek prior authorisation if at all possible. The effect was to create 'a recipe for delay and lethargy'.[20] Turning to the other two key factors identified in Chapter One, FSR II (1935) placed significant emphasis on the need for decision-making to be rapid, even in the context of imperfect knowledge, and highlighted the importance of this as a means to achieve surprise over the enemy. There was, however, little to suggest commanders should place themselves forward, and there was a strong expectation commanders would in practice issue detailed instructions to their subordinates.

In summary, Wavell saw the problems generated in warfare as inherently unpredictable and hence subject to friction through creating a wide Knowledge Gap. Consequently, speed of reaction was an essential means by which to inflict surprise on the enemy, thereby widening his Knowledge Gap in turn. Conversely, it appears

---

20   David French, *Raising Churchill's Army: The British Army and the War Against Germany, 1919-1945* (Oxford: Oxford University Press, 2000), p. 23.

Wavell lacked confidence in the ability of subordinates to close the Alignment Gap by responding beyond narrow limits to the changing opportunities of warfare through the exercise of initiative. This was because he assumed these subordinates would be inexperienced civilians drafted into the army at the start of a major war. This may have been a well-founded concern in the context of the British Army, which was a small professional force focused on the defence of the Empire, rather than a large conscript force directed towards European-scale national conflict. FSR therefore expected commanders to assign detailed tasks to their subordinates, who were required to follow those orders, even though the situation might have rendered them 'unsuitable or impracticable', other than in exceptional circumstances. This may be broadly aligned to Restrictive Control.

As was the case with *Truppenführung*, the text in FSR II (1935) regarding initiative closely reflected that presented in the successive previous editions, dating back to 1909. Unlike the German manuals, however, there was a significant discontinuity in the British doctrine, with the philosophy expressed in FSR (1909) differing in a number of fundamental aspects from that presented in FSR (1905). Comparing the two texts, it is clear the authors of FSR (1905) considered warfare much more unpredictable and full of unexpected situations than did their successors. As a consequence, the emphasis on the need for subordinates to be able to exercise their initiative, without constraint, was much stronger in the earlier manual than in later editions. As such, while FSR (1905) clearly considered warfare as chaotic and therefore presented a doctrine broadly equivalent to Directive Command, FSR (1909) and its successors described warfare in terms implying it was likely to be linear, and therefore leaned towards Logistic Control. In that sense, Wavell broke new ground in FSR II (1935). He returned to an understanding of warfare as inherently chaotic, but he recognised British commanders would be constrained by the inexperienced nature of any mass army raised to fight a major European war. The command approach set out in the doctrine was therefore Restrictive Control.

In summary, from at least 1885, the successive editions of the *Felddienst-Ordnung* and the *Instructions for Large Unit Commands* suggest the German doctrine saw warfare as inherently unpredictable, such that commanders could not extrapolate from their greater knowledge of the broader context in order to understand the local situation (widening the Knowledge Gap). As a consequence, the doctrine demanded commanders give their subordinates a clear sense of direction, but leave the achievement of that intent to their initiative (narrowing the Alignment Gap). When compared to the different options open to commanders when faced with the three dimensions of friction, this philosophy equates best with that command approach termed Directive Command.

By contrast, the British Army maintained a strong emphasis on the need to minimise the chaos of warfare, by dint of commanders retaining tight control over their subordinates, a philosophy equating to the command approach of Logistic Control. Central to the development of the army's command doctrine during this period was Colonel G.F.R. Henderson, who taught successive cohorts of Staff College students throughout the 1890s. From the mid-1890s, however, his detailed study of the battles of 1870, coupled with his analysis of the German doctrine of command developed over the following decades, led him to reject the previous orthodoxy. This was expressed in his draft text, which became FSR (1905). While by no means a simple paraphrase of the German *Felddienst-Ordnung*, the new manual drew very similar conclusions about the nature of warfare and accordingly promulgated similar solutions.

Reflecting on the experience of the First World War, the German Army concluded Directive Command remained an appropriate response to the reality of modern warfare and this was expressed in its first post-war statement of command doctrine – *Das FuG*. However, following further analysis and the development of thinking around armoured forces, the view the nature of warfare was fundamentally chaotic became even more central to the army's thinking. This led to the conclusion the existing tradition of forward command needed to be strengthened still further. This would enable rapid decision-making at the decisive point of the battle, which would allow commanders to achieve tempo and inflict surprise on the enemy. As a result, *Truppenführung* exhorted senior commanders to adopt a command approach equating to Directive Control.

By contrast, in the British Army, Henderson's own former students led a revision of his manual that saw his emphasis on decentralisation severely weakened, with FSR (1909) effectively reverting to the former tradition of Logistic Control. Although there is much evidence to demonstrate a correlation during the First World War between the BEF's progressive adoption of decentralised command and its increasing combat effectiveness, the official doctrine remained at heart true to this approach. This was expressed in a belief in the importance of commanders minimising the chaos of warfare by retaining tight control over their subordinates. This change was sustained through successive editions of FSR after the war, until Wavell returned to an understanding of warfare as inherently chaotic. The impact of this on the approach to command, however, was limited by his concerns about the reliability of the hastily trained civilians he expected to form the bulk of the army during any major European conflict, as had of course been the case during the First World War and would again happen in the Second World War. He therefore promoted an approach equivalent to Restrictive Control in FSR (1935).

Rommel and German Doctrine

Chapter Three considered the case of one of the German Army's most famous generals, Erwin Rommel. It is recognised historians of the Second World War, perhaps especially those who are British, display something of an obsession with Rommel. In this case, he was chosen as the subject for examination due to his reputation as a maverick, whose success up to 1940 was the result of his disregard of the official doctrine.

The first thing to note about Rommel is, although he was never a member of the prestigious General Staff and there is no question that this exclusion long irked him, this should not be taken as indicating he was an outsider to the military establishment. Rommel was definitely a well-respected and valued figure, though he was certainly not a member of the army's most inner elite. Nonetheless, few of Rommel's contemporaries had as great an influence on the subalterns and field officers of the Wehrmacht at the start of the Second World War.

Rommel spent most of the 1930s in a series of increasingly senior posts as an instructor, first at the Infantry School in Dresden (1929 to 1933), then at the War School in Potsdam (1935 to 1938), and finally as commandant of the War School at Wiener Neustadt (1938 to 1940). In these successive roles, he played a key part in the initial command training of perhaps a thousand Reichswehr officer candidates and up to five thousand in the Wehrmacht. Rommel left a lasting impression on his students, given his exceptional reputation as a teacher, drawing extensively on his personal experiences during the First World War. And his influence went much further, as his lecture notes formed the basis of a book, *Infanterie Greift An!* (*Infantry Attacks*), which became a set text for all officer candidates. By early 1940, therefore, Rommel had personally instructed perhaps a quarter of all the Active officers in the German Army, and a higher proportion still of those below field rank, while the book of his lectures had been read by almost every single recently-commissioned officer.[21]

Far from being considered controversial, Rommel was regarded with favour by his superiors, receiving promotion and further key appointments in the officer training system. It would be difficult to find a career path closer to the military establishment for an officer who was not a member of the General Staff, or one with greater potential to shape the thinking and command approach of junior officers throughout the army.

Rommel's command approach, as presented in his lectures and books, was received with favour by the military establishment. It is therefore necessary to identify its key elements in practice, as demonstrated in the action that brought him to international attention in May 1940 – the crossing of the Meuse at Dinant, at the head of 7th Panzer Division. In just four days (12-15 May), Rommel undertook a successful opposed river crossing, surprised and destroyed the powerful French 1st Armoured Division, and punched through the enemy defences to advance more than 50km beyond the Meuse, all at a cost of fewer than six hundred casualties.

Examination of this action reveals three key aspects of Rommel's conduct:

- His personal presence at the key points of the battle, even in the face of great physical danger
- His insistence on speed, both of action and movement, and hence maintaining tempo
- His coolness and decisiveness in the face of unexpected and changing situations

---

21   Peter Caddick-Adams, *Monty and Rommel: Parallel Lives* (London: Arrow, 2012), p. 190.

These characteristics are most typical of the command approach here termed Directive Control, where the commander recognises he can best reduce the Knowledge Gap through his personal presence at the key point, but reduces the Alignment Gap by expecting his subordinates elsewhere to act on their own initiative. The combination of this forward command and reliance on initiative permits a very rapid tempo of operations, allowing the commander to get inside the enemy's decision loop and hence achieve surprise, thereby increasing the level of friction experienced by the enemy and so reducing their combat effectiveness.

The impact of Rommel's approach on his French opponents was overwhelming. Although it is clear the French Army had reached a nadir in its military culture, fixated by the dogma of the methodical linear defence, nonetheless these weaknesses might not have proven fatal had Rommel not employed such a rapid and dynamic approach. Despite the courage of the French troops and the superior quality of much of their equipment, Ninth Army was left flat-footed by the tempo of 7th Panzer Division's advance. The psychological confusion this generated in its senior commanders meant their formations acted with extreme timidity, leaving themselves open to be repeatedly surprised by Rommel's bold moves and hence defeated in detail.

While it has often been suggested the German high command was almost as taken aback by Rommel's behaviour as were the French, the evidence suggests his behaviour was condoned. There was ample opportunity for his superiors to rein him in, but they did not. Indeed, they reinforced his successes at the expense of other formations, evidence they regarded his behaviour as entirely satisfactory. Rommel's approach may have left his own superiors as uncertain of 7th Panzer Division's location as were his opponents, but the outstanding results that came from this behaviour gave him the right to continue in that same vein. Rommel's application of Directive Control was therefore certainly not considered unacceptable.

Rommel's achievements are all the more remarkable when it is noted he had only taken up command of 7th Panzer twelve weeks earlier, and this was both his first divisional command and his first direct experience with armoured forces. It has often been suggested, therefore, Rommel simply drew upon his experience as a mountain infantryman during the First World War – an experience he had spent much of the previous decade recounting to the German Army's officer candidates.

Rommel's most famous exploit as a member of the Royal Wurttemberg Mountain Battalion (WMB) was his capture of Mount Matajur, during the opening stages of the Caporetto campaign in October 1917. In just three days, his force of just a few hundred men seized the lynchpin of the entire Italian defensive position and captured over nine thousand prisoners, along with eighty-one guns, at the cost of just six dead and thirty men wounded. Detailed examination of Rommel's actions through the operation demonstrates the characteristics he displayed as a Generalmajor commanding a panzer division in May 1940 were indeed equally apparent when he was an Oberleutnant commanding a group of mountain infantry companies in October 1917.

As was to be the case with the French in 1940, Rommel's approach at Mount Matajur was almost perfectly designed to inflict the maximum surprise on the Italians. His personal presence and intervention at the key points of the engagement, his emphasis on maintaining tempo, and his calmness in the face of the chaos and opportunity of battle together combined to increase the likelihood of the men of the WMB appearing at places, deep within the defensive zone, where they were least expected. Rommel then acted with a speed and decisiveness that increased the threat posed by his attack and denied the defenders time in which to develop an effective response. The result was the units facing his small group of men crumbled.

Again, as in 1940, Rommel ensured he acted closely within the scope allowed by his superiors. He took considerable pains to remain in close contact with his superiors throughout most of the battle, seeking their approval for his next actions, indeed, the commander of the WMB explicitly instructed him to 'try his luck' in the unfolding situation. Even when he did disobey orders, this was not done without significant (if still rapid) reflection, and his initiative received strong approval from his superiors.

Finally, however, while it is clear that Rommel's approach to command in both 1917 and 1940 was firmly within the bounds set out in the German Army's doctrine, this serves to highlight the great tension that lay at its heart. This was the delicate balance between commanders displaying independence, within the context of the whole, or descending into wilfulness, disregarding the wider context. Rommel's behaviour in 1940 has been characterised as representing 'überbietende Eigenmächtigkeiten' ('surpassing wilfulness'), breaking out completely from the scope of his orders. Yet, this was fully consistent with the German military culture as it had developed over the previous three centuries, where 'even getting [a commander] to follow the mission was difficult enough'.[22] Against enemies as fragile and inflexible as the Italians in 1917 and the French in 1940, the risks (personal and tactical) this involved were justified and brought success. But against a more resilient foe, this emphasis on independence at the expense of the wider plan might not have been sound.

Accordingly, if Rommel's command approach throughout his career up to May 1940 represents a near perfect example of the German Army's command doctrine in practice, his behaviour thereafter may provide a case study of the limits of that doctrine, perhaps especially of Directive Control as an approach. Even within the official manuals, there had long been evidence of a concern that the accepted culture might have its limits. As *Truppenführung* noted, repeating a mantra included in almost every iteration of the German doctrine since before Rommel was first commissioned:

> Willingness to accept responsibility is the most important quality of a leader. It should not, however, be based upon individualism without consideration of the whole, nor used as a justification for failing to carry out orders where seeming

---

22 Robert Citino, *The German Way of War: From the Thirty Years' War to the Third Reich* (Lawrence, KS: University Press of Kansas, 2005), p.302.

to know better may affect obedience. Independence of spirit must not become arbitrariness. By contrast, independence of action within acceptable boundaries is the key to great success.[23]

Doctrine in Practice: Amiens 1918 and Arras 1940

Chapters Four and Five completed the analysis of doctrine and its relationship with friction, through close examination of key elements of two important battles. Chapter Four considered the British tank attack at Amiens on 8 August 1918, the largest such offensive undertaken during the war and arguably the worst defeat suffered by the German Army in the whole war. Chapter Five explored the British armoured counterattack at Arras on 21 May 1940, which was the first time British tanks encountered the Germans during that war. Not only do both operations provide insights into the command approaches adopted by the two armies, they also offer excellent case studies of the impact of friction, and especially shock, at multiple levels.

Amiens, 8 August 1918

Looking first at the battle of Amiens, Chapter Four noted the explanations for the collapse of the German forward zone presented by commanders and historians from the two sides were very different. The British generally focused on their own actions, emphasising a variety of different elements of the tactics employed. The implication was any response by the defenders was largely irrelevant, as the tactics would have overwhelmed any opposition. By contrast, the Germans concentrated on the key factors causing the apparent collapse of morale of the forward troops. They focused on the combination of surprise, which was multiplied by the thick fog shrouding the battlefield during the initial phases, and the massed use of tanks.

That the morale of the defenders had indeed collapsed is demonstrated by the British and French forces taking more than eighteen thousand prisoners on 8 August, two-thirds of the total German losses for the day. Yet, although the British suffered fewer than nine thousand casualties, the attack bogged down during the afternoon and made only limited, costly progress thereafter. The poor quality reserve divisions of those same corps whose men had surrendered in droves in the morning successfully sealed the gash in the German defensive line in the afternoon. After four days, it was clear the front had stabilised and the offensive was closed down.

This contrast demands an explanation beyond simply the superiority of British tactics or the exhaustion of the German defenders. It illustrates the central importance of friction and shock. As Leo Murray noted, 'The real trick, the heart of combat, is to

---

23   *HDv 300/1: Truppenführung* (Berlin: Mittler, 1933), para.9, and *On the German Art of War Truppenführung*, ed. by Bruce Condell and David T. Zabecki (London: Rienner, 2001), p.18.

do those things that make the enemy fight less. [...] If the conditions are right then almost any man will fight, but change those conditions and almost everybody will stop fighting.'[24] At Amiens, the British created conditions causing the German defenders to stop fighting during the early stages of the battle. But those conditions were only temporary and, only a few hours later, they were resisting with some effectiveness.

When considered from the perspective of command, certain conclusions can be drawn with respect to the preferences displayed by the two armies and the consequences for the level of friction experienced and the tempo of operations achieved.

Despite the dramatic loss of ground and manpower suffered since March, Haig had maintained his forces in a state where they were now able to combine a suite of technological and tactical innovations into a system capable of obliterating the German defences. Within this system, the British displayed a strong tendency towards close control by senior officers. The move of the Canadian Corps from Flanders to Amiens provides a good example. Although the degree of secrecy with which this was undertaken was understandable and represented the application of Logistic Control, the reluctance to let even fairly senior officers and their logistics staffs into the secret meant there were instances where the plans went awry, resulting in the approach actually adopted being more akin to Restrictive Control. Only prompt initiative by relatively junior officers mitigated this friction and avoided significant delays that might have hindered the move. Equally, when Rawlinson's attempt to respond to the unexpected collapse of the German defences by deploying 32nd Division sooner than planned was blocked by his own chief of staff, on the grounds that the formation was not yet fully deployed, this may also be taken as an example of Restrictive Control. The increase in friction and drop in the tempo of operations that resulted from this strict control demonstrated the weaknesses of this approach.

Conversely, the reluctance of British forces to take advantage of the gap in the German lines created by the destruction of the forward defences and the rapid advance of the cavalry to the final objective before the available reserves could be deployed, may provide an example of Umpiring. Rawlinson had ordered the attack be pursued vigorously, with the aim of achieving a deep penetration of the German position. Despite this, none of his senior cavalry commanders sought to push the troops forward once it became clear they were digging in despite the limited resistance beyond. Rather, there is evidence to suggest these senior officers held their forces back, even though the commanders on the ground could see there was little in front of them and a deeper advance could have been made. While this reliance on the original battle plan lowered the level of friction experienced by the British formations, it also led to a reduction in the tempo of the offensive, giving the Germans vital time in which to restore their position, and thereby generate friction that prevented achievement of the broader British objectives.

---

24   Leo Murray, *Brains & Bullets: How Psychology Wins Wars* (London: Biteback, 2013), p. 34.

Looking at the German experience, it is notable officers at all levels sought to move forward in order to influence the battle effectively through personal observation. Conversely, commanders behind the lines saw their role as primarily focused on deploying reserves to support the most threatened sectors of the line, and providing guidance to their subordinates over how these forces might be employed in order to achieve the overall intent. These senior commanders all left the final decision to the 'man on the spot', given his better knowledge of the local situation. Taken together, these characteristics may be considered representative of Directive Command at the senior level, and Directive Control at more junior levels.

It may therefore be seen the approaches employed by both British and German commanders in practice, in the heat of a desperate battle, aligned closely with those set out in the written doctrines of the two armies. This thereby validates the analysis, in Chapter Two, of the manuals in which those doctrines were set out, while also indicating there was a strong alignment between the espoused doctrines and the actual practice of both armies. In addition, the actions of the German commanders, and the command approaches they used, were sufficiently similar to those adopted by Rommel at Caporetto as to provide further confirmation his practice was indeed broadly consistent with the expected norms, rather than representing the actions of a genius maverick.

But this contrast between the command approaches of the two armies provides only a partial explanation of events. Far more important was the impact of shock. Surprised by the appearance of hundreds of tanks, against which they were helpless due to the blinding of their anti-tank artillery by thick fog, the German defenders surrendered en masse. It seems highly unlikely this was a rational decision by demoralised troops. Rather, they were psychologically overwhelmed and became incapable of effective response, fleeing in panic or surrendering with barely a fight, as shown by the few fatalities suffered by the regiments in the front line and the limited casualties inflicted on the attackers.

Once the initial surprise wore off and the fog lifted, however, decisive action by German commanders at all levels mitigated the psychological impact of the attack. The weak reserve divisions successfully held off the somewhat half-hearted attempts by the British cavalry and Whippets to push deeper into the German position, despite a massive counter-battery and interdiction effort by Rawlinson's artillery, a major ground support commitment by the RAF, and the rampaging armoured cars of 17th Tank Battalion.

But perhaps the most important facet of the battle was its psychological impact on Ludendorff personally: far behind the front, he was stunned by the British attack and the successes gained. The shock convinced him the German Army had suffered a fundamental loss of combat motivation – a conviction with limited foundation.

Clausewitz argued victory was achieved through putting the enemy's forces 'in such condition that they can no longer carry on the fight'. In this context, he noted, rather than such a result being a question primarily of physical destruction, 'the loss of morale has proved the major decisive factor.'[25] Marshal Foch, quoting Joseph de Maistre, suggested, 'A battle lost is a battle one thinks one has lost; for a battle cannot be lost physically'.[26] When considering the course of the battle of Amiens from the German perspective, one is driven to conclude the psychological shock of the initial British armoured thrust, greatly magnified through the combination of surprise and fog, proved the key factor, not only for the immediate behaviour of the defending troops in the front line, but also for Ludendorff, far away at OHL.

Arras, 21 May 1940

Turning next to the Arras counterattack, it was noted in Chapter Five most previous accounts of the operation have relied on first order explanations for the British defeat. These largely focus on external factors, such as Rommel's ability to build a gun-line able to shatter the armour even of the heavy Matilda tanks, and the breakdown of communications within the British units, which meant that those tanks advanced without infantry support able to overcome the German artillery. Instead, the focus of the chapter here was on deeper issues emerging from the battle offering the potential to cast a wider light.

The British attack was, from the start, affected by a wide Knowledge Gap. Having issued his initial instructions, which envisaged little more than a mopping-up operation in the immediate vicinity of Arras, Gort then agreed the attack should be expanded into a decisive thrust southwards, designed the cut off the panzers and regain touch with the French forces to the south. Yet not only did Gort not inform Franklyn of this fundamental change of plan, Franklyn made only half-hearted attempts to obtain clarification, despite growing indications something had changed. In doing so, he may have felt restrained by FSR II (1935), which only allowed an officer to depart from his orders if there was no opportunity to consult with his commander. Whether intentionally or not, Gort and Franklyn therefore adopted a command approach equivalent to Restrictive Command. This Knowledge Gap led to friction: Franklyn issued orders inconsistent with the intent of his commander-in-chief.

The Knowledge Gap was made wider still when neither Franklyn nor Martel included in their orders information about the strong enemy force reported by British reconnaissance. Instead, they continued to refer only to the weak enemy forces known when Gort issued his original instructions a day and a half earlier. It is possible both officers were already uncertain regarding the purpose of the operation and were struggling with a sense the forces available to them were insufficient for the more expansive objectives being hinted at. Consciously accepting there was a contradiction between forces and objectives would have required them to accept that their orders

---

25   Clausewitz, *On War*, pp.230-231.
26   Marshal Ferdinand Foch, *The Principles of War*, trans. by Hilaire Belloc (New York, NY: Holt, 1920), p. 286

were no longer practical. Since implementing orders known to be inappropriate would stretch the loyalty even of officers brought up to rigid obedience, Franklyn and Martel may have found it easier instead to disregard the reconnaissance reports. In a situation of a conflict between orders and reality, a subordinate brought up within the Restrictive Control approach to command may find it simpler to adjust reality than to question his orders.

The level of friction experienced by the British was further increased as a result of a wide Alignment Gap. The task assigned to Martel's units was well outside that envisaged in the army's doctrine. Instead of the heavy "I" tanks working in close support of a dense infantry assault on a defended position, they were ordered to sweep a large area believed to contain only scattered enemy forces. Further, the units involved had no experience of working in combined infantry / tank columns. This was made worse by Martel's orders being ambiguous regarding the command arrangements for his two columns, and the rushed nature of the operation meant that the battalion commanders had minimal opportunity to sort this out between themselves prior to the start of the counterattack. Finally, Pratt's insistence the tanks maintain radio silence in the days before the battle meant communications across his brigade broke down almost immediately, rendering both himself and his battalion and company commanders virtually irrelevant and leaving his subalterns to fight as best they could, a further instance of the negative impact of a reliance on Restrictive Control.

Despite the significant level of friction experienced by the British attack, the surprise achieved by Martel's initiative, coupled with the Matildas being proof against the German 37mm PAK guns, led to the defenders suffering a severe psychological jolt, pushing them into shock and, in many cases, flight. This could have led to a disastrous collapse of the German position, an event avoided largely through Rommel's personal intervention. Demonstrating his usual mix of personal bravery and resolute decisiveness, he established a gun-line from his artillery, personally directing fire that brought the British tank advance to a halt. The absence of such Directive Control by a senior commander was apparent in the reaction of the SS Totenkopf Division, when it was engaged by the handful of tanks that managed to penetrate Rommel's gun-line. As had been the case with 7th Panzer Division, the SS men initially fled in panic, though perhaps not on the scale subsequently suggested. Their divisional commander, however, was notable by his absence. His reliance on strict obedience to orders, implying the application of Restrictive Control, meant, lacking such direction, his men had to revert to the instinctive aggression he had inculcated into the formation. The limits of this as an approach to combat were indicated by the division's heavy casualties.

It is clear forward command by senior German commanders, especially Rommel himself, was central to the ability of 7th Panzer Division to recover from its initial shock. The picture on the British side was rather more mixed. On the one hand, Martel, Churchill and Pope all went forward from their headquarters and spent the day roaming across the battlefield, moving from one unit to another. By contrast, Pratt decided to remain with his headquarters, despite the fact communication with his units broke down almost immediately, a situation made worse by the early deaths of both tank battalion commanders. Yet, whereas the German commanders went forward right to the front-line, exposing themselves to significant personal danger, none of the British commanders went beyond battalion headquarters. Their influence on the course of the battle may therefore be questioned.

As at Amiens, the British approach at Arras was characterised by reliance on control from above, even when senior commanders were aware their knowledge of the situation was very limited. Conversely, when Franklyn did give Martel his head, it was more a case of giving up, in the form of Umpiring, than of releasing him to apply his initiative. Although several senior officers did go forward, they did not venture especially close to the fighting troops. There was limited evidence of actions expressive of Directive Control. By contrast, the heavy reliance of the German commanders on Directive Control was everywhere apparent, forming the decisive factor in avoiding a setback becoming a disaster. Arras again underlined the importance of shock as a central factor in determining the level of friction experienced by troops, and the influence that reliance on Directive Control as a command approach could have on countering this.

But perhaps the most important facet of the battle was its psychological impact on Rundstedt personally. Even though the British counterattack was quickly defeated, he was convinced the French were about to follow the obvious course and launch a powerful thrust against the lengthy and exposed flanks of the deep penetration created by the panzers in their headlong rush to the sea. He may have been influenced by the longstanding tradition in the German Army that penetration of the enemy line merely offered the defenders the chance to surround the attackers, whereas encirclement from the flanks was the only sure route to success. The shock persuaded him the offensive was about to suffer a decisive counterstroke, a conviction with limited foundation, nonetheless Rundstedt clung onto the idea for several days, hiding in his headquarters and ignoring the clearer appreciation of his subordinates. Yet, as has been noted, shock is only a temporary phenomenon. The British and French did not take advantage of the German paralysis, so Rundstedt recovered his nerve: the German offensive restarted, the panzers rolled forward again, the forces encircled in Belgium were crushed. Although hundreds of thousands of men were evacuated from Dunkirk, thereby allowing the British to hope for a future victory, an opportunity to avoid the current defeat had perhaps been lost.

Arras demonstrated once again the correctness of Clausewitz's belief victory is achieved through putting the enemy's forces 'in such condition that they can no longer carry on the fight'.[27] Rather than such a result being a question primarily of physical destruction, 'the loss of morale has proved the major decisive factor.' When considering the course of the British counterattack at Arras from the German perspective, it was the psychological shock of the initial British armoured thrust, apparently proving

27   Clausewitz, *On War*, pp.230-231.

the high command's worst fears were about to be realised, that was decisive. As with Ludendorff at Amiens, it was not the troops on the ground that felt defeated, it was Rundstedt, scores of miles away in his headquarters at Charleville, who convinced himself he was defeated.

Beyond 1940

Williamson Murray argued the success of German arms in France was in large measure made possible by the analysis of lessons from the conquest of Poland the previous autumn, and their inculcation across the army through a major programme of training. He identified two critical features of the military system made this possible. First, OKH was open to the reality the army's operational performance had fallen short of expectations, even in a campaign that had obliterated Germany's most hated enemy in a matter of weeks. Second, the trust and confidence between levels of command was such units and formation did not hesitate to share the deficiencies the experience of combat had revealed.[28]

With regard to the factors highlighted in this book, concerning command, surprise, and shock, a number of key issues were highlighted through this learning process:[29]

- Commanders at all levels needed to exercise leadership from the front
- Subordinates should not be deprived of the scope to exercise their initiative, notwithstanding that attacks should be carefully prepared, with a lack of action considered a more serious fault than ignoring orders
- Attacks should seek to maintain their momentum, exploiting success, and not be allowed to bog down

These lessons were ingrained in the troops through focused, highly realistic training. The importance placed on realism was highlighted when most of the staff of the infantry school were redeployed, to be replaced by men who had gained combat experience in the recent campaigns and could therefore connect the army's doctrine with practice. The aim of training exercises was to test the men to breaking point, developing their offensive spirit and initiative, so they would not shatter when faced with the reality of combat.[30]

A similar process was undertaken following the victory against France. This may be illustrated through reference to recently released documents captured by the Soviet

---

28 Williamson Murray, 'The German Response to Victory in Poland: A Case Study in Professionalism', *Armed Forces and Society*, 7(2) (Winter 1981), 285-298 (pp.286-287 & 294-295).
29 Murray, 'German Response', pp.287-293.
30 Murray, 'German Response', pp.291-294.

armed forces later in the war.[31] Analysis was undertaken by OKH of the doctrine and practice of the defeated enemy. A report on the defensive principles employed by the British, for example, noted although these paralleled the German approach in many respects, there were important differences. These included an emphasis on holding positions to the last man without thought of retreat, less focus on the immediate counterattack than found in German manuals, and a tendency in practice to use tanks defensively and in penny packets, even though the doctrine promoted their employment in sudden massed counterattacks.[32] Arras, of course, was the sole occasion when the BEF managed to mass its armour, if 'mass' is the right word for just 74 heavy tanks.

The lessons drawn by OKH from the performance of German troops in the western campaign were set out in a series of reports, distributed down to division level. One of these,[33] opened with the assessment that the after action reports submitted by the operational formations had reaffirmed the validity of the key principles set out in the pre-war manuals. The lessons drawn from the practical experience gained during the campaign echoed those promulgated after Poland:

- 'Boldness in making decisions and in their execution, rapid, agile action, and concentration of forces to establish a clear *Schwerpunkt*, have once again proved themselves to be the basis of success. The achievement of surprise [...] also helped decisively.'
- 'Unhesitating penetration, without any reluctance to expose flanks, brought the enemy's front to collapse.'
- 'The personal influence in combat of commanders at all levels, especially in the exploitation of a success, often proved decisive. To this end, the commander must foresee in advance the point in the changing situation at which he can most effectively bring to bear his influence on the course of the engagement.'
- 'Clearly defined combat missions [...] give the subordinate the opportunity to act independently within the framework of the assigned task. Personal interventions in the conduct of subordinate units are only justified where the situation [...] makes them necessary.'
- 'In order to maintain the tempo of the attack, the infantry must above all put their own heavy weapons into full force. These, which should be trained for independent action, must ensure they are closely engaged, even without orders.'

---

31 Russisch-deutsches Projekt zur Digitalisierung deutcher Dokumente in den Archiven der Russischen Föderation http://www.germandocsinrussia.org/de/nodes/1-russisch-deutsches-projekt-zur-digitalisierung-deutscher-dokumente-in-den-archiven-der-russischen-foderation [accessed 16 April 2017], hereafter RdP.
32 RdP: Akte 115: OKH, Fremde Heere West, 4 September 1940, Die englischen Kampfgrundsätze in der Abwehr.
33 RdP: Akte 165: OKH, Ausbildung Abteilung (Ia), 20 November 1940, Taktische Erfahrungen im Westfeldzug.

- 'All commanders must know that where the attack is making progress, they must continue straight ahead until the cohesion of the enemy's front is torn apart. [...] Assaulting units that have broken through must not allow themselves be held up by concerns about their flanks.'

Central to these reports were two longstanding principles of the German way of warfare: commanders should place themselves far to the front, at the decisive point of the battlefield, and subordinates should be given the maximum scope for exercising their initiative, within the framework set by their superiors' overall intent.

The experience of the coming years was to demonstrate the limits of these principles. One of the documents subsequently captured by the Soviets was a list of general officer (*Generalmajor* and above) casualties suffered by the German Army during the war.[34] This recorded that, up to 1 April 1945, 416 generals were lost, of whom more than half were killed in action or died from wounds or other operational causes. The document reveals the escalating pace of the losses, as the fighting became increasingly desperate and the personal example of senior commanders ever more necessary. Just 14 generals were lost in the twenty-one months from the start of the war to the middle of 1941, but the rate leapt following the launch of Operation Barbarossa: 23 generals were lost during the second half of that year, and a further 48 in 1942 (an average rate of four a month). The turn of the strategic tide at that point in the war was expressed in a dramatic increase in the figures: 93 generals fell in 1943 (almost eight a month) and fully 188 during the following year (almost sixteen a month), a rate maintained in the 46 lost in the first three months of 1945.

The German doctrine may have called upon commanders at all levels, including those at divisional level and above, to place themselves close to the decisive point, but the inevitable consequence was many became casualties: a total of 110 divisional commanders, 23 corps commanders, and even three army commanders.[35] Few armies could withstand the loss of such a large number of commanders without significant reduction in their operational combat capacity. By contrast, the US Army (excluding the Army Air Corps) suffered fewer than a dozen generals killed in action during the Second World War,[36] while the British lost just five.[37]

---

34 RdP: Akte 47: OKW/Org. Abt. und Heerespersonalabt., 5 June 1945, Zusammenstellung der in diesem Kriege gefallenen, tötlich verunglückten, verstorbenen, vermissten und in Gefangenschaft geratenen Generale.

35 Major French L. MacLean, German General Officer Casualties in World War II – Harbinger for U.S. Army General Officer Casualties in Airland Battle? (unpublished master's thesis, US Army Command & General Staff College, Fort Leavenworth, KS, 1988), pp.4-6.

36 Jörg Muth, *Command Culture: Officer Education in the U.S. Army and the German Armed Forces, 1901-1940, and the Consequences for World War II* (Denton, TX: University of North Texas, 2011), p.100.

37 Richard Mead, *Churchill's Lions: A Biographical Guide to the Key British Generals of World War II* (London: Spellmount, 2007), p.31.

Parallel to this heavy price in blood, although *Truppenführung* remained the prime source of doctrine until the end of the war, Robert Citino suggested the culture of leadership it expressed in such clear language had been abandoned long before that point. He dated this pivotal change to December 1941, when the incredible encirclement victories achieved during the war of movement that characterised the first phase of Operation Barbarossa came to an end and the German forces had become bogged down in the unyielding Russian winter. Although the change in command approach is normally associated with Hitler's infamous *Haltbefehl*, demanding the German forces stand fast in the face of General Zhukov's counteroffensive, Citino argued it had a much more significant origin, within the army itself and as a response to the changing nature of warfare. In essence, the growth in the importance of airpower, and hence the need for close cooperation between ground and air forces, coupled with the increased importance of logistics in a theatre the size of Russia, meant that the actions of individual formations needed to be far more closely controlled and coordinated than before. There was therefore no longer scope within the more orchestrated campaign plans for the application of initiative. As Halder wrote in January 1942, 'The duty of soldierly obedience leaves no room for the sensibilities of lower headquarters. On the contrary it demands the best and most rapid execution of orders in the sense that the one issuing them intended.'[38]

Of course, the position was not quite as sudden and coherent as this. As demonstrated in Marco Sigg's recent magisterial study of Auftragstaktik, the practice of individual formations within the German Army varied, both before and after December 1941, with clear differences evident between elite, motorised, and line divisions.[39] His analysis revealed, even though the commanders of all three types of divisions outwardly continued to espouse the principles of Auftragstaktik well after the date identified by Citino as representing the pivotal shift in German thinking, their actions in practice were often contrary to those principles. Sigg suggested a key to this was the loss of professionalism of the officer corps as the war continued, due to the impossibility of replacing growing losses suffered during 1943.[40]

Nonetheless, in broad terms, and in the sense of the model of command approaches developed here, the Germans came to the conclusion Directive Command, supplemented by Directive Control at the decisive point, was unsuited to the context of massed technological warfare of the Eastern Front, whether due to its scale or to the loss of the subordinate commanders able to apply the doctrine in practice. Instead, they concluded it was necessary to switch to a more centralised approach, in theory Logistic Control, though often in practice sliding into Restrictive Control, yet still

---

38 Robert M. Citino, *The German Way of War: From the Thirty Years' War to the Third Reich* (Lawrence, KS: University of Kansas, 2005), pp.299-304.

39 Marco Sigg, *Der Unterführer als Feldherr in Taschenformat: Theorie und Praxis der Auftragstaktik im deutschen Heer, 1869 bis 1945* (Paderborn: Schöningh, 2014), pp.16-18.

40 Sigg, *Unterführer als Feldherr*, pp.459-464.

coupled with dramatic personal leadership from the front by commanders at all levels. Of course, if this assessment was wrong, then OKH might in fact have been adopting the command approach of the Enthusiastic Amateur, an approach shown in Chapter One to be, by definition, ineffective.

On the other side of the hill, the British also sought to learn the lessons from the debacle of May 1940. On Wednesday, 5 June, only the day after Dunkirk fell to the Germans, the BEF's commander, Lord Gort, wrote to Sir Edmond Ironside, Chief of the Imperial General Staff: 'I am sure that you will agree that we must, as quickly as possible, review the lessons learned from our recent fighting in order to make the best use of our experience'.[41] Ironside replied the following day: 'I agree that we must review the lessons learned in the recent fighting as quickly as possible. I think, however, that [... a]t the present juncture we obviously cannot make big changes in our organisation.'[42] In contrast to the detailed analysis of collated after action reports characterising the equivalent exercise in the German Army, however, Ironside felt the work needed to be done much more quickly. He proposed establishing a small committee of senior officers, which 'after about a week would be able to produce an exceedingly valuable report on which it should be possible to base some immediate action.'[43] His urgency was understandable, given the risk the Germans might launch an invasion of the British mainland in the very near future.

Work did indeed progress very quickly. On Sunday, 9 June, a letter was sent to General Sir William Bartholomew, GOC Northern Command, appointing him chair of the committee.[44] The file now in the National Archives does not indicate why he was selected, but one factor may have been he was one of the eight members of the famous Kirke Committee on the lessons of the First World War.[45] In a parallel to Ironside's comments regarding the need to avoid recommendations that might require substantive changes in organisation, it may be noted the published version of the Kirke report had omitted 'any matter which might engender in the regimental officer a lack of confidence in the equipment with which the Army is at present supplied.'[46]

Four other officers were quickly appointed to the committee: the Director of Military Training at the War Office, the commander of 2nd Division, and the senior staff officers of two of the BEF's corps.[47] The work progressed briskly: on Wednesday, 12

41   WO32/9581: Committee to Review the Lessons Learnt from the Recent Fighting in Flanders (Bartholomew Report 1940), 1A: Letter from Lord Gort to CIGS (5 June 1940).
42   WO32/9581: Bartholomew Report, 2A: Letter from CIGS to Lord Gort (6 June 1940).
43   WO32/9581: Bartholomew Report, 2A.
44   WO32/9581: Bartholomew Report, 5A: Letter from DMT to General Bartholomew (9 June 1940).
45   WO32/3116: Report of the Committee on the Lessons of the Great War (Kirke Report), 10A: (October 1932), p.3.
46   WO32/3116: Kirke Report, Minute 16 (12 January 1934).
47   French, Churchill's Army, p.189.

June, only a week after Gort's original letter, these five officers began taking evidence, beginning with Brigadier Oliver Leese, the BEF's Deputy Chief of the General Staff. Over five consecutive working days, the committee heard from thirty-seven officers.[48] They submitted their final report a fortnight later, on 2 July.[49]

The Bartholomew committee's report opened with the statement, 'It must be appreciated that the operations on which this report is based consisted almost entirely of a series of withdrawals'.[50] Given that the Arras counterattack was the only point in the whole campaign when the BEF had attempted a significant offensive action, and the sole occasion when more than a handful of tanks had been involved in a single operation, it might have been expected the operation would feature heavily in the body of the report. This was all the more so, given the officers who had given evidence included Major-Generals Howard Franklyn, Giffard Martel, and Vyvyan Pope, as well as Brigadier Douglas Pratt, effectively the entire senior command hierarchy for the battle. Yet, in fact, the report made not even passing mention of it. Indeed, there was no section on offensive operations at all. Perhaps the members of the committee were too focused on what was expected to be a passive defence against a German invasion. The minimal number of armoured vehicles available to the British after Dunkirk meant that there could be little thought of counterattacks.

The report went on to underline the difficulties of the campaign, notably the need to keep withdrawing in order to maintain touch with allies on the flanks, the larger number of German armoured formations than had been expected, and the psychological effect of dive-bombing. Perhaps surprisingly, it nonetheless drew the conclusion, 'our organization as planned [...] and our tactical conceptions have on the whole stood the test.'[51]

Since the basics of the army's approach were considered sturdy, the major lessons drawn were rather more specific:[52]

- 'The inculcation of a fiercer, aggressive spirit' into the troops,
- 'Rigid discipline',
- Improved cooperation between the army and the RAF in order to achieve air superiority, and
- An increase in the number of tanks and anti-tank guns as a counter to the scale of German armoured vehicles.

Lessons concerning command and control filled just one and a half pages of the twenty pages of the report.[53] Almost half of this section was focused on communications,

---

48   WO32/9581: Bartholomew Report, 22A: Programme, p.1.
49   French, *Churchill's Army*, p.189.
50   WO32/9581: Bartholomew Report, 22A: Part 1, General, p.2.
51   WO32/9581: Bartholomew Report, 22A: Part 1, General, p.2.
52   WO32/9581: Bartholomew Report, 22A: Part 1, General, p.3.
53   WO32/9581: Bartholomew Report, 22A: Part 2, Lessons, pp.12-14

including the use of radios, codes, and light signals. In terms of the exercise of command, four main points were made:

- The BEF had too often slipped into the use of ad hoc formations, which lacked the capacity for control or administration,
- Headquarters had become too large,
- Orders were often issued verbally, without being confirmed to commanders unable to be present, and
- Commanders were insufficiently mobile.

The solutions, however, were hardly revolutionary:

- The need for ad hoc formations should be avoided by the adoption of all-arms brigade groups within the division, capable of independent operations,[54]
- Large headquarters should be split into forward and rear elements,
- Verbal orders should be confirmed to those commanders not present, and
- Units should be issued with more carriers, scout cars and motorcycles with pillions, so that commanders were less reliant on staff cars.

The pace of seeking to draw lessons from the recent campaign, which might bolster the defence against the imminent German seaborne invasion of England, was maintained after Bartholomew's committee submitted their report. On that very day, their conclusions formed the core of *Army Training Memorandum No.33*,[55] issued to every officer across the entire army.[56]

Analysing the British Army's reaction to May 1940, Timothy Harrison Place and David French drew similar conclusions: senior commanders returned from Dunkirk convinced their basic approach was correct, and defeat had been due to the failings of the troops, the weakness of the Belgians and French, and the overwhelming numerical and technological superiority of the Germans. They retained the mindset victory would be won through 'thorough planning and preparation'. This was one factor that led to a preference for tactics based on artillery timetables and set-piece assaults. As Harrison Place summarised it:

> In the conduct of training and operations in the British Army, preparing for the expected [...] took priority over expecting the unexpected. What could not be made comprehensible on a planning desk remained uncomprehended. What could not be tidily put across on the printed page of a training manual remained

---

54 WO32/9581: Bartholomew Report, 22A: Part 2, Lessons, pp.4-5.
55 Timothy Harrison Place, *Military Training in the British Army, 1940–1944: From Dunkirk to D-Day* (London: Cass, 2000), p.10.
56 *Army Training Memorandum No.33 (War), June, 1940* (2 July 1940), p.1.

beyond the scope of practical training. Neat system smothered all that was chaotic and unpredictable [...].[57]

French noted the Bartholomew committee explicitly rejected the suggestion its report should match the organisational flexibility of its proposed brigade group structure with a parallel decentralisation of command. In part, this appears to have been due to a fear, if senior commanders allowed their subordinates to exercise their initiative and this led to mistakes, it would be the superior who would take the blame.[58] The contrast is stark with the trust and confidence between superiors and subordinates in the German Army at the time, allowing commanders to submit reports that were highly critical of the performance of their own formations.

Instead of allowing subordinates to exercise their initiative, the British became convinced they could achieve a faster tempo of operations than could the Germans if they simply adopted more efficient staff practices, and switched from a reliance on written orders to giving verbal instructions.[59] Through greater use of radio, commanders were able to retain far closer control over their subordinates. Yet, although this certainly enabled orders to be issued far more quickly, it may also have served to restrict the initiative of their subordinates even more strongly,[60] developing a propensity to 'hesitate to proceed without instructions. If the radio networks breakdown [they tended to] feel lost.'[61]

One expression of this retention of close control may be found in the 1941 edition of *Military Training Pamphlet No.23: Operations, Part III - Appreciations, Orders, Intercommunication and Movements*. This little booklet, which in practice replaced the relevant section of *Field Service Regulations: Part II – Operations* (1935), once again included the text that had been a part of British military doctrine since 1909:

> 3(5) Notwithstanding the greatest skill and care in framing orders, unexpected circumstances may render the precise execution of an order unsuitable or impracticable. In such circumstances the following principles will guide the recipient of an order in deciding his course of action.
>
> i.   A formal order will never be departed from either in letter or spirit so long as the officer who issued it is present, or there is time to report to him and await a reply without losing an opportunity or endangering the force concerned.
>
> ii. If the above conditions cannot be fulfilled, a departure from either the spirit or the letter of an order is justified if the subordinate who assumes the

57 Harrison Place, *Military Training*, p.174.
58 French, *Churchill's Army*, pp.192-193.
59 French, *Churchill's Army*, p.198.
60 French, *Churchill's Army*, pp.282-283.
61 Brigadier David Belchem, quoted in French, *Churchill's Army*, p.283.

responsibility bases his decision on some fact which could not be known Jbo the officer who issued the order, and if he is satisfied that he is acting as his superior would order him to act were he present.

iii. If a subordinate neglects to depart from the letter of his orders when such departure, in the circumstances of sub-para. ii, above, is clearly demanded, he will be held responsible for any failure that may ensue.

iv. Should a subordinate find it necessary to depart from an order, he will immediately inform the issuer of it, and the commanders of any neighbouring units likely to be affected.

The copy in the National Archives is stamped with the words CANCELLED and the date: 1945.[62]

---

62 WO231/167: Military Training Pamphlet No.23: Operations, Part III - Appreciations, Orders, Intercommunication and Movements (17 September 1941).

Bibliography

Archives

David Irving's Private Research Collection <www.britishonlinearchives.co.uk>

Beurteilungen, 1929-1938, in Selected Documents on the Life and Campaigns of Field-Marshal Erwin Rommel, Rommel's Career as Recorded in His Personnel File and His Words, imgs.112-135.

Gefechts-Bericht über die Zeit vom 04.-31.10.1917 (1 November 1917), in Items Chronicling Rommel's Career, 1917-1941, imgs.257-267.

Kluge to Rommel, 30 November 1940, in Items Chronicling Rommel's Military Career, 1917-1941, img.112.

Kurt Hesse, Wandlung eines Mannes und eines Typus (1945), in Documents Discussing Rommel Mostly by Those Close to Him, img.320

Kurzer Gefechtsbericht der 7.Pz.Div. für die Zeit v.10.-29.5.40, in Rommel's Career, imgs.142-143

Letter from von Kluge to Rommel, 30 November 1940, in Selected Documents on the Life and Campaigns of Field-Marshal Erwin Rommel, Rommel 1917-1941, imgs.109-112

Imperial War Museum, London

92nd Field Regiment, RA, War Diary, 21 May 1940

Enemy Documents Section: AL596, 7th Panzer Division, Kriegstagebuch, 21 May 1940

Enemy Documents Section: War Diary, Army Group A, 25 May 1940

Private Papers of Lieutenant-General Sir Giffard le Quesnel Martel

Libraries and Archives of Canada, www.collectionscanada.gc.ca

RG9/III-D-3/4840/T-1923: War Diaries – 1st Canadian Division - Administrative Branches of the Staff

RG9/III-D-3/4861/T-1939: 4th Canadian Division, Narrative of Operations, Battle of Amiens

RG9/III-D-3/4878/T-10676: War Diaries – 3rd Canadian Infantry Brigade, August 1918

RG9/III-D-3/4883/T-10680: 4th Canadian Infantry Brigade, August 1918, War Diary and Appendix 10

RG9/III-D-3/5072/T-11350: War Diary, 1st and 3rd Cavalry Divisions, 8 August 1918.

National Archives, Kew, London

CAB44/67: The BEF in France and Flanders, Part II, (a) and (b)

WO32/3116: Report of the Committee on the Lessons of the Great War (Kirke Report)

WO32/9581: Committee to Review the Lessons Learnt from the Recent Fighting in Flanders (Bartholomew Report 1940)

WO95/106: 3rd Battalion, Tank Corps, May 1917 to March 1919

WO95/109: War History of the 1st Tank Battalion, 1916-1919.

WO95/110: 4th Battalion, Tank Corps (August 1916 to September 1919)

WO95/116: 17th Battalion, Tank Corps, April to December 1918

WO95/437: War Diary, General Staff, Fourth Army: 1st to 31st August 1918.

WO95/575: Cavalry Corps, 24th March 1916 to 8th October 1918

WO95/1053: Canadian Corps Headquarters

WO95/1109: War Diaries 1st Cavalry Division, 1st Cavalry Brigade

WO95/2372: 32nd Division, War Diary, August 1918

WO95/2397: War diaries of 2/Manchester, 15/Lancashire Fusiliers and 16/Lancashire Fusiliers

WO167/244: G Branch, 5th Division, January – June 1940

WO167/300: 50th Division War Diary, May 1940

WO167/300: GS Branch, 50th Division, February – May 1940

WO167/404: 151st Infantry Brigade War Diary

WO167/414: 1st Army Tank Brigade, April to June 1940

WO167/452: 12th Lancers, 21 May 1940

WO167/459: War Diary, 4th Royal Tank Regiment, May 1940

WO167/460: War Diary, 7th Royal Tank Regiment, May 1940

WO167/729: 6th Durham Light Infantry, January to June 1940

WO167/730: 8th Durham Light Infantry, January to June 1940

WO167/800: 4th Royal Northumberland Fusiliers, January to June 1940

WO231/167: Military Training Pamphlet No.23: Operations, Part III - Appreciations, Orders, Intercommunication and Movements (17 September 1941).

Russisch-deutsches Projekt zur Digitalisierung deutcher Dokumente in den Archiven der Russischen Föderation, <*http://www.germandocsinrussia.org/de/nodes/1-russisch-deutsches-projekt-zur-digitalisierung-deutscher-dokumente-in-den-archiven-der-russischen-föderation*>

Akte 47: OKW/Org. Abt. und Heerespersonalabt., 5 June 1945, Zusammenstellung der in diesem Kriege gefallenen, tötlich verunglückten, verstorbenen, vermissten und in Gefangenschaft geratenen Generale.
Akte 115: OKH, Fremde Heere West, 4 September 1940, Die englischen Kampfgrundsätze in der Abwehr.
Akte 165: OKH, Ausbildung Abteilung (Ia), 20 November 1940, Taktische Erfahrungen im Westfeldzug.

Tactical Doctrine Retrieval Cell, Staff College, Camberley (former)

TDRC-7030A: Brian Bond, Arras 21 May 1940: A Case Study in the Counteroffensive (1984)
TDRC-7148: HQ 20 Armoured Brigade, 4 Armoured Division Study Period, Arras – 21 May 40 (1985)
TDRC-7778B: Battlefield Guide, Arras, 21 May 1940 (1986)
TDRC-8666: Captain R.J. Edmondson-Jones, Arras and the Modern Counter-Stroke (1988)

Primary Sources

Altrichter. Major Friedrich, *Die seelischen Kräfte des Deutschen Heeres im Frieden und im Weltkriege* (Berlin: Mittler, 1933)
Anonymous, 'The Mobilization of the Army, and National Defence', *Blackwood's Edinburgh Magazine*, 120 (July to December 1876), 509-520 (p. 511).

Balck, Lieutenant General William, *Development of Tactics – World War*, trans. by Harry Bell (Fort Leavenworth, KS: General Service Schools, 1922)
Bateman, Lieutenant-Colonel B.M., *Trench's Manoeuvre Orders 1914*, 12th rev. ed. (London: Clowes, 1916)
Boraston, Lieutenant-Colonel J. H., ed., *Sir Douglas Haig's Despatches (December 1915 – April 1919)*, (London: Dent, 1919)

Clausewitz, Carl von, *On War*, ed. and trans. by Michael Howard and Peter Paret (Princeton, NJ: Princeton University Press, 1976), pp. 120-121.

Cochenhausen, Oberstleutnant [Friedrich] von, *Die Truppenführung: Ein Handbuch für den Truppenführer und seine Gehilfen*, 3rd ed. (Berlin: Mittler, 1926)

Cron, Hermann, *Imperial German Army 1914-18: Organisation, Structure, Orders-of-Battle*, trans. by C.F. Colton (Solihull: Helion, 2001)

Currie, Lieutenant-General Sir Arthur W., *Canadian Corps Operations During the Year 1918* (Ottawa: Department of Militia and Defence, 1919)

Doumenc, General Joseph Edouard Aimé, *Histoire de la Neuvième Armee* (Paris: Arthaud, 1945)

Ellison, Gerald F., 'Lord Roberts and the General Staff', *The Nineteenth Century* (December 1932), 722-732

Eon, General Joseph Marie, *The Battle of Flanders: Sedan - The Operations, and the Lessons to be Learned from Them* (London: Hachette, 1943)

Foch, Marshal Ferdinand, *The Principles of War*, trans. by Hilaire Belloc (New York, NY: Holt, 1920)

Franklyn, General Sir Harold E., *The Story of One Green Howard in the Dunkirk Campaign* (Richmond: Green Howards' Gazette, 1966)

Frederick Charles, Prince of Prussia, 'The Origins and Development of the Spirit of the Prussian Officer, its Manifestations and its Effect' (1860), reprinted in K. Demeter, *The German Officer Corps in State and Society: 1650-1945* (London: Weidenfeld & Nicolson, 1965), pp. 257-266

Frederick Winslow Taylor, *The Principles of Scientific Management* (New York, NY: Harper, 1911)

Fuller, Brevet-Colonel J.F.C., *Tanks in the Great War, 1914-1918* (New York, NY: Dutton, 1920)

Fuller, Colonel John F.C., *The Reformation of War* (London: Hutchinson, 1923)

Fuller, Major-General J.F.C., *Lectures on F.S.R. II* (London: Praed, 1931)

Fuller, Major-General J.F.C., *Memoirs of an Unconventional Soldier* (London: Nicholson & Watson, 1936)

Gall, Captain Herbert Reay, *Questions and Answers on Field Service Regulations: Part I (Operations) 1909* (London: Rees, 1910)

Generals Balck and Von Mellenthin on Tactics: Implications for NATO Military Doctrine, edited by General William DePuy (McLean, VA: BDM, 1980)

Großen Generalstab, Abteilung für Kriegsgeschichte I, ed., *Moltkes Militärische Werke: II, Die Thätigkeit als Chef des Generalstabes der Armee im Frieden, 2. Moltkes Taktisch-Strategische Aufsätze aus den Jahren 1857 bis 1871* (Berlin: Mittler, 1900)

Großen Generalstab, Abteilung für Kriegsgeschichte I, ed., *Moltkes Militärische Werke: IV, Kriegslehren, 2. Die taktischen Vorbereitungen zur Schlacht* (Berlin: Mittler, 1911)

Großen Generalstab, Abteilung für Kriegsgeschichte I, ed., *Moltkes Militärische Werke: IV. Kriegslehren, 3. Die Schlacht*, (Berlin: Mittler, 1912)

Guderian, General Heinz, *Panzer Leader*, trans. by Constantine Fitzgibbon (1952, reprinted London: Futura, 1974)

Guderian, Generaloberst Heinz, *Die Panzertruppen und ihre Zusammenwirken mit den anderen Waffen*, 3rd ed. (Berlin: Mittler, 1940)

Guderian, Heinz, *Achtung-Panzer! The Development of Tank Warfare*, trans. by Christopher Duffy (London: Cassell, 1992)

Henderson, Colonel G. F. R., *The Science of War: A Collection of Essays and Lectures, 1891-1903*, ed. by Captain Neill Malcolm (London: Longmans Green, 1912)

Henderson, Colonel G. F. R., 'War', reprinted in Henderson, *Science of War*, pp. 1-38

Henderson, Colonel G. F. R., 'Military Criticism and Modern Tactics', *United Services Magazine* (1891), reprinted in Henderson, *Science of War*, pp. 108-164

Henderson, Lieutenant-Colonel G.F.R., *Stonewall Jackson and the American Civil War* (London: Longmans Green, 1898)

Henderson, 'The Training of Infantry for the Attack', *United Services Magazine* (1899), reprinted in Henderson, *Science of War*, pp. 338-64

Hindenburg, Marshal Paul von, *Out of My Life*, trans. by F.A. Holt (London: Cassell, 1920)

Hüttmann, Oberstleutnant, *Die Kampfweise der Infanterie auf Grund der neuen Ausbildungsvorschrift für die Infanterie vom 26.10.1922* (Berlin: Mittler, 1924)

Kett, Henry, *The Flowers of Wit* (Hartford: Cooke, 1825)

Lossberg, General der Infanterie Fritz von, *Meine Tätigkeit im Weltkriege 1914-1918* (Berlin: Mittler, 1939)

Luck, Hans von, *Panzer Commander: The Memoirs of Colonel Hans von Luck* (London: Cassell, 2002)

Ludendorff, General Erich, *Ludendorff's Own Story, August 1914-November 1918; the Great War from the siege of Liège to the signing of the armistice as viewed from the grand headquarters of the German Army*, 2 vols. (New York, NY: Harper, 1919)

Ludendorff, General Erich, *My War Memories 1914-1918* (London: Hutchinson, 1920), vol.2

Ludendorff, General Erich, *Urkunden der Obersten Heeresleitunq über ihre Tätigkeit, 1916-18* (Berlin: Mittler, 1920)

Martel, Lieutenant-General Sir Giffard Le Quesnel, *An Outspoken Soldier: His Views and Memoirs* (London: Praed, 1949)

Martel, Lieutenant-General Sir Giffard Le Quesnel, *Our Armoured Forces* (London: Faber & Faber, 1945)

Marwitz, General von der, *Weltkriegsbriefe*, ed. by General der Infanterie a.D. von Tschischwitz (Berlin: Reimar Hobbing, 1940)

Monash, Lieutenant-General Sir John, *The Australian Victories in France in 1918* (London: Hutchinson, 1920)

Montgomery, Major-General Sir Archibald, *The Story of the Fourth Army in the Battles of the Hundred Days, August 8th to November 11th, 1918* (London: Hodder and Stoughton, 1920)

Moser, General Otto von, *Feldzugsaufzeichnungen als Brigade-, Divisionskommandeur und als kommandierender General, 1914-1918* (Stuttgart: Belsersche, 1920)

Niemann, Oberstleutnant a.D. Alfred, *Kaiser und Revolution: Die entscheidenden Ereignisse im Grossen Hauptquartier* (Berlin: Scherl, 1922)

Rohrbeck, Major, *Tactics: A Handbook Based on Lessons of the World War*, trans. by US General Service School (Fort Leavenworth, KS: General Service School, 1921)

Rommel, Field Marshal Erwin, *The Rommel Papers*, ed. by Basil H. Liddell Hart, trans. by Paul Findlay (London: Collins, 1953)

Rommel, General Field Marshal Erwin, *Infantry Attacks* (Barton-under-Needwood: Wren's Park, 2002)

Rommel, Generalfeldmarschall Erwin, *Aufgaben für Zug und Kompanie (Gefechtsaufgaben, Gefechtsschiessen, Geländebesprechung), Ihre Anlange und Leitung*, 5th edn (Berlin: Mittler, 1944)

Rupprecht von Bayern, Kronprinz, *Mein Kriegstagebuch* (Munich: Deutscher National, 1929), vol.3

Schittenhelm, Helmut, *Wir zogen nach Friaul: Erlebnisse einer Kriegskameradschaft zwischen Isonzo und Piave* (Stuttgart: Thienemanns, 1939)

Scott, Douglas, ed., *Douglas Haig: The Preparatory Prologue, 1861-1914. Diaries and Letters*, (Barnsley: Pen & Sword, 2006)

Sun Tzu, *The Art of War*, ed. by James Clavell (London: Hodder & Stoughton, 1981)

Treaty of Peace with Germany, International Conciliation, 142 (New York, NY: American Association for International Conciliation, September 1919)

Wavell, General Sir Archibald, *Generals and Generalship: The Lees Knowles Lectures Delivered at Trinity College, Cambridge in 1939* (Harmondsworth: Penguin, 1941)

Westphal, General Siegfried, *The German Army in the West* (London: Cassell, 1951)

Official Publications

British Empire

*Army Doctrine Publication: Army Doctrine Primer (*Army Code *71954)* (May 2011)
Army Doctrine Publication: Operations (Army Code 71632) (2010)
Army Training Memorandum No.33 (War), June 1940 (2 July 1940)
Army Training Memorandum No.36 (War) (September 1940)

Bean, Charles Edwin Woodrow, *Official History of Australia in the War of 1914-1918: vol. VI: The Australian Imperial Force in France During the Allied Offensive, 1918* (Sydney: Angus and Robertson, 1942)

Combined Training (Provisional) (London: HMSO, 1902)

Design for Military Operations: The British Military Doctrine (Army Code 71451) (London: HMSO, 1989).
Design for Military Operations – The British Military Doctrine (Army Code 71451 (1996)

Edmonds, Brigadier-General James E., *The Official History of the Great War: Military Operations: France & Belgium, 1915, vol. 2: Battles of Aubers Ridge, Festubert, and Loos* (London: Macmillan, 1928)
Edmonds, Brigadier-General Sir James E., *The Official History of the Great War: Military Operations: France & Belgium, 1916*, vol. 1 (1932, repr. Woking: Shearer, 1986)
Edmonds, Brigadier-General Sir James E., *The Official History of the Great War: Military Operations: France & Belgium, 1918, vol. 3: May-July – The German Diversion Offensives and the First Allied Counter-Offensive* (London: HMSO, 1939)
Edmonds, Brigadier-General James E., *The Official History of the Great War: Military Operations: France & Belgium, 1918, vol.4: 8 August to 26 September - The Franco-British Offensive* (London: HMSO, 1947)
Ellis, Major L.F., *History of the Second World War: United Kingdom Military Series: The War in France and Flanders* (1953, reprinted Uckfield: Naval & Military, 2004)

Field Service Regulations: Part I – Combined Training (London: HMSO, 1905)
Field Service Regulations: Part I - Operations (London: HMSO, 1909)
Field Service Regulations: Part II - Organization and Administration (London: HMSO, 1909)
Field Service Regulations: Vol. II - Operations (Provisional) (London: HMSO, 1920)
Field Service Regulations: Vol. I - Organization and Administration (Provisional) (London: HMSO, 1923)

Field Service Regulations: Vol. II - Operations (London: HMSO, 1924)
Field Service Regulations: Vol.II - Operations (London: HMSO, 1929)
Field Service Regulations: Vol. I - Operations (London: HMSO, 1930)
Field Service Regulations: Vol.II - Operations – General (London: HMSO, 1935)
Field Service Regulations: Vol.III - Operations – Higher Formations (London: HMSO, 1935)

German Military Training: A Study of German Military Training. Produced at GMDS by a combined British, Canadian and US Staff (May 1946)

Hinsley, F.H., with E.E. Thomas, C.F.G. Ransom and R.C. Knight, *British Intelligence in the Second World War: Its Influence on Strategy and Operations*, vol.1 (London: HMSO, 1979)
Historical Section (Military Branch) CID, 'A German Account of the British Offensive of August, 1918', *Army Quarterly*, 6 (April 1923), 11-16

Infantry Drill (London: HMSO, 1889)
Infantry Drill (London: HMSO, 1896)
Infantry Training (Provisional) (London: War Office, 1902)

Jones, H.A., *The War in the Air: Being the Story of the Part Played by the Royal Air Force*, vol.VI (Oxford: Clarendon, 1937)

Military Training Pamphlet No.8: Notes on the Tactical Handling of Army Tank Battalions (August 1938)
Military Training Pamphlet No.22: Tactical Handling of Army Tank Battalions, Part III: Employment (September 1939)
Military Training Pamphlet No.23: Operations, Part III. Appreciations, Orders, Intercommunication and Movement (October 1939)

Nicholson, Colonel G.W.L., *Official History of the Canadian Army in the First World War: Canadian Expeditionary Force, 1914-1919* (Ottawa: Duhamel, 1962)

Report of a Conference of General Staff Officers at the Staff College, 9th to 12th January 1911, Held Under the Direction of the Chief of the Imperial General Staff
Report of a Conference of General Staff Officers at the Royal Military College, 13th to 16th January 1913, Held Under the Orders and Direction of the Chief of the Imperial General Staff (Camberley, 1913)

SS 109: Training of Divisions for Offensive Action (May 1916)
SS 135: Instructions for the Training of Divisions for Offensive Action (December 1916)
SS 135: The Training and Employment of Divisions (January 1918)
SS 135: The Division in Attack (November 1918)

Statistics of the British Military Effort During the Great War, 1914-1920 (London: HMSO, 1922)

Training and Manoeuvre Regulations (London: HMSO, 1913)

Wise, S.F, *Canadian Airmen and the First World War: The Official History of the Royal Canadian Air Force*, vol.1 (Toronto: University of Toronto, 1980)

German

(Includes translations of official German publications)

Ausbildungsvorschrift für die Fußtruppen im Kriege (n.p.: Reichsdruckerei, January 1917)
Ausbildungsvorschrift für die Fußtruppen im Kriege, 2nd ed. (n.p.: Reichsdruckerei, January 1918)

Bemerkungen des Chefs der Heeresleitung, Generaloberst von Seeckt, bei Besichtigungen und Manövern aus den Jahren 1920 bis 1926 (Berlin: 1927).
Bose, Major Thilo von, *Die Katastrophe des 8.August 1918* (Schlachten des Weltkrieges, vol. 36) (Berlin: Stalling, 1930)

Command and Combat Use of Combined Arms (German Field Service Regulations), September 1, 1921, trans. by Captain P.B. Harm (np: Army War College, 1925)

Dellmensingen, General der Artillerie Konrad Krafft von, *Der Durchbruch am Isonzo, Teil 1: Die Schlact von Tolmein und Flitsch (24. bis 27. Oktober 1917)* (Berlin: Stalling, 1926)
Dellmensingen, General der Artillerie Konrad Krafft von, *Der Durchbruch am Isonzo, Teil 2: Die Verfolgung* über *den Tagliamento bis zum Piave* (Berlin: Stalling, 1926)
Der Angriff im Stellungskriege, (1918)
Die Abwehr im Stellungskrieg, 4th edn (20 September 1918), in Erich Ludendorff, *Urkunden der Obersten Heeresleitung* über *ihre Tätigkeit 1916/18* (Berlin: Mittler, 1920) pp.604-640
DVE 53: Grundzüge der höheren Truppenführung vom 1. Januar 1910 (Berlin: Reichsdruckerei, 1910)
DVE 130: Exerzier Reglement für die Infanterie vom 29. Mai 1906 (Neuabdruck) (Berlin: Mittler, 1909).
DVE 267: Felddienst-Ordnung (Berlin: Mittler, 1908)
DVE 438: Felddienst-Ordnung (Berlin: Mittler, 1894)

Einführung und Stichwortverzeichnis zu Abschnitt I-XVII von Führung und Gefecht der verbunden Waffen (F.u.G.) (Berlin: Mittler, 1924)

Exerzir Reglement für die Infanterie (Berlin: Mittler, 1888)

Felddienst-Ordnung (Berlin: Mittler, 1887)
Felddienst-Ordnung (Berlin: Mittler, 1900)
Field Service Regulations (Felddienst Ordnung, 1908) of the German Army, trans. by
    General Staff, War Office (London: HMSO, 1908)

Grundsätze für die Abwehr im Stellungskriege (March 1917)
Grundsätze für die Abwehr im Stellungskriege (September 1918)

*HDv 130/2b: Ausbildungsvorschrift für die Infanterie, Heft 2: Die Schützenkompagnie,
    Teil b: Der Schützenzug und die Schützenkompagnie* (Berlin: Offene Worte, 1936)
*HDv 130/9, Ausbildungsvorschrift für die Infanterie, Heft 9: Führung und Kampf der
    Infanterie. Das Infanterie-Bataillon* (Berlin: Offene Worte, 1940)
HDv 130: Ausbildungsvorschrift für die Infanterie (Berlin: Reichsdruckerei, 1922)
HDv 130: Ausbildungsvorschrift für die Infanterie: Heft V, unaltered reprint (Berlin:
    Reichsdruckerei, 1934)
HDv 300/1: Truppenführung (Berlin: Mittler, 1933)
HDv 487/1: Führung und Gefecht der verbundenen Waffen (Berlin, 1921).

Kriegsgeschichtlichen Forschungsanstalt des Heeres, *Der Weltkrig, 1914 bis 1918,
    Band 13: Die Kriegführung im Sommer und Herbst 1917, Die Ereignisse außerhalb
    der Westfront bis November 1918* (Berlin: Mittler, 1942)

Neues aus der Felddienstordnung (Oldenburg: Stalling, 1900)

Oberkommando des Heeres, *Der Weltkrieg, 1914 bis 1918: Die militärischen Operationen
    zu Lande*, vol.14 (Berlin: Mittler, 1944)
On the German Art of War: Truppenführung, ed. by Bruce Condell and David T.
    Zabecki (London: Rienner, 2001)

Regulations for Manoeuvres (Manöver-Ordnung, 1908) German Army, trans. by General
    Staff, War Office (London: HMSO, 1908)

*SS 561: Manual of Position Warfare for All Arms: Part 8: The Principles of Command in the
    Defensive Battle in Position Warfare* (1 March 1917, trans. May 1917)

The Field Service Regulations (Feld Dienst Ordnung, 1900) of the German Army, trans. by
    Colonel H. S. Brownrigg (London: HMSO, 1900)
The New German Field Exercise, trans. by G.J.R. Glünicke (Bedford: Hockliffe, 1888)
The Order of Field Service of the German Army, trans. by Major J. M. Gawne and Spenser
    Wilkinson (London: Stanford, 1893)

Verordnungen über die Ausbildung der Truppen für den Felddienst und über die größeren Truppenübungen (Berlin: Königlichen Geheimen Ober-Hofbuchdruckerei, 17 June 1870)

Was bringen Felddienst-Ordnung und Manöver-Ordnung vom 22. März 1908 Neues? (Berlin: Mittler, 1908)

United States

Headquarters, Department of the Army, *FM 100-5: Operations* (5 May 1986)

Infantry in Battle, 2nd ed. (Washington, DC: Infantry Journal, 1939)

US Army, Special Bulletin No.11: British Tank Operations in the Vicinity of Arras, May 19-23, 1940 (22 August 1940) <http://cgsc.contentdm.oclc.org/cdm/singleitem/collection/p4013coll8/id/2739/rec/17> (Accessed 23 December 2016)
US Foreign Military Studies, C:053: Campaign in the West (1950)

War Department, *Field Service Regulations: FM 100-5: Operations* (22 May 1941)
War Department, *Field Service Regulations: FM 100-5: Operations* (15 June 1944)

Unit Histories

Anonymous, *Das k.B. 23. Feldartillerie-Regiment*, Erinnerungsblätter deutscher Regimenter, Bayerische Armee, vol. 23 (Munich: Bayerisches Kriegsarchiv, 1923)

Barclay, Brigadier C.N., *The History of the Royal Northumberland Fusiliers in the Second World War* (London: Clowes, 1952)
Braun, Major Heinrich, *Das k.B. 25. Infanterie-Regiment*, Erinnerungsblätter deutscher Regimenter, Bayerische Armee, vol. 44 (Munich: Bayerisches Kriegsarchiv, 1926)

Clay, Major Ewart W., *The Path of the 50th: The Story of the 50th (Northumbrian) Division in the Second World War, 1939-1945* (Aldershot: Gale & Ploden, 1950)

Gottberg, Generalmajor Döring von, *Das Grenadier-Regiment König Friedrich Wilhelm IV (1.Pommersches) Nr.2 im Weltkriege*, Erinnerungsblätter deutscher Regimenter, vol.256 (Berlin: Kolk, 1928)
Göz, Major August, *Das k.B.8.Infanterie-Regiment Grossherzog Friedrich II von Baden*, Erinnerungsblätter deutscher Regimenter, Bayerische Armee, vol.43 (Munich: Bayerisches Kriegsarchiv, 1926)

Groos, Generalmajor Carl and Hauptmann Werner von Rudloff, *Infanterie-Regiment Herwarth von Bittenfeld (1.Westfälisches) Nr.13 im Weltkriege 1914-1918*, Erinnerungsblätter deutscher Regimenter, vol.222 (Berlin: Stalling, 1927)

Hase, Major Dr Armin, *Das 17. Königliches Sächsisches Infanterie-Regiment Nr.183*, Erinnerungsblätter deutscher Regimenter, Sächsische Armee, vol.5 (Dresden: Baensch, 1922)

Heidrich, Fritz, *Geschichte des 3. Ostpreußischen Feldartillerie-Regiments Nr. 79*, Erinnerungsblätter deutscher Regimenter, Artillerie vol. 2 (Berlin: Stalling, 1921)

Hofmiller, Hauptmann Hubert, *Das k.B.4.Infanterie-Regiment "König Wilhelm von Württemberg" im Weltkriege 1914-1918* (Munich: n.p., 1921)

Holroyd, Jack, *Images of War: SS-Totenkopf France 1940: Rare Photographs from Wartime Archives* (Barnsley: Pen & Sword, 2012)

Lewis, Major P.J., *8th Battalion, The Durham Light Infantry, 1939-1945* (Newcastle upon Tyne: Bealls, 1949)

Liddell Hart, Captain B.H., *The Tanks: The History of the Royal Tank Regiment and its predecessors, Heavy Branch Machine-Gun Corps, Tank Corps and Royal Tank Corps, 1914-1945*, vol.1 (London: Cassell, 1959)

Liddell Hart, Captain B.H., *The Tanks: The History of the Royal Tank Regiment and its Predecessors, Heavy Branch Machine-Gun Corps, Tank Corps & Royal Tank Corps, 1914-1945*, vol.2 (1939-1945) (London: Cassell, 1959)

Mann, Chris, *SS-Totenkopf: The History of the 'Death's Head' Division 1940-45* (Staplehurst: Spellmount, 2001)

Meyer, Oberleutnant Werner, *Das Infenterie-Regiment von Grolman (1.Posensches) Nr.18 im Weltkriege*, Erinnerungsblätter deutscher Regimenter, vol.285 (Berlin: Stalling, 1929)

Moses, Harry, *The Faithful Sixth* (Durham: County Durham, 1995)

Plato, Generalleutnant Anton Detlev von, *Die Geschichte der 5. Panzerdivision, 1938 bis 1945* (Regensburg: 5. Panzerdivision, 1978)

Riebensahm, Generalleutnant Gustav, *Infanterie-Regiment Prinz Friedrich der Niederlande (2. Westfälisches) Nr.15 im Weltkriege 1914-18* (Minden: Self-Published, 1931)

Rissik, D., *The DLI at War: The History of the Durham Light Infantry, 1939-1945* (Durham: DLI, 1954)

Scheibert, Horst, *Die Gespenster-Division: Die Geschichte der 7. Panzer-Division* (Eggolsheim: Dörfler, 2006)

Schulz, Oberstleutnant, *Infanterie-Regiment Graf Bülow von Dennewitz (6. Westfälisches) Nr. 55 im Weltkriege* (Detmold: Meyerschen, 1928)

Sprösser, Generalmajor Theodor, *Die Geschichte der Württembergischen Gebirgsschützen* (Die württembergischen Regimenter im Weltkrieg 1914-1918, Band 49) (Stuttgart: Belser, 1933)

SS Totenkopf-Division, *Damals: Erinnerungen an Grosse Tage der SS Totenkopf-Division im Französischen Feldzug 1940* (Stuttgart: Belser, 1941)

Stewart, Captain Patrick Findlater, *The History of the XII Royal Lancers (Prince of Wales's)* (London: Oxford University, 1950)

Stolfi, Russel H., *A Bias for Action: The German 7th Panzer Division in France & Russia, 1940-41* (Quantico, VA: Command & Staff College Foundation, 1991)

Sydnor, Charles W., *Soldiers of Destruction: The SS Death's Head Division, 1933-1945* (Princeton, NJ: Princeton University Press, 1990)

Tiede, Generalleutnant, Hauptmann Himer and Oberleutnant Röhricht, *Das 4.Schlesische Infanterie-Regiment Nr.157*, Erinnerungsblätter deutscher Regimenter, vol.14 (Berlin: Stalling, 1922)

Trang, Charles, *Totenkopf* (Bayeux: Heimdal, 2006)

Tschimpke, Alfred, *Die Gespenster-Division. Mit der Panzerwaffe durch Belgien und Frankreich* (München: NSDAP, 1940), p.116.

Ullrich, Karl, *Like a Cliff in the Ocean*, trans. by Jeffrey McMullen (Winnipeg: Fedorowicz, 2002)

Vopersal, Wolfgang, *Soldaten, Kämpfer, Kameraden: Marsch und Kämpfe der SS Totenkopf-Division, Vol 1: Aufstellung, Frankreichfeldzug, Bereitstellung für Rußlandfeldzug* (Bielefeld: Truppenkameradschaft der 3. SS-Panzer-Division, 1983)

Secondary Sources

Alfoldi, Laszlo M., 'The Hutier Legend', *Parameters*, 5 (1976), 69-74

Anonymous, 'Army and Super-Army', *Infantry Journal*, 49(2) (August 1941), 2-15

Anonymous, 'Obituary of General v.d. Marwitz', *Army Quarterly*, 19(2) (January 1930), 238-241

Anonymous, 'Publishers' Note', in Rommel, *Infantry Attacks*, xi-xiii

Anonymous, 'The British Army and Modern Conceptions of War', *Edinburgh Review*, 213 (1911), 321-346

Anonymous, 'The British Campaign in the West, Part I: August – November 1918', *Army Quarterly*, 5 (January 1923), 314-330

Anonymous, 'The German Catastrophe of the 8th of August 1918', *Army Quarterly*, 25 (October 1933), 65-71

Anonymous, 'Über militärisches Schrifttum im preußisch-deutschen Heere von Scharnhorst bis zum Weltkriege', *Militärwissenschaftlische Rundschau* 3(4) (1938), 463-482

Antal, Major John F., 'Combat Orders: An Analysis of the Tactical Orders Process' (unpublished master's thesis, US Army Command & General Staff College, Fort Leavenworth, KS, 1990)

Atkins, Ronald, *Pillar of Fire: Dunkirk 1940* (London: Sidgwick and Jackson, 1990)

Auchinleck, Field Marshal Sir Claude, 'Foreword', in Young, *Rommel*

Aylwin-Foster, Brigadier Nigel, 'Changing the Army for Counterinsurgency Operations', *Military Review* (November-December 2005), 2-15

Badsey, Stephen, *Doctrine and Reform in the British Cavalry, 1880-1918* (Aldershot: Ashgate, 2008)

Barnett, Corelli, *The Swordbearers: Supreme Command in the First World War* (London: Cassell, 2000)

Barr, Niall, 'Rommel in the Desert, 1942', in Beckett, *Rommel*, pp.81-112

Beach, Jim, 'Issued by the General Staff: Doctrine Writing at British GHQ, 1917-1918', *War in History*, 19(4) (2012), 464-491

Beckett, Ian F.W. (ed), *Rommel: A Reappraisal* (Barnsley: Pen and Sword, 2013)

Beyerchen, Alan, 'Clausewitz, Nonlinearity, and the Unpredictability of War', *International Security*, 17(3) (Winter 1992/93), 59-90.

Biddle, Stephen, *Military Power: Explaining Victory and Defeat in Modern Battle* (Princeton: Princeton University, 2004)

Bidwell, Brigadier Shelford and Dominic Graham, *Firepower: British Army Weapons and Theories of War, 1904-1945* (London: Allen & Unwin, 1982)

Blaxland, Gregory, *Amiens: 1918* (London: Star, 1981)

Blaxland, Gregory, *Destination Dunkirk: The Story of Gort's Army* (London: Kimber, 1973)

Blumentritt, Guenther, *Von Rundstedt: The Soldier and the Man* (London: Odhams, 1952)

Bond, Brian, *France and Belgium, 1939-1940* (London: Purnell, 1975)

Bowman, Timothy and Mark Connelly, *The Edwardian Army: Recruiting, Training, and Deploying the British Army 1902-1914* (Oxford, 2012)

Box, George E.P. and Norman R. Draper, *Empirical Model Building and Response Surfaces* (London: Wiley-Blackwell, 1986)

Boyd, John R., Organic Design for Command and Control This and other related briefings by Boyd are available at <http://dnipogo.org/strategy-and-force-employment/boyd-and-military-strategy/> (Accessed 5 April 2012)

Boyd, John R., Patterns of Conflict

Boyd, John R., The Essence of Winning and Losing

Boyd, John R., The Strategic Game of ? And ?

Brett-Smith, Richard, *Hitler's Generals* (London: Osprey, 1976)

Brice, Christopher, *The Thinking Man's Soldier: The Life and Career of General Sir Henry Brackenbury, 1837-1914* (Solihull: Helion, 2012)

Brinkmann, Jürgen, *Die Ritter des Ordens "Pour le Merité" 1914-1918* (Bückeburg: self-published, 1982)

Brown, Ian M., 'Not Glamorous, But Effective: The Canadian Corps and the Set-Piece Attack, 1917-1918', *Journal of Military History*, 58(3) (July 1994), 421-444

Brown, Ian Malcolm, *British Logistics on the Western Front, 1914-1919* (Westport, CT: Praeger, 1998)

Bungay, Stephen, *Alamein* (London: Aurum, 2002)

Bungay, Stephen, *The Art of Action: How Leaders Close the Gaps between Plans, Actions and Results* (London: Brealey, 2011)

Butler, Daniel Allen, *Field Marshal: The Life and Death of Erwin Rommel* (Havertown, PA: Casemate, 2015)

Caddick-Adams, Peter, *Monty and Rommel: Parallel Lives* (London: Arrow, 2012)

Chapman, Guy, *Why France Collapsed* (London: Cassell, 1968)

Citino, Robert M., *The German Way of War: From the Thirty Years' War to the Third Reich* (Lawrence, KS: University Press of Kansas, 2005)

Citino, Robert, *The Path to Blitzkrieg: Doctrine and Training in the German Army, 1920-39* Mechanicsburg, PA: Stackpole, 2008)

Clark, Jason Patrick, The Many Faces of Reform: Military Progressivism in the US Army, 1866-1916 (unpublished PhD thesis, Duke university, 2009)

Condell, Bruce, and David T. Zabecki, 'Editors' Introduction', in *On the German Art of War: Truppenführung*, ed. and trans. by Bruce Condell and David T. Zabecki (London, 2001), pp.1-14.

Coningham, Simon, 'The Battle of Amiens: Air-Ground Co-operation and its Implications for Imperial Policing', in *Changing War: The British Army, the Hundred Days Campaign and the Birth of the Royal Air Force, 1918*, ed. by Gary Sheffield and Peter Gray (London: Continuum, 2014), pp.207-229

Connell, John (pseudonym of John Henry Robertson), *Wavell: Scholar and Soldier – To June 1941* (London: Collins, 1964)

Connelly, Mark, 'Rommel as Icon', in *Rommel: A Reappraisal*, ed. by Ian F.W. Beckett (Barnsley: Pen and Sword, 2013), 157-178

Conti, Robert F., 'Frederick Wilmslow Taylor', in *The Oxford Handbook of Management Theorists*, ed. by Morgen Witzell and Malcolm Warner (Oxford: Oxford University Press, 2013), pp.11-31

Coram, Robert, *Boyd: The Fighter Pilot Who Changed the Art of War* (Boston: Little Brown, 2002)

Cordingley, Colonel P.A.J., 'Armoured Forces and the Counter Stroke', in Mackenzie, *British Army*, pp.94-107

Corrigan, Gordon, *Blood, Sweat and Arrogance and the Myths of Churchill's War* (London: Phoenix, 2007)

Corum, James S., *The Roots of Blitzkrieg: Hans von Seeckt and the German Military Reform* (Lawrence, KS: University Press of Kansas, 1992)

Creveld, Martin van, 'On Learning from the Wehrmacht and Other Things', *Military Review* (January 1988), 62-71

Creveld, Martin Van, *Command in War* (Cambridge, MA: Harvard University Press, 1985)

Creveld, Martin Van, *Fighting Power: German and U.S. Army Performance, 1939-1945* (Westport, CT: Greenwood, 1982)

Creveld, Martin van, *The Culture of War* (Stroud: Spellmount, 2009)

Doughty, Robert Allan, *The Breaking Point: Sedan and the Fall of France, 1940* (Hamden, CT: Archon, 1990)

Douglas-Home, Charles, *Rommel* (London: Book Club Associates, 1973)

Dunlop, Colonel John K., *The Development of the British Army: 1899-1914* (London: Methuen, 1938)

Echevarria, Antulio J., *After Clausewitz: German Military Thinkers Before the Great War* (Lawrence, KS: University Press of Kansas, 2000)

Eisel, Major George W., 'Befehlstaktik and The Red Army Experience: Are There Lessons for Us?' (unpublished master's thesis, US Army Command & General Staff College, Fort Leavenworth, KS, 1993)

Elliott-Bateman, Michael (in conjunction with Spencer Fitz-Gibbon and Martin Samuels), 'Vocabulary: the Second Problem of Military Reform – I. Concepts', *Defense Analysis*, 6(3) (1990), 263-275

Evans, Richard J., *David Irving, Hitler and Holocaust Denial*, electronic edition <http://hdot.org/en/trial/defense/evans/6.html> (Accessed 28 July 2015)

Falls, Captain Cyril, *Caporetto, 1917* (London: Weidenfeld & Nicholson, 1966)

Falls, Cyril, 'An Aspect of the Battle of Amiens, 1918', *Army Quarterly*, 6 (Jul 1923), 298-306

Fitz-Gibbon, Spencer, *Not Mentioned in Despatches... The History and Mythology of the Battle of Goose Green* (Cambridge: Lutterworth, 1995)

Foley, Robert T., *German Strategy and the Path to Verdun: Erich von Falkenhayn and the Development of Attrition, 1870-1916* (Cambridge, 2005)

Fong, Giordan, 'The Movement of German Divisions to the Western Front: Winter 1917-1918', *War in History*, 7(2) (2000), 225-235

Forty, George, *The Armies of Rommel* (London: Arms & Armour, 1997)

Fraser, David, *And We Shall Shock Them: The British Army in the Second World War* (London: Book Club Associates, 1983)

Fraser, David, *Knight's Cross: A Life of Field Marshal Erwin Rommel* (London: HarperCollins, 1994)

French, David, 'Doctrine and Organization in the British Army, 1919-1932', *Historical Journal*, 44(2) (2001), 497-515

French, David, *Raising Churchill's Army: The British Army and the War against Germany, 1919-1945* (Oxford: Oxford University Press, 2000)

Frieser, Colonel Karl-Heinz, with John T. Greenwood, *The Blitzkrieg Legend: The 1940 Campaign in the West* (Annapolis, MD: Naval Institute Press, 2005)

Fuller, Major-General J.F.C., *The Conduct of War, 1789-1961* (1961, reprinted London: Methuen, 1972)

Gabriel, Richard A. and Paul L. Savage, *Crisis in Command: Mismanagement in the Army* (New York, NY: Hill & Wang, 1978)

Gleick, James, *Chaos: The Amazing Science of the Unpredictable* (London: Vantage, 1998)

Gooch, John, *The Italian Army and the First World War* (Cambridge: Cambridge University Press, 2014)

Gooch, John, *The Plans of War: The General Staff and British Military Strategy c.1900-1916* (London: Routledge & Kegan Paul, 1974)

Green, Andrew, *Writing the Great War: Sir James Edmonds and the Official Histories, 1915-1948* (London: Cass, 2003)

Grieves, Keith, *Sir Eric Geddes: Business and Government in War and Peace* (Manchester: Manchester University Press, 1989)

Griffin, Nicholas J., 'Scientific Management in the Direction of Britain's Military Labour Establishment During World War I', *Military Affairs*, 42(4) (December 1978), (197-201)

Grint, Keith, *Leadership, Management and Command: Rethinking D-Day* (Basingstoke: Palgrave, 2008)

Gross, Gerhard P., *The Myth and Reality of German Warfare: Operational Thinking from Moltke the Elder to Heusinger*, ed. by Major-General David T. Zabecki (Lexington, KY: University Press of Kentucky, 2016)

Gruss, H., 'Aufbau und Verwendung der deutschen Sturmbataillone im Weltkrieg' (unpublished doctoral thesis, Berlin University, 1939),

Gudmundsonn, Bruce Ivar, *Stormtroop Tactics: Innovation in the German Army, 1914-1918* (New York, NY: Praeger, 1989)

Gudmundsson, Bruce Ivar, *On Armor* (Westport, CT: Praeger, 2006)

Hammond, Bryn, *Cambrai 1917: The Myth of the First Great Tank Battle* (London: Weidenfeld & Nicolson, 2008)

Hammond, Grant T., *The Mind of War: John Boyd and American Security* (Washington, DC: Smithsonian, 2001)

Harman, Nicholas, *Dunkirk: The Necessary Myth* (London: Hodder and Stoughton, 1980)

Harris, J.P., *Amiens to the Armistice: The BEF in the Hundred Days' Campaign, 8 August–11 November 1918* (London: Brassey's, 1998)

Harris, J.P., *Men, Ideas and Tanks: British Military Thought and Armoured Forces, 1903-1939* (Manchester: Manchester University Press, 1995)

Harrison Place, Timothy, *Military Training in the British Army, 1940-1944: From Dunkirk to D-Day* (London: Cass, 2000)

Herbert, Major Paul H., *Deciding What Has to Be Done: General William E. DePuy and the 1976 Edition of FM 100-5, Operations* (Fort Leavenworth, KS: Combat Studies Institute, 1988)

Hillgruber, Andreas, 'Field-Marshal Gerd von Rundstedt', in *The War Lords*, ed. by Field Marshal Sir Michael Carver (London: Weidenfeld and Nicolson, 1987), pp.188-201

Holmes, Richard, *Army Battlefield Guide: Belgium and Northern France* (London: HMSO, 1995)

Holmes, Terence M., 'Planning versus Chaos in Clausewitz's *On War*', *Journal of Strategic Studies*, 30 (1) (February 2007), 129-151.

Hones, Captain William, The German Infantry School (unpublished student paper, US Army Command & General Staff School, 1931), <http://cgsc.contentdm.oclc.org/cdm/singleitem/collection>

Horne, Alistair, *To Lose A Battle: France 1940* (1969, republished Harmondsworth: Penguin, 1979)

Horstmann, Harry, *Die Entwicklung deutscher Führungsgrundsätze im 20. Jahrhundert: Eine vergleichende Betrachtung zwischen Beständigkeit und Wandel* (Norderstedt: Grin, 2009)

Howard, Michael, 'The Influence of Clausewitz', in Clausewitz, *On War*, pp. 27-44

Howard, Michael, *The Franco-Prussian War* (London: Routledge, 1988)

Hughes, Daniel J., ed., *Moltke on the Art of War: Selected Writings*, trans. by Daniel J. Hughes and Harry Bell (New York, NY: Ballantine, 1993)

Irving, David, *The Trail of the Fox: The Life of Field-Marshal Erwin Rommel* (London: Weidenfeld and Nicolson, 1977)

Jacobsen, Hans-Adolf, 'Dunkirk 1940', in *Decisive Battles of World War II: the German View*, ed. by Hans-Adolf Jacobsen and Jürgen Rohwer (London: Deutsch, 1965), pp.29-69

Jeffery, Keith, *Field Marshal Sir Henry Wilson: A Political Soldier* (Oxford: Oxford University Press, 2008)

Johnson, Major John D., 'Mission Orders in the United States Army: Is the Doctrine Effective?' (unpublished master's thesis, US Army Command & General Staff College, Fort Leavenworth, KS, 1990)

Johnston, Paul, 'Doctrine is Not Enough: The Effect of Doctrine on the Behavior of Armies', *Parameters* (Autumn 2000), 30-39

Jones, Spencer, *From Boer War to World War: Tactical Reform of the British Army, 1902-1914* (Oklahoma, OK: University of Oklahoma, 2012)

Kabisch, Generalleutnant Ernst, *Der schwarze Tag: Die Nebelschlacht vor Amiens (8./9. August 1918)* (Berlin: Schlegel, 1933)

Kenyon, David, *Horsemen in No Man's Land: British Cavalry and Trench Warfare, 1914-1918* (Barnsley: Pen & Sword, 2011)

Kesselring, Agilof, *Die Organisation Gehlen und Die Verteidigung Westdeutschlands: Alte Elitedivisionen und neue Militärstrukturen, 1949-1953* (Marburg: Bundesnachrichtendienst, 2014)

Kirkland, Faris R., 'The French Officer Corps and the Fall of France, 1920-1940' (unpublished doctoral dissertation, Pennsylvania University, 1982)

Lee, John, *A Soldier's Life: General Sir Ian Hamilton, 1853-1947* (London: Pan, 2001)

Leistenschneider, Stephan, *Auftragstaktik im preussisch-deutschen Heer 1871 bis 1914* (Hamburg: Mittler, 2002)

Lemelin, Major David J., 'Command and Control Methodology: A Sliding Scale of Centralisation' (unpublished master's thesis, US Army Command & General Staff College, Fort Leavenworth, KS, 1996)

Lewin, Ronald, *Man of Armour: A Study of Lieut-General Vyvyan Pope and the Development of Armoured Warfare* (London: Cooper, 1976)

Lewin, Ronald, *Rommel as a Military Commander* (New York, NK: Barnes & Noble, 1968)

Liddell Hart, Captain Basil. H., *The Other Side of the Hill: Germany's Generals, Their Rise and Fall, with Their Own Account of Military Events 1939-1945* (London: Cassell, 1948)

Liddell Hart, Basil H., *The Other Side of the Hill: Germany's Generals, Their Rise and Fall, with Their Own Account of Military Events 1939-1945*, 2nd ed (1951, reprinted London: Pan, 1978)

Lind, William, *Maneuver War Handbook* (Boulder, CO: Westview, 1985)

Livesay, J.F.B., *Canada's Hundred Days: With the Canadian Corps from Amiens to Mons, Aug. 8 – Nov. 11, 1918* (Toronto: Allen, 1919)

Lossow, Lieutenant-Colonel W., 'Mission-Type Tactics versus Order-Type Tactics', *Military Review* (June 1977), 87-91

Lupfer, Captain T.T., *The Dynamics of Doctrine: The Changes in German Tactical Doctrine During the First World War* (Fort Leavenworth, KS: Combat Studies Institute, 1981)

Luvaas, Jay, *The Education of an Army* (London: Cassell, 1965)

Macksey, Kenneth, *Guderian: Panzer General* (London: Macdonald & Jane's, 1974)

Macksey, Kenneth, *Rommel: Battles and Campaigns* (London: Book Club Associates, 1979)

Macksey, Major Kenneth, *The Shadow of Vimy Ridge* (London: Kimber, 1965)

MacLean, Major French L., German General Officer Casualties in World War II – Harbinger for U.S. Army General Officer Casualties in Airland Battle? (unpublished master's thesis, US Army Command & General Staff College, Fort Leavenworth, KS, 1988)

Mahnken, Thomas G., *Uncovering Ways of War: U.S. Intelligence and Foreign Military Innovation, 1918-1941* (Ithaca, NY: Cornell University Press, 2009)

Marshall, Colonel S.L.A., *Men Against Fire: The Problem of Battle Command* (Norman, OK: University of Oklahoma Press, 2000)

Matuschka, Edgar Graf von, 'Organisationsgeschichte des Heeres', in *Handbuch zur deutschen Militärgeschichte, 1648-1939, vol. VI: Reichswehr und Republik (1918-1933)*, ed. by Militärgeschichtliches Forschungsamt (Munich: Bernard & Graefe, 1970)

McRandle, James and James Quirk, 'The Blood Test Revisited: A New Look at German Casualty Counts in World War I', *Journal of Military History*, 70(3) (July 2006), 667-701

McWilliams, James and R. James Steel, *Amiens 1918: The Last Great Battle* (Stroud: History, 2008)

Mead, Richard, *Churchill's Lions: A Biographical Guide to the Key British Generals of World War II* (London: Spellmount, 2007)

Mearsheimer, John J., *Liddell Hart and the Weight of History* (London: Brassey's, 1988)

Meier-Welcker, Hans, 'Der Entschluss zum Anhalten der Deutschen Panzertruppen in Flandern 1940', *Vierteljahrhefte für Zeitgeschichte*, 2(3) (1954), 274-290

Melvin, Mungo, 'The German Perspective', in *The Normandy Campaign 1944: Sixty Years On*, ed. by John Buckley, (London: Routledge, 2006), (22-34)

Melvin, Mungo, *Manstein: Hitler's Greatest General* (London: Phoenix, 2011)

Messenger, Charles, *The Day We Won the War: Turning Point at Amiens, 8th August 1918* (London: Phoenix, 2009)

Messenger, Charles, *The Last Prussian: A Biography of Field Marshal Gerd von Rundstedt, 1875-1953* (London: Brassey's, 1991)

Mitcham, Samuel W., *Rommel's Lieutenants: The Men Who Served the Desert Fox, France, 1940* (Mechanicsburg, PA: Stackpole, 2009)

Murray, Leo, *Brains & Bullets: How Psychology Wins Wars* (London: Biteback, 2013)

Murray, Williamson, 'Leading the Troops: A German Manual of 1933', *Marines Corps Gazette* (September 1999), 95-98

Murray, Williamson, 'The German Response to Victory in Poland: A Case Study in Professionalism', *Armed Forces and Society*, 7(2) (Winter 1981), 285-298

Muth, Jörg, *Command Culture: Officer Education in the U.S. Army and the German Armed Forces, 1901-1940, and the Consequences for World War II* (Denton, TX: University of North Texas, 2011)

Naveh, Shimon, *In Pursuit of Military Excellence: The Evolution of Operational Theory* (London: Cass, 1997)

Oetting, Dirk W., *Auftragstaktik. Geschichte und Gegenwart einer Führungskonzeption* (Frankfurt: Report-Verlag, 1993)

Oliver, Colonel R.A., 'Training for the Friction of War', in *The British Army and the Operational Level of War*, ed. by Major-General J.J.G. Mackenzie and Brian Holden Reid (London: Tri-Service, 1989), pp.166-191

Osinga, Frans, *Science, Strategy and War: The Strategic Theory of John Boyd* (Delft: Eburon, 2005)

Pappila, Lieutenant-Colonel Ove, 'Rommel and the German 7th Panzer Division in France 1940: The Initial Days of the Campaign', *Kungl Krigsvetenskapsakademiens Handlingar Och Tidskrift* (2009), 73-101

Perrett, Bryan, *The Matilda* (London: Allan, 1972)

Philpott, William, *Bloody Victory: The Sacrifice on the Somme* (London: Abacus, 2009)

Prior, Robin and Trevor Wilson, *Command on the Western Front: The Military Career of Sir Henry Rawlinson, 1914-1918* (Barnsley: Pen & Sword, 2004)

Province, Charles M., *The Unknown Patton* (New York, NY: Hippocrene, 1983)

Pugsley, Christopher, 'We Have Been Here Before: the Evolution of the Doctrine of Decentralised Command in the British Army, 1905-1989', *Sandhurst Occasional Papers* (9) (2011)

Raths, Ralf, *Vom Massensturm zur Stoßtrupptaktik: Die deutsche Landkriegtaktik im Spiegel von Dienstvorschriften und Publizistik, 1906 bis 1918* (Freiburg: Rombach, 2009)

Remy, Maurice Philip, *Mythos Rommel* (Munich: List, 2002)

Reuth, Ralf Georg, *Rommel: The End of a Legend*, trans. by Debra S. Marmor and Herbert A. Danner (London: Haus, 2005)

Riebicke, Otto, *Was brauchte der Weltkrieg? Tatsachen und Zahlen aus dem deutschen Ringen 1914/18* (Leipzig: Hase & Köhler, 1936)

Rittel, Horst W.J. and Melvin M. Webber, 'Dilemmas in a General Theory of Planning', *Policy Sciences* 4 (1973), (155-169)

Roberts, Field-Marshal Earl, 'Memoir', in Colonel G.F.R. Henderson, *The Science of War*, ed. by Captain Neill Malcolm, 5th imprint (London: Longmans Green, 1912), xiii-xxxviii

Rowland, David, *The Stress of Battle: Quantifying Human Performance in Combat* (London: TSO, 2006)

Ryder, Rowland, *Oliver Leese* (London: Hamilton, 1987)

Samuels, Martin, *Command or Control? Command, Training and Tactics in the British and German Armies, 1888-1918* (London: Cass, 1995)

Samuels, Martin, *Doctrine and Dogma: German and British Infantry Tactics in the First World War* (Westport, CT: Greenwood, 1992)

Schmidt-Richberg, Wiegand, *Die Generalstäbe in Deutschland 1871-1945* (Stuttgart: MGFA, 1962)

Schreiber, Shane B., *Shock Army of the British Empire: The Canadian Corps in the Last 100 Days of the Great War* (Westport, CT: Praeger, 1997)

Searle, Alaric, 'A Very Special Relationship: Basil Liddell Hart, Wehrmacht Generals and the Debate on West German Rearmament, 1945-1953', *War in History*, 5(3) (1998), 327-357

Searle, Alaric, 'Rommel and the Rise of the Nazis', in Beckett, *Rommel*, 7-29

Sebag-Montefiore, Hugh, *Dunkirk: Fight to the Last Man*, rev. ed. (Harmondsworth: Penguin, 2015)

Seligmann, Matthew S., '*Hors de Combat?* The Management, Mismanagement and Mutilation of the War Office Archive, *Journal of the Society for Army Historical Research*, 84 (2006), 52-58

Shamir, Eitan, *Transforming Command: The Pursuit of Mission Command in the U.S., British and Israeli Armies* (Stanford, CA: Stanford University Press, 2011)

Sheffield, Gary and John Bourne, 'Introduction', in *Douglas Haig: War Diaries and Letters, 1914-1918*, ed. by Gary Sheffield and John Bourne (London: Phoenix, 2006), pp.1-43

Sheffield, Gary, *Forgotten Victory: The First World War: Myths and Realities* (London: Headline, 2001)

Sheldon, Jack, *The German Army at Cambrai* (Barnsley: Pen & Sword, 2009)

Shils, E. A. and Morris Janowitz, 'Cohesion and Disintegration in the Wehrmacht in World War II', *Public Opinion Quarterly* (Summer 1948), 280-315

Showalter, Dennis E., *Tannenberg: Clash of Empires, 1914* (Washington, DC: Brassey's, 2004)

Showalter, Dennis, *Patton and Rommel: Men of War in the Twentieth Century* (New York, NY: Berkley Caliber, 2005)

Sigg, Marco, *Der Unterführer als Feldherr in Taschenformat: Theorie und Praxis der Auftragstaktik im deutschen Heer, 1869 bis 1945* (Paderborn: Schöningh, 2014)

Simkins, Peter, *Kitchener's Army: The Raising of the New Armies 1914-16* (Manchester: Manchester University Press, 1988)

Simpkin, Richard E., *Human Factors in Mechanized Warfare* (London: Brassey's, 1983)

Simpkin, Richard E., *Race to the Swift: Thoughts on Twenty-First Century Warfare* (London: Brassey's, 1985)

Smithers, A.J., *A New Excalibur: The Development of the Tank, 1909-1939* (London: Grafton, 1988)

Spiers, E. M., 'The Regular Army in 1914', in *A Nation in Arms: A Social Study of the British Army in the First World War*, ed. by Ian F. W. Beckett and Keith Simpson (Manchester: Manchester University Press, 1985), 37-62

Spires, David N., *Image and Reality: The Making of the German Officer, 1921-1933* (Westport, CT: Greenwood, 1984)

Starry, General Donn A., 'Foreword', in Richard E. Simpkin, *Race to the Swift: Thoughts on Twenty-First Century Warfare* (London: Brassey's, 1985), pp. vii-ix.

Stone, Jay, 'The Anglo-Boer War and Military Reforms in the United Kingdom', in *The Boer War and Military Reforms*, by Jay Stone and Erwin A. Schmidl (London: University Press of America, 1988)

Storr, Colonel Jim, *The Human Face of War* (London: Continuum, 2009)

Storr, Major Jim, 'A Command Philosophy for the Information Age: The Continuing Relevance of Mission Command', *Defence Studies*, 3(3) (Autumn 2003), 119-129

Strachan, Hew, 'The British Army, its General Staff and the Continental Commitment, 1904-14', in *The British General Staff: Reform and Innovation, c.1890-1939*, ed. by David French and Brian Holden Reid (London: Cass, 2002), pp. 75-94

Strachan, Hew, *Clausewitz's On War: A Biography* (New York, NY: Atlantic Monthly, 2007)

Strohn, Matthias, *The German Army and the Defence of the Reich: Military Doctrine and the Conduct of the Defensive Battle, 1918-1939* (Cambridge: Cambridge University Press, 2011)

Telp, Claus, 'Rommel and 1940', in *Rommel: A Reappraisal*, ed. by Ian F.W. Beckett (Barnsley: Pen and Sword, 2013), 30-59

Terraine, John, *To Win a War: 1918, The Year of Victory* (London: Papermac, 1986)

Terraine, John, *White Heat: The New Warfare 1914-18* (London: Sidgwick & Jackson, 1982)

Thompson, Major Paul W., *Modern Battle: Units in Action in the Second World War* (Harmondsworth: Penguin, 1942)

Thompson, Major-General Julian, *Dunkirk: Retreat to Victory* (London: Pan, 2009)

Thompson, Mark, *The White War: Life and Death on the Italian Front, 1915-1919* (London: Faber & Faber, 2008)

Travers, Timothy H.E., *The Killing Ground: The British Army, The Western Front and The Emergence of Modern Warfare, 1900-1918* (London: Allen & Unwin, 1987)

Travers, Timothy, *How the War Was Won: Factors that Led to Victory in World War One* (Barnsley: Pen & Sword, 2005)

Uhle-Wettler, Franz, *Erich Ludendorff in seiner Zeit: Soldat – Stratege – Revolutionär: Eine Neubewertung* (Berg: Vowinckel, 1995)

Urwick, Lyndall, *The Development of Scientific Management in Great Britain* (London: Management Journals, 1938)

Vandergriff, Donald, *The Path to Victory: America's Army and the Revolution in Human Affairs* (Novato, CA: Presidio, 2002)

Wallach, Jehuda, *The Dogma of the Battle of Annihilation: The Theories of Clausewitz and Schlieffen and Their Impact on the German Conduct of Two World Wars* (Westport, CT: Greenwood, 1986)

Watson, Alex, '"For Kaiser and Reich": The Identity and Fate of the German Volunteers, 1914-1918', *War in History*, 12(1) (2005), 44-74

Watson, Alexander, *Enduring the Great War: Combat, Morale and Collapse in the German and British Armies, 1914-1918* (Cambridge: Cambridge University, 2008)

Wilks, John and Eileen Wilks, *Rommel and Caporetto* (Barnsley: Cooper, 2001)

Williams, John, *The Ides of May. The Defeat of France, May-June 1940* (London: Constable, 1968)

Wittmann, Jochen, *Auftragstaktik – Just a Command Technique of the Core Pillar of Mastering the Military Operational Art?* (Berlin: Miles, 2012)

Wynne, Captain Greame C., *If Germany Attacks: The Battle in Depth in the West* (1940, reprinted Westport, CT: Greenwood, 1976)

Wynne, Captain Greame C., 'The Development of the German Defensive Battle in 1917, and its Influence on British Defensive Tactics, Part III: Field Service Regulations (1935)', *Army Quarterly*, 35 (1) (October 1937), 14-27

Wynne, Captain Greame C., 'The Hindenburg Line', *Army Quarterly*, 37(2) (January 1939), 205-228

Young, Desmond, *Rommel* (London: Collins, 1950)

Young, Desmond, *Try Anything Twice* (London: Hamilton, 1963)

Zabecki, Major-General David T., *The German 1918 Offensives: A Case Study in the Operational Level of War* (London: Routledge, 2006)

Zwehl, General der Infanterie Hans von, *Die Schlachten im Sommer 1918 an der Westfront* (Berlin: Mittler, 1921)

Index

Lightning Source UK Ltd.
Milton Keynes UK
UKHW021250190522
403200UK00003B/283